D0909210

Estranged Bedfellows

Studies in Middle Eastern History
Bernard Lewis, Itamar Rabinovich, and Roger Savory
General Editors

THE TURBAN FOR THE CROWN
The Islamic Revolution in Iran
Said Amir Arjomand

LANGUAGE AND CHANGE IN THE ARAB MIDDLE EAST
The Evolution of Modern Arabic Political Discourse
Ami Ayalon

ISLAMIC REFORM
Politics and Social Change in Late Ottoman Syria
David Dean Commins

KING HUSSEIN AND THE CHALLENGE
OF ARAB RADICALISM
Jordan, 1955–1967
Uriel Dann

EGYPT, ISLAM, AND THE ARABS
The Search for Egyptian Nationhood, 1900–1930
Israel Gershoni and James Jankowski

EAST ENCOUNTERS WEST
*France and the Ottoman Empire
in the Eighteenth Century*
Fatma Müge Göçek

THE FERTILE CRESCENT, 1800–1914
A Documentary Economic History
Edited by Charles Issawi

ESTRANGED BEDFELLOWS
*Britain and France in the Middle East
during the Second World War*
Aviel Roshwald

OTHER VOLUMES ARE IN PREPARATION

ESTRANGED BEDFELLOWS

Britain and France in the Middle East
during the Second World War

AVIEL ROSHWALD

New York   Oxford
OXFORD UNIVERSITY PRESS
1990

Oxford University Press

Oxford   New York   Toronto
Delhi   Bombay   Calcutta   Madras   Karachi
Petaling Jaya   Singapore   Hong Kong   Tokyo
Nairobi   Dar es Salaam   Cape Town
Melbourne   Auckland

and associated companies in
Berlin   Ibadan

Copyright © 1990 by Oxford University Press, Inc.

Published by Oxford University Press, Inc.,
200 Madison Avenue, New York, New York 10016

Oxford is a registered trademark of Oxford University Press

All rights reserved. No part of this publication may be reproduced,
stored in a retrieval system, or transmitted, in any form or by any means,
electronic, mechanical, photocopying, recording, or otherwise,
without the prior permission of Oxford University Press.

Library of Congress Cataloging-in-Publication Data
Roshwald, Aviel.
Estranged bedfellows :
Britain and France in the Middle East during the Second World War
/ Aviel Roshwald.
p.   cm.—(Studies in Middle Eastern history)
Includes bibliographical references.   ISBN 0-19-506266-3
1. Middle East—History—20th century.   2. Great Britain—Foreign relations—France.
3. France—Foreign relations—Great Britain.
4. World War. 1939–1945—Middle East.   5. World War 1939–1945—Diplomatic History.
6. France—Foreign relations—1940–1945.
7. Great Britain—Foreign relations—1939–1945.
I. Title.   II. Series: Studies in Middle Eastern history (New York, N.Y.)
DS63.R67   1990 940.53′2241′0944—dc20   89-26669

2 4 6 8 9 7 5 3 1

Printed in the United States of America
on acid-free paper

LIBRARY
ALMA COLLEGE
ALMA, MICHIGAN

To My Parents
Miriam and Mordecai Roshwald

Preface

During the Second World War, the international alliance against Hitler presented itself to the world as a cohesive coalition of nations that agreed on how the war was to be conducted and held a common vision of the postwar world. In fact, behind the façade of the United Nations lay a fractured alliance whose members were pursuing very different objectives beyond the immediate defeat of the Axis powers. Britain was struggling not just to survive, but to save its empire; the United States was fighting for a new world order based on its own principles of political and economic organization; the Soviet Union viewed its democratic allies with deep suspicion and made repeated overtures to the Germans well into 1943. Perhaps the most ambivalent relationship was that between Britain and France, whose quest for grandeur had caused them to clash in the previous fifty years as often as their need for security had brought them together.

This study examines the course of this wartime relationship within the context of the Levant. It begins with a look at the ambivalent British policy toward Vichy-controlled Syria and Lebanon during 1940–1941. Finding their resources overstretched, the British sought to avoid a direct military confrontation by attempting to negotiate a local modus vivendi with the Beirut authorities, while simultaneously supporting the Free French in their attempts to undermine Vichy's control of the region. This in turn had a major impact on the internal political dynamics of the French colonial administration. Following Vichy's offer of Syrian air bases to the Germans during the anti-British revolt in Iraq, British and Free French troops seized control of the Levant in a bloody, five-week campaign. An ambiguous situation then arose in which judicial authority was exercised by de Gaulle's movement, while effective power lay in the hands of the British.

This period is of interest both because of its very anomalousness and because it brought into focus in a striking manner the underlying tensions that had characterized Franco-British relations in the Middle East ever since the end of the First World War. The defeat of France on the continent enhanced the importance of its colonies as a source of national self-esteem. For their part, the British found it difficult to restrain themselves from meddling in local affairs once their forces had gained control of the Levant. With their overlapping authority in the region creating a virtual condominium, British and Free French turned on each other with a vindictiveness that belied their commitment to the wartime alliance.

In later years, the French blamed the ultimate collapse of their rule in Syria and Lebanon on the intrigues of Major-General Sir E. L. Spears, the British chief of mission there. They tended to perceive his conduct as the logical culmination of British imperial policy in the Middle East.[1] The British either argued that the French had been defeated largely by their own short-comings or insisted that Spears had acted on his own and without Whitehall's authority in undermining the French foothold in the region.[2]

What was the true nature of Spears' role in the Levant? Did the Anglo-French confrontation in the region arise from a clash of personalities or of policies? Did an element of continuity exist between Vichy and Free French views of the British? What impact did the recurrent crises in Syria and Lebanon have on the overall conduct of Anglo–French relations? To what extent, conversely, did Levantine tensions reflect wider problems in the alliance? How did the British and French interact with the nationalist movements in Syria and Lebanon? These are some of the questions with which this book grapples.

It should be noted that although the book does deal with key events on the Arab political scene, it is intended primarily as a case study in the history of European colonial rivalry. The definitive work on Syrian and Lebanese political development during World War II has yet to be published.

This study is based largely on the archival sources of Britain, France, and Israel. The Public Record Office in London was found to be a rich treasure house of information about all aspects of British policy in the Middle East, including the background minutes and discussions among officials that lay beneath the surface of formal policymaking. Insight into the personal perspective of E. L. Spears was provided by the Spears Papers at the Middle East Centre, Oxford. It should be noted, however, that various sensitive files from the FO 371 and other series have been withheld from public scrutiny for twenty or forty-five years beyond the normal thirty-year rule. In addition, intelligence papers remain closed to the general scholarly community, although copies of some intelligence reports did find their way to the files of other departments and thus to the Public Record Office.

The material found in the Quai d'Orsay archive is far less comprehensive in scope; while admitting that papers from the Beirut High Commission under Vichy have indeed been preserved, the archivists refuse to release them for scholarly research. Material from the Free French General Delegation in the Levant also remains hidden away in locked drawers. As for the deliberations of the Free French leadership, while a series entitled "Séances du C.F.L.N." does indeed exist, it contains lists of official decisions taken by the committee without providing a clue regarding the heated discussions that often lay behind those decisions. Nonetheless, several series of documents relating both to Vichy and Free French foreign policy had been opened just before I went to work on the topic, and these were found to contain much new information. The Service Historique de l'Armée de Terre also made hitherto unopened *Deuxième Bureau* records from 1940–1941 available to me.

The Central Zionist Archive in Jerusalem afforded useful insight into the field of study from the perspective of a third party. The Haganah Archive in Tel-Aviv contains some interesting material on the wartime activities of the Jewish underground in the Levant; however, for no apparent reason, some of these papers were not made available, while others were opened only on condition that they would not be specifically cited. (Copies of some of these were later found at the Central Zionist Archive, where access to them was perfectly unrestricted.) In addition, recently declassified OSS documents in the National Archives, Washington, D.C., shed some light on the murky, intelligence-related aspects of the subject.

In references to unpublished sources, it is to be understood that—unless otherwise indicated—all British documents are from the Public Record Office and all French papers from the Ministère des Affaires Étrangères (MAE). All translations of quotations from French sources are mine, unless otherwise indicated.

A key to the various abbreviations used throughout the text is to be found before the Notes at the end of the book. I have referred to de Gaulle's movement as the Free French throughout, ignoring the formal, wartime name change to Fighting French. The Levant refers specifically to the territory of Syria and Lebanon as defined by the 1922 League of Nations mandate.

I would like to thank Professor Ernest R. May and Professor Bradford Lee of Harvard University for taking the time to read this manuscript and comment on it. Professor Albert Hourani of St. Antony's College, Oxford, went out of his way to go over the text with meticulous care, making many valuable comments and suggestions, both general and specific. My parents also provided me with critiques that were as useful as they were extensive.

John E. Taylor of the National Archives and Records Service in Washington, D.C. was kind enough to locate various intriguing OSS files for me. Madame Bompard of the Quai d'Orsay archive told me about "la danse des canards." Material from the Public Record Office is cited by permission of Her Majesty's Stationery Office.

I am grateful to Harvard University's Sheldon Fund and to Harvard's Center for European Studies for funding my year of research in foreign archives. The Hebrew University in Jerusalem was kind enough to fund my year there as a post-doctoral fellow, enabling me to devote myself to the revision of the manuscript.

A number of participants in and observers of the events dealt with in this book were kind enough to relate their experiences and impressions to me. They helped to flesh out characters and bring to life events in a way that dry documents cannot always do. I am grateful to them all: Sir Richard Beaumont, Yerucham Cohen, Sir P. M. Crosthwaite, Dr. Eliahu Elath, Lord Hankey, Prof. Maxime Rodinson, and Richard Usborne.

The following people have also at one time or another provided me with useful advice and welcome encouragement: Dr. C. M. Andrew, Prof. E. Badian, Madame la général Catroux, Dr. Joseph Heller, Prof. Patrice Higon-

net, Prof. Philip Khoury, Dr. Henri Lerner, Prof. Wm. Roger Louis, Prof.
Nisan Oren, Prof. Itamar Rabinovich, Dr. Raghid al-Solh, Dr. Asher Susser,
and Prof. Bernard Wasserstein.

Sarah and Natan Gilboa showered me with their warm hospitality during
my stay in Tel-Aviv, and I am glad to have this opportunity to thank them.

I am grateful to the members of the Diplomatic History Workshop at
Harvard for their feedback on thematic aspects of my work. Last but not
least, I remain indebted to the Good Companions of Sumner Road for making Cambridge what it was for me.

As usual in these cases, I retain a monopoly on the blame for whatever
flaws may mar this study.

Claremont, Calif.   A. R.
December 1989

Contents

Estranged Bedfellows

INTRODUCTION

This study focuses on a rather odd episode in the history of Anglo–French colonial rivalry, a curious Middle Eastern sideshow that took place against the tumultuous backdrop of the Second World War, but which nonetheless had serious repercussions on the overall pattern of Franco–British relations.

Anglo–French competition in the colonial sphere dates back at least to the eighteenth century, when it reflected an equally intense antagonism between the two powers on the European continent. After its humiliating defeat in the Franco–Prussian war of 1870–1871, France sought to compensate for its decline as a continental power by engaging in colonial adventures in Africa and Indochina, pursuing the illusion of power for want of its substance. This culminated in the well-known confrontation between Marchand and Kitchener at Fashoda in 1898, when French national pride once again suffered a painful blow at the hands of the nonchalant British.

In the Middle East, France fared rather poorly in its attempts to gain direct political influence, as in 1840, when the other European powers supported the Ottomon Empire in its successful resistance to the expansionist efforts of the French-backed Egyptian ruler, Muhammad Ali. One exception was the case of Lebanon in 1860–1861, when French military intervention in the wake of the massacre of Christian communities in the region was supported by the other European powers, and agreement was reached among them on the creation of a new, Maronite-dominated *mutasarrifate* in Mount Lebanon.[1] However, the main thrust of French activity in the Ottoman Empire during this period came in the form of cultural expansion, which served as a modest compensation for Britain's political control in Egypt and commercial ascendancy throughout the region. This *mission civilisatrice* was carried out through the establishment of schools by Catholic missionaries, the *Alliance Israelite Universelle,* and the *Mission Laïque,* with both encouragement and, except in the case of the *Alliance,* financial support from the government. Although the closest and most lasting contacts thus established were with the non-Muslim minorities of the region, a significant number of Muslims did attend French schools, with the result that French became the European language most commonly spoken by the area's educated elite.[2]

With the entry of Turkey into World War I on the side of the Central Powers in November 1914, the prospect of a partition of the Ottoman Empire among the Allies once victory had been achieved immediately arose. Although the Sykes–Picot agreement of 1916 was intended to settle the division of the Middle East into British and French spheres of influence in advance, it was a British army under General Allenby that conquered Palestine and the Levant in the course of the following two years. Whether under orders from

London or Cairo, or on his own initiative, Allenby allowed Faisal's army of the Hejaz to take the credit for liberating Syria's major towns. A protracted standoff ensued between the French, who occupied the Lebanese coastal region, and the Syrian nationalists, who sought to create an independent state with Faisal as their monarch.

By September 1919, British Prime Minister Lloyd George had decided that the growing tension between his country and France was too high a price to pay for the fulfillment of Sherifian ambitions in the Levant. An ambiguous Anglo–French agreement on the disposition of the territories was concluded, after which British forces were withdrawn from Syria, leaving General Gouraud free to move in from the coast in July 1920, dispersing Faisal's ill-organized troops before him. The British compensated Faisal with the throne of Iraq and the League of Nations subsequently legitimized this division of spoils by recognizing French mandates in Syria and Greater Lebanon, while Britain was entrusted with the mandates for Palestine (including Transjordan) and Iraq.[3]

For Britain, the creation of military bases in these territories facilitated protection of the Suez Canal and thus enhanced the safety of the trade route to India, still the United Kingdom's single largest export market. Control of the Mosul oil fields in northern Iraq was a welcome bonus.[4] As for the French, their eagerness for mandates in the Levant was a direct outgrowth of their traditional interest in the region as patrons of the Maronites and propagators of French culture. To be left out of the division of spoils in the Middle East would have been a humiliating blow to France's international prestige. Control of the Levant, it was hoped, would also strengthen France's position as a Mediterranean power and provide it with an arena for lucrative financial investment. (These illusions were to be left unfulfilled, although the Iraq Petroleum Company's pipeline to Tripoli, Lebanon, did come to supply 40 percent of metropolitan France's oil needs by the end of the interwar period.[5])

More or less overnight, then, France's mode of action in the Middle East was transformed from the general propagation of its cultural influence throughout the region, to the exercise of direct political control over a relatively confined area.[6] The transition was an awkward one and led to contradictions. Retaining their sense of possessing a *mission civilisatrice,* the French were loath to grant the Syrians and Lebanese anything but the most rudimentary degree of self-rule. Officially, Syria and Lebanon were categorized as "Class A" mandates by the League of Nations—that is, they were slated for an early independence, toward which they were to be led by France's guiding hand. But the French tended to lay the emphasis on imbuing the local populations with French culture, and protecting the Christian minorities in the region. This was quite different from the League of Nations' Wilsonian conception of a political tutelage aimed at fostering the development of independent nation-states. From a more down-to-earth perspective, the French saw in the Levant one of the few prizes won as the result of a horrendous war, and they had no intention of abandoning it within a few years. To grant real independence to Syria and Lebanon, it was thought, would set a dangerous precedent for French North Africa, and would thus endanger France's entire position as a Mediterranean power.[7] Ultimately, the French saw the mandate as a form of legitimization for their rule, not a reason for giving it up.

Adopting the model of Lyautey's acclaimed system of colonial administration in Morocco, General Gouraud (appointed as the first high commissioner) and his successors in the Levant sought to establish an easily controlled system of indirect rule through native collaborators. At the same time, the resumption of organized resistance to French domination was to be forestalled by a policy of *divide et impera*. The French looked to the Lebanese Maronites as their most reliable base of support in the region, and sought to cultivate various other disaffected or threatened minorities such as the Alawites, Druze, Kurds, and Syrian Christians as buttresses of their influence.

Sectarianism was confirmed as the basis of political culture in Lebanon by the addition of predominantly Muslim areas to the old Maronite stronghold of the *mutasarrifate*. In Syria, the Damascene elite's aspirations to political power on a national scale were blocked by the creation of autonomous zones in the Alawite and Druze regions, and the further division of this truncated Syria into a state of Damascus and a state of Aleppo. (The administrative structure of Syria was periodically reshuffled over the course of the following twenty years, but the basic objective—to prevent the centralization of power in the hands of the Sunni Muslim elite—remained fairly constant.)[8]

While the Levant was divided into ministates and autonomous regions, effective political and economic power was centralized in a rigid, and increasingly corrupt, French administrative bureaucracy that monopolized decision making and controlled most of the Levant states' fiscal resources. All the departments that served the common needs of the territories, including customs, telecommunications, the railways, and public utilities, were labeled "Common Interests" and came under the direct control of the High Commission. Little effort was made to train a native elite that could gradually assume responsibility for some of these functions.

Whereas the Levant had an almost mystical appeal for the imperialist ideologues who had steered France into the region during and after World War I, it ranked quite low on the order of colonial priorities once the territory had actually been secured. In contrast to Algeria, the French community in Syria and Lebanon never rose above a few thousand souls in number. These were an ill-assorted group of teachers and scholars (both lay and clerical), businessmen, and the civil servants and officers who were stationed in the region.

As in metropolitan France, political opinion tended to grow increasingly polarized in the course of the interwar period in the French community in the Levant. The sharpest division appeared among the educators, with the lay teachers tending toward the left wing of republican politics, while the Jesuit missions were a bastion of antirepublican sentiment. For their part, the 300–400 French bureaucrats and functionaries in Syria and Lebanon appeared to concern themselves primarily with protecting the perquisites of office under whatever coalition happened to be governing in Paris.[9]

Lacking a trained corps of regional experts to run its administration and short of funds in a period of fiscal austerity, the French High Commission in Beirut was ill-equipped for its task. More fundamentally, its entire conception of how to establish and maintain French influence in the region was flawed. The Syrian elite of urban notables and absentee landlords—on whose cooperation any system of indirect rule was ultimately bound to depend—was not receptive to the patronizing techniques of political domination that Lyautey had more effectively exercised in Morocco. During the last two decades of Ottoman rule, many of the Syrian notables had turned to the ideology of Arab nationalism in response to the centralizing tendencies of the Young Turk regime. The nationalist dream of an independent Arab homeland appeared to have been fulfilled by the success of the Hashemite-led rebellion, and many of the notables had assumed influential positions in Faisal's fledgling government, when the French intervened militarily and imposed their own authority on the country. The subsequent division of Syria into ministates and the decision to carve a Greater Lebanon out of Syrian territory, only further antagonized the nationalists instead of undermining their movement.[10]

France's position was yet further compromised by the geopolitical context of its rule in the Levant: that of British control in the neighboring territories. More flexible in their approach than the French, the British were prepared to minimize their direct political role in Iraq and Egypt, provided their main strategic and economic interests were protected. Daily intervention in the running of affairs in the Arab countries was seen as an unnecessary burden, and Arab nationalism was viewed as a strongly rooted political force that should be given room to grow and that would only be radicalized if its demands were completely ignored.

A process of gradual disengagement culminated in the granting of independence to Iraq in 1932 and Egypt in 1936, on the basis of negotiated treaties that allowed the British to retain military bases and transit rights and guaranteed them unlimited access to all necessary facilities in the event of war. In practice, the British retained a supervisory role in the governance of Iraq and Egypt through the sheer weight of their military presence and through the advisers who were assigned to key ministries and services; however, a sufficient degree of self-rule was granted to these countries to undercut nationalist demands temporarily, and an aura of political stability was created around the British sphere of influence in the Middle East. In Transjordan, the British retained their mandatory administration, but in the Hashemite Emir Abdullah they had a loyal ally who hoped (in vain) to use the support of his British patrons to extend his sway over Syria and Iraq. The main source of friction between Britain and its regional client states in the 1930s was not so much the conduct of bilateral relations as the issue of Palestine.[11]

Britain's policy of disengagement from Egypt and Iraq created a destabilizing precedent for Syria. Chafing under the yoke of French bureaucratic domination and eager to take the first steps toward the fulfillment of their dream of a unified Arab homeland, the Syrian nationalists demanded a greater role in running their country's affairs. They backed their demand with periodic general strikes and the instigation of popular unrest. In 1925, French mishandling of relations with the semifeudal leadership of the Jebel Druze sparked off an armed uprising in the region, which rapidly spread to Damascus and many other parts of Syria. The foundation of French *divide et impera* policy was shaken as the Druze leaders forged a working alliance with the nationalist leadership of Damascus in a bloody challenge to French rule that was not completely suppressed until 1927.

The 1925 revolt was a major turning point in the history of Syria under the mandate. It left a legacy of intensified bitterness against the French, who had twice bombarded Damascus during the height of the conflict. It was also a watershed in the development of nationalist politics. The revolt brought Dr. Abd al-Rahman Shahbandar to the fore as the main leader of the nationalist movement, and simultaneously sowed the seeds of discord within that movement. Shahbandar, a Damascene political activist with close ties to the British-sponsored Hashemite regime in Transjordan, had formed the People's Party just before the outbreak of the conflict, and dominated the Syrian–Palestine Congress Executive that served as the umbrella organization coordinating the revolt from Palestine. As the inevitability of French military victory became apparent in the latter half of 1926, Shahbandar urged his colleagues to follow a practical course and come to terms with the French while concessions were still to be had. This placed him at odds with more intransigent figures such as Adil and Shakib Arslan, and Shukri al-Quwatli, a veteran of the pre-1918, anti-Turkish secret societies. This group, which was to forge increasingly close ties with the German government in the following decade, became known as the Istiqlali party (from the Arabic word for independence).

In the aftermath of the revolt, the French authorities realized that they would have to coopt a portion of the nationalist leadership if they were to govern Syria successfully in the future. After the promulgation of a relatively liberal constitution for Lebanon in 1927, a group of Syrian nationalists who had avoided exile issued a conciliatory statement indicating their readiness to work out a similar arrangement for Syria as a first step toward a more permanent solution. This group was the kernel of what was to be called the National Bloc, a broadly based coalition of Syrian nationalists who were ready in principle to do business with the French if the latter would give them political power within the framework of Syrian self-rule. Strengthened by the return of some exiles in 1928, the National Bloc came to be dominated by notables such as Jamil Mardam and Hashem al Ata-si. Soon after his return from exile in 1931, Shukri al-Quwatli led his Istiqlalis into the National Bloc as a means of challenging Jamil Mardam's leadership from within his own movement. The People's Party continued to maintain its separate identity, while Shahbandar himself remained in exile until 1937. Although none of these groups were modern political parties with well-structured, grass-roots organizations, they were able to wield influence through the personal clientele of their individual members. The nationalists depended on this vital connection to urban street life if they were to pressure the French into coming to terms with them. On the other hand, the mandatory authorities were in a position to determine who would emerge at the head of the nationalist movement by choosing the group to which their concessions would be made. It was with these cards in their hands that the two sides slowly edged toward the negotiating table.[12]

In 1930, the French followed the precedent they had set in Lebanon two years earlier by unilaterally imposing a constitution on Syria that granted it a large measure of parliamentary self-rule, but preserved the principle of mandatory tutelage and imposed strict curbs on Syrian jurisdiction in the country's autonomous regions. These were conditions that the National Bloc refused to accept, although some of its members did join the unstable coalitions that came to power in Syria in the first half of the 1930s as the result of an electoral process that was closely monitored and controlled by the French. The National Bloc's influence in the Syrian legislature and government was strong enough to scuttle all French attempts to negotiate a treaty of independence that would preserve the Alawite and Druze regions as sectors of effective French control in a legally independent Syria. Meanwhile, the accession of Iraq and Egypt to the ranks of the League of Nations in 1932 and 1936, respectively, increased the pressure on the French authorities to grant a similar measure of self-rule to Syria.

Although Lebanon tended to be much more quiescent under French rule than was Syria, the Muslim community in the areas annexed in 1920 had never reconciled itself to its inclusion in the Maronite-dominated state. Throughout the interwar years, the Sunni political leadership continued to advocate reabsorption into Syria of the predominantly Muslim territories. The most vocal Sunni leader in Lebanon was Riad al-Solh, whose espousal of pan-Arab nationalism earned him the particular suspicion of the French authorities. Within the Maronite community, the traditional pro-French orientation was represented by a loosely organized political coalition known as the National Bloc (which bore no relation to its Syrian namesake), led by Emile Edde. But even among the Maronites there were those in the 1930s who were influenced by the growth of Arab nationalism in the region and conscious of the need to adapt to changing circumstances. Most notably, al-Khoury's Constitutional Bloc began to distance itself from the conception of Lebanon as a Western outpost in the Middle East, and to press for the negotiation of a new constitution for the country that would grant it a much greater degree of self-rule. Although personal feuds and clan rivalries were crucial elements in the formation of these alignments, the ideological factor lent clearer definition to the parties and was to play an even more substantive role during the crucial war years.[13]

In 1936, the left-wing Popular Front came to power in France, and quickly set a new tone in French colonial policy by inviting a delegation of National Bloc leaders headed by Hashem al-Atasi and Jamil Mardam to Paris for treaty negotiations. The delegation returned triumphantly to Damascus with a treaty in hand, along the lines of the Anglo–Iraqi model. (A similar treaty was negotiated with the Lebanese.) The High Commission was instructed to take the first steps toward the implementation of the treaty: the Druze and Alawite territories, as well as the northeastern frontier zone known as the Jezireh, were integrated into the Syrian state and parliamentary elections were held in which the French allowed the National Bloc to gain an overwhelming majority. Under a government headed by Hashem al-Atasi as president and Jamil Mardam as prime minister, Syria seemed headed toward legal independence and a large measure of effective self-rule. Only one element was missing: ratification of the treaty by the French Senate. Despite revisions demanded and obtained from the Syrians, a majority in favor of the treaty could not be mustered in France's upper chamber, especially under the more centrist governments that succeeded the shortlived Popular Front.

Remaining in power without moving Syria any closer to independence, the National Bloc found its position increasingly embarrassing, as Shahbandar and his supporters accused it of having surrendered Syria's birthright for the sake of a French-brewed pottage. In 1938, the French further compromised the National Bloc (and discredited themselves) in Syrian eyes by ceding the *sanjaq* of Alexandretta (a district in the northwest of the country with a large proportion of Turkish speakers among its inhabitants) to Turkey. In the following year, consideration of treaty ratification was formally suspended by the French government.[14] In the wake of this decision, Hashem al-Atasi resigned, followed soon after by Jamil Mardam. With the outbreak of war in September, the new high commissioner, Gabriel Puaux, suspended the Syrian and Lebanese constitutions and replaced the elected governments with administrative directorates immediately answerable to his authority.[15]

British policy in the Middle East disturbed the French not only because of the problems created for them by the force of its example, but also because it was perceived as being deliberately aimed at the undermining of French rule in the Levant. Faisal, after all, had been a British protégé, and he and his successors on the Iraqi throne, as well as his brother the Emir Abdullah of Transjordan, continued to cultivate support for their dynasty among the Syrian population. During the 1925–1926 revolt, some Syrian guerrilla fighters crossed the border into Transjordan at their convenience and their leaders found refuge there. Surely this could not happen without the connivance of the British mandatory authorities?[16] The latter insisted that they were restraining Abdullah and were refusing to lend assistance to the Druze rebels across the border, but the French were never completely convinced.[17] (The Druze themselves were not averse to exacerbating Anglo–French tensions by exaggerating their reports of assistance from across the border.[18]) During the Arab Revolt in Palestine of 1936–1939, the French reciprocated by allowing the leaders of the uprising to use the Levant as a base of operations against the British.[19] An assessment by the British consul in Damascus indicated that French resentment may not have been completely misplaced:

> It is a noteworthy fact that the British authorities in Palestine and particularly in Transjordan showed a hospitality to Syrian bandits and rebels which now we must truthfully regret. A sharp thorn in our side today is Mahomet al Ashmar. A bandit chief . . . who was directly responsible for the death of two French officers and three French noncommissioned officers in 1925, he had a previous criminal record and was condemned to death by French court martial. He escaped into Palestine where we insisted on treating him as a

political refugee. His case like that of Fawzi Kawokji, a deserter from the French forces, was only one of many. Most of those [who] then benefited from British asylum are now planning to go, or had already gone, to Palestine, to continue their acts of terrorism, this time directed against the British administration.[20]

The continual friction marking Anglo–French relations in the region appears all the more remarkable in view of the common threats that the two powers faced, both from the local nationalists and from other aspirants to the position of imperial overlord of the Middle East. Fascist Italy's grand strategy, after all, was aimed at creating a latter-day Roman Empire on the banks of the Mediterranean (*mare nostrum*) and toward this end a major effort was invested in education and propaganda among the native populations of the eastern Mediterranean. Italy also cultivated direct political influence in Yemen and struck a not insignificant blow to Britain's regional prestige through the conquest of Abyssinia in 1935, carried out in complete disregard of the concentration of British naval forces at Alexandria. Germany also maintained contacts with nationalist circles throughout the Middle East, and, though it was more discreet, Berlin seemed to hold a greater attraction for the Arab nationalists than did Rome. In general, the fascist mystique seemed to exert a much more powerful fascination over the minds of political activists in the Arab world than did the example of Western democracy. Particularly in the Levant, the late 1930s witnessed the sprouting of a number of political parties (such as Antun Sa'adeh's Parti Populaire Syrien and Pierre Gemayel's Maronite Falange movement) that were transparent imitations of the Italian or German model; existing parties sought to move with the times by setting up fascist-style youth movements that clashed with each other on the streets.[21]

And yet, although larger strategic considerations may have occupied the minds of planners in London and Paris, local representatives of the two powers seemed much more obsessed with combating each other's influence than with cooperating against common dangers. French resentment against the British was fed not only by incidents recalled from the previous decade, but also by developments in the 1930s. During those years, the Iraqi and Transjordanian branches of the Hashemite dynasty began to campaign actively—and in competition with one another—for the creation of a pan-Arab federation that was to include Syria. This aspiration struck a sympathetic chord among some of the British officials based in the region, who considered that such a federation might provide a more stable basis for British influence in the Middle East. (Whitehall took a much more cautious view of the matter.) French control over the Levant obviously constituted a hindrance to the fulfillment of such a plan, and the French were convinced that local British officials such as Glubb Pasha, the commander of Transjordan's Arab Legion, were conspiring with nationalist elements in Syria to overthrow French rule there.[22]

There is no doubt that many of these officials did indeed regard the French presence in the Levant as an unnecessary complication in a region already crowded with overlapping interests and contradictory policies. But the real source of French malaise seemed to be a sense of insecurity born of weakness. In Europe, France had been forced for years to follow the British lead in foreign policy.[23] The Levant, with its historical ties to France, provided an imperial arena in which the latter could play the role of a Great Power; it could serve as a source of prestige that would make it worth its upkeep. Yet even here, the French role was being dwarfed by the regional influence of the United Kingdom. One British diplomat, writing two months before the out-break of the 1925 Syrian revolt, put it as follows:

> I have the honour to report that since my return from leave I have noticed a considerable intensification of anti-British feeling among the French Officials and Officers at Damascus. This feeling appears to me to arise from no local causes but from a vague, general perception of France's helplessness in the world to-day and from an exasperated realisation of the inevitable progress of Anglo–Saxon predominance.[24]

Unable to accept the reduction of their country to the rank of a second-rate power, the French sought to cast all the blame for their troubles on Britain, and seemed almost gratified when local British officials obliged them by behaving in a suspect manner. One French naval commander in the Levant assessed the situation in 1934 as follows:

> Everywhere from Aden to Alexandretta, England is, perhaps through the activity of her local agents rather than in the execution of a general plan, engaged in activities every day and in every way, which are tending to under-mine and cramp French influence, to destroy our traditional position and to eliminate us from the East.[25]

Unwilling to confront the reality of nationalism as a potent new force in Middle Eastern politics, the French persuaded themselves that popular unrest was entirely the product of British subversion. The romanticization of Law-rence's wartime exploits combined with a fascination with intelligence and espionage to convince the French of the existence of a vast network of British agents whose sole purpose was to topple the French edifice in the Levant. This myth was even popularized in a poorly written novel, *La Châtelaine du Liban*, whose protagonist, an officer in the *Deuxième Bureau* by the name of Domevre, is pitted against a devious British agent who tirelessly hatches anti-French plots. Domevre's fictional musings seem to have been all too typical of many of his real-life counterparts:

> Here, in a narrow office of the Grand Sérail [headquarters of the French High Commission in Beirut], . . . I sensed the pride and the grandeur of the task which devolved upon me. In these hundreds of dossiers, of notes, of multicolored files which I ceaselessly examined and classified with a meticu-lous love, it was the entire French epic in Syria which rose up and unfolded, ever exposed to the monstrous intrigues of our enemies, of our allies. . . . With a sense of exaltation bred of horror and of pride, something of the sentiment which one feels when laying a bomb, I handled the tragic blue, red,

green, white files: Sherifian plots, English plots, American plots. . . . Ah! A
world of underground enemies against whom I must, dear country of mine,
protect you![26]

During the period when the rest of the world was engulfed by the confla-
gration of the Second World War, it was with their multicolored files on each
other that both British and French in the Levant remained obsessed.

1

Initial Ambiguities

The Impact of the Armistice

On June 16, 1940, in the last days of the Battle of France, Prime Minister Reynaud resigned and was replaced by the aged World War I hero, Marshal Pétain. The Pétain Government immediately requested armistice terms from the German military command and the final document was signed at Compiègne on June 24. Hostilities were thus brought to a halt and France entered a prolonged period of domination by and collaboration with the occupying forces.

Despite the juridical legitimacy of the new regime, the situation did not immediately appear clear-cut from the perspective of some of the French colonies. Hardly any of the colonial administrators were willing at this stage to follow the example of General de Gaulle's intransigent repudiation of Pétain's political authority. It did take some time for the spirit of defeatism to seep through to the colonies, however, and there were quite a few figures who were initially inclined to distinguish between the desperate situation in which metropolitan France found itself and the options that remained open to the French Empire. The belief also seems initially to have been prevalent that Pétain and his cabinet secretly favored a continued role for the empire in the prosecution of the war.

In the Middle East, where the British and French had engaged in close military coordination and planning from the onset of war, the initial inclination of the local French authorities was to maintain the joint war effort. The distance separating the Levant from metropolitan France was a psychological as well as a geographical one. Gabriel Puaux, high commissioner in Beirut, was later to contrast the spirit of defeatism prevailing in France with

> the perspective of most of the Frenchmen in the Levant, who had not measured the extent of the disaster with their own eyes, who had not felt its weight and whose intact nervous system lent itself more easily to indignation than to resignation.[1]

In his diary entry for June 16, 1940, Puaux noted:

> This morning, General Mittelhauser [commander-in-chief of French forces in the Eastern Mediterranean] was indignant at the idea of a separate peace.

13

"One does not treat with Hitler, says he; better to let oneself be killed in the last trench."[2]

Two days before the signature of the armistice, General Wavell, British commander-in-chief in the Middle East, flew to Beirut to confer with Mittelhauser on the possibility of establishing a joint Anglo–French supply center in the region. On the day the armistice was signed, Mittelhauser told the head of the British military mission in Beirut that he recognized that his determination to remain in the war would probably result in a break with Pétain and Weygand.[3] Gabriel Puaux made public his commitment to the war effort regardless of the armistice in a radio address on June 23.[4] He also assured Godfrey Havard, the British consul-general in Beirut, "that French authorities in Syria and the Lebanon are determined to fight on, whatever instructions they receive from French Government."[5]

Puaux and Mittelhauser did not expect the Levant to be the only French-controlled territory to adopt this stance. Rather, they hoped that an anti-armistice front could be established among the French Middle Eastern and African territories and they sent telegrams to this effect to General Noguès in Algeria as well as to Peyrouton in French West Africa. It is clear, however, that Mittelhauser and Puaux expected the leading role in the French colonial war effort to be played by the most important French-held territory in the region. In his telegram to Noguès, Mittelhauser emphasized that the commitment Puaux and he had made to a continuation of the war effort was based on the assumption that

> a Government of Imperial France will constitute itself in North Africa as well as a Commander-in-Chief of the forces of the Empire. . . . It seems to me urgent that someone take into his hands the conduct of military operations . . . in liaison with the British Command and organize the general supply effort.[6]

While Noguès was initially inclined to support the idea of continued colonial commitment to the war effort, he was loath to accept the responsibility of leadership himself. Instead, he wrote to General Weygand, Pétain's minister of national defense, seeking to win him over to the idea:

> Only you can assume responsibilities here which will extend over all of Overseas France and channel individual initiatives.
>
> Your personality would bring about the union of all and your status as member of the Government would make it possible to keep the decisions taken within a national framework.[7]

Weygand was quick to send disciplinary telegrams to both Noguès and Mittelhauser making it clear that imperial resistance was quite incompatible with the terms of the armistice.[8] In the absence of support from above, Noguès promptly fell into line with the Pétain government's official policy.

Puaux and Mittelhauser thus found themselves isolated and forced to choose between an independent political initiative and a return to bureaucratic discipline. They chose the latter, albeit with reluctance. Puaux wrote to Foreign Minister Baudoin:

> Contrary to what Your Excellency thinks, it was not easy for me clearly to perceive where my duty lay. The maintenance of resistance by our Empire seemed to me the most effective means of coming to the aid of the British armies, whose victory alone can deliver France from the definitive subjugation with which she is menaced. . . . I cannot conceal from your Excellency that my disappointment as a patriot was profound.[9]

In the rather defensive account that he gives of this period in his memoirs, Puaux claims that the decisive factor that led him to accept the armistice was the fear that if the Levant continued on its own with the war effort, it would become little more than a pawn in the hands of the British. A conversation with Consul-General Havard had left him with the impression that the British were willing to envision the cession of northern Syria to the Turks in exchange for Turkish military cooperation. Therefore, as long as the Axis powers did not threaten to annex the Levant, France's interests in the region would best be served by a policy of neutrality as dictated by the terms of the armistice.[10] As he put it in a postwar attempt to justify his decision:

> A Franco–British condominium in Damascus and Beirut could not fail to be the prelude to our eviction from the Middle East. . . . There was no room for two in Syria, and we were not the strongest ones.[11]

A more cynical interpretation of Puaux's behavior might be that, having failed to find a responsive chord for his ideas either in North Africa or in France, he judged it safer not to stick his own neck out. The true nature of his predicament is probably best described by Mittelhauser's chief of staff, Colonel de Larminat, who writes:

> The High Commission was very defeatist, apart from that good Mr. Puaux, who was full of good intentions, but who felt altogether overtaken by events for which he had some trouble finding valid precedents.[12]

Confronted with a situation in which the distinction between treachery and patriotism was completely obscured, Puaux avoided taking a leap of faith, and chose instead to try and ride out the storm.

Despite his commitment to observance of the armistice terms, Puaux initially assured Havard that he would continue to aid the British war effort indirectly by leaving French troops free to join British forces in Palestine if they wished and by turning over as much war materiel as possible to the British.[13] Action was not suited to words, however. Colonel de Larminat did manage to convince Mittelhauser to permit him to furnish a Polish brigade stationed in the Levant with supplementary equipment from French stocks and to facilitate its passage over the border to Palestine.[14] When de Larminat tried to organize a mass defection of fully equipped French units to Palestine, however, he was promptly arrested.[15] (He managed to escape, with outside help, within thirty-six hours and ultimately joined de Gaulle's forces.) As early as July 2, 1940, the U.S. consul-general reported:

> The attitude of these [local French] authorities appears now to be primarily one of determination to support the Bordeaux Government unreservedly in carrying out the terms of the armistice in the hope of avoiding the presence there of an armistice commission with Italian and German members; secondarily, but increasingly one of distrust of the British.[16]

The final breach in Anglo–French cooperation in the eastern Mediterranean came on July 3, in the form of Britain's preemptive attack on the French fleet at Mers el-Kebir, Algeria. This seemed to provide ex post facto justification for the armistice, allaying any unease Puaux and Mittelhauser may still have felt over their abandonment of the joint war effort. Puaux reported:

> The aggression of the British navy stirred all of the French of the Levant profoundly. This is in any case a blow struck at the movement of rallying to the British forces of Palestine.[17]

Puaux did add significantly that "if the assurance could be given that no Italian or German commissioner will come to the Levant, no further incident is to be feared."[18] Given the past history of colonial rivalry in the region, Mers el-Kebir "crystallized in the most durable manner the sentiments of defiance and hostility of the French of the Levant, and above all of the officers, towards Great Britain."[19]

The British Consider Their Options

The British were thus confronted with a very ambiguous situation in the Levant. The high commissioner in Beirut was a man who had whole-heartedly cooperated with them up to the fall of France and who had accepted the armistice with the greatest of reluctance. Yet the government whose authority he accepted was under the German heel and seemed more inclined to strike bargains with the enemy than to maintain ties with its former ally. Would Vichy be willing to offer the Axis bases in the Levant? Would Puaux actually obey orders to that effect if they were given? Would Puaux be able to maintain a firm grip on Syria and Lebanon or was a power vacuum likely to develop in the region? The British were not sure that they could afford the risk of letting time provide the answers to these questions.

British representatives in the Arab world reported the existence among the ruling circles of widespread sentiment in favor of immediate British intervention in Syria and Lebanon. The Arab regimes in the British sphere of influence clearly perceived this juncture as a golden opportunity for destroying the French mandate in the Levant. Each one hoped to reap direct or indirect benefits from the collapse of French rule. The Iraqi prime minister, doubtless hoping to bring Syria under the wing of a Baghdad-based, pan-Arab confederation, urged the British to force the French to grant Syria and Lebanon independence. The Saudis expressed their fear of an Italo–Turkish partition of Syria and implied that military action should be undertaken to prevent this.[20] The Emir Abdullah of Transjordan feared that the emergence of a power vacuum in Syria might lead to the enthronement of a Saudi monarch there, and he hoped an immediate British takeover might result in the annexation of Syria to his emirate.[21] From Damascus, the British consul himself urged immediate intervention, arguing that French troops were in a state of bewilderment and would rally to the British in large numbers.[22] No doubt the eagerness among the Arab states for a British military takeover in the Levant must have appealed to the imperialist instinct of some of His Majesty's representatives in the Middle East.

In fact, however, the British government was in no mood for political or military adventurism in the region. All available resources had to be conserved for the struggle with the Axis powers and it was hoped that the situation in the Levant would remain stable enough to obviate British intervention. There was certainly no need to drive a further wedge between France and Britain by reviving the old colonial rivalry in the Middle East. The only immediate reaction to the Levant's adherence to the armistice was the extension to it of the economic embargo against Vichy France.[23] In a memorandum prepared by the Eastern Department of the Foreign Office just before Puaux's acquiescence in the armistice, it was emphasized that caution was necessary in dealing with the authority of the French in the Levant "so long as they continue to act, even if only in a passive way, in the Allied interest."[24] If the French actually lost political control of Syria and Lebanon, British forces would, of course, have to step in to prevent an Axis incursion:

> But any such measures should, so far as possible, be temporary in the strictest sense of the word. . . . It is . . . at least possible . . . that a state of affairs will return [after the war] in which cooperation throughout the world between Great Britain and a revivified France will be essential to each. The fact that France has a stake in the Middle East has upon the whole been an advantage in recent years. . . . Furthermore, the interest of France in the Levant, and especially her sentimental interest has always been very great and nothing would be more likely to prejudice future Anglo–French unity in a wider field than the suspicion that His Majesty's Government had taken advantage of the difficulties of France to whittle down the French position there— especially as similar suspicions have persisted in some French circles from the last war down to the present day. . . . His Majesty's Government must endeavour to avoid doing or saying anything which will make it impossible for the "true France" to resume her former position there when the war is over.[25]

The subsequent course of events was to demonstrate how well-founded this warning was.

With both ambitions and fears being awakened throughout the Middle East by the potential prospect of a power vacuum emerging in the Levant, the War Cabinet decided to issue a public declaration clarifying the British approach to the problem.[26] This served as a warning to the French not to allow any Axis inroads on the region as well as an assurance that Britain had no interest in undermining long-term French control there:

> His Majesty's Government declare that they could not allow Syria or the Lebanon to be occupied by any hostile Power or to be used as a base for

attacks upon those countries in the Middle East they are pledged to defend, or to become the scene of such disorder as to constitute a danger to those countries. . . . Any action which they may hereafter be obliged to take in fulfillment of this declaration will be entirely without prejudice to the future status of the territories now under French mandate.[27]

A wait-and-see attitude was thus adopted by London; all options were kept open in the event British strategic interests in the Levant were prejudiced. As for Arab or Turkish hopes of exploiting the situation for their own purposes, Foreign Secretary Halifax pointed out:

The declaration has been drafted so as to avoid constituting a promise or commitment to anybody. It is intended as a reservation of the right of His Majesty's Government to do whatever they may think necessary in or in regard to Syria and Lebanon.[28]

In the absence of any decisive action to clarify the situation in the Levant, the British authorities began vacillating between different approaches in their dealings with Beirut. The first issue to arise immediately in the wake of the armistice was whether or not to encourage the defection of French troops to Palestine. As has been seen, Colonel de Larminat failed in his attempt to organize a mass defection, but with a British military mission still in Beirut, the situation might be redressed. Yet how could an active attempt to subvert military discipline in the Levant be reconciled with a policy of preserving the stability of the region? General Wavell argued that to encourage the disintegration of the French army in Syria was to create conditions under which Britain would be forced to intervene militarily. He insisted that the only hope of gaining a cooperative attitude from the French authorities lay in avoiding any disruption of their control over the Levant.[29] Uncertain over the pros and cons of this cautious approach, the War Office responded with a series of conflicting telegrams that finally ended with a vaguely worded authorization "to take action as you consider required"[30]; that is, to take no action at all!

When Winston Churchill was informed of this decision he saw it as undercutting his attempt to build up a Free French force under General de Gaulle. He fired off an angry telegram to Wavell countermanding the War Office authorization: "Do not . . . on any account discourage the rallying of good men to our cause upon consideration local to your own command."[31] Two days later came Mers el-Kebir and the closing of the British military mission in Beirut. As of that date only about 200 French troops had crossed to Palestine and from that point on, the French attitude toward the British hardened and discipline was tightened in the ranks of the military.[32] The opportunity created by the earlier state of confusion in the Levant had been lost.

The ambivalence that had characterized Britain's handling of the troop-defection issue was to mark its policy toward the Vichy-occupied Levant throughout the following year. Italy's autumn 1940 offensive in the Western Desert added to the logistical complications that direct British intervention in Syria would have entailed. In any case, London still hoped to cultivate contact with anti-German elements in Vichy and had no desire to seek unnecessary confrontation with the metropolitan French regime.[33] Although Vichy had broken off direct diplomatic relations with London on July 8, Britain retained consular representation in Beirut and Damascus. (Consul-General Havard was eventually forced to move his residence to the village of Aley, on the outskirts of Beirut.) It was hoped that the distance separating Syria and Lebanon from France, combined with the Levant's heavy dependence on trade with its British-controlled neighbors, would help foster a cooperative spirit in the Beirut High Commission.[34]

Britain's primary concern was to ensure that the Beirut authorities would not permit Axis forces to gain a foothold in the Levant. Although active French resistance to any Axis move seemed unlikely, the British wanted at least to be assured that they would not be prevented from intervening in the event of a German or Italian attack on Syria.[35] The Foreign Office asked Consul-General Havard to secure Puaux's acceptance of such an understanding, regardless of Vichy's orders. In addition, London wished Puaux to respect the British embargo on metropolitan France by not shipping any oil to Marseilles. Railroads connecting Turkey with Iraq and Palestine via the Levant were to be kept open. British ships held at Beirut harbor were to be exchanged for French ships at Haifa. Ideally, the French authorities would also be willing to afford His Majesty's government the opportunity to spread anti-German propaganda in Syria and Lebanon. In return for such cooperation, Britain was willing to permit trade between the Levant and Palestine and to restrain the pan-Arab nationalists (particularly the Iraqi regime) from stirring up unrest in Syria. In addition, a monthly subsidy of up to 150,000 pounds sterling might be offered to the French authorities, depending on the degree to which they were willing to satisfy British desiderata.[36] Thus, London hoped that for a small price, Britain's basic strategic interests in the Levant would be safeguarded, obviating the need for an invasion of the territory.

Puaux's Position

Up to a point, the British were right to think that the peculiarly vulnerable position of the Levant would render Puaux amenable to some sort of local modus vivendi with them. Puaux's initial response to the overture was quite favorable, and Havard gained the impression that Vichy was allowing its high commissioner considerable freedom of action in handling the situation as he saw fit.[37] Certainly, in his telegraphic correspondence with Vichy, Puaux continually emphasized that Syria and Lebanon were dependent on trade with Palestine for their economic well-being. If the British-imposed trade boycott were to continue indefinitely, an economic crisis might develop and popular unrest could ensue. Given the poor state of morale among French reservists in the Levant, Puaux clearly doubted his ability to handle widespread trouble.[38] He accordingly asked the Foreign Ministry "to leave me a certain latitude of action to settle this problem."[39]

Such freedom of action was never actually granted to Puaux, however, for Vichy's perception of the Levant dilemma was quite different from that of the high commissioner. Vichy's main concern was to appease the German authorities and convince them that at no level did there exist any French collusion with the British. When Puaux broached the possibility of satisfying the British demand for an exchange of ships detained in Beirut and Haifa, Vichy initially rejected it out of hand: "It is important to avoid any dealings between the two navies. The project must therefore be discarded."[40] Puaux was never authorized to make any significant decisions on his own and, when push came to shove, his obedience was commanded by Vichy. That was a decision he had made just after the armistice and the British were mistaken in thinking they could wean him away from it.

With the initial prospects for reaching an understanding with Puaux looking bright, London authorized the Palestine High Commission to send its economic adviser Walsh to Beirut to hammer out an economic clearing agreement with the French. These talks were to be coordinated with Havard's continuing political discussions with Puaux.[41] In the meantime, meetings were held between French and British district officers on the Syria–Transjordanian border and the British resident in Amman met with the French commander of the Jebel Druze in an effort to defuse long-standing local tensions and reassure each other of their good intentions.[42] Amid this atmosphere of pragmatic good will, the economic talks proceeded smoothly and rapidly. By the end of July, an agreement had been reached that provided for a resumption of trade between the Levant and Palestine under regulations designed to prevent an adverse balance of trade for either side and circumventing problems created by inconsistent monetary exchange rates. Havard eagerly urged London to put the agreement into effect immediately in order to reward and further encourage the cooperative attitude of the French.[43]

Attitude did not seem to reflect itself in action, however. On August 1, the three British ships detained in Beirut were officially requisitioned by the French and the crews (numbering forty men in all) were interned on orders from Vichy.[44] A few days later, Vichy ordered Puaux to declare a ban on the issuing of exit visas to all British and Allied males of military age resident in the Levant. With Beirut carrying out orders inimical to British interests, it was decided that immediate implementation of the clearing agreement was out of the question despite Havard's continued eagerness to reward Puaux for his personal good will.[45] One Eastern Department official noted:

It will be necessary for the French administration to begin to feel some of the economic difficulties which we have every reason to hope they will feel without our aid, before they begin to face realities and realize that what Vichy says is not the last word in territories where, in the long run, they cannot make their authority felt.[46]

Ill at ease with Vichy's orders and continually fearful of the potential consequences of the British economic boycott, Puaux did all he could to convince Vichy to change its approach. He continually repeated his request that the decision against the ship exchange be reviewed, and did secure Vichy's approval for the release of the interned British crews. In response, the British agreed to sell the Levant authorities a two weeks' supply of petroleum, with the understanding that Puaux would continue his efforts on behalf of a ship exchange.[47] Puaux also requested the annulment of the exit visa ban and was authorized to inform Havard that the ban did not extend to transit visas. Furthermore, Puaux permitted British military cargoes to traverse the Levant by rail. The British were thus able to maintain easy communication with Turkey and felt accordingly relieved.[48] In response to Havard's consistently apologetic interpretation of Puaux's behavior, however, Churchill remained resolutely in favor of a continued economic boycott of Syria:

> All this idea of "subjugation without tears" is wrong. . . . The economic distress is much more likely to make them turn to us . . . than to be a help to the Germans. The maxim should be to help and feed our friends, to hinder our foes and let indifferent or unhelpful neutrals suffer the full consequences of their pusillanimity.[49]

The Arab Nationalist Factor

While the British maintained a fairly tight trade boycott of the Levant, they remained careful to avoid any policies likely to threaten Puaux's grip on the region directly. Throughout July and August, Iraqi Foreign Minister Nuri Pasha was cultivating contacts with the National Bloc leaders in Syria and trying to coordinate action with the Saudi and Egyptian governments in an effort to pressure Vichy into granting independence to Syria.[50] The Foreign Office emphasized to its representatives in the area that Britain had no interest in undermining French rule in Syria:

> His Majesty's Government cannot take part in manoeuvres to wring independence for Syria from them against their wishes. Similarly, unless events force His Majesty's Government to abandon all hope of co-operation with the French authorities, they must do everything in their power to dissuade their Arab friends from making position of French authorities more difficult than it is already.[51]

While avoiding direct interference in Nuri Pasha's activities, the British found it easy to rely on the mutual suspicion of the various Arab regimes under their control or influence to help undermine Iraq's efforts.[52] Thus, Ibn Saud, while willing to back Syrian demands for independence, was reluctant to see any other Arab country gain leverage in the Levant as a result. He was particularly suspicious of Nuri Pasha's plans for the formation of an Arab federation including Syria, fearing that the Hashemite regime would use such a federation as a cover for expanding its own regional influence. The Saudi monarch appealed to British sympathy by suggesting to Stonehewer-Bird, the minister in Jedda, that the Iraqis were willing to contemplate the cultivation of ties with Germany. Stonehewer-Bird was instructed to encourage Ibn Saud's attitude and make it clear that His Majesty's government was itself opposed to the convening of a pan-Arab congress at that juncture.[53] By the end of August, Nuri Pasha's eager overtures to the Saudi and Egyptian governments over the possibility of a joint *démarche* to Vichy had still elicited no more than a dull and unenthusiastic response. The British minister in Baghdad reported that Nuri had become "depressed and uncommunicative." An Eastern Department official commented tersely that Nuri's latest trip (to Cairo) "seems to have been quite educative."[54]

Puaux and the Shahbandar Murder

At the beginning of July, just as Nuri Pasha's diplomatic efforts were getting under way, Dr. Abd al-Rahman Shahbandar was assassinated in Damascus and suspicion fell on the National Bloc's leadership. The investigation of the murder immediately became a highly charged political issue, over which Puaux's and Vichy's views diverged sharply and which led to a demonstration of considerable self-assertion on the high commissioner's part.

From the very start, Puaux suspected that the instigators of the crime were to be searched for "in the nationalist circles favorable towards an Iraqi–Syrian union."[55] In August, five suspects were arrested, religious zealots who appeared to have had obscure reasons of their own for the deed, but who implicated Jamil Mardam's chief aide, Asim al-Na'ili, as an instigator.[56] The Saudi consul-general in Beirut (whose government had close ties with Shukri al-Quwatli) immediately interceded on behalf of the National Bloc leadership, asking Puaux not to implicate it in the assassination.[57] The Iraqi consul soon added his own voice to this delicate request. Puaux dutifully reported to his government on these interventions, and was shocked by an answering cable from Vichy instructing him to respond favorably by halting the entire investigation on grounds of insufficient evidence, or at least by arranging for the proceedings to be drawn out indefinitely. Charles-Roux of the Foreign Ministry argued that, in addition to the difficulties of France's current position in the Middle East,

> the ever so suspect behavior of Shahbandar was too systematically harmful to us, for us to believe ourselves morally obliged to commit ourselves, at whatever cost, to punish the authors, still less the instigators, of his murder. The opening of the trial entails the risk, moreover, of furnishing a number of local as well as external elements with an opportunity for new intrigues.[58]

Clearly, Shahbandar's friendly ties with the Emir Abdullah and his British backers were central factors in determining Vichy's attitude toward his murder. The fact that the Axis powers were reported to be providing financial support to the National Bloc may also have carried weight with a French government reluctant to antagonize the Germans.[59] In any case, Jamil Mardam and his associates had proved useful negotiating partners in the past, and could well play a similar role in the future. Why alienate them for the sake of a dead man who was, in French eyes, no better than an agent of British influence in the Levant?

Puaux appears to have been outraged by this approach. He immediately pointed out that, in view of the confessions that had just been obtained from the five assassins, it would be impossible to close the investigation. In addition, the protraction of the investigation would pose a direct threat to internal security, for it would encourage Shahbandar's followers to take justice into their own hands and thus result in retaliatory murders, agitation, and popular unrest. Above all, it was Vichy's fear of confrontation and lack of moral backbone that seems to have been alien to Puaux:

> As long as the French flag flies in Syria, I consider that our duty as well as our interest is to maintain order there without weakness, and not to let the reputation for impartial justice which forms an integral part of our patrimony in the Levant be tarnished.[60]

Although conceding the need to go ahead with the investigation, Vichy remained extremely reluctant to allow the French authorities to associate themselves directly with the proceedings. In any case, Puaux was instructed not to conduct the investigation under the auspices of the long-dormant Cour de Justice over which both French and Syrian judges would preside:

> Such an initiative would be difficult to reconcile . . . with the reserve dictated to us by circumstances. I would, in addition, see an advantage in the disengagement of our direct responsibility in so far as possible. To this end, investigation of this affair should be left to the indigenous justice system.[61]

Once again, however, Puaux was too quick for Vichy. He reported that the Cour de Justice had already been reconstituted for the Shahbandar murder investigation, albeit with a majority of Syrian justices presiding. He could thus reassure the Foreign Ministry that French authority would not be too closely associated with the proceedings. In an angry finale, Puaux objected to the tone of Vichy's communications on the subject:

> After a mission of 20 months, carried out in sometimes critical circumstances, I believe I can demand of the Government to place confidence in my evaluation of local contingencies.[62]

In addition to securing the conviction of the five assassins, the investigation also pointed to direct involvement by nationalist leaders in the authorship of the crime. Puaux was advised by Hautecloque, his delegate in Damascus, to exploit this opportunity to decapitate the nationalist movement and restore constitutional government under a coalition of Shahbandarist and nationalist figures selected and controlled by the High Commission.[63] Three National Bloc leaders, Jamil Mardam, Saadullah Jabri, and Lutfi Haffar, were charged in mid-October with complicity in the murder, but managed to evade arrest and flee to Iraq.[64] Havard reported that there were some indications of French complicity in their flight;[65] it is known that Perissé, the fervently pro-Vichy head of the *Sûreté Générale* in Damascus, was on much closer terms

with the National Bloc than was Puaux.[66] In February, four of the five assassins were executed under Puaux's successor, General Dentz, whose decision
not to commute the sentences was, at the last minute, left unquestioned by
Vichy.[67] The three National Bloc leaders were exonerated in abstentia, though
they remained in exile. In Jamil Mardam's absence, Shukri al-Quwatli
emerged as the most powerful figure in the National Bloc.[68]

On a more important issue, Vichy and Puaux had similar views, but were
unable to effect their objective. In the fall of 1940, on the eve of Italy's
offensive against the British in Egypt, Germany regarded the eastern Mediterranean as Italy's field of action in the war. The Levant accordingly fell into the
sphere within which the terms of the Franco–Italian armistice came into
force. In the second week of August 1940, rumors began circulating of the
impending arrival in the Levant of a subcommission of the Italian armistice
commision at Turin.[69] Vichy needed no prompting from Puaux to realize what
a damaging effect this would have on French morale in the Levant as well as
on French prestige in the eyes of the native population. The French protested
to the Italians that this sort of intrusion could only serve to provoke the
British into an invasion of the Levant.[70] The Italians were insistent, however,
and were backed by the Germans, who also announced their intention of
sending a "representative" of their own to oversee the release of all remaining
German detainees in Syria and Lebanon.[71] The Italian Control Commission[72]
arrived at Beirut at the end of August with the formal task of overseeing the
full implementation of the armistice terms in the Levant. It was suspected that
the Italians would exploit their presence to cultivate contacts with nationalist
elements and generally pursue their long-held ambitions in the eastern Mediterranean.[73] The effect on French morale as well as on British policy was
almost immediately noticeable.

2

The Coup Plot and Its Aftermath

Plans for a Free French Coup

Within days of the Italian Control Commission's arrival in Beirut, reports began to circulate of subversive activity by the Italians. It was confirmed that they had established contact with the notorious anti-British Palestinian leader, the Mufti al-Husseini, in Baghdad, and possibly with the Syrian nationalist leadership that had taken refuge there as well. The Italian Control Commission was also trying to organize Syrian guerrilla bands that could be used to foment trouble for the British in Iraq and Palestine.[1] In its official capacity, the commission was also making itself obnoxious, as it began actively demanding the transfer to its control of large stocks of French military equipment, in accordance with the terms of the Franco-Italian armistice agreement.[2]

The arrival of the Italian Control Commission not only seemed to confirm Britain's fears about the possible consequences of leaving the Levant in the hands of Vichy, it also caused many Frenchmen in Syria and Lebanon to question the wisdom of continued allegiance to the Pétain government.[3] Havard reported that

> support for Vichy Government is now on the wane amongst the younger military officers and civilian officials, many of whom are wondering whether joining de Gaulle would not be the better course. Small groups are working in all the principal centres to spread propaganda on behalf of de Gaulle.[4]

Two French officers defecting from Syria who reached London at the end of August reported to General de Gaulle that

> though the administration and senior army officers were accepting directions from Vichy, there were a large number of both troops and officials who would be prepared to continue the struggle with us, but that we should adopt a far more forceful attitude, both in the political and military spheres, in an endeavour to swing them over to us.[5]

Reports of this kind were coming to London at a time when the Free French had just had their first major success against Vichy. During August 26–28, a handful of Free French officers including Edgard de Larminat had induced the main colonies of French Equatorial Africa to rally to de Gaulle.[6]

A number of factors thus combined to dispose His Majesty's government toward the adoption of a more aggressive stance toward the Levant. The arrival of the Italian Control Commission seemed to confirm Britain's worst fears over the possible consequences of leaving the Levant in the hands of Vichy, especially since it came at a time when General Wavell was bracing his forces for the expected Italian offensive against British forces in Egypt.[7] The Control Commission's arrival had also sowed dissension in the ranks of the French colony in Syria and Lebanon. The precedent of Equatorial Africa seemed to indicate that the appearance on the scene of the right men at the right time could render the conversion of a colony to the Gaullist cause a relatively easy matter. Moreover, Britain was pursuing an aggressive policy toward the Vichy Empire in general at this time, with Operation "Menace" (aimed at Dakar, in French West Africa) planned for later in September. Puaux was showing no signs of flexibility on any of the outstanding issues Havard had raised in their discussions. Clearly, the policy of waving carrots before the eyes of the French was not paying off.

In two meetings on August 29 and September 2, the cabinet's Committee on Foreign (Allied) Resistance (CFR)[8] concluded that Britain should assume an active, though covert, role in encouraging and helping organize the various uncoordinated groups of junior officers in the Levant that were reported to favor a Gaullist coup.[9] On September 3, the War Cabinet's Middle East Committee endorsed the recommendations of the CFR and specifically supported

> the proposal for a *coup d'état* provided that it can be carried out with a reasonable prospect of success.[10]

It was again stressed that the coup must be made to appear as the result of a purely Free French initiative (presumably so as to avoid unnecessary friction with Vichy and in order not to undermine the legitimacy of the Free French movement). Importance was also stressed on the need for de Gaulle to appease Syrian nationalist opinion once his forces had seized power in Syria.

It was agreed that the dispatch of a prominent Free French leader to the region could help galvanize the sympathetic elements in the Levant officer corps into a determined group of conspirators. Havard stressed in his telegrams from Beirut that the

> main difficulty at present is that these [pro-Gaullist] groups lack leadership and are not always aware of each other's existence. If their efforts could be directed and co-ordinated, they might spread very rapidly.[11]

It was not easy to settle on the right man for the job, however. De Gaulle himself was en route to Dakar for Operation "Menace." De Larminat was busy consolidating Free French control of Equatorial Africa, although it was proposed that he make a radio broadcast calling on the French of the Levant to follow the example of the African colonies.[12] Havard recommended that General Catroux, the high commissioner of Indochina who had defected to the Free French cause, should be sent to the Middle East to take charge of

Gaullist plans in Syria.[13] Catroux had actually passed through Palestine and Egypt at the end of August, just at the time when the idea for a coup was taking form. Unfortunately, the British had not briefed him on the Levant situation at that time, and he had been allowed to sail on to London, where he remained for consultations throughout September.[14]

Part of the problem was that in the choice of the man lay the choice of the approach. The Free French were eager to act immediately and, in de Gaulle's absence, proposed that Admiral Muselier—the commander of the movement's makeshift navy—be sent immediately to Alexandria to examine the possibility of an effective coup in Syria. If he found conditions to be favorable, he would carry out a plan to sail to a Levant port in a sloop with British naval support and rally the territory to the Free French cause like a latter-day Garibaldi. The Free French emphasized the urgency of the situation, writing:

> In view of the present situation in Syria (the arrival and establishment of the [Italian] Disarmament Commission) it would appear that any attempt to win Syria for free France will only have some chance of success if it is carried out in the immediate future.
>
> *Every day's delay considerably diminishes the chances of success* [italics in original].[15]

The Chiefs of Staff took a very dim view of this sort of precipitate approach. Whereas the Free French had little to lose by trying whatever they could in the Levant, British strategic considerations dictated a large measure of caution. The Chiefs of Staff did not want to involve British forces openly in a Levant operation and they feared the consequences of an unsuccessful attempt on the part of the Free French:

> The possibility of exploiting the situation in Syria is complicated by the presence of considerable French forces, which might constitute a threat to Palestine and Egypt, by the inflammable qualities of the Pan-Arab movement, and by the possible reactions of any deterioration of the situation in Turkey. So long as we are building up our resources to meet the enemy threat to Egypt and the Sudan we shall have no forces to spare for Syria. . . .
>
> The fact remains . . . that an unsuccessful revolt might provoke the hostility of those French Divisions on our flank in Palestine at a most critical time or might be the signal for a Syrian native rising. We have no forces to meet these eventualities. Any internal unrest in Syria will undoubtedly have repercussions in Palestine and Iraq. . . . Whilst we should welcome a coup d'état from within, therefore, we consider that we should not ourselves take any action which might run the risk of provoking the active hostility of the French in Syria or lead to a serious deterioration in the internal security situation.[16]

At the September 7 meeting, the Chiefs of Staff agreed that implementation of the Free French plan as it stood was completely out of the question and Admiral Muselier was tactfully informed that no means were currently available to transport him to Egypt.[17]

Even de Larminat's radio appeal became a controversial issue when the message he proposed to broadcast included a call for the mass defection to Palestine of troops in the Levant. This contradicted Wavell's standing policy once again and the British finally broadcasted a message in de Larminat's name that had actually been drafted by the Foreign Office. It called on the French of Syria and Lebanon to follow the example of Equatorial Africa, but avoided any suggestion of cross-border defection.[18] (Churchill's July outburst against this cautious approach seems to have been either forgotten or ignored.[19])

The issue of de Larminat's broadcast highlights the continued ambiguity of British policy toward the Levant. While eager for the Free French to seize control of Syria and Lebanon, the British were unwilling to take any halfway measures likely to leave Puaux with a weakened grip on the region, for fear of the chaos that might ensue. Either the coup d'état would take the form of a carefully engineered, swift, political takeover or else the status quo would have to be maintained. The British were not willing to take the risk involved in a drawnout sapping of Puaux's political control prior to the actual coup itself. Thus, the 1,250 tons of oil that had been promised to Puaux as an inducement for greater political cooperation were duly delivered in early September.[20] It was only late in that month that the decision was actually made to halt discussion of a clearing agreement and to requisition the French ship held at Haifa harbor.[21]

The reluctance to antagonize or undermine Puaux's administration prevented any decisive action from being taken. When the high commissioner of Palestine, seconded by the CFR, suggested that the entire Italian Control Commission be kidnapped as an easy propaganda exercise,[22] the Foreign Office did not question the operation's feasibility, but called for caution on political grounds. Lacy Baggallay of the Eastern Department was not willing to envision such a daring gesture unless it actually came in conjunction with a successful coup.

> While a nicely planned, quiet, workmanlike kidnapping, which would make the Italians look ridiculous, would be very welcome, such a kidnapping is in no sense vital to our policy vis-à-vis Syria and the Lebanon, is in particular quite secondary in importance to the "Free French" coup *and is not worth drawing down upon us the active resentment of the present French administration and forces* [italics added].[23]

In truth, the Free French were themselves quite uncertain over what approach to adopt in the Levant once the Muselier project had effectively been vetoed by the British. Des Essars, a Free French officer who had been sent to Cairo to investigate the situation, reported that the dissidence in the Levant was "developing not in the first instance as a de Gaulle movement but as a move against being disarmed [by the Italian Control Commission]."[24] This view was backed up by Colonel Bouvier, the quasi-dissident commander of the Jebel Druze, who met in a Syrian border town with Kirkbride, the British resident in Transjordan, to discuss the political climate in the Levant. He reported that the French authorities had already heard of the coup conspiracy and that a successful coup could not be based on an explicitly Gaullist foundation. He also argued that the chances of success would be improved once the 100,000 reservists still in Syria had been demobilized and returned to France, for these older men, eager to rejoin their families in France, were the least interested in a Gaullist takeover.[25] Indeed, it appears that even among leftist and pro-British elements in the Levant, de Gaulle was not yet a familiar figure in the fall of 1940.[26]

Des Essars accordingly recommended that a disturbance be engineered from within the Levant and that General Catroux, who had not yet publicly associated himself with the Free French movement, could then seize political control of the territory in response to an appeal from the coup organizers. "He would not go in as representative of General de Gaulle but would declare support of him afterwards."[27] At the same time, de Larminat telegraphed from the French Congo presenting himself as the officer best qualified to organize the coup.[28] In the absence of any direction from General de Gaulle, however, the Free French Committee appeared reluctant to make any important decisions on the matter.

The initiative was finally taken by His Majesty's government. Having already had occasion to run up against the calculated arrogance with which General de Gaulle asserted his movement's freedom from external intervention, the British were at this time considering the possibility of replacing him with a more malleable figure at the head of the Free French. Their favorite candidate for the job was none other than General Catroux, who, before his assignment as high commissioner in Indochina, had held various posts in the Middle East, including that of delegate in Damascus under General Gouraud in 1920–1922. Apart from his considerable administrative experience, Catroux was also a higher-ranking and better-known officer than de Gaulle, as well as a more courtly figure, a tactful diplomat with whom it would be easier to do business than with the bristly, intransigent de Gaulle; however, when Churchill made these sentiments known to Catroux, he turned down what he took to be a suggestion that he usurp de Gaulle's authority.[29] The British then decided to settle for second best by following Des Essars' and Havard's advice and sending Catroux secretly to Cairo to take charge of planning the Levant coup. As an old Syrian hand and a distinguished officer who was not yet identified with de Gaulle's controversial organization, it was thought he would have the best chance of winning the hearts and minds of the French army and administration in Syria and Lebanon.

This was an assignment that Catroux gladly accepted, but even this development was not without its complications. Although de Gaulle was accessible by telegraph throughout the third week of September, he was not consulted about Catroux's assignment, which was decided on during this period. Churchill simply informed him of the decision once it had been made. De Gaulle immediately protested that this represented an infringement on his authority as head of the Free French movement, although he fully approved of the choice of Catroux in and of itself.[30] Churchill apologized and asked that de Gaulle approve the decision retroactively, which he did while reserving the option of replacing Catroux with de Larminat at a later date.[31]

This pattern of indecision and poor communication at the highest levels had a disastrous effect on the actual implementation of coup plans in the Levant. As has been pointed out, the dissident elements in the Levant army and administration were poorly organized and can hardly be said to have attained the minimal standards of any self-respecting conspiracy. There was a Free French captain in Palestine by the name of Repiton-Preneuf whom Des Essars had placed in charge of establishing liaison with Gaullist sympathizers in Syria and Lebanon.[32] Free French propaganda leaflets were distributed in the region through an operation supervised by a joint Special Operations Executive (SOE)–Free French–Jewish Agency board in Palestine.[33] Pending the arrival of Catroux, however, no major initiative was undertaken by the low-ranking Free French figures on the scene.

In the absence of decisive action, rumors began to abound. Word had already begun to spread in Beirut of Catroux's impending arrival on the scene during the first days of September, before the actual decision had been made to assign him to the job.[34] This premature rumor had apparently been set off by a chance encounter between Catroux and an old acquaintance during Catroux's brief stopover in Palestine on his way to London in late August.[35] It made a mockery of the Foreign Office's instructions to Ambassador Lampson in Cairo in late September:

> It is vital . . . that Gen. Catroux's presence in Egypt should be kept abso-
> lutely secret and that his identity should be known to the minimal number of
> essential officials.[36]

It is clear that pro-Gallist sentiment was growing increasingly rife among junior officers as well as high functionaries at the High Commission.[37] The second-in-command in the army, General Arlabosse, and the delegate in Damascus, Hautecloque, were reported to be sympathetic.[38] (On the other hand, General Mittelhauser had been replaced in mid-July as military commander-in-chief by General Fougère, a hard-line, anti-British officer who was unlikely to stand for any nonsense from dissidents.) The actual line separating sympathetic from conspiratorial elements appears to have been rather vague, however. Many people who sided wholeheartedly with de Gaulle or at least wished the Levant to contribute to the British war effort, did not seem to have any clear idea of how their hopes could be realized. Thus Gennardi, a counselor at the High Commission, sent de Gaulle a secret letter of support in which he conceived of a grand, Napoleonic entry by the general, in the course of which the Levant would spontaneously rally to his cause:

> I am . . . convinced that [despite the hostility of the military command] the
> officer corps, as well as the rank-and-file, will rally on their own to your
> standards, in the same manner as the troops of the Empire received their
> emperor at the time of the 100 days.[39]

The role played by other pro-British figures, such as the chief financial counselor in the High Commission, Lucien Ehrhardt, and the afore-mentioned military commander of the Jebel Druze, Colonel Bouvier, remains ill-defined.

Ehrhardt was later to defend himself successfully against charges of conspiracy, while openly avowing his opposition to the armistice.[40] Bouvier was reported at one point to be on the verge of pledging his allegiance to de Gaulle, yet he never quite came through.[41]

Amid this atmosphere of political effervescence, an emissary from the Free French arrived on the scene, a Monsieur Vermeulen, sent from Cairo to establish better contact with the Gaullist elements in the Levant and to mold them into a more coherent conspiracy.[42] Vermeulen spent a few days in Beirut and Damascus in the second week of September, sounding people out and distributing money from a fund of 20,000 pounds provided by the British "to secure connivance of certain venal but essential [elements?]."[43] Unfortunately, venality and discretion were two qualities that did not go hand in hand, at least not in the Levant. Word soon spread "that an 'emissary of de Gaulle' was in Beirut."[44]

In his effort to bring key figures into the plot, Vermeulen ended up sabotaging the whole movement. Before his departure from Beirut, he met with Marcel Cuinat, who was an official in the political department of the High Commission involved in the Gaullist conspiracy. Vermeulen urged Cuinat to approach Colombani, the joint head of the *Sûreté Générale* and of military intelligence, and try to win his support by offering him a one million-franc bribe. Colombani was a seedy character who had been implicated in the Stavisky scandal of 1933 (and, it was said, had had a hand in Stavisky's "suicide" as well), and whose venality was notorious. For some reason, he also seems to have been regarded by some as sympathetic toward the Free French cause.[45] Unfortunately, this was a fatal miscalculation. Colombani had fallen out of Puaux's good graces and was worried about losing his job. When, on September 12, Cuinat revealed to him the existence of the plot, he appears to have seen in it an opportunity for proving his merit to the local military command as well as to the Vichy government. Although he is reported to have accepted the proffered bribe, he immediately betrayed Cuinat's confidence to General Fougère and to the High Commission. All the essential details of the plot were soon known to the French authorities, including the roles played by Repiton-Preneuf and Vermeulen as well as the involvement of the British behind the scenes. The Gaullist conspiracy was revealed before it was ready to execute.[46]

The Bourget Purge

The Beirut administration's immediate response to the Gaullist movement was of a purely defensive nature. On the very day of Cuinat's meeting with Colombani, General Fougère assembled his senior officers and warned them harshly against any cooperation with the British. (He is reported to have encountered a disconcerting silence.) As the coup attempt had originally been scheduled for September 15, though later put off until more of the reservists had been repatriated, special security measures were taken on the night of

September 14, and armed guards were placed outside all government offices as well as General Fougère's house.[47]

In his report to Vichy on the situation, Puaux was quite frank:

> A number of counterchecks confirm [the existence of] very strong agitation among the junior officers. An impulsive action by a number of them remains a possibility. General Fougère has taken appropriate measures. Certain civil functionaries appear to sympathize [with the] movement and are under surveillance. According to unconfirmed information General Catroux is or will arrive in Egypt and will eventually assume leadership of the movement.[48]

Puaux, however, did not draw the conclusion that a crackdown was necessary to deal with the Gaullist movement. Instead, he argued:

> Under these circumstances, it is to be recommended that the Italian Commission not prolong its stay, since there is no doubt that its arrival in Syria sharply changed a theretofore altogether calm situation.[49]

Puaux seems to have been implying that responsibility for the coup plot lay not so much with the plotters themselves as with the political context in which they found themselves. He was later to describe his attitude as follows:

> I confess I did not take this conspiracy at all seriously. I saw in it nothing but an adventurous project born in the imagination of a few patriots who were more ardent than reflective, more enthusiastic than experienced.[50]

Puaux's easygoing approach to the Gaullist movement struck a raw nerve in Vichy. It came at a time of repeated complaints from dissatisfied elements in the Levant over the high commissioner's lack of energy in implementing Pétain's "National Revolution."[51] According to these reports, selfishness, luxury, graft, and laziness were rampant among both military and civil personnel in Syria and Lebanon. The loose morals associated in Pétainist minds with the Third Republic were said to prevail unchallenged among the French community in the Levant. People could publicly insult the Pétain government without fear of punishment.[52] Xavier Vallat, then secretary-general for Veterans' Affairs and later to become Vichy's first commissioner-general for Jewish Affairs, seems to have had his own sources of information in the region and he wrote to Pétain accusing a number of Puaux's subordinates of financial improprieties and sexual immorality. Pétain took all this very seriously and demanded a major housecleaning in the Levant, with exemplary punishment to be meted out to anyone found guilty of improper conduct.[53]

Graft, bribery, and sexual license had long been notoriously rampant in the Levant administration and it can safely be assumed that this remained the case under Puaux; however, whispered accusations and rumors were equally widespread and could easily be turned to political purposes. It seems quite clear that the main source of dissatisfaction with Puaux among right-wing elements in the Levant as well as Vichy was his lack of enthusiasm for the National Revolution. Certainly, the harsh measures taken in Vichy France against leftists, freemasons, and Jews did not seem to have much of an impact in the Levant even when formally implemented.[54] The continued prevalence of a comparatively liberal atmosphere in the region seems to have antagonized hard-line Vichyites who saw in Puaux a holdover from the Third Republic. It is noteworthy that none of the accusations of impropriety were directed at Colombani, a notorious bribetaker and wheeler-dealer, but one who had long been at odds with Puaux. Likewise, when Puaux was finally relieved of his post in December 1940, the man chosen to replace him as high commissioner was Jean Chiappe, who had been forced to resign as Paris chief of police in 1934 because of his implication (like Colombani) in the Stavisky scandal, but whose right-wing credentials were beyond dispute.

Puaux hotly denied any wrongdoing by his immediate subordinates and insisted that impropriety was being punished wherever it was uncovered in the administration.[55] His low-key response to the discovery of the coup plot was too much for Vichy, however. The high commissioner who had himself wavered before accepting the armistice was clearly not the man to rid the Levant of the Gaullist movement. Within days, the decision was made to dispatch Colonel d'Artillerie Bourget to the region as a sort of latter-day version of the Committee of Public Safety's representatives-on-mission, charged with bringing the Levant fully into line with the National Revolution. Colonel Bourget was instructed to investigate the extent of dissidence and the state of morale in both army and civil administration. He was authorized to make arrests, order dismissals, and implement whatever other measures he considered necessary over the head of the high commissioner.[56] The minister of war, General Huntziger, ordered that Bourget should lay a heavy emphasis on the importance of loyalty to the current government of France:

> He will remind all of the necessity . . . of "thinking French" in regard to the political problems posed by Germany's pursuit of the war against England. He will show that the defections [to Palestine] brought about by English propaganda . . . entail grave risks for the actual future of the Empire, and thereby for the equilibrium of the nation. He will show that the action of a few arrogant, wayward men leads their dupes towards *treachery* by abusing their generosity [italics in original].

If reason did not prevail, Bourget was not to abstain from cruder devices: "He will not hesitate any the more to make everyone aware of the dangers his defection would create for his family and property left behind in France."[57]

Pending Bourget's arrival in the Levant, Vichy continued to badger Puaux about the reliability and loyalty of his subordinates, urging him to dismiss all suspect elements.[58] In response, Puaux protested that he could not adopt a single line of action toward all those whose loyalty had wavered. Nearly everyone in the French colony in the Levant hoped for the ultimate defeat of Germany. Some, like Hautecloque, the delegate in Damascus, had simply become overly exuberant in the expression of their hopes for a British victory:

> If necessary, I will not hesitate to impose sanctions against certain functionaries, but I would prefer to avoid measures which would provoke a still more

marked schism among Frenchmen or which might be badly interpreted even by the loyalists.[59]

Puaux did declare himself willing to repatriate those who clearly could not be disciplined. Baudoin promptly promised to provide a ship for this purpose and reemphasized to Puaux the importance of assuring himself of the loyalty of his closest collaborators. In particular, he pointed out that, judging by Puaux's own descriptions, Hautecloque's attitude did not sound satisfactory. In a telegram sent on September 20, he urged Puaux to demand a formal assurance from Hautecloque of his loyalty to the Pétain government.[60] On the very same day, Colonel Bourget arrived by plane in Beirut and Vichy no longer had to rely exclusively on Puaux for the implementation of its policy.

Within days of Bourget's arrival, the atmosphere in the French community in the Levant had been radically transformed. Bourget immediately ordered the arrest of figures suspected of involvement in the coup plot. General Fougère and Colombani promptly jumped on the bandwagon and began carrying out arrests of their own, while Puaux stood by, powerless to intervene even if he wanted to.[61] By mid-October, thirteen top-echelon members of the High Commission as well as several army officers and a dozen or more low-ranking officials had been arrested and charged with plotting against the state.[62] Colombani, in his eagerness to demonstrate his usefulness to Bourget as well as to discredit Puaux and settle personal political scores, was said to rely on hearsay evidence if necessary in order to get his hands on as many high officials as possible.[63] (Bourget was appropriately impressed, reporting that he could not be sure about charges that Colombani was corrupt, but that he certainly was effective at cracking down on Gaullists).[64] Suspect figures like Hautecloque, on whom it proved impossible to pin any charges, were summarily dismissed from their posts or transferred to less important positions. Colonel Bouvier was court-martialed for his apparent involvement in the conspiracy, although he was eventually acquitted and returned to his post.[65] Puaux complained in vain to Vichy that he was suffering from a severe personnel shortage in the wake of Bourget's purge.[66]

While Bourget's intervention clearly dealt a severe blow to the Gaullist movement, he was far from complacent about the future loyalty of the Levant. In his report to Vichy, he described Gaullist and pro-British sentiments as being widespread in the French community. Bourget warned that despite the crackdown on active conspirators, most army units (apart from the reservists) still contained suspect elements, the general staff seemed evenly divided between Gaullists and loyalists, and the civil administration was similarly riddled with dissenters. Therefore, the sudden appearance in the Levant of a Catroux or a de Larminat might still have dangerous consequences.

Although in some cases venality was seen as the source of disloyalty, Bourget recognized that what he himself referred to as "noble motives" lay behind much of the dissent. He argued that General Mittelhauser's original equivocation over the armistice had set a terrible example to the rest of the armed forces in Syria and Lebanon:

This crisis has not been entirely surmounted and a pure and simple appeal to discipline does not suffice for people who remain very troubled and are still in a feverish state. . . .

The best [among them] cannot be consoled over not having fought [in the Battle of France] and live in the hope that the opportunity for them to engage in warfare will still arise. The question I was often asked—"what would the Government do in the event of a British victory?"—is an indication of the anxiousness that such an opportunity [for resuming warfare] be exploited. From that, to [actually] creating that opportunity by rallying to the English cause right away is sometimes an easy step.[67]

While such "noble motives" seemed to be the almost exclusive cause of dissidence among officers, less honorable sources of disruption existed among the rank-and-file of the army and in the civil administration. The fear of early demobilization or retirement under Vichy created restlessness, as did the promise of financial reward for deserters to Palestine who took their equipment (particularly airplanes) with them. Members of the officially dissolved masonic lodges were also reported by Bourget to be engaging in "oblique manoeuvres." Of particular concern to Bourget was information "pointing to the existence of elements loyal in appearance, but committed to the 'Gaullist' movement at heart." Thus, Colonel Bouvier had originally impressed Bourget as a steadfastly loyal officer, but had in the meantime been implicated in the coup plot.[68]

Bourget reported the French colony in the Levant (that is, those French residents not employed in the administration or army) to be by and large sympathetic to de Gaulle. Many people continued to entertain the notion that Pétain himself secretly supported de Gaulle while publicly playing the role demanded of him by the Germans.

To remedy this situation would clearly be no easy matter. Most immediately, Bourget called for heightened vigilance against any further Gaullist plots. In particular, the Beirut garrison was reported to be unreliable and would have to be watched. Steps would have to be taken to strengthen ties with metropolitan France and to provide "tangible signs of the new France" such as putting up more portraits of Marshal Pétain in troops' quarters and in mess halls. An effort could be made to enable the families of officers to join them in the Levant and to offer other "proofs of solicitude" from Vichy. Disciplinary measures would also have to be more rigorously enforced.

Bourget did not limit himself to these superficial measures. Rather, he sought to strike at what he saw as the social roots of the Gaullist cancer in the Levant, to eradicate the moral laxity and the lack of discipline that, he was convinced, lay at the bottom of the disaffection with Vichy. He urged Puaux to purge all corrupt officials from the High Commission in addition to those of doubtful loyalty. Puaux's refusal to dismiss officials without legal proof of wrongdoing on their part was resented by Bourget as an obstacle to implementing the National Revolution in the Levant. In an attempt to instill the officer corps with the virtues Vichy purported to represent, Bourget started what the British consul in Damascus called a "hearth and home campaign" that stressed the centrality of the family to French society and sought to discipline married officers who kept mistresses (estimated at 50 percent of the officer corps).[69] As a means of creating a corporate base for the transformation of the French colony, Bourget recommended that a local chapter of Vichy's *Légion Française des Combattants* be formed, consolidating the most loyal elements of the French community into an elite grouping that could lead the rest of the colony in the right direction. A crackdown on illegal masonic activities would help undermine organized dissidence.[70]

If Bourget's conceptions of political indoctrination and social reform seem simplistic, his analysis of the native population's attitude will appear hopelessly naïve. He reported to Vichy that the defeat of France had actually reinforced the attachment of the Levantines to the mandatory power. Everyone he met with in Syria and Lebanon expressed feelings of good will toward the Marshal, and many Lebanese Christians had gone to church to pray for France after the fall of Paris. Only "people who are ill informed about the oriental soul" would deny the importance of such sentimental factors.[71] Although political stagnation was certainly to be avoided, Bourget saw no need to move in the direction of granting independence to Syria and Lebanon or indulging nationalist fantasies about pan-Arab unity. This account can be contrasted usefully with a report written in late August by the French intelligence service in the Levant, which described Lebanese public opinion as completely disillusioned with France in the wake of her dismal performance against Germany and the apparent insouciance with which the defeat had been received by the local French population.[72]

Bourget's ideas about how to conduct relations with the British appear to have been the most far-fetched of all. Echoing charges that had already been made by the Italian Armistice Commission,[73] Bourget argued that the continued presence of Consul-General Havard in Beirut represented an intolerable nuisance. He accused Havard of exercising a pernicious influence over the local political scene by coordinating the diffusion of British propaganda in the Levant and facilitating the defection of French troops to Palestine.[74] The solution to this problem was simple—Havard was to be expelled from the country. When Puaux pointed out that this would at the very least result in the intensification of Britain's economic blockade of Syria, Bourget was not at all disconcerted. He simply argued that if the British took hostile measures against the Levant, the French would have to respond in kind. Bedouin saboteurs could be sent to cut off the Baghdad-to-Haifa oil pipeline and an Arab revolt could be fomented in Palestine![75]

If the French colony in the Levant had not come to grips with the fact of French defeat by the Germans, Vichy's plenipotentiary representative had certainly failed to grasp the extent of French vulnerability in the Levant. Puaux was up in arms over his proposals. He telegraphed desperately to Vichy in an attempt to persuade the government of the folly of Bourget's line. Even if the reprisals Bourget had suggested were feasible, they would inevitably provoke the British into devastating countersabotage at the very least. The

French were in no position to deal with any consequent popular revolt or unrest in the Levant. The result would be the disintegration of the French position in Syria and Lebanon. To try and limit the effectiveness of British propaganda was one thing, but a complete rupture with Britain in the Middle East was quite another:

> If we were here in force and solidly backed up I would recommend energetic action, but we live on the basis of a precarious and fragile equilibrium. We must therefore conduct a policy commensurate with our means.[76]

Puaux proposed to limit himself to measures restricting access to the British consulate-general and providing for surveillance of the building and the monitoring of British telephone conversations.[77]

On this issue at least, Vichy adopted Puaux's advice. Bourget's counsel was accepted only to the extent of ordering the expulsion of Ogden, the British vice-consul in Damascus. Havard was to be denied diplomatic bag service and forced to move still further away from Beirut, but no further provocation was to be offered. It was subsequently decided to let Havard stay at his current residence at Aley, provided strict surveillance of the building was maintained.[78] Puaux was also ordered to stop turning a blind eye to British transportation of supplies from Turkey to Palestine via Levant railroads. In addition, Vichy firmly rejected the Turin Armistice Commission's demands for Havard's expulsion and Puaux's replacement, characterizing this as unwarranted intervention in French administrative affairs.[79] Vichy's later response to German intervention was not to be quite as firm.

The Impact of the Bourget Purge

By the time of Colonel Bourget's departure from the Levant on October 11, British and Free French hopes for a dramatic reversal of fortune in the Levant had been dealt a very severe blow. De Gaulle's expedition to Dakar had ended in a demoralizing fiasco at the end of September, and this combined with Italy's initial advance into Egypt's Western Desert to tarnish the image of the Allies even among their supporters. Above all, Bourget had succeeded in breaking up the loosely organized Gaullist movement and introducing conditions under which Gaullist sympathizers feared taking any action or making any statement likely to expose their sentiments.[80] Havard reported:

> The High Commissioner, in conversation . . . [with me] on October 28, . . . continued to display good-will but showed clearly that his authority had been largely usurped by the military by whom he himself was spied on. In this Gestapo atmosphere which Colonel Bourget and his Deuxième Bureau imitators have created it is not surprising that the French as a whole give an impression of dispirited resignation to the existing order of things. There is much good-will for the British war-effort . . . but it seems even more disorganised than before and there are no signs whatsoever of any rallying to the cause of Free France.[81]

General Catroux, who had finally arrived in the region on September 30, thus found his range of options severely limited. He made public his presence in the Middle East in a radio address on November 14, in which he called on the Levant to rejoin the war effort. He then made various direct appeals to prominent Levant figures, including Puaux himself, vainly seeking to win them over to the Free French cause.[82] The dissemination of propaganda and collection of information through *Haganah* channels continued apace; the operation had been expanded in mid-September to include Free French broadcasts directed at the Levant from a radio station concealed in the Haifa apartment of the Jewish Agency liaison with the SOE, David ha-Cohen.[83] Plans for an actual coup, however, had to be placed on hold until more propitious circumstances had arisen.[84]

The British found it best not to be unduly provoked by the restrictive measures imposed against their diplomats in the Levant. Initial reports by French intelligence of an imminent British military move against the Levant border in mid-November proved to be a false alarm.[85] Not even diplomatic retaliation was resorted to, the French consul in Palestine being allowed to maintain his residence in Jerusalem.[86] While the economic pressure on the Levant was maintained and even tightened, ships carrying demobilized reservists were allowed to continue plying the Beirut–Marseilles route. Despite the fact that the French were using these ships to transport Gaullist sympathizers back to Vichy, and reports that Syrian produce was also being shipped to France, the British refrained from demanding inspection calls at Haifa. They remained satisfied with verbal assurances from the Levant authorities that no one was being transported to France against his will and that the rules of Britain's economic blockade of France were being strictly observed.[87]

Meanwhile, Bourget's attempt to introduce structural change in the French community of the Levant appeared increasingly to be a failure. While support for Free France waned, enthusiasm for Vichy did not grow. The prevalent attitude was one of *attentisme:* in the absence of any clear-cut developments, there was little point in committing oneself wholeheartedly to one side or the other.[88] The formation of a regional branch of the *Légion Française des Combattants* merely created a forum for complaint and accusation by cantankerous, right-wing elements, much to the annoyance of Puaux's successor;[89] however, Bourget did succeed in fatally undermining Puaux's position. Although he never directly accused Puaux of any wrongdoing, Bourget did call into question the whole thrust of his policy and raised suspicions concerning the loyalty of his very top aides including Conty, the number-two man in the High Commission.[90] At the end of November 1940, one month after Laval's replacement of Baudoin as Vichy's minister of foreign affairs, Puaux was informed that he was to be relieved of his functions and replaced by the extreme right-winger, Jean Chiappe.[91] Turning down a British suggestion that he seize this opportunity to break the Levant away from Vichy's authority without necessarily recognizing de Gaulle's leadership, the high commissioner prepared to leave the country.[92] Puaux's only consolation was that his longtime enemy Colombani was to lose his job as well.[93]

An Assessment of Puaux's Role

In view of the severe constraints on Puaux's freedom of action during the period we have examined, it is difficult to arrive at a fair assessment of his policy. He has been portrayed as a fence-sitter whose ambiguous behavior was designed to furnish a basis for credible ex post facto self-justification in the eyes of whichever side won the war.[94] However, the fact that an ambiguous policy lends itself to such purposes does not in and of itself prove that this is what actually motivated it. An examination of the available records leaves one with an impression of Puaux as a man of conscience who had lost his bearings in the turbulence of national disaster and global war. De Larminat's portrayal of him sounds a true note:

> A Protestant of puritan tendency, a man of the best company, cultivated and well spoken, and in addition courageous and capable of firmness, this was a highly admirable personage, but out of its element in an episode which was revolutionary . . . in character.[95]

Once his recognition of his isolation had prevented him from taking the bold step of repudiating the armistice, Puaux's policy became inextricably linked with that of Vichy. Puaux had recognized the ultimate authority over the Levant as lying in Vichy, which had itself mortgaged the principle of French self-determination to the Germans. There was no middle ground for him to follow, and to perform a sudden about-face and support a Free French coup later on would have involved a much more painful act of self-assertion than an original decision not to recognize the armistice.

Within the narrow bounds imposed on him by circumstances, Puaux does seem to have acted as indulgently as possible toward the Free French conspirators and to have done all he could to preserve ties with the British. When word of the conspiracy leaked out, it reached General Fougère at least as quickly as Puaux, making it impossible for the high commissioner to feign ignorance of what was going on. Nevertheless, the main thrust of his reaction was to use the coup conspiracy to bolster his continued demands that Vichy allow him greater leeway in his relations with the British, the argument being that alleviation of the British trade boycott was the only way to prevent a total collapse of French authority in the Levant.[96]

All this is not to portray Puaux as some sort of secret resistance fighter planted within the Levant administration on behalf of the Allied cause. It is merely to reject the depiction of him as an opportunist whose behavior was determined by calculations of narrow self-interest. Certainly, Puaux was at least partially responsible for some anti-British actions such as the jamming of BBC broadcasts after the discovery of the coup plot.[97] He also delivered a number of anti-British speeches over the radio and to military officers.[98] Given his position, however, Puaux was bound to display some resentment, be it spontaneous or contrived, over the economic boycott and British backing for the coup plot. The overall thrust of his policy continued to be directed at preventing a rupture with the British, both in the short-term interests of the

French Levant and the long-term interests of France. In one of the last tele-grams he sent before receiving word of his dismissal, Puaux expressed his fear of a British–Turkish demand for troop-passage rights in the Levant in the event Axis forces advanced further into the Middle East. The only way of preventing such a development, which could well lead to an actual incursion, was, he argued, to assure Britain and Turkey that France would actively resist any attempt by Germany or Italy to gain bases in the area:

> If this assurance could be given to Syria's neighbors, we would at least be able to gain time and maintain the status quo; this is the only means by which we can preserve our positions in the Levant, for any initiative on our part would risk rupturing the fragile equilibrium.[99]

As became clear six months later, the notion of catering to Axis war needs was less unthinkable for the Vichy government than it was for Puaux. His telegram remained unanswered, unless he was right in surmising that his dismissal was a direct response to the cable.[100] Puaux's successor was to prove a less questioning instrument of Vichy's foreign policy.

3

Limited Resources
and Makeshift Arrangements

Britain's Blockade Policy

In the wake of the coup plot's failure, British policy toward the Levant was at a standstill. On the one hand, Anglo–French relations in the region had soured, Puaux was soon to be replaced by an aggressively right-wing, Vichy loyalist, and reports persisted of Axis ambitions in the region. On the other hand, the options for active intervention remained extremely limited, although some hope persisted that Catroux would yet manage to engineer a coup. The Chiefs of Staff were able to contemplate the possibility of a military operation in Syria and Lebanon in the spring of 1941, but even then, the success of the operation would depend on its orchestration with a Turkish occupation of nothern Syria.[1] Given the Arab world's latent fears of Turkish expansionist designs, such an option was regarded in London as appropriate only in a worst-case scenario, that is only in the event of an immediate threat of an Axis incursion into the region.[2]

His Majesty's government thus found itself largely disabused of its earlier hopes of gaining active cooperation from the Levant administration, but bereft of effective means to counter Beirut's stonewalling. Even the decision to tighten the economic blockade was reached with the greatest of difficulty. From Beirut, Havard actually called for the lifting of economic sanctions, having decided that Vichy policy in the Levant was not so inimical to British interests after all and that popular unrest there could prove dangerous.[3] The War Cabinet's Middle East Committee, which continued to entertain vague hopes of a coup, weighed the pros and cons of the blockade:

As regards the application of economic pressure on Syria, this was in accordance with His Majesty's Government's general policy towards the French Empire, which was directed to persuading the French Colonies to throw in their lot with the Free French movement. If, however, General Catroux's project were to be postponed, there might be a case for recommending a more lenient treatment of Syria as an exception to that policy in order to further British interests. In this connection it was pointed out that the effect of the economic weapons would not be realised immediately and that relaxa-

41

tion of pressures might diminish the prospects of a favourable coup d'état at a later date if it were decided that the time was not ripe for an attempt at present. On the other hand, the application of severe blockade measures might prejudice success if they were pushed too far.[4]

While the British government remained preoccupied with this maddeningly insoluble dilemma, the Levant administration was actively seeking ways of circumventing the existing trade boycott. Feelers were extended to the government of Turkey and Iraq concerning the possibility of barter arrangements,[5] and unofficial overland barter across the Palestine frontier was stepped up. High Commissioner MacMichael was loath to crack down on this trade because he was concerned over the effects of the boycott on the Palestine economy.[6] In an effort to boost the Levant's economic self-sufficiency, the French were rapidly completing work on a small oil refinery in Tripoli with the United States providing the caustic soda needed to make the plant operational.[7]

By the end of November, the British government had finally reached a decision on the question of the blockade. Talks had been held during October between the British and French ambassadors in Madrid, and between Pétain's unofficial representative Professor Rougier and His Majesty's government in London, over the possibility of relaxing the British blockade on Vichy France in return for firm guarantees from the French that they would furnish no aid to the German war effort. Nevertheless, the meetings at Montoire between Laval and Hitler on October 22 and Pétain and Hitler on October 24 cast a long shadow over the prospects for fostering an Anglo–French understanding.[8] The blockade on metropolitan France was maintained to the extent that the British fleet was able to impose it and in the last days of November it was decided to tighten sanctions against the Levant as well. Foreign Minister Halifax informed MacMichael:

> I consider stringency of economic pressure is more important than incidental advantages arising from continuance of trade. Trade should therefore be stopped, subject to such small relaxations as you may consider absolutely necessary for administrative reasons.[9]

Besides tightening existing sanctions, the decision was also made to extend the scope of the blockade by applying the navicert (navigation certificate) and certificate-of-origin system to the Levant. This meant that no shipment of goods would be allowed to leave or enter the Levant without prior approval from Britain, regardless of whether or not the particular trading partner happened to be a neutral. Thus, even trade with the United States could be limited if Britain refused to issue the appropriate navicerts. In the estimation of the U.S. consul in Beirut,

> while Syria has not been formally listed as territory under enemy control, Consul General Havard thinks that the measures taken amount to practically the same thing and that trade between the United States and Syria as well as Iraq will be made most difficult if not impossible. He said that from the

instructions he has received he can only deduce that London's policy is to asphyxiate economically this territory until "they decide to come around."[10]

Of course, throughout this period, the repatriation of French reservists from the Levant continued apace, as it was considered to serve Britain's interest; London only had the high commissioner's word that these ships were not being used to transfer goods between France and the Levant.

The Arrival of Dentz

Although Puaux had been expected to leave Beirut in early December, his stay was prolonged by the unexpected demise of Chiappe, whose plane was mistakenly shot down by the Italians as it made its way toward the Levant. Relations with the British remained sour during this interlude, with General Fougère delivering a virulently anti-British address to his officers, describing Britain as France's true, hereditary enemy.[11] Fearing a British incursion in the wake of Chiappe's death, the French tightened security in the Levant. Gardener reported that "Syria is now run by military, especially Second Bureau. Gestapo atmosphere reigns."[12] Last-minute, written appeals from Catroux to Puaux and General Arlabosse, calling on them to rally to the war effort, were politely rejected.[13] Contacts were maintained with various sympathetic elements in the High Commission, but prospects for political change remained bleak.[14] Reports of Italian aircraft being authorized to land and refuel in the Levant raised considerable fears in London.[15] Soon after Chiappe's unexpected demise, the Vichy government chose a new man for Puaux's job: General Dentz, who had served as chief of military intelligence in Syria and Lebanon in 1923–1926, during General Weygand's first tenure there as high commissioner.[16] More recently, he had served as the military commander of the Paris region who had carried out the order to surrender the capital to the Germans at the time of the armistice negotiations.

Unlike his civilian predecessor, General Dentz was to combine the functions of Levant military commander with those of high commissioner. General Fougère's role would accordingly be eclipsed. How Dentz would use this power remained unclear to the British. He was certainly an improvement over Chiappe, whose appointment had appeared to be related to the archcollaborationist Laval's accession to the post of minister of foreign affairs. Dentz's association with the staunchly anti-German Weygand seemed to bode well for British interests. (Laval himself was dismissed from his position on December 13.) Brigadier Fraser, the former British military attaché in Paris, described Dentz as anti-German, although strictly loyal to Pétain and Weygand. He suggested that "it might be possible for us to do quite a lot with him." Yet, Dentz was reported to have told the Turkish ambassador to Bulgaria that the French Empire would benefit from a protracted struggle between Britain and Germany. Shortly after Dentz's arrival in Beirut on December 29, the Foreign Office seriously considered the possibility of making a friendly overture to

him in the form of some easing of blockade restrictions. It was finally concluded that this might be seen as a sign of irresolution and that the best tactic
was to let Dentz make the first move.[17]

The Erosion of the Blockade

While Britain's tough new blockade policy remained officially in place, it did
not take long for short-term, tactical considerations to erode it. As it was, the
French were doing what they could to facilitate the smuggling of basic com-
modities like sugar, gasoline, and kerosene across the long Transjordanian–
Syrian border.[18] Harold MacMichael continued to complain about the strain
on Palestine's economy caused by the absence of trade with Syria. He argued
that the cutoff in commerce was actually more harmful for Palestine than for
Syria and that food prices in Palestine were steadily rising.[19] General Wavell
complained that the British army in Greece was suffering from a shortage of
trucks which the Levant authorities could supply in exchange for British gasoline. In view of Wavell's pressing logistical requirements, it was decided to
make an exception and authorize him to negotiate the barter. (The deal fell
through when it turned out that the French were only willing to supply Wavell
with mules.[20]) In addition to its own considerations, the British government
was coming under increasing pressure from the United States to ease up on
anti-French trade restrictions in general and on the blockade against Syria in
particular. It was the American view that the provision of essential supplies to
the French would strengthen the hands of anti-German elements in Vichy
against collaborationists like Laval and Darlan. It was also in the period of
January–February 1941 that the U.S. government informed the British of its
decision to establish trade links with French Morocco and French North Africa, where Weygand had just been sent as delegate-general. It was hoped that
this would improve the chances for defection by Weygand to the Allied side
and would in any case increase the French capacity and resolve to resist any
Axis move against North Africa.[21] As for the Levant, the American government pressed the British to allow the export of Syrian wool and silk to the
United States in exchange for newsprint and foodstuffs. Faced with the threat
of export of this material to Germany by way of Turkey, the British government tentatively agreed to the deal in February.[22]

In general, however, London remained opposed to the American notion
of gaining Vichy's favor through economic concessions. Blockade was a more
effective means of keeping the French in line:

> We are trying to exercise the maximum economic pressure on Syria. This
> does not mean that we desire or expect an immediate uprising. A weak Syria
> is, however, a safeguard against any possibility of hostile French action of
> some kind against us. This seems to us essential in view of the strategical
> importance of Syria and of the unreliability of the Vichy Government. This
> seems to His Majesty's Government to involve less danger than any other
> course, and does not amount to their working for the collapse of Syria.[23]

In the very justification of their conduct, the British seemed to be exposing its inconsistency. They hoped to pressure the Levant into good behavior, yet were reluctant to push it to the brink of collapse. The result was a policy that was neither here nor there, a partial blockade that affected Palestine as adversely as it did the Levant and that, as we shall see, had no effect at all on the behavior of Dentz.

The *Providence* Affair

A further illustration of the dilemmas faced by the British and the contradictions inherent in their responses during this period is provided by the *Providence* affair. As mentioned in Chapter 2, it had been Britain's standing policy to allow the French to repatriate their reservists from the Levant in accordance with the Franco–Italian armistice terms. The reservists were regarded by the British as the most Anglophobe elements in the French army of the Levant, and their departure was considered desirable. There had been occasional reports of Vichy troop-transport ships being used to carry merchandise as well as Gaullist sympathizers back to France, but the vessels had been allowed to pass freely between Beirut and Marseilles for the sake of Britain's higher interests. By January 1941, only about 3,000 reservists still remained in Syria and Lebanon out of an original 100,000. A large contingent from this group was due to be transported back to France on board the *Providence*.

Just as the *Providence* was on its way to Beirut to pick up the reservists, reports reaching Havard indicated that 100–200 noncommissioned officers and regulars who were suspected of ties with the Free French or who had been caught trying to desert to Palestine were to be transported back to France aboard the ship. The Foreign Office immediately instructed Havard to inform the High Commission in Beirut that, unless the *Providence* submitted itself to inspection at Haifa, it would not be granted free passage to Marseilles. Dentz protested that this would never be permitted by the German armistice commission at Wiesbaden and gave Havard his word that no prisoners were to be shipped to France. At the same time he admitted that past convoys had indeed included Free French sympathizers who had been repatriated in order to prevent them from causing trouble, but who were not slated for any sort of punishment.[24]

In fact, Dentz was convinced that the British government was using this issue as a pretext for increasing their pressure against the Levant:

> There is reason to consider this new measure as a hostile act which is to come on top of the economic blockade from which the Levant suffers. Faced with this policy of systematic pressure, we still dispose of means of reprisal.[25]

Dentz asked Vichy to authorize him to threaten Havard with the closing of all British consulates, the barring of British citizens from transit through the Levant, and the halting of all rail transport through Syria destined for British mandatory territories unless the *Providence* were allowed to sail freely.[26] At the same time, he pointed out to Vichy that no Free French sympathizers were actually scheduled for transport aboard the *Providence*.[27] Reversing the role it had played during Puaux's tenure, Vichy now urged restraint on Dentz. Reporting that the British had conveyed (via their ambassador in Madrid) their continued refusal to allow free passage to the *Providence,* Foreign Minister Flandin pointed out to Dentz:

> Among the retaliatory measures which you propose, the closing of consulates would be all the more ineffective for backfiring against us.
>
> As for the halting of transit, that of people as well as of merchandise, it would also risk provoking a reaction by our neighbors, the gravity of which I cannot even measure.[28]

Meantime, however, Dentz had already instructed the director of his political cabinet, Conty, to threaten Havard with retaliatory measures unless His Majesty's government became more forthcoming over the freedom-of-passage issue. On the other hand, Dentz gave Havard vague assurances of an improvement in relations if the *Providence* were permitted direct passage to France. Confronted with the prospect of having his consulate shut down, Havard recommended to the Foreign Office that it reconsider its demand for an inspection call at Haifa, arguing that it was not an issue over which it was worth rupturing relations with the Levant.[29]

Faced with this request from Havard, the Foreign Office referred the matter to the CFR for consideration. A heated debate arose between the members of the committee representing ministries and Major-General Edward L. Spears, who was the British liaison officer to the Free French. As on other occasions during this period, it was Spears who vigorously upheld de Gaulle's position, arguing that it would be a disservice to Britain's interests as well as a blot on its honor to allow Dentz to ship Free French supporters back to France. The Foreign Office representative urged that Britain's demands be limited to a request for a formal guarantee from Dentz that no Gaullist sympathizers would be placed aboard the *Providence*. Spears scoffed at this as a shamefully inadequate solution to the problem, but the majority on the committee overrode his objections, and Havard duly obtained Dentz's solemn promise not to put anyone but the reservists aboard the ship. The high commissioner also assured Havard that British diplomatic-bag privileges, which had been suspended after the Bourget purge, would be restored.[30]

Infuriated by this decision, Spears vented his rage in a letter to Sir Alexander Cadogan, the undersecretary at the Foreign Office:

> You asked me to inform General de Gaulle of the F.O.'s decision to allow the "Providence" to sail without calling at Haifa, and I shall, of course, do so. I had postponed doing this until to-day in the hope that the matter might have been reconsidered. . . .
>
> My general responsibility in all questions affecting the Free French will, I hope, be accepted as a sufficient reason for justifying my expressing deep regret at the decision taken. It must, I fear, adversely affect and cause discour-

agement to the whole Free French movement. . . . My own feelings as an old soldier impel me to state that I am deeply moved by the prospect of the risk being run . . . by persons [the 100–200 attempted deserters] whose sole crime is that of wishing to fight by our side.

That this risk should be inflicted on them with our knowledge and consent seems to me like abandoning a comrade, and I fear that it will so strike the Free French. . . .

Admittedly it was considered important to repatriate the reservists in Syria, but this has been done with the exception of some 3000 men, and the War Office representative [to the CFR] . . . expressed the view that so comparatively small a number was immaterial.

The F.O. took a different view. It was "plus royaliste que le roi" in what would appear to be mainly a military matter. . . .

. . . The Foreign Office . . . agreed to the "Providence" sailing direct for France, if General Dentz . . . guaranteed that no Free French sympathisers would be on board.

Everything, therefore, depends upon whether General Dentz's word can be accepted or not.

His predecessor, M. Puaux, considered to be an Anglophile and held in considerable esteem by the F.O., gave exactly the same guarantee in respect of previous sailings but it is admitted by the French themselves that this was violated and that both contraband and Free French were conveyed in ships certified by the High Commissioner as only carrying reservists.

Mr. Havard believed then as he believes now, that the Syrian authorities would keep their word. . . . Unfortunately he was misinformed. His powers of verification were small at best. . . . How could he tell who, out of a long list of privates and N.C.O.s, were adherents of de Gaulle? . . .

The very latest information I have seen does not tend to increase my faith in General Dentz.

The High Commissioner in Palestine telegraphed on the 12th instant that Dentz, exasperated at his failure to secure the release of the "Providence," threatens to hand over Free French prisoners to General Fougères [sic] with the intention that the utmost rigour of the law shall be applied to them.

This is blackmail. . . . We had been given to understand that there was very little against the persons concerned and that they would be dealt with gently. . . .

The further consideration . . . was that the consequence might be that the Armistice Commission would refuse to allow further ships to sail between France and Syria. No one has, so far, argued that this would be a disadvantage from our point of view.[31]

While the Eastern Department staff rejected Spears' indictment of Foreign Office policy, Cadogan noted that "I hope . . . [Spears'] grievance *is* imaginary.—Otherwise I must confess that this business makes me feel rather uncomfortable [italics in original]."[32] Meanwhile, Dentz was triumphantly reporting to Vichy that the threats he had been warned not to make had borne fruit just as he had expected.[33]

Although ready to be aggressive in his dealings with the British, Dentz took his engagements toward them very seriously. When Vichy instructed him not to apply to future shipments his promise to avoid all transportation of merchandise,[34] he protested that this would undermine the whole basis of his understanding with the British. His guarantee that no war materiel or merchandise would be transported aboard the *Providence* was the reaffirmation of a standing commitment:

> The engagement therefore holds for future convoys as for those in the past. To place it in doubt would doubtless result in the disintegration of the negotiations conducted by this High Commission and which resulted in the lifting of the categorical refusal which the English Government had communicated to the Ministry.[35]

As it turned out, however, Dentz was not in full control of his own administration. In the first week of March, the British discovered that the *Providence* had actually been used to transport aircraft parts to the Levant. With 1,400 reservists still remaining in Syria, the British decided to revert to their original policy of blocking all maritime communication between the Levant and France unless ships stopped at Haifa for inspection.[36] Dentz complained to Vichy that the *Providence* had in fact been used to transport two planes as well as spare parts for hydroplanes at a Levant naval base. No one at the High Commission had been informed of this shipment in advance and Dentz demanded an investigation. In the meantime, there was no point in trying to send any more vessels to Beirut.[37]

Von Hentig's Visit

Concurrently with the *Providence* affair, a more ominous development was affecting Anglo–French relations in the Levant. This was the four-week visit to the region by the German Foreign Ministry representative, Werner Otto von Hentig.

In the 1930s, Germany had adhered to a cautious policy toward British interests in the Middle East. Hitler's primary consideration during this period was to reach a general accommodation with Britain that would leave him a free hand in central and eastern Europe in exchange for a German undertaking not to disturb the equilibrium of the British Empire. At the time of the Czechoslovak crisis of 1938, the Germans did begin channeling funds to the Arab rebellion in Palestine, and unsuccessfully tried to smuggle arms to the rebels via Saudi Arabia. But even then, the main thrust of this policy seems to have been to divert British resources from the European continent, rather than to seriously undermine Britain's grip on its Middle Eastern sphere of influence.[38]

After the outbreak of war, of course, Berlin no longer had any motive to respect Britain's imperial interests. Although the Arab countries had broken off formal diplomatic relations with Germany, indirect contact was maintained in some cases, and Iraq actually maintained diplomatic relations with Italy. With the formation of a new Iraqi government under Rashid Ali al-Kilani at the end of March 1940, Baghdad became increasingly interested in what Berlin had to offer, and the Germans also kept in touch with the Mufti al-Husseini, the former leader of the Arab revolt in Palestine who now lived in exile in Baghdad. Even then, the Germans were careful not to commit themselves to any specific program of pan-Arab liberation and unification lest they antagonize the Italians, who claimed the region as their own sphere of interest. Instead, they limited themselves to issuing a joint declaration with Italy in October 1940, expressing general sympathy with Arab nationalist aspirations.[39]

In the Levant, German policy was further complicated by its interest in supporting Vichy's control of the area at least until the Axis was itself in a position to take the region over; however, in the wake of the December 1940 government crisis in Vichy, which resulted in the dismissal and brief arrest of their favorite son Laval, the Germans were no longer inclined to indulge the Pétain regime in any of its pretensions. Moreover, the decision in late 1940 to commit German troops to the support of Italy on the North African front raised the Germans' stake in the eastern Mediterranean, and relieved them of some of their earlier qualms over interfering in the Italian sphere of interest.[40] The time had come to send someone to the Levant to spy out the land.

In the summer of 1939, the Germans had already sent Baron von Oppenheim on what was purported to be an archaeological expedition to Syria. A noted academic, and the author of the standard scholarly work on the Bedouin, von Oppenheim also had close contacts with German intelligence and was treated as an "honorary Aryan" despite his Jewish origin.[41] Von Oppenheim had actively cultivated contact with local notables and political leaders, especially in Syria's northeastern Jezireh region, during his two-month stay.[42] In August 1940, the German military had sent a representative by the name of Roser to Beirut to oversee the release of German detainees. He had stayed on and filed regular reports about the political situation in the Levant.[43] In late September, the Wiesbaden Commission had demanded that the diplomat and Middle Eastern expert Otto von Hentig be authorized to travel to the Levant, ostensibly in order to investigate the possibility of a trade agreement between Germany and the French authorities in Beirut.

It was obvious to the French that von Hentig's mission would be more than economic in nature. He had already traveled extensively throughout the Middle East and Central Asia on behalf of the German Foreign Ministry during World War I in an effort to counter and undermine British influence in the Muslim world. The suggestion of a visit by him to the Levant raised the spectre of German political interest in the region, and the Vichy authorities procrastinated until late November, when it was finally decided to refuse the German request outright.[44] After the ouster of Laval in December, the German authorities renewed their request, making it clear that " 'in the difficult phase which Franco–German relations are currently going through,' the response which is made to this *démarche* will be regarded as an indication of France's intentions."[45] Further procrastination would clearly be counterproductive for Vichy, and the decision was made reluctantly to issue von Hentig a visa for Syria and Lebanon. He promptly departed from Ankara, where he had spent six weeks awaiting the go-ahead, and traveled overland to Beirut, arriving in the second week of January 1941.[46]

Von Hentig's formal instructions from the German Foreign Ministry did not call for any political intervention or provocation in the Levant. His mission was designated as strictly informational. He was to report on the political and military situation in Syria and the surrounding region and to assess French chances for a successful defense of the territory against a British invasion. He was also to gather information relevant to German policy toward the Arab states. In addition, von Hentig was instructed to report on German economic and cultural interests in the Levant. (As noted earlier, a trade agreement between Germany and the Levant was secured in February 1941.) He was explicitly requested "to avoid, for your part, anything that might be construed as approval or support of any tendencies directed against the French Government."[47]

In practice, however, it proved difficult to distinguish reconnaissance from intervention. The simple fact of von Hentig's presence in the Levant undercut French authority and raised the hopes of Arab nationalists. Immediately on his arrival in Beirut, von Hentig began to meet with Lebanese and Syrian political figures, who sounded him out on Germany's intentions in the Middle East and urged him to recommend more active support by Berlin for the Arab nationalist movement. Von Hentig even received a group of Stern Gang representatives from Palestine who offered to cooperate with Germany against the British if the Germans promised to support an independent Jewish Palestine.[48] In Lebanon, von Hentig was reported to have encountered a particularly warm reception among Muslim circles. Sunni political leaders such as the pan-Arab nationalist Riad al-Solh and Umar al-Dauk were particularly eager to cooperate with the Germans. The Maronites tended to keep their distance.[49]

After a two-week sojourn in Beirut, von Hentig was accompanied by Roser on a tour of the Levant states, meeting notables throughout the region and renewing many of von Oppenheim's contacts. Although the French authorities resented his presence and feared its consequences, there was little they could do to limit his activities. The *Services Spéciaux* in the Jezireh reported that von Hentig had arrogantly rebuffed an attempt by local French officers to establish his identity, claiming that the Germans would soon be in control of the Levant anyway. Whether as the result of indirect suggestion or explicit encouragement, notables such as Khalid Bey of the Jezireh began spreading pro-German propaganda and rumors of an impending German takeover soon after meeting with von Hentig.[50]

Although von Hentig did cultivate contact with those members of the Syrian nationalist movement still in Damascus, such as Shukri al-Quwatli, he found their response unsatisfactory. While professing support for the German cause, the Syrian nationalists were not as forthcoming as their Lebanese counterparts when it came to practical cooperation in propaganda or contingency plans for insurrection. They apparently considered it safer to wait for the final outcome of the battle in North Africa. Consequently, von Hentig concentrated on winning the cooperation of less prominent figures such as the pan-Arab guerrilla leader Fawzi al-Qawuqji and Saadi Keilani (known as the Shami Pir), a shadowy, conspiratorial figure who was an Afghan nobleman by birth, was married to a German woman, and who had fomented trouble among the tribes of Waziristan in northwestern India until the British paid him to leave in 1938.[51] The impression gained by French and British intelligence was that von Hentig preferred to establish a network of paid agents in the Levant to dealing with an autonomous Arab nationalist movement.

Strong indications also existed of collusion between pro-Nazi agitators in the Levant and the Mufti al-Husseini in Baghdad.[52] Jewish Agency reports indicated that the Mufti and his collaborators in Iraq were the focus of a German contingency plan for inciting an Arab rebellion in the Levant and Palestine in the event of a German invasion of Turkey. This would help forestall any attempt by the British to move into the Levant before the Germans got there.[53] As long as Vichy managed to maintain its grip on the territory and the German war effort had not extended to Turkey, Berlin had no interest in undermining French authority in the area.[54]

Von Hentig himself did press for a more dynamic German policy in the Middle East, and chafed under the restraint imposed by the Reich's tolerance of Italian ambitions in the region. Ridiculing the Italian Control Commission in Beirut as hopelessly ineffective and Mussolini's expansionist dreams as preposterously grandiose, von Hentig hoped to see German influence in the Levant and Iraq grow unhindered by Italian demands. Weizsäcker, the state secretary of the Foreign Ministry, seemed to share this view. The Realpolitik of the professional diplomats did not seem to accord with the party's views, however, either because of Hitler's continuing indulgence toward his erstwhile role-model, Mussolini, or because plans for the invasion of the Soviet Union were the first order of business in Berlin. Von Hentig was warned that he risked facing the firing squad if he continued to criticize Hitler's policy toward Italy.[55] Nonetheless, the Foreign Ministry did go so far as to recommend the conversion of the exclusive Italian control of French forces in the Levant into mixed German–Italian control through negotiation with Rome. This came at a time when Germany was also preparing to bring French Morocco under the control of a German armistice commission.[56]

Feeling threatened by von Hentig's activities, the Vichy government complained ineffectually to the German armistice commission at Wiesbaden while seeking ways of repairing the damage to their position in Syria and Lebanon. The High Commission perceived a marked change in the attitude of Syrian politicians in the wake of von Hentig's visit. In February, the self-exiled leaders of the National Bloc were exonerated of any involvement in the murder of Shahbandar and it was apparently hoped that this would render the nationalists more amenable to cooperation with the mandatory authorities. Instead, the Shahbandar party was alienated while the National Bloc maintained its distance. Only one of its exiled leaders, Lutfi Haffar, chose to return to Syria at this juncture.[57] Attempts by Dentz to replace the Syrian directorate with a more regularly constituted government ran aground. Politicians who had earlier seemed eager to cooperate now refused to join a new cabinet unless Syrian independence was declared.[58] A report in February by the French intelligence service in the Levant pointed out that any concessions Dentz chose to make to Syrian nationalism at this juncture would simply be perceived as a response to German pressure and hence a sign of weakness. The report continued by arguing that the only way to salvage the French position in the Levant was to formulate an Arab policy of wide scope with a view to securing a treaty guaranteeing French privileges in the region once the war was over. Such a policy could be worked out through consultations in Vichy with ambassadors from Arab countries as well as with U.S. Ambassador Leahy:

> In any case, since it is absolutely clear that Germany and Britain are preparing in these countries [of the Arab world] not only their spring campaign but [also] the "post-war" [scenario] . . . we cannot ourselves remain insensible to the projected liquidation of all our interests.[59]

In principle, Vichy had long been in favor of assuaging nationalist sentiment in the Levant. In the fall of 1940, the Foreign Ministry had responded to appeals from the Iraqi and Saudi ambassadors for a restoration of constitutional government in Syria by pestering Puaux with vague demands for administrative reform and blanket amnesties for political prisoners. Puaux had resisted taking precipitate action but had finally recommended that Ata Bey al-Ayubi be appointed head of a new government, replacing the unpopular Syrian directorate.[60] Things had drifted during the interim between Puaux's dismissal and Dentz's arrival on the scene, but in January, the new high commissioner had begun to reexamine the question. Deciding that Puaux's candidate for prime minister was too obscure a political figure for the job, Dentz recommended instead the appointment of Hashem al-Atasi, who had been Syria's president during the period of National Bloc rule in 1936–1939.[61] This was too much for Vichy. Flandin objected:

> The program which you present us with is too summary to assure me that it is strictly inspired by the essential principles of Marshal Pétain's policy. Regardless of all else, it is important that, in the development of your projects you do not stray from these principles in any way. In view of the fact that, as of 1 July 1939, we put an end in Damascus to the parliamentary system and that, since the defeat, metropolitan France has deliberately followed an analogous orientation, it would not seem appropriate to restore the system whose functioning we have suspended.[62]

Thus, despite its intention of creating a more solid foundation for French rule in the Levant, what amounted to ideological considerations prevented Vichy from approving any bold measures. Certainly Pétain's government lacked either the will or the energy necessary for the formulation of the sort of long-term policy recommended in the Levant intelligence-service report of February 1941. Dentz was left to try and get along by means of cosmetic changes in the structures and personnel of the Syrian and Lebanese governments.

In fact, Dentz himself does not seem to have regarded the appointment of Atasi to the premiership as a move necessarily leading to the reintroduction of a parliamentary system. He simply saw in Atasi a figure commanding the sort of political following necessary to lend a measure of stability to any new government.[63] In the wake of von Hentig's visit, however, Atasi was demanding impossible preconditions for his cooperation, and Dentz was forced to look elsewhere for a head of government. Indeed, it seems quite clear that the National Bloc would have avoided reaching any definitive agreements with the Vichy authorities even if the latter had been more forthcoming and ready to make concessions. The defeat of France had left it completely bereft of prestige in Arab eyes and it seemed only a matter of time before either Germany or Britain became the arbiter of power in the Levant. Moreover, Jamil Mardam's exile had enabled Shukri al-Quwatli to gain control over the National Bloc, and he had always had a much more intransigent attitude toward the French than Mardam. Thus, the notion that the reestablishment of cabinet rule could assuage nationalist sentiments in Syria was, like so much else in Vichy's policy, mere self-deception.

Unrest in Syria and the Revision of Britain's Blockade Policy

The political stability of the Levant was hardly furthered by the economic situation in February–March 1941. Despite the various breaches in Britain's blockade of the French-held territories, the impact of the trade restrictions was clearly felt. In particular, the gasoline shortage impinged on all other sectors of the economy, since limited fuel meant limited transportation facilities. Most significantly, the provision of wheat stocks for the urban centers was severely hindered by the fuel shortage as well as by corruption among those in the French administration responsible for the wheat supply.[64]

The increasing tenuousness of Dentz's position did not induce him to become any more forthcoming to overtures from the British. Another of Catroux's personal appeals for cooperation was merely forwarded to Vichy, and in conversation with Havard, Dentz refused to promise to continue allowing the passage of supplies for the defense of Turkey through the Levant in the event Germany invaded Anatolia; the matter would have to be referred to Vichy.[65] Horace Seymour, the undersecretary in charge of the Eastern Department, noted:

> All this leaves us where we were: the High Comm[issioner] will do what Vichy tells him, and Vichy will presumably do what the Germans tell them in such a matter as communications through Syria.[66]

Meanwhile, the bread shortage was growing increasingly acute, and at the end of February, demonstrations and riots began to rock the major towns of Syria. The situation was quickly exploited by the nationalist parties, which whipped up unrest and transformed the crowds' cries for more bread to demands for political independence. In Damascus and Aleppo, shops were forced to close in protest over French policies.[67] More than ever, Dentz felt compelled to do away with the directorship and appoint a regular government.

The impact of the riots on the British was more startling. Faced with the possible prospect of a collapse of French authority in the Levant, they rapidly contemplated a complete revision of their already heavily eroded blockade policy. In meetings with the American and British consuls in Beirut, Dentz and Conty expressed their fear that the Germans might try to exploit the unrest for their own purposes.[68] The British government quickly approved an increase in trade between Syria and the United States.[69] In addition, General Wavell renewed his demands for a revival of direct trade links with the Levant and this time his views were echoed by Ambassador Lampson in Cairo. They reemphasized the economic plight the blockade had created in Palestine and warned that there were no British troops to spare for an occupation of the Levant in the event a vacuum was suddenly created there.[70]

By the end of the third week of March, reports were coming in of primitive bombs exploding in the streets of Damascus and of the distribution of pamphlets threatening to blow up shops that had remained open in defiance of the strike; German radio contributed to the trouble by directing inflammatory broadcasts at the Levant. Shukri al-Quwatli, who was now recognized as leading the strike movement, seemed to have no intention of letting up the pressure.[71] He was said to have chaired a meeting of Arab nationalists and German agents on March 4, at which the nationalists agreed to help further the German cause and oppose any attempt by Britain to take over Syria.[72] In addition, Roser had been seen in Damascus in the company of the Shami Pir.[73] The blockade policy seemed to be backfiring and the decision was made in London to renegotiate a clearing agreement with the French authorities.[74]

Free French Policy and Activities

Throughout this period, the Free French continued their attempts to set up an independent propaganda and intelligence network in the Levant, but met with relatively little success. They were in fact almost totally dependent on British support, while the distribution of Free French propaganda leaflets seems to have been carried out largely by agents of the *Haganah* and the Jewish Agency. One such agent, Tuviah Arazi, was arrested in December by the Vichy French authorities and subjected to brutal interrogation before managing to escape. Nevertheless, other propaganda and espionage networks run by *Haganah* agents continued to operate right through the British invasion of the Levant in June–July 1941.[75]

The Jewish Agency had made tentative overtures toward the Free French movement as early as July 1940. In addition to suggesting cooperation in the Levant, the agency had suggested that the World Jewish Congress (WJC) could assist the Free French propaganda effort in the United States and provide the Gaullists with information on the climate of political opinion in America. Although Free French representatives in New York actually signed an agreement at the end of April 1941 providing for broad political cooperation between the Gaullist movement and the WJC, this was subsequently disavowed by the Free French authorities in London who wished to limit themselves to the exchange of information with the WJC. The suggestion of wider cooperation, possibly involving financial support by the WJC for the Free French, seems to have provoked the bitter opposition of anti-Semitic elements in the French National Committee (FNC) who feared a Jewish takeover of the pro-Gaullist, France for Ever committees in the United States. It was also feared that Vichy would be able to exploit such cooperation for its own propaganda.[76]

Meanwhile, a more specific agreement between the Free French and the Jewish Agency regarding information exchange on Levant affairs was reached in London in September 1940 with the tacit approval of the British. This provided a direct framework for local Gaullist–Zionist cooperation beyond the indirect one already established via the SOE. It was on the basis of this agreement that the Jewish Agency helped distribute the Free French propaganda leaflets in Syria and Lebanon.[77] François Coulet, in charge of operating the secret Free French radio station in Haifa, was an ardent advocate of expanding the cooperation with the Zionists, and he badgered members of the FNC with letters on the topic over a period of several months.[78] His efforts seemed to bear fruit in November, when Commandant Passy, head of the Free French intelligence service, proposed to Catroux the creation of a wider framework of cooperation with the Jewish Agency. Catroux balked at the idea, however, fearing that the British would suspect the Free French of meddling in Palestine politics.[79] When evidence continued to surface of contacts behind Catroux's back between Free French intelligence and the Zionists, he protested vigorously to de Gaulle:

> I have learned from a reliable source that secret communications are taking place between our central services and the delegate [in London, Albert Cohen] of the Zionist organization in Palestine and that, in addition, an officer under my direct command [presumably Coulet], stationed in Haifa, passes information to London via the same procedure.
>
> This exchange of communications dealing in particular with our propaganda and our policy with regard to the Levant, can no longer be justified since my assumption of responsibility for the direction of affairs.
>
> I consider it irreconcilable with my position and authority and I am sure that, sharing my sentiment, you will have an end put to it.[80]

Catroux thus stood in the way of a development that might have won the Free French a slightly greater measure of operational autonomy in Syria and Lebanon. Yet his reluctance to antagonize the British is understandable, given the utter dependence of the Free French movement on London's support. Besides, as the Jewish Agency itself pointed out, if the *Haganah* continued to do the Gaullists' work for them in Syria, the Free French could easily be portrayed by Vichy propaganda as nothing but a pack of English spies or Zionist agents.[81]

Acutely aware of the limited scope of action available to him, Catroux pursued a very cautious policy during the period of popular unrest in Syria. Repiton-Preneuf reported to him that the nationalist agitation was not furthering Free French interests since the movement was directed against French rule as such, not just against Vichy.[82] The prospects of the Levant army rallying to the Free French cause now seemed remote. The only chance for change lay with British military plans, but General Wavell was too busy fending off the Germans in the Western Desert and preparing for their anticipated attack in the Balkans to deal with Syria for the time being.[83] Only the Germans stood to benefit from an immediate collapse of Vichy French authority in Syria. Accordingly, Catroux expressed his support for an easing of the blockade, arguing that General Dentz "would appreciate support, from which we might later derive some benefit."[84] In a dispatch to Repiton-Preneuf on March 26, Catroux again emphasized the need to coordinate policy with the British even if that meant avoiding for the time being any action that Vichy might regard as provocative.[85]

Catroux's reluctance to take any risks did not sit well with General de Gaulle, who was further antagonized by Catroux's tendency to consult independently with the British. During a brief sojourn in Khartoum, on his way to Cairo, de Gaulle told Spears:

> He [de Gaulle] won't accept that C[atroux] sh[ould] come to understandings with people like Eden and that he s[houl]d hear about it not from C[atroux] but from Eden. He told me that C[atroux] had told him that Eden approved he s[houl]d be high Commissioner for Syria in case of occupation and left it at that without submitting it f[or] approval. . . .

> The curse is of course Mme Catroux who works against de G[aulle]: she declared publicly that her husband at least had no Fr[ench] blood on his hands![86]

The Pressure for Action Mounts

The month of April 1941 witnessed an alarming series of events that gravely threatened Britain's entire position in the eastern Mediterranean. In North Africa, Rommel's first offensive pushed British forces 400 miles back to the Egyptian border in less than two weeks, reversing their earlier gains over the Italians save for their continued occupation of the stronghold at Tobruk. On April 6, Germany invaded Greece and Yugoslavia, while Rashid Ali's coup d'état toppled the pro-British government in Iraq. With danger looming on every flank in the Middle East, the British government faced some very tough choices over the allocation of its overstretched resources. During the months that followed, General Wavell advocated the concentration of the effort on the struggle in the Western Desert at the expense of lesser theaters, whereas Churchill sought to press forward aggressively on every front. It was within this context that the Levant problem was discussed in the spring of 1941.

On April 1, de Gaulle and Spears arrived in Cairo to examine first hand the possibility of removing the Levant from Vichy's control. They immediately began to lobby against General Wavell's reluctance to risk confrontation with Vichy's forces in Djibouti and Syria while simultaneously battling the Germans. Wavell's approach was also perceived as overly prudent by Churchill, who rejected his proposal for a compromise in Djibouti whereby the British blockade would be lifted in return for access to the colony's railway system. Churchill ordered the Chiefs of Staff to tighten the blockade and starve the French out, emphasizing that de Gaulle's views on the matter could not be disregarded. The British government had "signed a solemn undertaking to support him and due weight must be given to his views and advice." However, Churchill remained reluctant to take any precipitate action in the Levant at that juncture.[87]

For his part, Spears vigorously advocated the extension of British support to a Free French invasion of Syria and Lebanon to take place as soon as possible. Precisely *because* of the multiple threats to its position in the Middle East, Britain could not afford to leave the Levant so vulnerable to a German takeover. To do so was to invite a German pincer movement from Libya in the west and Syria and Iraq in the north and east. Spears furiously criticized Wavell for being blind to the strategic implications of leaving Syria in Vichy hands. If only he had actively encouraged the defection of troops from the Levant over the past year, he argued, the territory might already have been in Free French hands. In his diary, the exasperated Spears wrote that Wavell's "blindness is frightful—but what is fundamentally wrong is that soliders are in charge [of] policy and don't know anything about it."[88]

Over the course of April and May, a series of conferences including Wavell, the heads of the British military services in the Middle East, Ambassador Lampson, Spears, de Gaulle, and Catroux, was held in Cairo to discuss the situation in Syria and Lebanon. The participants argued endlessly over various possible courses of action without arriving at any clear-cut agreement. Wavell was opposed to a Gaullist move into the Levant because he feared British forces might get drawn into the conflict. Of the service chiefs, only Air Chief Marshal Longmore, in charge of the Royal Air Force, seemed impressed with the potential liability of Syria as a landing site for German aircraft enroute to support an Iraqi revolt.[89] Spears vented his frustration with the military in his diary, writing:

I felt strongly that none [of the participants in the Cairo conferences] really revealed their full mind, and that each was thinking of considerations affecting his own service he did not care to inform the other services about. . . . [I]t was clear that here were different watertight compartments facing each other and not blending. Lack of one authority was painfully apparent. . . . The Ambassador [was] quite helpless in face of technical opinion; what is more he is told little or nothing of milit[ar]y situation.[90]

Lampson agreed with Spears' indictment of General Headquarters Middle East, and supported him when Wavell complained to the War Office about Spears' habit of criticizing Wavell's policy in his telegrams to London:

Michael [Wright of the Cairo embassy] suggested that this was a first-class opportunity on which to challenge what appeared to be a claim by our military to complete dictatorship in the Middle East. He asked [and received] my leave to go over with Spears and see Arthur Smith [Wavell's Chief of Staff] and take this line.[91]

In arguing the case for intervention, the Free French were hampered by their own lack of a well-thought-out plan of attack. They could not even agree among themselves on whether or not it was desirable that British forces participate in the operation. Their estimate was that while the Levant army was unlikely to rally spontaneously to de Gaulle's banner, it would also be reluctant to offer more than token resistance to a Free French invasion; the appearance of British troops on the scene would provoke much stiffer opposition.[92] De Gaulle seemed to feel that his forces could really go it alone in the Levant, whereas Catroux felt some concrete assistance from the British would be vital.[93] At the April 15 meeting in Cairo to discuss the Free French plans for an invasion, Catroux surprised both de Gaulle and Spears by asking Wavell for two British mechanized divisions as part of the invasion force. Spears felt this was an unrealistic demand, given existing circumstances, and de Gaulle was angered by Catroux's apparent eagerness to rely on direct British support for a Free French operation, telling Spears "how angered he was with Catroux for putting forward his idiotic plan this morning."[94] Lampson observed:

Throughout all these discussions one fact stands out, namely, how jealous de Gaulle is of any suggestion that Free France is being run in any way with British assistance. Rather stupid, but I fear characteristic.[95]

De Gaulle insisted that only minimal support would be needed from the British, as Lampson reported sympathetically to the Foreign Office.[96] Catroux's plan, however, had played right into Wavell's hands, lending support to his argument that essential British troops and materiel would be drawn off into the Levant if the Free French were allowed to invade the territory. On May 2, the situation was yet further complicated by the outbreak of an anti-British revolt in Iraq. The hard-pressed Wavell felt he could not spare troops from the Western Desert to deal with Rashid Ali's forces, and he telegraphed to London urging a negotiated settlement with the Iraqis. As for Syria, even if Germany started landing troops there, he could envisage intervening only if assured beforehand of General Dentz's cooperation.[97]

Dentz's Concern about German Intentions

The British and the Free French were not the only ones to be concerned about the German threat. The French authorities in the Levant suffered from very similar worries. The counterproductive role played by the Germans in the Syrian riots of March had awakened fear of a concerted attempt by Berlin to subvert French authority in the Levant. Dentz telegraphed to Vichy:

> If one connects this [Syrian] agitation with the campaign recently unleashed by the official German press agency on the subject of the Syrians, the question arises whether Berlin does not have the intention of securing certain positions in the French mandatory territories.
>
> One cannot hide from oneself the dangers entailed in such a development. From the internal point of view, German interference would gravely damage French authority. . . . From the external point of view, it would inevitably provoke intervention by the British army.[98]

During this time, Vichy's ambassador in Switzerland reported that, according to a reliable source, there was open talk among official circles in Berlin of the possibility of a German takeover of iron mines in Lebanon in the course of 1941.[99]

By the beginning of April, Dentz had managed to bring the situation in the Levant under fairly good control. As the strike movement started to wane, the nationalists became more amenable to political compromise, and agreed to lend their support to a government led by Khalid al-Azm, an able public figure not associated with any political party but not regarded as a stooge of the French either. The formation of a consultative assembly composed of representatives of the major Syrian interest groups lent the new arrangement a veneer of constitutionality.[100] In response to unrest in Lebanon, a similar arrangement was instituted there, with Alfred Naccache as head of the politically neutral government.[101]

The temporary subsiding of popular unrest did not allay Dentz's fear of German interference. When word came that von Hentig was planning to return to the Levant, the High Commission became alarmed. A report by the Muslim Affairs section of the Levant army's *Deuxième Bureau* suggested that von Hentig's activities could be seen as the expression of a long-standing German ambition to gain control over the Muslim world. In a long dispatch to Darlan, Dentz emphasized that the recent trouble in Syria had come directly in the wake of von Hentig's visit, whereas the British seemed to have done their best to restrain the nationalist agitation. If the Germans tried to gain a foothold in the Levant, the British response would be "immediate et brutale," and the Turks might well move in from the north as well:

> It is imperative that, at any price, von Hentig does not return to Syria.
>
> And *a fortiori* other German emissaries.[102]

While Vichy sought to convince the German authorities not to send von Hentig to the Levant, the Germans continued to interfere in Dentz's affairs from afar. On April 18, Jacques Benoist-Méchin, a close aid to Darlan, was presented with a formal German demand for the expulsion from the Levant of six officials (including the head of Dentz's political cabinet, Conty) who were described as agents of British propaganda.[103] Despite Dentz's complaints about personnel shortages, Vichy remained adamant that the German demand be complied with, although the sudden change in circumstances in mid-May prevented the order from being carried out.[104]

During this period of impending crisis, the Vichy French and British seemed to be moving closer toward cooperation with each other in the Middle East than at any time since the armistice agreement. Conty let Consul-General Havard know of Dentz's concern about the German threat, and actually requested that His Majesty's government induce the American Ambassador in Vichy to impress on Pétain's government how important a strategic asset Syria was for France! Conty also claimed that the military authorities in the Levant were contemplating the possibility of accepting British support against the Germans in the event of an invasion.[105]

This was good news to the British, whose forces in the Eastern Mediterranean were being driven back on all fronts. The collapse of resistance to the Germans in Yugoslavia and Greece now appeared to herald a German assault on Crete and then Cyprus or Syria. In the Western Desert, Rommel's army posed a dire threat to British control of Egypt.[106] The outbreak of the Iraqi revolt threatened to create a base for the Germans in the very heart of the Middle East, and this issue involved the Levant directly, for it constituted the natural supply route to Iraq. Short of an all-out attack on Syria, it seemed likely that the Germans would attempt to seize bases in the Levant for use in the channeling of troops or supplies to the Iraqi rebels. An alternate hypothesis was that the Iraqi revolt was but a diversion designed to facilitate a German occupation of Syria followed by a quick march on Palestine.[107] In any case, if Dentz really intended to resist a German assault, Britain must clearly do all it could to strengthen his position. Accordingly, the CFR decided to give the final authorization for the negotiation of an economic clearing agreement between Palestine and Syria.[108] Wavell was instructed by the War Office to promise Dentz British support against a German attack, and to assure him he would not be obliged to recognize General de Gaulle's authority in exchange for British aid.[109]

Predictably, the Free French were vehemently opposed to Britain's apparent rapprochement with Dentz. Catroux and de Gaulle insisted that it would be self-defeating for the British to grant Dentz the clearing agreement without any tangible quid pro quo or concrete commitment from Beirut in return. Given the history of Vichy's behavior over the past year, it made no sense to build up the regime's position in the Levant at such a crucial moment.[110] De Gaulle (now in Brazzaville) wrote to Wavell:

> To imagine that Dentz would be able to issue orders of resistance against the
> Germans is a pure illusion. Dentz will not take a stand against Vichy, and the

arrival of the Germans in Syria, if it takes place, will be the result of a collaboration agreement between Vichy and the Germans.[111]

The British government remained unmoved. On May 11, the Foreign Office reported to Ambassador Halifax in Washington that "negotiations with the French [for a clearing agreement] will shortly open at Jerusalem."[112] De Gaulle also received indications that Wavell was about to be authorized to relax the blockade on Djibouti. On May 12, de Gaulle wrote Catroux:

> Given the negative policy which our British allies have believed themselves obliged to adopt toward our interests in the Orient, I consider that the presence in Cairo of an important personage such as yourself and a High Commissioner representing Free France is no longer justified.[113]

Catroux was instructed to depart immediately from Cairo. On the very same day, German planes began landing at Syrian airfields.

4

Invasion and Armistice

Darlan's Paris Talks

Throughout the tortuous course of Vichy's relations with Germany since the Armistice, there had existed the possibility of broad cooperation between the two states based on an active French contribution to the war effort against Britain in return for a significant alleviation of the armistice terms. The dismissal of Laval in December 1940 had destroyed the hopes of the more ardent collaborationists in the Pétain regime, but only temporarily. The appointment of Admiral Darlan to the vice-presidency of the council in February 1941 marked Vichy's reversion to a more active pursuit of military cooperation and diplomatic reconciliation with Germany.[1] After a number of feelers had been extended by Darlan without much success, the events of May in Iraq suddenly created a new climate for cooperation. Although Rashid Ali's revolt was premature and Hitler's attention was largely concentrated on planning the invasion of the Soviet Union, he was convinced by Ribbentrop that it was worthwhile to send aid to the Iraqis, whose success could help precipitate the collapse of Britain's entire position in the Middle East.[2]

To extend substantial assistance to Rashid Ali was easier suggested than implemented. Neutral Turkey was not about to agree to the passage of German arms over its territory and plans for a circuitous supply route through Iran proved impractical. It became clear that the quickest and surest way of sending aid to Iraq was by air. To facilitate this, it would be essential to secure landing rights in Syria for refueling purposes.[3]

Over the previous several months, Darlan had been exploring the possibility of limited military cooperation with Germany in exchange for an easing of the armistice terms. He had authorized the sale of French trucks to Rommel's army in North Africa and had entertained the idea of breaking the British blockade through the employment of escorted convoys.[4] So far the Germans had shown little interest in Darlan's overtures. Now the situation had altered, and Ribbentrop authorized the German ambassador in Paris, Otto Abetz, to seek Vichy's agreement to make Syrian airfields available for German planes and arms enroute to Iraq. Also on the agenda was a request for the transfer to Iraq of French military equipment held by the Italian Control Commission in the Levant. In return, the French would be allowed to rearm a number of naval vessels.[5]

The initial overture was made by Abetz on May 2 in a meeting with Darlan's righthand man, Jacques Benoist-Méchin. An intellectual with strong fascist sympathies and a flair for grandiose designs, Benoist-Méchin was enthusiastic about the proposal, which he saw as a potential turning point in Franco–German relations:

> I had always foreseen that . . . the military operations would end up crossing one of the territories under our control and I thought that at that moment we would be able to play our luck to the full, provided we grasped the opportunity: that moment had come. . . .
>
> . . . There was a strong possibility that England would use the transit of German airplanes as a pretext for attacking Syria. For my part, I was convinced that she would attack *in any case* [italics in original]. . . .
>
> By acquiescing in the German request and by aiding the Iraqi nationalists, the eventual loss [of Syria] would acquire a positive value: it would place us among the defenders of Arab liberties, which would favorably impress the Muslim populations of our Empire; it would make the Germans parties to the loss, thereby facilitating its restitution [to France] at the time of the peace treaty.[6]

Barely able to contain his glee over the German request, Benoist-Méchin promised to convey the proposal to his government. Once back in Vichy, he had little trouble winning Darlan over to the idea. Pétain also gave his approval, provided that the Germans were willing to offer substantive concessions in return.[7]

Meeting with Benoist-Méchin and Darlan in Paris on May 5, Abetz was now authorized to offer a reduction in indemnity payments and the repatriation of a substantial number of prisoners of war in addition to the rearmament of six French destroyers and seven torpedo boats. The promise was also held forth of an easing of restrictions on postal communication between the occupied and unoccupied zones of France. In addition to the cooperation already requested, the French were also asked to share all of their intelligence on British military movements in the Middle East.[8] Darlan accepted the general outline of this arrangement and it was agreed that the technical details would be worked out in subsequent talks with the German military staff. But at the last moment, Abetz received a telegram from Berlin which, he said, reported a substantial deterioration in Rashid Ali's military position. Could Darlan order Dentz immediately to facilitate the landing of German aircraft at Syrian airfields? Benoist-Méchin later claimed to have resisted such precipitate action, but Darlan overrode his objections and sent off the appropriate orders to Beirut forthwith. It was also agreed that Rudolf Rahn of the German embassy in Paris be sent to Syria in the company of a Vichy representative, Jacques Guerard, to oversee the transfer of French arms to the Iraqis.[9]

On May 11, Darlan and Benoist-Méchin sought to consummate their policy of collaboration by meeting with Hitler at Berchtesgaden. Much to

Benoist-Méchin's chagrin, the Führer seemed mysteriously preoccupied (it later emerged that he had just learned of Rudolf Hess' flight to Britain) and would agree only to a cautious quid pro quo arrangement rather than a broad restructuring of Franco–German relations. This was to be the basis for the ill-fated Paris Protocols of late May 1941.[10]

The Initial British Response

Darlan's attempt to ensure the secrecy of his deal with the Germans by avoiding use of the Wiesbaden channel proved to be of no avail. Only three days after Darlan's first meeting with Abetz, the British government was already informed of the probable substance of the Paris talks.[11] In fact, it was feared that the arrangement called for the complete occupation of Syria by German forces rather than just the use of airbases there.[12] The first German planes, painted over with Iraqi markings, began landing at three different bases in Syria on May 12. Any illusions Havard may have still entertained over General Dentz's attitude were dispelled in a conversation on May 13. The high commissioner told him "that his instructions did not at present provide for a German occupation of Syria, but if those orders came he would obey them."[13] When U.S. Consul-General Engert tried to press Dentz on the issue, he was told that

> politicians had been the ruination of France and he was glad Pétain was a soldier everybody trusted; and if, as seemed to be the case, the Marshal found it necessary to yield, he (Dentz) for one was not prepared to question the decision and he would continue to obey instructions.[14]

In fact, in his telegraphic correspondence with Vichy, Dentz did at least question the wisdom of Darlan's decision. He feared that the British might respond to German aircraft landings by destroying the new Tripoli oil refinery, thereby crippling the Syrian economy.[15] But when it was made clear to him that the decision was an irrevocable one, Dentz followed orders and gave Rahn and Guerard his full cooperation.

In London, there was a strong sentiment favoring preemptive military action, but, as always, viable options were painfully limited. Feeling hopelessly beleaguered, Wavell continued to preach extreme prudence, asking that he be authorized to negotiate a compromise settlement with Rashid Ali in Iraq. The War Cabinet's Defence Committee, under Churchill's chairmanship, decided compromise was out of the question and authorized the prime minister to send Wavell a telegram ordering him to press on with the campaign, "not hesitating to try to break into Baghdad even with quite small forces and running the same kind of risks as the Germans are accustomed to run and profit by."[16] Syria was another matter, however. As long as operations were under way in Iraq, it made no sense to dissipate British forces yet further by committing them to an armed intervention in the Levant. The only hope for preemptive action in May lay with the Free French and the SOE.

Much uncertainty clouded the issue of a move by Catroux into Syria. The Free French themselves had presented conflicting plans for military operations, and it seemed likely that British forces would be drawn into any operation by General Catroux.[17] Various proposals were aired involving stalling for time or winning over the support of the Syrian population. Churchill was the only one at the meeting who rejected the notion of mundane responses to an extraordinary situation:

> The Prime Minister thought the time had passed for trying to liquidate matters by political settlements or promises to the Arabs. The immediate problem was to oppose the imminent German arrival. As we had no troops ourselves to do it with the right course seemed to be to give General Catroux the lorries he required for his troops and to tell him to go in and attempt to win the French over.[18]

In a minute of the same date to Major-General Ismay, the prime minister wrote:

> A supreme effort must be made to prevent the Germans getting a foothold in Syria with small forces and then using Syria as a jumping-off ground for air domination of Iraq and Persia. It is no use General Wavell being vexed at this disturbance on his eastern flank. The Catroux plan should certainly not be excluded. . . . In addition we ought to help in every way without minding what happens at Vichy.[19]

The meeting, however, finally decided to adopt the course of action suggested by Air Chief Marshal Longmore, who argued that "the best chance of success would be to let Catroux cross into Syria as soon as the landing [of German aircraft] was detected. He did not think that he would stand much chance of gaining support if he went in beforehand."[20]

After the confirmation of German aircraft landings in Syria, the decision was immediately taken to bomb the three airfields in question.[21] The Defence Committee also formally suspended the clearing agreement, the terms of which had just been finalized on May 13.[22] On May 14, Churchill sent de Gaulle a personal telegram assuring him that the blockade of Djibouti would be maintained and asking him to cancel his order for Catroux's departure from Cairo. In view of the new circumstances, de Gaulle promptly complied with this request.[23]

From Beirut, Havard reported:

> Reactions caused by recent arrivals of German aeroplanes show that there is a large body of Frenchmen to whom collaboration with Germany is anathema but who are getting discouraged through lack of counter-action by us.
>
> . . . Any air action by us should be followed up by military occupation.[24]

As soon as the bombing of airfields began, the British diplomatic corps was expelled from the Levant. For the time being, however, the main body of British forces in Palestine had been sent to fight in Iraq as "Habforce," placing a full-scale invasion of the Levant beyond the realm of immediate possibility.[25]

The Tripoli Sabotage Operation

The scarcity of regular forces did not preclude the possibility of launching sabotage operations in the Levant. Although the papers of the SOE remain classified, the details of one such operation are known because it was coordinated with the *Haganah* in Palestine. Despite the opposition of the British civil and military establishment to any significant participation by the Zionist movement in the war effort, the intelligence services were hard-pressed for human resources and less concerned over the possible political ramifications of their modus operandi. As was seen in the preceding chapters, the *Haganah*'s cooperation had already been central to the Gaullist propaganda effort in the Levant as well as to British intelligence gathering (activities that had been coordinated by Brigadier Clayton in Cairo). Now, given the dangerous turn of events in the Vichy-occupied territories, it was decided to embark on a more ambitious venture.

Before the outbreak of the war, the Levant had relied on refined oil imported from Iraq for the bulk of its fuel needs. In the wake of the British blockade, the Beirut administration had set up a small refinery of its own in Tripoli, Lebanon, which helped fulfill minimal military needs. If this installation could be knocked out, it would limit the amount of aviation fuel available for German aircraft as well as hinder the ability of the Vichy forces to resist a British invasion. The *Haganah*, which was just setting up its elite *Palmach* commando force at this time, was eager to benefit from the training and experience which participation in such an operation would provide. A unit of twenty-three men was hand-picked by the *Haganah* command from among a group that had been put through an intensive, British-run training course in amphibious commando attacks. On May 18, the squad set forth on its mission from Haifa aboard the *Sea Lion,* under the command of an SOE officer, Major Antony Palmer.[26]

Tragically, the mission failed and the unit was eliminated under unknown circumstances. Vague and conflicting eyewitness accounts gathered two months later, after the British occupation of Lebanon, gave rise to a number of hypotheses regarding the fate of the *Sea Lion.* Most indications seemed to suggest that the unit encountered stiffer security measures at the refinery site than had been anticipated and that an exchange of fire broke out in which a portion of the group was killed. There is good reason to believe that the rest of the squad, including the British commander, were captured and then shot by the Vichy authorities.[27] In any case, the French High Commission kept the incident a closely guarded secret rather than exploiting it for propaganda purposes.[28]

Certainly one of the major reasons for the mission's failure must have been the frail structure of the British and *Haganah* intelligence network in the Levant as well as poor coordination between the SOE and the military command. The *Sea Lion*'s information on security at the refinery was based on reports provided by the *Haganah*'s espionage unit in Tripoli. On the eve of the vessel's departure, British planes bombed the Tripoli refinery (failing to destroy it) and in response, the French tightened their security there.[29] Had this been reported to Haifa before the scheduled time of the sabotage operation, radio silence could have been broken in order to pass on the crucial information or even to call off the mission. As it was, twenty-four lives were lost in vain while the Vichy French were left with an important resource that helped sustain their resistance to the British one month later.[30]

British Invasion Plans

By the end of the third week of May, the sentiment of the British War Cabinet had swung decisively in favor of an invasion of Syria. With the German assault on Crete imminent, the Chiefs of Staff had been weighing the alternatives of reinforcing the defenses of Cyprus or preemptively occupying Syria.[31] Reports by Free French intelligence on May 18 indicated that General Dentz was withdrawing his forces from Syria into Lebanon, presumably in anticipation of a German occupation of Syria.[32] It was also feared that neutral Turkey would join the Axis camp if it appeared that Syria was about to fall into German hands.[33] On May 20, the War Cabinet's Defence Committee, chaired by Churchill, decided to accede to Catroux's request for authorization to move his military contingent up to the Syrian frontier and across the border at his own discretion.[34] The Chiefs of Staff reported to Wavell:

> Defence Committee considered that opportunity is too good to miss and the advance [into Syria] must be regarded as a political coup, in which time is all important, rather than as a military operation. You should do everything you can to give Catroux not only the lorries and drivers which he requires but also as much military and air support as possible.[35]

In conjunction with this "political coup," the Free French were to issue a declaration of Syrian and Lebanese independence, backed by London, as a means of winning over the support of the native populations.[36]

In Cairo, General Wavell had remained extremely reluctant to give in to the mounting chorus of demands for immediate action.[37] Churchill's willingness to send the Free French into the Levant without any clear notion of how much resistance they would encounter was bound to draw British forces into the fray. To risk such a waste of resources when Britain's position in the region was already so precarious struck Wavell as being extremely foolhardy. He was also personally antagonized by Spears' continuing habit of sending critical telegrams to London over his head. In response to new orders from London, Wavell protested that the Free French could not act alone. He was preparing contingency plans for a combined operation,

> but you must trust my judgement in this matter or relieve me of my Command. I am not willing to accept that Catroux, De Gaulle or Spears should dictate action that is bound seriously to affect military situation in Middle East.[38]

Wishing to avoid the disruption that would be created by Wavell's sudden resignation,[39] Churchill assured him that the decision to undertake a Syrian operation had been made by the War Cabinet and not by Catroux. He reiterated that what was envisaged was not a regular military operation, but an "armed political inroad." If he liked, Wavell could mix some British troops in with the Free French contingent, although not at the cost of a diversion of resources from the Western Desert or Crete. If Wavell remained reluctant to undertake such an operation, then he should indeed submit his resignation.[40]

By the time Wavell had received this reluctantly appeasing telegram, the point of contention had become irrelevant to the situation. On May 21, General Catroux met secretly at the Syrian border with Colonel Collet, who commanded the Circassian cavalry in southern Syria. The purpose of the meeting was to arrange for the forthcoming defection to the Free French of Collet along with his 18,000 men. When asked about the reported evacuation of Syria by Vichy forces, Collet insisted that this was totally incorrect and that, in fact, Dentz was reinforcing the defenses around Damascus.[41] The prospects of success for an "armed political inroad" by Catroux suddenly seemed much dimmer, and he became convinced that a conventional military operation in coordination with the British was the only viable option.[42] Catroux's continuing inclination to conform to British policy infuriated de Gaulle, who flew back from West Africa for another visit to Cairo a few days later. He ordered Catroux not to meet on his own with Wavell, warning him that "if you take orders from the English go to them and get out of F[ree] F[rench] movement."[43] Presented with the hard facts, however, de Gaulle was also forced to agree that Catroux's small contingent could not go forth into Syria on its own.

The renewed delay in military action was acutely frustrating for de Gaulle and Spears because all indications pointed to the current moment as the ideal time for striking. The landing of German planes and the arrogance of German military personnel had created consternation and resentment in the Levant army and it was a pity not to be able to capitalize on this immediately. Spears had warned on May 20 that "in a fortnight . . . divisions will be needed where battalions would suffice within the next few days."[44] The American consul-general in Beirut similarly reported that "best information is to the effect that majority of French and natives would welcome British occupation but with every hour that passes pro-British sentiment is losing ground."[45]

Political Aspects of the Invasion

A military takeover of Syria and Lebanon could not be considered in isolation from its political ramifications. May 1941 was a month of acute crisis for the British position in the Middle East and there was a sense of urgent need for engendering greater political support for Britain in the Arab world. The most crucial step in this direction would be to reestablish an image of strength by crushing Rashid Ali's forces in Iraq. Over and beyond this, it was felt that some indication should be given of Britain's sympathy for Arab nationalist aspirations. This created a dilemma for London's policy in the Levant. The

British felt they would be hurting themselves if they seized control of the Levant from Vichy merely in order to hand over power to the Free French. This would reawaken the bitterness and suspicion that had been stirred up by the disclosure of the Sykes–Picot agreement and the subsequent British abandonment of Syria to the French after the First World War. On the other hand, Churchill had formally declared his intention of restoring the French Empire in all its greatness at the end of the current war and the Free French had been intimately involved in British policy toward the Levant ever since the fall of France. From a strictly military point of view, given the painful shortage of troops available for an operation in the Levant, Gaullist forces could prove useful in the campaign. As had happened before and as it would again, British policymakers were confronted with a painful predicament in the Levant.

Curiously, although Churchill had originally been one of de Gaulle's most committed supporters, he now seemed to be the most inclined to dispense altogether with the recognition of French mandatory rights in Syria and Lebanon.[46] In a note written on May 19, he envisaged the possibility of declaring that the French mandate had lapsed and proclaiming the birth of

> an Independent Sovereign Arab State in Syria in permanent alliance with Turkey on the one side and Great Britain on the other. All this unless French in Syria seize this, their last, chance to rally to Britain.

As for the Free French, "none of our promises to de Gaulle cover mandated territories."[47] Eden suggested to the cabinet that the Free French be given another chance to win over Syria and Lebanon, provided they declared those territories independent. If they refused to do so or their attempt to rally the Levant failed, "we should hold ourselves free to turn from the Free French towards the Syria Arabs." Britain would then move in on its own and become the guarantor of Syrian and Lebanese independence.[48] Contradicting itself once again, the cabinet was also considering coordinating the invasion of Syria with the Turks, who would seize the northern half of the country while Wavell's limited forces occupied the south.[49]

The solution chosen for this dilemma was that of ambiguous rhetoric. In his note of May 19, Churchill had suggested that the declaration of Syrian and Lebanese independence come within the context of a wider scheme of Arab federation and of an agreement with Ibn Saud on the inclusion of an independent Jewish political entity in Palestine as part of such a federation.[50] On May 29, Eden delivered a speech at Mansion House in which he paid lip service to the federation formula. Emphasizing that the military campaign against Rashid Ali would not affect Britain's respect for Iraqi independence, he added:

> Some days ago I said in the House of Commons that His Majesty's Government had great sympathy with Syrian aspirations for independence. I should like to repeat that now. But I would go further. The Arab world has made great strides since the settlement reached at the end of the last War, and many Arab thinkers desire for the Arab peoples a greater degree of unity than they now enjoy. In reaching out towards this unity they hope for our support. No such appeal from our friends should go unanswered. It seems to me both

natural and right that the cultural and economic ties between the Arab countries and the political ties too, should be strengthened. His Majesty's Government for their part will give their full support to any scheme that commands
general approval.[51]

The general lines of this policy were approved by the cabinet four days later.[52]
His Majesty's government thus avoided any definite commitments by expressing its general support for Arab nationalist aspirations without actually specifying what the ramifications of such a policy would be for French or Zionist
interests in the Middle East. Nowhere was it said that Syrian independence
would entail the termination of the French mandate or that the creation of an
Arab federation would preclude the formation of an independent Jewish
state.

De Gaulle himself was not unmindful of the need to gain at least the
acquiescence of the Arab population in a transfer of the territories to Free
French control. He was prepared to issue a declaration of Syrian and Lebanese independence on the eve of the military incursion, as long as this did not
entail the abolition of French mandatory rights. Intent on establishing an
independent power base for Free France in whatever colonies he could seize,
de Gaulle was not willing to contemplate a substantive modification of
France's imperial role, at any rate not until the war was over:

> Our position in Syria will be as follows: We will proclaim independence. But
> we will not declare the mandate purely and simply abolished. . . . We will
> only say that we are coming in order to put an end to the mandatory regime
> and to conclude a treaty guaranteeing independence and sovereignty.[53]

It was not quite so simple, however. Although the British were gratified by
de Gaulle's willingness to proclaim Levantine independence, they insisted
that they must be associated with the declaration in order to lend it credibility
in the eyes of the Arab world. Britain, after all, would be providing the main
military contingent for the campaign. In Cairo, Catroux had already conceded
this point to Ambassador Lampson, agreeing to include a formal British
guarantee in his proclamation. On arriving in Egypt on May 25, de Gaulle
balked at this arrangement, seeing in it an infringement on French sovereignty
and a tacit acceptance of British political responsibility for a territory mandated to France. After nearly two weeks of wrangling, the British suggested
that they could issue a separate statement guaranteeing the independence of
Syria and Lebanon. De Gaulle responded by submitting a letter to Lampson
dissociating the Free French from any such gratuitous endorsement of their
policies. Spears wrote in alarm that this set a disturbing precedent in so far as
the British had to reserve the option of pressuring the Free French over the
independence issue in the event they later tried to disavow their commitment.
Soon afterwards, de Gaulle discussed the matter with Spears and reassured
him by promising to consult with the British during the actual negotiation of
the Levant states' independence.[54] At Spears' suggestion, Churchill sent de
Gaulle a conciliatory telegram assuring him that Britain did not seek to exploit the situation in order to gain territory at French expense and asking that

a British guarantee of Levant independence be accepted in good faith.[55] Spears' role as peacemaker was successful on this occasion, and de Gaulle dropped his objections to a separate British guarantee.[56] He also finally gave in on another issue over which he had been holding out, that of Catroux's title. He had insisted that Catroux be named high commissioner of Syria and Lebanon, whereas the British had demanded that he be named delegate-general instead, as an expression of the change in tone and attitude which the Free French takeover was supposed to introduce.[57] With a mixture of exasperation and relief, Spears remarked in his diary that "it has been a homeric struggle amounting to so little."[58]

The Levant Gears up for Conflict

Despite the initial shock created by the landing of German aircraft at Syrian airfields, Dentz managed to keep a grip on the situation throughout May 1941. The German military staff coordinating the operation was subject to the authority of the Foreign Ministry representative Rudolf Rahn, who was a protégé of Otto Abetz and was much better attuned than the military to the French sense of pride. He did his best to keep the German airmen confined to barracks during their transit through Syria so as to minimize any potential friction with the French.[59] For his part, Dentz did what he could to convince his officers that the transit of German planes in no way infringed on French sovereignty and that the English blockade posed the real menace to French well-being. Above all, loyalty to the Marshal was the key to surviving this period of hardship. The text of one of the circulars distributed at this time concluded with these remarkable lines:

> You have now been briefed and oriented. There are therefore . . . no individual cases of conscience. Your sole duty consists of obeying the orders of the Marshal.[60]

Although many officers may have questioned this line of reasoning, this did not mean they were ready to throw all sense of discipline to the wind and remain passive if the British invaded. This was emphasized to the British by Colonel Collet, who had made good his defection along with only a handful of troops after a premature broadcast by Radio Brazzaville gave the Levant military command advance knowledge of his intentions.[61] He told Spears that the gut instinct of an officer was to open fire on an invading army even if his political sympathies lay with the adversary. Only in the first hours after news of the German landings had first spread would an immediate British or Free French intervention have encountered no resistance, and that moment of opportunity had now passed:

> Colonel Collet himself cannot be taken as typical of the mentality of his late comrades for he has an English wife [she was actually Irish-born] who, although he does not say so, has evidently considerable influence over him. He is genuinely pro-British and really likes the English, which is very rare

amongst Frenchmen. He never has varied in his belief that the future of France depends on a British victory. Nevertheless Collet himself, when put the question by his wife, "Could you possibly fire on British troops advancing across the frontier into Syria?" answered that he would. He told me that he thought in fact he himself would have bolted rather than do so, but that he could not have given the order to his officers not to resist.

> This gives the cue [clue?] to the whole position in Syria. Collet himself the day before he came over would have resisted us. French soldiers entrusted with the defence of a position will defend it, and cannot even, in the excitement of the moment, be relied upon not to fire to kill. In the excitement of action and the fear of being themselves shot, they will defend themselves to the best of their ability.[62]

Although the Beirut administration did not know when or in what form British intervention would come, there was little doubt that action of some sort would take place.[63] As noted earlier, Rahn convinced Dentz to reinforce his Syrian defenses rather than withdraw troops to Lebanon. After Collet's defection, Rahn assumed a direct role in further revising French defensive plans in Syria.[64] Complacency did not reign among those responsible for internal security either. Denunciations of suspected Gaullist conspirators and British spies were rife. Some were signed and seemed to reflect sober observation; others were anonymous and sounded like tales from the *Arabian Nights*.[65] The *Deuxième Bureau* took it all very seriously and became convinced that the possibility existed of a British-engineered putsch taking place at any time. Evidence of pro-Gaullist sentiment among various circles was taken as the sign of an active conspiracy coordinated by the Jews, the Free Masons, and the Protestants (not to mention the Rotary Club!).[66] Surveillance of all potentially suspect persons was ordered and preventive measures were taken at crucial military bases to forestall the growth of dissidence.[67] Colonel Collet informed Spears that Dentz had also broken up large troop concentrations as a means of reinforcing discipline:

> General Dentz's action in dispersing the troops has turned out to be a very cunning move. Officers are not in touch with each other; the one paper from which they glean some information has been suppressed; they do not know what is going on and are unable to consult each other. The result is that the usual lethargy has set in and they have become susceptible once more to Vichy influence and propaganda.[68]

With the final collapse of Rashid Ali's revolt at the end of May, Dentz and Guerard telegraphed to Vichy arguing that the continued presence of German military elements in the Levant constituted a liability for its defense against the British. Darlan sent Benoist-Méchin to Paris to request Abetz for the withdrawal of the German military staff. As Benoist-Méchin argued, "pending the start of massive German–French military collaboration, France must be left in a position to denounce any English attack on Syria as a clear case of aggression against France alone."[69] The Germans, whose attention was now narrowly focused on the imminent launching of Operation "Barbarossa," complied promptly, leaving Rahn behind "as unofficial representative of the German Goverment in Syria."[70] The last-minute attempt to alter the script proved useless, however. The stage was already set for "Exporter"—the Anglo–Free French invasion of Syria and Lebanon.

Operation "Exporter"

The military force assigned to carry out Operation "Exporter" was an ill-assorted group including Australian, Indian army and Free French units, and the Transjordanian Frontier Force, under the overall command of General "Jumbo" Wilson. Having been formed only a few weeks before the launching of the ill-fated Operation "Battleaxe" against Rommel's North African army in mid-June, Wilson's 30,000-man force did not even enjoy numerical parity with Vichy's army of 35,000–40,000 regulars and native troops. In equipment, the British were at a distinct disadvantage. One armored squadron and a handful of Free French tanks faced ninety Vichy tanks and the initial British inferiority in air power was aggravated in the course of the campaign by the arrival of aircraft reinforcements to the Levant from French North Africa. Only in naval gunfire did the British have almost uncontested superiority. London's request that Turkey move into northern Syria was turned down by Ankara, which agreed only to reinforce its garrison along the Syrian frontier. (Turkey was to sign a limited friendship treaty with Germany on June 18).[71]

Despite this adversity of circumstances, it was decided to go ahead with the planned invasion on June 8. In the long run, the British naval blockade would ensure that French resources would be depleted without any hope of replenishment. It was hoped that, realizing this, the Vichy forces would rapidly lay down their arms after offering token resistance for a few days. Simultaneously with the invasion, Catroux's declaration of Syrian and Lebanese independence was read over the radio.

The three-pronged advance into Lebanon and Syria beginning in the early hours of June 8 proved successful initially, due in part to effective topographical reconnaissance that had been carried out by the *Haganah* over the preceding several weeks.[72] Within days, however, the operation encountered major difficulties. Given the lengthy period of tension preceding the invasion, the element of surprise had been totally absent. Indeed, information provided by a mole in close touch with both the British and the Free French general staff had given the Vichy command a rough idea of the British plan of attack.[73] Attempts by the British to induce Vichy troops to lay down their arms proved useless. All along the front, Allied forces began to experience fierce resistance and effective counterattacks. The Free French forces under General Legentilhomme seemed to provoke particularly stubborn opposition tinged with the bitterness of civil war.[74] There were some indications that the Vichy government was itself surprised by the tenacity with which the Levant army was carrying out its official order to resist.[75]

In addition to the unexpectedly fierce defense put up by the Vichy forces, operation "Exporter" was also hampered by poor tactical and strategic planning. The Australian troops were described as courageous in battle but lacking in training and discipline. The progress of British forces was hindered by their overly static approach to warfare; they wasted time and manpower on storming fortified positions rather than passing them up in a rapid advance and leaving them to fall later.[76] Strategically, Wilson's frontal assault has been criticized as an unimaginative attempt by the British to bludgeon their way up the three obvious routes into the Levant without resorting immediately to a flanking movement from Iraq.[77]

In the second week of the operation British forces suffered major setbacks at Merjayoun and Kuneitra, the former of which destroyed any immediate prospect of taking Beirut. By June 21 however, both Sidon and, more significantly, Damascus, had fallen into British hands and an assault had finally been launched against Vichy's eastern flank by Habforce, which crossed over from Iraq and started advancing toward Palmyra in central Syria.[78]

Despite its superiority in equipment, the Levant army under the operational command of General Verdilhac was beginning to suffer from its isolation from outside sources of support. Apart from the airplanes transferred from North Africa, any significant replenishment of manpower, fuel, or equipment would be difficult to achieve, given Britain's naval superiority. For their part, the British were able to augment their forces now that their units in Iraq had been regrouped and an unsuccessful counteroffensive in North Africa called off. In a war of attrition, the ultimate defeat of Dentz's forces was inevitable.

And yet both Dentz and Darlan refused to put an early end to the fighting. In a memorandum written on June 19, Dentz rejected the possibility of ordering a general disengagement and retreat of his forces toward the Turkish frontier, arguing that, under the circumstances, this could easily turn into a general rout:

> The retreat of the army . . . will signify the veritable abandonment of the country by France.
>
> It will result in the unleashing of the appetites of the native population as well as of French civilians eager to pledge their loyalty to "Free France."
>
> In order that the sacrifices already made bear their fruit, it is necessary to hold out for as long as possible—which can only be done by clinging on to terrain and holding on to the largest possible portion of Lebanon and the coast.
>
> We can thus hold out long enough to permit the arrival of reinforcements with which we will win—or if these cannot be sent us—to conduct negotiations with dignity and security, permitting the settlement of numerous questions involving the safeguarding of French interests and the protection of families.[79]

As the military position steadily worsened, a desperate Dentz, urged on by Rahn, asked Vichy to authorize German bombers to reestablish themselves at

Syrian airbases and carry out concerted attacks against the British forces; however, given the Germans' unwillingness to make any political concessions in the talks then under way on the implementation of the Paris Protocols, Vichy was reluctant to take this step toward a Germanization of the Levant battle. For their part, the Germans refused to undertake a major intervention without first securing access to Syrian airfields. A few limited strikes were carried out by the *Luftwaffe* against British naval forces off the coast of Lebanon and against British installations in Haifa, in northern Palestine.[80] Germany's invasion of the Soviet Union on June 22 would probably have made it difficult for Berlin to commit more resources to the Levant in any case.

Vichy's reluctance to introduce German forces directly into the conflict was not a symptom of defeatism on its part. On the contrary, the Pétain government cast about for any possible means of sustaining Dentz's military effort for as long as possible. A troop-carrier attempting to reach the Levant with reinforcements was sunk by the British northwest of Cyprus on July 1.[81] Darlan also contemplated the possibility of using German logistical, intelligence, and military support to break the British blockade. The Germans proved forthcoming, but leakage of information on the operation to the British and increasing doubts within the Vichy government over the political value of a military collaboration that might result in the widening of the conflict with Britain led to the abandonment of the scheme.[82]

The most serious attempt to reinforce the Levant forces was made by the overland route. Troops were sent by train as far as Salonika, Greece, where they awaited Ankara's permission to traverse Turkey on their way to Syria. Jacques Benoist-Méchin was dispatched to Ankara at the end of June to try and persuade the Turks to acquiesce in the passage of French troops, but to no avail. Despite Benoist-Méchin's attempt to convince Ambassador von Papen to use his leverage with the Turkish government to good effect, the Germans proved unwilling to spend much political capital on what they must have realized was a lost cause. The most Turkey would agree to was the transportation of fuel oil over its territory, and even this was effectively limited by various contrived technical delays.[83]

With fuel oil running dangerously low, all hope of external reinforcement fading and the steadily increasing number of British and Free French forces seizing more and more territory, Dentz started actively to seek an honorable armistice. Although diplomatic feelers in this direction had been extended through the medium of Engert, the American consul-general in Beirut, as early as June 18, it was not until the end of the month that Dentz decided to send a mission to Vichy to convince the government of the need to terminate hostilities. At this point, Darlan was still entertaining his pipe dreams of a massive reinforcement of the Levant army and was only willing to consider an armistice that would leave Vichy in control of the positions it still held.[84] Meanwhile in the Levant, Rahn was doing his best to keep the conflict going by organizing Arab irregulars under Fawzi al-Qawuqji to harass the British forces that were assaulting Palmyra; however, al-Qawuqji was wounded before his group was ready to go into action and Palmyra fell on July 3.[85] Another diplomatic feeler had been extended on June 29 by Benoist-Méchin to Knatchbull-Hugessen, the British ambassador in Ankara, but the British preferred to conduct talks through the Engert channel.[86] On the night of July 11/12, a ceasefire finally went into effect as a prelude to the settlement of a conclusive armistice agreement.[87]

This anomalous military conflict between two former allies had lasted a full five weeks and cost the British and Free French forces approximately 4,500, and the Vichy forces 6,000, casualties.[88] The British decision to proceed with the campaign despite the inadequacy of their forces has been criticized as unsound, especially in view of the fact that signals intelligence indicated the Germans had no immediate intention of occupying Syria;[89] and yet, until May 1941, Britain's caution in its Levant policy had been based not just on a sense of its own limited resources, but on the hope, if not assumption, that the Levant would remain neutral territory. The moment German planes began refueling at Syrian airbases, London felt it had little to lose and much to gain by throwing all available resources into the seizure of what had become a potential springboard for German military power. The fact that Germany did not have immediate plans for an occupation of the region was less important. After all, if Hitler were to invade and defeat the Soviet Union and only then turn his attention to the Middle East, a Levant still occupied by a collaborationist Vichy would not pose any less of a threat to Britain's grip on the region. Only with the gift of hindsight can we ascertain that the invasion of Syria and Lebanon was not, in fact, necessary.

The intensity of the military resistance put up by the Levant forces surprised nearly everyone. Although Darlan clearly pressed Dentz to commit all of his resources to the fight, it is by no means certain that all of the members of Pétain's government were equally enthusiastic about the enterprise. Benoist-Méchin was to complain bitterly that during his late June visit to the Levant to evaluate the desirability of introducing the *Luftwaffe* directly into the fighting, the Vichy air minister, General Bergeret, sowed doubt in the minds of air force officers about the value of continued resistance. He reportedly informed them that the talks with the Germans over the Paris Protocols were not proceeding smoothly and that Pétain had had his hands tied when he issued the order for fierce resistance.[90] However that may be, not only Dentz, but the great majority of the rank-and-file seem to have taken the order most seriously.[91]

Doubtless, an important factor in the Levant army's will to resist was a simple sense of discipline as well as the conviction that the Germans would crack down on the remaining liberties of unoccupied France unless a good fight was put up against the British in Syria and Lebanon. There seems to have been more to it than this, however. The Levant troops did not just fight well, they fought zealously. Throughout the pronouncements by Dentz and the statements in the press during the period of the conflict, heavy emphasis was laid on the theme of French honor being redeemed on the battlefields of the Levant. There seems to have been a sense that the humiliation of France at the hands of Germany could somehow be compensated for by a heroic battle against the British, who had for years been France's colonial rival in the Middle East and who had, as it was perceived, "stabbed France in the back" at Mers el-Kebir just after the degrading armistice with Germany. (More than a decade after the end of the war, a French history of this period accused Britain of having invaded the Levant out of greed for more colonies rather than any legitimate strategic concerns.[92]) Even before the launching of Operation "Exporter," it was reported that "every French officer [in the Levant] has an underlying desire to vindicate his military qualities to wipe out the stain of past defeats."[93] It seems that the weakness of the British military force also contributed to the tenacity of Verdilhac's army, which would have felt it particularly humiliating to submit meekly to so puny an antagonist. General Wavell, reporting to the War Office shortly before his transfer to the Indian army command, pointed out:

> Vichy French expected to be attacked in overwhelming force both on ground and in air and were probably prepared to capitulate after token resistance. On discovering our weakness and that we had no tanks they put up very stout and skillful resistance.[94]

Despite the apparent futility of fighting the British over the Levant while metropolitan France squirmed under the German jackboot, this battle for a piece of their empire was full of historical and psychological significance for the French. As C. M. Andrew and A. S. Kanya-Forstner have noted, France had long seen its empire as a great reservoir of strength that helped make up for French weakness on the European continent. The empire thus held a special significance for Vichy, as well as for de Gaulle, in the wake of the defeat of France in Europe.[95] In the words of one French newspaper in the Levant:

> That which is being contested between Merjayoun and Kuneitra is not a ridiculous territorial stake, it is not the possession of and sovereignty over a few provinces: it is the safeguarding or crumbling of French unity and continuity, the maintenance or collapse of Continental and Imperial France.[96]

As mentioned earlier, the participation of Free French forces in the fighting lent it a bitter edge and a quality of *acharnement* that had not been anticipated even in the most pessimistic prognostications. The resentment of the British troops at the pointless stubbornness of Vichy resistance added to the ferocity of the battle, and tales abound of bestial conduct on either side in the course of the campaign.[97]

Thus, in the heat of battle, the tunnel vision that afflicted Vichy was extended with a vengeance to its colonial outpost in the Middle East. The larger issues of the war were forgotten as Frenchmen sought to redeem their honor by firing on the very armies that were battling elsewhere against France's real foe. The mentality of the Levant army can best be described in the words Spears used in his indictment of the defenders of Vichy-held Djibouti: "That strange class of Frenchmen who had developed a vigour in defeat which had not been apparent when they were defending their country, and [who] . . . embrace their downfall as if it was a new religion of which Pétain was the Prophet and Laval the High Priest."[98]

The Negotiation of the Armistice

From the very moment when the British had begun to consider what sort of terms they would set for an armistice in the Levant, the Free French factor had complicated the issue. In the initial discussion of the question in Cairo during mid-June, Spears argued vehemently on behalf of the Free French that no provision should be made for the repatriation of Vichy personnel, since they could simply be transferred to North Africa where they might later be used to fight against the Allies once again. The Middle East service chiefs took a dim view of Spears' objections, insisting that the prime concern was to put a speedy end to the conflict by offering Dentz an honorable solution.[99]

After Dentz's initial armistice feeler on June 18, however, de Gaulle managed to work out a compromise on the Allied terms with the commanders-in-chief in Cairo according to which the repatriation clause was retained, but provision was also made for the full participation of a Free French representative in the talks; it was also agreed that Vichy troops would be given a full opportunity to rally to the Free French cause if they so desired. In London, the Chiefs of Staff found the Cairo terms generally agreeable, while expressing their reservations regarding the "undue prominence . . . given to the part that the Free French were to play in negotiations."[100] His Majesty's government decided to transmit its own draft to Dentz via Washington and Engert. In this version the role of the Free French in negotiations and in recruiting Vichy troops was played down considerably. When de Gaulle heard of this he exploded, leaving even Spears stunned by his vehemence:

> "I don't think I shall ever get on with Les Anglais" he said.—"You are all the same, exclusively centred upon your own interests and business, quite insensitive to the requirements of others. Do you think I am interested in England's winning the war, I am not—I am interested only in France's victory." "They are the same," I said "Not at all. . . ."
>
> He was entitled to be annoyed and discouraged, but even I, who know his mind and am not taken in by his occasional niceness about us, was taken aback.[101]

Of course, the real bone of contention here was not the technical issue of which terms would best serve the Allied war effort. At the heart of the dispute lay the question of who was to gain primacy in the Levant once the armistice had been concluded. This problem came out into the open at the beginning of July with the publication of a letter de Gaulle had sent Catroux on June 24. In it, de Gaulle invested him with all the powers that had previously been held by the high commissioners, pending the negotiation of treaties with Syria and Lebanon. Reference was also made to Catroux's role as military commander-in-chief without the slightest mention of General Wilson or the British army.[102] The implications of this letter were completely unacceptable to the British, as Churchill made clear:

> It was never our intention that the de Gaullists should virtually step into the places of the Dentz administration, or that they should govern Syria in the name of France. Their losses and contribution have been only a small fraction of ours. They should be given a certain prominence in order to show that French interests in Syria are safeguarded against any other European power, and that we have no desire to supplant France in her privileged and favoured position in Syria. However, all this is but about one to four or five in our Syrian policy, which remains the independence of Syria and all its peoples. No French policy which conflicts with this major decision can be accepted. It is therefore for de Gaulle or Catroux to make the same kind of arrangements with Syria as we made in the case of Iraq [which had been granted independence by Britain in 1932], with the important difference that in the ultimate issue we have military force behind us, and he has not, to any extent.[103]

In London, the Free French Committee was able to work out an abstruse, legalistic understanding with the Foreign Office by the terms of which supreme military and civil authority would be exercised by the British general officer commanding (G.O.C.), but the French administrative personnel would derive its authority solely from Catroux's position as delegate-general.[104] This was not acceptable to de Gaulle, who insisted:

> The supreme authority in Syria belongs to France, and not in the slightest degree to a foreign commander-in-chief. The British troops in Syria are not occupying a conquered land; they are collaborating in battle on allied territory. When Marshal Haig fought in France, the authority in the departments where his troops were found continued to belong entirely to the Government of the Republic.

De Gaulle concluded by announcing that he was returning to the Middle East from Brazzaville in order to clarify the issue once and for all with Oliver Lyttelton, who had just been appointed to the newly created post of minister of state in the Middle East.[105]

What might have been a sober discussion of the structure of authority in the Levant turned into a fiery confrontation due to the terms of the armistice convention signed at Acre on July 14. When Dentz had made his serious overture for an armistice on July 9, Whitehall's initial intention had been to offer the London terms drafted two weeks earlier as the basis for a ceasefire. Predictably, de Gaulle insisted on an amendment to those terms that "would guarantee that the rights and interests of the French in the Levant would be maintained." Balking at this, the British government preferred to revert to the original Cairo terms that de Gaulle and the Middle East commanders-in-chief had already agreed on.[106] De Gaulle was thus reassured and the stage seemed set for the negotiation or a satisfactory armistice.

Unfortunately, Dentz was not a party to the agreement and neither General Wilson nor Winston Churchill seemed to take it too seriously. The Vichy authorities appeared adamantly opposed to any contact with the Free French, insisting that the negotiations be conducted with the British alone.[107] Lyttelton, who was formally in charge of coordinating all major political and military decisions in the region, ordered Wilson to stick to the letter of the Cairo terms. Concurrently, Churchill telegraphed instructions in just the opposite sense to Lyttelton:

> Negotiations should not be allowed to break down merely on the point of form as to who Dentz will surrender to. We have adopted terms agreeable to the Free French, but their presence should not constitute a fatal obstacle to our getting them. Of course if you can get them in all the better.[108]

As it turned out, Lyttelton chose to disregard this cable, leaving Wilson with instructions to resume hostilities unless Dentz accepted participation by Catroux in the talks.[109] Wilson decided to sidestep the whole issue by letting Catroux attend the talks without actually participating in them. According to the final terms, Verdilhac agreed to hand over all war materiel to the British, Vichy forces were to be granted full honors of war, and the matter of repatriation was to be left to the free choice of the troops. At no point was any mention made of the Free French and General Catroux was only allowed to sign a separate document informing the British command of his acceptance of the terms.[110] Most serious of all was a secret protocol annexed to the agreement that effectively negated the spirit of the repatriation clause by prohibiting any direct contact between Gaullist and Vichy personnel. Since the Vichy troops were all to be kept under the watchful eyes of their commanding officers, the protocol ensured that virtually none of them would be given the opportunity of choosing freely between Pétain and de Gaulle. Loudspeakers and pamphlets would be the only means of access available to the Free French.[111] Moreover, Catroux had actually given Wilson his verbal agreement to the substance of the protocol.[112]

It was not only de Gaulle who was taken aback by the secret protocol. The Foreign Office cabled Lyttelton that "we ourselves find that Protocol hard to understand, since although the first objective of the policy of His Majesty's Government is military security and the second the fulfillment of undertakings to Syria and the Lebanon, the third undoubtedly remains the enhancement of the Free French movement."[113] Churchill seemed rather less sympathetic, bluntly pointing out to de Gaulle that Free French participation in the military campaign, for all its gallantry, had helped stiffen Vichy resistance "and that the antipathy of the Syrian people to the French, whether Vichy or Free, is strongly marked."[114] The Free French delegation in London, afraid of the consequences of de Gaulle's wrath, sent him soothing telegrams assuring him that the Foreign Office sympathized with their objections to the armistice and asking him not to overreact or publicize the dispute, since

> for us to break ranks with Great Britain would be playing Vichy's and Germany's game. In view of this, we insist once again that nothing of our present difficulties pass into the public domain.[115]

De Gaulle did not take heed of this advice. On arrival in Cairo on July 20, he confided to Spears that he intended to withdraw his troops from British command in Syria. Spears tried to mollify him by expressing sympathy with his outrage and noted in his diary that "it may be that I have taken the edge off his despite."[116] At his formal meeting with Lyttelton the following morning, however, Spears recorded:

> de Gaulle was in the worst mood I have ever known him in, he looked frightful and as if he had not slept for a week. He was completely intransigent and often extremely rude. He handed to Lyttelton an ultimatum which declared that at 12 noon on the 24th the Free French troops in Syria would no longer consider themselves as being under British command.[117]

Trying to remain calm, Lyttelton simply tore up the document, saying that he could not accept it. After a furious tirade by de Gaulle, the meeting was adjourned until 6 P.M. During the interlude, Michael Wright of the British embassy and de Larminat sought to calm de Gaulle, while Spears, Lyttelton, and his assistant Henry Hopkinson consulted with Ambassador Lampson.[118] Lampson noted that "they were all out for de Gaulle's blood." He tried to place the issue into the broader context of Anglo-Free French relations and "after O.L. and Henry Hopkinson had left I had some talk with Louis Spears on the above lines but I found that he was even more violently disposed than the others."[119] Spears argued that, sooner than allow de Gaulle to create chaos in the Levant, it would be necessary to deny him access to any telegraph or radio communications that he could use to

> turn the whole Free French movement against us. . . .

> If it comes to a pinch we could depose him and nominate Catroux, notifying all in the Free French movement that all pay and emoluments will be made through Catroux. If we are reduced to this, it may be necessary to shut up de Gaulle for a time.[120]

With the coolness of the evening came a certain easing of tension and de Gaulle proved much less abrasive at the resumption of discussions. The outline of what was to become the juridical basis of Anglo-Free French relations in the Levant now began to take form. Lyttelton emphasized that the secret protocol would be effectively nullified as soon as Dentz had provided an excuse through some violation of the armistice terms. For his part, de Gaulle conceded that the Levant had to be viewed as part of the Middle Eastern theater of war, within which the British exercised the supreme operational command; however, in the event a particular military plan or operation involved a greater number of French than British troops, the command should be exercised by a French officer. As for the civil administration, it was agreed that British military security considerations would always take precedence over the prerogatives of the delegate-general, but that otherwise Catroux would be formally in charge of decision making.

After all the details had been worked out, an exchange of letters between

Lyttelton and de Gaulle took place on July 24 and 25 that defined the precise terms of their agreement. The Free French were in effect made retroactive parties to the armistice convention, with the British handing over to them part of the Vichy war materiel as well as recognizing their right to assume command over the native levies (*troupes spéciales*). The Free French were promised the opportunity of rallying as many Vichy troops as possible to their cause. In addition, operational command was recognized as belonging to the British while the Free French exercised territorial command ("direction or military control of public services, general security, gendarmerie, police, exploitation of local resources, etc.") over Syria and Lebanon. An ambiguously worded clause also linked local military command to the relative proportions of French and British troop strengths.[121] With the framework of political and military authority finally fixed, de Gaulle proceeded to the Levant on a tour of inspection. It seemed for the moment as though the crisis had been an aberration produced by the irresponsibility of General Wilson and the poor state of communications between Acre and Cairo. Unfortunately, events were soon to establish this sort of incident as the norm rather than the exception.

Before July 1941, the Free French and British had shared a common goal in the Levant—the ouster of Vichy. With the termination of hostilities, the future status of Syria and Lebanon immediately became the source of intense disagreement between the two allies. For de Gaulle, control of the territories was crucial if his movement was to gain stature as the wartime embodiment of France's national identity and the guardian of French interests. In British eyes, the Levant formed part of a larger, Middle Eastern theater of operations under British command, and what transpired there had immediate repercussions in the parts of the Arab world under London's control or influence. At the personal level, de Gaulle's unbridled outbursts over the terms of the armistice appear to have cost him the backing of his would-be mentor and most ardent supporter among the British, Louis Spears. If the conflict between Vichy and Britain over the Levant had had about it a certain anachronistic air of chivalry between enemies, the falling out between British and Free French was to be characterized by all the bitterness of friendship betrayed.

5

The Widening Rift

Initial Clashes

Within days of the conclusion of the de Gaulle–Lyttelton agreements, a gap began to emerge between the theory and practice of Anglo–Free French relations in the Levant. Catroux's effort to rally Vichy troops to the Cross of Lorraine was frustrated by their confinement to military camps to which the Gaullists had no access. The situation was slightly improved when it became known that Dentz had flown a number of captured British officers out of the Levant before the armistice. The British were incensed, placing Dentz and some of his leading aides under arrest until the British prisoners of war returned.[1] They also became much more amenable to Catroux's demands and saw to it that Vichy officers allowed their men freedom to move outside their camps, facilitating personal contact with Free French recruiters. Clearly, though, haphazard encounters at bistros were unlikely to produce very favorable results, and only a few thousand troops agreed to join the Free French cause.[2] This fell far short of the major accretion to his forces de Gaulle had hoped for, which would have both strengthened his grip on the Levant and rendered the Free French a more credible, independent factor in the war. In de Gaulle's eyes, "the commitments which the British Government had made to us regarding the interpretation of the St. Jean d'Acre armistice thus remained a dead letter."[3]

Unfortunately, the perceived failure of the British to cooperate wholeheartedly in the effort to win over Vichy troops seemed to form part of a wider pattern of disregard by the British military for the de Gaulle–Lyttelton agreements. In fact, General Wilson and his staff went out of their way to display deference and respect for the defeated Vichy forces well beyond the formal honors of war promised them in the armistice convention, while the Free French were treated as though they did not exist. Lyttelton himself had the impression that

> the British seemed at the time to be more in sympathy with the regular Vichy officers, who had respected their oath at the expense of their country, than with the Free French, who had, with deep heart-searchings, set it aside for the greater good and glory of France.[4]

On July 27, Collet issued a report in which he charged that the British were playing into the hands of Vichy and Axis propaganda by usurping Free French power in all the outlying regions of Syria. Indeed, a Vichy political officer who had rallied to the Gaullists reported that those members of the *Services Spéciaux* remaining at their posts had been instructed by Vichy to spread disorder among the populace and to accept orders only from British officers. (Arms had been widely distributed to Bedouin and villagers in eastern Syria by Vichy forces just before the armistice.) The Emir Abdullah of Transjordan was spreading propaganda calling for his ascent to the Syrian throne; Glubb Pasha—the British commander of Transjordan's Arab Legion—was cultivating support among the Bedouin in the Syrian desert; and in Jezireh, Colonel Slim of the Tenth Indian Division was issuing direct orders to the Free French delegate. Everywhere, British officers were behaving as though they were the sole masters of the land.[5]

Most serious of all was the confrontation that arose in the sensitive Jebel Druze region. A warlike, semifeudal area, the Jebel was dominated by the Atrash clan, which had long maintained ties with the British across the border in Transjordan and had entertained hopes of throwing off the French yoke either through the independence of Jebel Druze or its annexation to Transjordan by the Emir Abdullah. (It was in Jebel Druze that the bitter Syrian revolt of 1925 had been centered.) Due to the region's volatility, a special clause in the armistice convention had provided for the continued stationing of Vichy troops there until the British were ready to replace them, so as to ensure a smooth transition. In the de Gaulle–Lyttelton agreements, Article 8 provided for prior consultations betwen Catroux and Wilson on all matters affecting the maintenance of order in the Jebel. Disregarding this agreement, Brigadier Dunn of the British Fifth Cavalry Brigade unilaterally disarmed the Vichy troops under Colonel Bouvier and occupied the Residence at Soueida on July 24. When Catroux learned of this, he ordered General Monclar of the foreign legion to march to Soueida with a Senegalese battalion and assume formal control of the region. On July 30, Monclar's forces camped outside the town and demanded that Dunn lower the Union Jack and allow the French to occupy the Residence. Dunn refused, warning that he would open fire if Monclar advanced any further. The scene was set for a showdown that evening, when Wilson's headquarters finally ordered the brigadier to let the French have their way. The situation remained extremely tense, however, as both Free French and British troops remained in occupation of the town without any clear understanding over whose authority was supreme.[6]

Not surprisingly, de Gaulle saw in these incidents clear evidence that the British intended to usurp Free French authority in the Levant and integrate the region into their imperial sphere. The British, in turn, were alarmed and antagonized by Catroux's decision to send Monclar to Jebel Druze without prior consultation and his renewed assertions that the British military command had no special rights in the Levant. Spears thought:

> Catroux is so frightened of General de Gaulle that he is standing up to us in a way he has never done before and against his own better judgment. He even

put forward the claim that barracks in Syria, being French property, should be allocated to us by the French. This made me really angry. The thought of Senegalese installed in comfort while our white troops are under canvas is not only ridiculous but would create very bad blood between the officers.[7]

With Generals Wilson and Catroux incapable of resolving their differences and Spears reporting that the Free French were getting completely out of hand, Oliver Lyttelton decided to try and regain control over the situation. In a telegram sent to Churchill just before his departure from Cairo, Lyttelton expressed his concern over reports that de Gaulle's efforts at recruiting Vichy troops and officials in Syria "was dictated . . . by the desire to swell the ranks of the Free French at all costs, whether new adherents are anti-British or not." In view of the danger of native revolts being set off by the retention of the "old corrupt administration," it might prove advisable to apply direct British military administration to certain outlying regions of the country.[8]

On his arrival in Beirut, Lyttelton appeared to have revised his views in favor of the Free French. Outraged by the flagrant favoritism displayed by the British army toward the defeated Vichy forces, Lyttelton held a series of meetings with de Gaulle and Catroux at which he readily conceded that the Cairo agreements had not so far been carried out "either as regards opportunities for presenting to the Vichy troops the Free French point of view, the recognition that civil authority in Syria and Lebanon is Free French, or other matters." Lyttelton lamely explained that this was largely due to the time lag created by the slow percolation of new guidelines down to the level of the officers and officials in charge of the day-to-day running of affairs. That situation, said Lyttelton, had now been corrected by his personal visit. Most importantly, the problem of the Jebel was resolved by an agreement on joint evacuation of the region, leaving it in the hands of the French-commanded Druze squadron. A similar squadron that had been raised by the British was to be disbanded. For their part, the Free French promised to be more careful in their selection of former employees of the Vichy administration for the new General Delegation; those against whom charges of disloyalty could be proved would be dismissed.[9] An exchange of letters between Lyttelton and de Gaulle formalizing the settlement of outstanding differences and announcing the transfer of a number of administrative services to the Free French was published in the local newspapers after the conclusion of the meetings in the second week of August.[10] With the sense of Anglo–French tension largely alleviated, de Gaulle prepared to return to London while Lyttelton proceeded to Transjordan, where he asked Glubb Pasha to refrain for paying any more visits to Syria and diplomatically informed the Emir Abdullah that Britain could not currently support his claim to the Syrian throne.[11]

The Formation of the Spears Mission

After the departure of de Gaulle and Lyttelton, Catroux and Wilson were left behind to manage affairs in the Levant, with Spears heading a liaison mission between them. On the face of it a simple and straightforward arrangement, the structure of the Spears Mission actually fostered the development of an ill-defined and dangerous duality of authority in Syria and Lebanon. Over the years that followed, the mission was to become the bane of the Free French in the region, although it was in fact de Gaulle who had originally favored its creation. To gain a proper understanding of this curious political evolution, it is necessary to take a look at the personality of the man in charge of the mission.

Major-General (Sir) E. L. Spears[12] was a close, personal friend of Winston Churchill whose reputation as fervent Francophile and fluent Francophone had repeatedly resulted in appointments to military and political liaison functions over the years. Spears' mercilessly pungent wit combined with his bilingual ability and what others took to be his affectation of Continental manners, made him something of a social outcast in the British political and diplomatic establishments, as well as in military circles. Consequently, his chances of professional success as well as his personal sense of worth became increasingly dependent on his friendship with Churchill, which was cemented in 1922, when he offered to step down from his newly won parliamentary seat so as to give Churchill a chance to win an easy byelection. (The offer was turned down.)[13]

During World War I, Spears had served as liaison officer between British and French military intelligence and later between the two military commands. This experience made him Churchill's natural choice for the role of personal liaison with French Prime Minister Reynaud during the Battle of France in May–June 1940. (Spears also continued to hold the position of member of Parliament for Carlisle throughout the war years.) It was Spears who first cultivated contact with de Gaulle and who actually whisked him away from Bordeaux to England in his airplane at the time of the fall of France.[14] The Spears Mission was then established to maintain contact between Whitehall and the Free French.

Spears' longstanding affection for things French had undergone a severe trial in June 1940. His disappointment over the military and moral collapse of France was as bitter as his original faith in the strength and glory of French arms, and the tenacity and courage of Pétain in particular, had been great. Describing the retreat of French air force convoys along the road from Tours to Bordeaux in June 1940, Spears wrote:

> During this horrible, depressing journey, I endured a kind of sorrow that withers faith. All that I had believed in, worked and hoped for during so many years, could not now be recalled without pain. The finger of memory touching the past hurt as if probing a wound. What would all the brave airmen I had known in the first war . . . think of these fat convoys and their sleek personnel ambulating like a herd of cows towards Bordeaux?[15]

Spears did see in de Gaulle "all that was now left of the spirit of France,"[16] and de Gaulle seems to have reciprocated Spears' confidence and trust to a large extent. As we have seen earlier, throughout the first year after the fall of

France, Spears was an ardent champion of Free French interests in the face of the occasional indifference of the British government. Writing in 1941, Colonel Collet's wife was still able to characterize Spears "as the apostle of Anglo–French union."[17] Ever since he had flown de Gaulle out of Bordeaux, Spears had behaved more like the patron saint of the Free French than the officer in charge of liaison with them. It was the ideal role to play for a man who had always felt excluded from the mainstream of the British establishment, and who was able to use this peculiar niche as a position from which to criticize the policies pursued by Whitehall, while building himself up as an independent actor on the political stage.

But the price Spears expected in return for his jealous guardianship of Free French interests was complete personal loyalty. The moment de Gaulle made a move that suggested self-assertion, Spears would threaten to cut off all ties with the Free French. Thus, during a tour in autumn 1940 of French West African colonies that had rallied to de Gaulle's movement, General de Larminat conveyed a suggestion to Spears that the number of liaison-staff members accompanying de Gaulle in public should be kept to a minimum, so that the general should not be made to look like a British stooge. Spears' acid response was paraphrased as follows:

> The French must really have the courage to stand by and defend the position which every thinking man knows to be inevitable, namely that the F[ree] F[rench] movement, although completely free and independent, is but a very junior partner of the British Empire and everybody knows it, and that if we are to help them we must do it in our own way. General Spears conveyed to General de Larminat the difficulties the French would find themselves in if they attempted to deal with all their needs themselves, the hint being of course that if difficulties were raised this Mission would simply be closed.[18]

Thus, despite the common front presented toward the British military and diplomatic establishments, insidious tensions had begun to mark Spears' relationship with de Gaulle well before Operation "Exporter."

During the military campaign in the Levant, the Spears Mission was assigned to act as liaison between Catroux and the British command until the completion of operations.[19] This merely begged the question of how liaison was to be organized after the occupation of the Levant. Predictably, Spears advocated keeping his mission in charge:

> In my view it is absolutely essential if serious difficulties are to be avoided in the future that there should be no British organisations in Syria which will not be part of or be affiliated to Mission. . . .
>
> Many French and British officials will have to deal with extremely difficult question[s] most of which if not carefully handled are certain to cause trouble. For this reason it is essential in my view that there should be no British delegation other than the Mission in Syria and that any individual that it is found necessary to send there should be attached to it.[20]

In response to Wavell's endorsement of this suggestion, Whitehall came down strongly against the idea. In its view, the mission ought to remain a strictly civilian affair and one limited to liaison functions, with no executive powers whatsoever. All technical experts were to be attached to the G.O.C.'s staff.[21] One War Office official wrote that

> it is . . . worth bearing in mind that the Spears Mission, as an organisation accredited to the Free French alone, seems an unsuitable body to have charge of British responsibilities on the political side in Syria. It seems not unlikely that the Free French may need some pressure to keep them up to the mark in fulfilling their promise of independence to Syria and the Lebanon, and for this purpose it appears to be important that our political officers in Syria should be independent of the Free French.[22]

In the meantime, uncertainty continued to prevail over who would actually head the Levant branch of the Spears Mission. Spears volunteered for the job himself, but immediately encountered resistance:

> It is evident Wavell does not want *me*, and my disinterested offer to start the thing they want—It is heartbreaking -

> Here are these people who are not even aware of what they are up against, sailing on, persuaded they know all the answers, and I who c[oul]d arrange it all, prevented from doing so.[23]

When Godfrey Havard was proposed for the post, however, the Free French rejected him, largely because of the stand he had adopted over the *Providence* affair.[24] John Hamilton of the British embassy in Cairo was put forward as an alternative, but he himself felt unqalified because of his inexperience in dealing with the French.[25] At least one other name was suggested for the post, but Spears was gradually winning Lampson and Lyttelton over to the idea of letting him take charge after all. He was the only man who met the pertinent criteria of being "closely associated with Free French and . . . capable of getting his views accepted by them." Once the Franco–Levantine treaty negotiations had been satisfactorily concluded, someone else could take over Spears' duties.[26] More significantly, Lyttelton and the Middle East Command continued to press for the attachment of political advisors directly to Spears' liaison mission. Despite the considerable misgivings of both the War Office and the Foreign Office, the combined weight of Cairo's demands and the prime minister's personal intervention had their effect and Lyttelton was authorized to proceed as he proposed. A charter was issued formally entrusting the Spears Mission with responsibility for all Anglo–French liaison functions in the Levant. Lyttelton was warned, however, to beware of the potential conflict of duty between Spears' effective role as Catroux's advisor and his new administrative responsibilities in the Levant.[27]

General de Gaulle could not have been happier with this arrangement, which he doubtless thought would restrict the political initiative of the British military to a minimum, leaving the sympathetic Spears in charge of British decision making. De Gaulle sent Lyttelton a message expressing satisfaction with Spears' appointment, writing that "Major General Spears has often proved to me his comprehension and ability."[28] During the first weeks after the occupation of the Levant, Spears did, for the most part, live up to his reputation as a vigorous defender of Gaullist interests. On July 8, for instance, he sent a telegram to London warning that the Syrians could be induced to sign a treaty guaranteeing French privileges in the country only if the British made it clear they stood fully behind the Free French. The Syrians must not be allowed to "form the opinion Catroux and the Free French are but puppets in our hands and that it is we who are really controlling the country." In words which, in retrospect, ring with irony, Spears added, "I much regret the interventions of individuals like De Gaury [a British officer] in the Jebel Druze. Whether they like it or not their action serves to incite the natives to play Britain against Free France. There are too many would-be Lawrences in these parts."[29]

The decisive turning point in Spears' attitude toward de Gaulle seems to have been the crisis over the armistice near the end of July 1941. As we have seen, Spears was so shocked by de Gaulle's hostile stance on this issue that he envisaged the possibility of arresting him and placing Catroux at the head of the Free French. Although relations were temporarily restored after the resolution of the crisis, a gulf of mutual suspicion and resentment continued to separate Spears from de Gaulle. The very closeness of their earlier association seemed to add to the bitterness of their estrangement. Spears doubtless felt that de Gaulle was biting the hand that had fed him;[30] de Gaulle suspected Spears of having deliberately misled him over the nature of the original armistice terms.[31]

By the time of de Gaulle's departure from the Levant in mid-August, the Free French leader clearly regretted his earlier support for Spears' appointment to the British mission in Beirut. Trying to undo the damage, he urged Spears to return to London with him, but Spears resisted adamantly:

> A signal came on the 18th August ordering me to go to London with de Gaulle but when Churchill returned to London after his visit to Roosevelt he cancelled this. Important though it would have been for me to be in London when de Gaulle arrived I think it would have been absolutely disastrous for me to leave this Mission at this stage; Hamilton [who had been appointed as Spears' deputy in Beirut], though excellent in native affairs, has not the gun to get hold of the French side of the business and if I had come back in a month's time many things would have assumed the wrong shape, habits would have been formed which it would have taken infinite trouble to break. I was, however, told to go to Cairo with de Gaulle.[32]

Frustrated in his attempt to get Spears out of the Levant, de Gaulle sought to minimize his power by ordering Catroux not to have any direct dealings with Lyttelton (to whom Spears reported). Instead, any substantive discussion of Levantine affairs would have to be carried on with de Gaulle himself in London. Spears advised Lyttelton not to make an issue out of this in Cairo, but to let it be dealt with by Whitehall on de Gaulle's arrival in England. Henry Hopkinson was being dispatched there to see to it that His Majesty's government realized the importance of leaving the initiative in Levantine affairs with Lyttelton (who, in turn, was inclined to follow Spears' advice).[33] Left alone in Beirut with the pliable Catroux, Spears doubtless felt he would be able to manage affairs to his satisfaction.

While Spears returned to consolidate his mission in the Levant, de Gaulle proceeded to London by way of Brazzaville, where he stirred up trouble by granting a newspaper interview in which he angrily assailed Britain's Levant policy. Naturally, this only served to undermine his cause, for Churchill was infuriated by the publication of de Gaulle's words and actually considered replacing him as head of the Free French movement, until his advisors persuaded him this would be an overreaction.[34] In a parliamentary address on September 9, 1941, the prime minister made it clear that his government meant business in Syria:

> We have no ambitions in Syria. We do not seek to replace or supplant France, or substitute British for French interests in any part of Syria. . . . However, I must make it quite clear that our policy, to which our Free French Allies have subscribed, is that Syria shall be handed back to the Syrians, who will assume at the earliest possible moment their independent sovereign rights. We do not propose that this process of creating an independent Syrian Government . . . shall wait until the end of the war. We contemplate constantly increasing the Syrian share in the administration. There is no question of France maintaining the same position which she exercised in Syria before the war. . . . There must be no question, even in war-time, of a mere substitution of Free French interests for Vichy French interests. . . .
>
> I was asked a question about our relations with Iraq. They are special; our relations with Egypt are special, and, in the same way, I conceive that France will have special arrangements with Syria. The independence of Syria is a prime feature in our policy.[35]

De Gaulle met with Churchill in London in an attempt to repair relations. He expressed regret for some of his more extreme recent utterances. He "begged the Prime Minister to understand that the leaders and members of the Free French Movement were necessarily somewhat difficult people; else they would not be where they were." Their basic loyalty to the alliance was not to be questioned. The prime minister seemed assuaged, and the two leaders agreed on the need to fulfill the promise of independence to Syria and Lebanon and the desirability of broadening the political base of the Free French movement in the near future.[36]

De Gaulle had not given up on his efforts to curtail the powers of the Spears Mission in the Levant, however. During September 1941, he sought to induce the British government to appoint Spears ambassador to Syria and Lebanon *instead of* retaining him as chief of the British mission to the Free French there. Spears immediately interpreted this as an attempt to have him kicked upstairs. As he had noted in mid-August:

> He [de Gaulle] looks askance at this mission as he does on all British organisations that deal with his subordinates. He would like to be the sole authority

through whom we deal with in Syria and to be the only source of information concerning this country.[37]

Within the Levant itself, Catroux was trying to ensure the autonomy of his administration by continuing the policy of retaining as many former Vichyites as possible in the General Delegation. In this respect, Free French and Vichy interests actually overlapped. Pétain's government was interested in retaining as large a body of functionaries as possible in the Levant as a potential means of reasserting its control in the region in the event of a German conquest of the Middle East. (It is, of course, difficult to envisage such a naïve image of German generosity actually being fulfilled, but the illusion seems to have been quite prevalent in Vichy.) For their part, the Free French were far from discriminating about the personnel they employed, as long as they were not British. They therefore made a point of announcing that no oath of loyalty would be required of French officials who chose to remain at their posts. They were also guaranteed exemption from military mobilization in the event of a direct Axis invasion of the region. The fulfillment of their professional duties and the avoidance of any collusion with or support for the Axis powers were all that was expected of them. Technically in accord with the clause in the armistice convention providing for administrative continuity in the Levant, these lenient guidelines were also perfectly compatible with Vichy's requirement that all personnel choosing to remain in the Levant sign a declaration recognizing the Pétain regime as the only legal government of France.[38] (In the end, about 48 percent of Vichy officials in the Levant chose to remain at their posts without rallying to the Free French, 30 percent pledged their allegiance to de Gaulle's movement, and 22 percent returned to France.[39])

Spears was quick to draw London's attention to this situation, using it as a means of undermining de Gaulle's effort to limit the powers of his mission. In fact, he turned the tables on de Gaulle by calling into question the wisdom of allowing the Free French to remain in charge in the Levant:

> Personal jealousies, corruption, the most astonishing cases of feminine influence are rife. In fact there are present here all the most distressing characteristics of the "Republique Des Camarades."
>
> . . . [British] influence is fought at every step with greater venom, one cannot help feeling, than either Vichy or the Germans would arouse.

Spears insisted that unless the British assumed direct control of Syria and Lebanon, the situation would become chaotic.[40]

Churchill was deeply disturbed by Spears' reports and appears to have taken his proposal for a British takeover quite seriously. Fortunately for de Gaulle, Oliver Lyttelton was in London for consultations at this time and at a ministerial meeting that took place on September 26 to discuss the Levant, he presented a more balanced picture of the situation. Although a tougher line could be taken with the Gaullists now that all of the Vichy troops had been evacuated and the situation stabilized, there was nothing inherently wrong with the existing administrative framework, at least for the time being.[41]

Lyttelton's judgment was accepted and both Spears and de Gaulle were forced to bide their time, awaiting the next opportunity for striking at each other's positions.

The Proclamations of Syrian and Lebanese Independence

In the interim, it had become apparent that the time was not yet ripe for the negotiation of Franco–Levantine treaties. The issue had already been the source of tension in August, when de Gaulle was angered by a British suggestion that Spears sit in on Catroux's talks with Syrian and Lebanese leaders.[42] Lyttelton then conceded that Catroux could hold his talks in private, provided he kept Spears fully informed of their content. As we have seen, however, de Gaulle was most reluctant to undertake any substantive modification of the mandate while the war lasted and British troops remained in the Levant. For its part, the National Bloc, over which Shukri al-Quwatli had gained a large measure of control,[43] was unwilling to commit itself to the acceptance of a treaty on the 1936 model, granting the French long-term privileges in Syria. After all, de Gaulle was the leader of a political movement rather than a recognized head of state and the British seemed to be the real occupying power in Syria.[44] In any case, it would serve the nationalist interest better to play off the two powers against each other rather than reach a definitive agreement with either one. Thus, both Free French and Syrians felt that could only gain by playing for time. The most Lyttelton could get out of de Gaulle was an assurance that he would proceed unilaterally with a gradual increase in the administrative autonomy of the Levant States.[45]

In setting up a Syrian government, Catroux had to contend with the same problem faced by Dentz before him—how to form a cabinet that would enjoy a reasonable measure of popular support without having to bargain away French power in advance? Just like his predecessor, Catroux turned first to the nationalist-supported Hashem al-Atasi, but could not accept his demands for either immediate elections or the reconvening of the nationalist-controlled, 1936 Parliament. It became apparent that with al-Atasi as president, the strings of power would lie in the hands of Shukri al-Quwatli, of whom the Allies remained wary in view of his ties to the Axis powers. Instead, Catroux decided to appoint Sheikh Taj al-Din to the presidency. Sheikh Taj was a Damascene political operator, who had twice served as prime minister in earlier years, and who had long since established a reputation as a willing tool in the hands of the French. Although his appointment was supported by the fragmented Shahbandarists, whose primary aim at this point was to keep the National Bloc out of power at all costs, he had no firm political base beyond the limits of the capital.[46] On September 27, Catroux issued a unilateral declaration of Syrian independence which received as apathetic a public response as had marked the creation of the new government two weeks earlier. Lest anyone had any doubts, de Gaulle made it clear to the British government that the declaration was of a provisional nature in view of the nongovernmental status of the Free French.[47]

If arranging Syrian affairs seemed difficult, regulating the political life of Lebanon was to prove a Sisyphean task. In appointing a Lebanese cabinet at the end of November 1941, Catroux chose to play it safe by simply appointing Alfred Naccache, Dentz's choice as head of government, to the presidency of the Lebanese Republic; however, he managed to antagonize the Maronite Patriarch Arida by failing to consult with him about the appointment of a president. Catroux thus started out on the wrong foot with one of the major pillars of political support for France in Lebanon, a fact that Spears was adroitly to exploit in the following year.[48]

The formulation of a proclamation of Lebanese independence was equally complicated. Whereas Catroux had acted to a large extent on his own in the issuing of the Syrian proclamation, both de Gaulle and the British authorities demanded that they be consulted before the Lebanese declaration was published; this was both on account of dissatisfaction with various phrases that had been included in the Syrian proclamation and because French political ties to Lebanon were at once more intimate and more complex. Needless to say, the participation of de Gaulle, Lyttelton, Spears, and the Foreign Office in the drafting of the text did not serve to simplify the matter. What ensued was a confused and ill-coordinated pattern of talks held simultaneously in London, Cairo, and Beirut, in which it seemed impossible even to establish what the points of agreement were, let alone to communicate them to either one of the other two negotiation sites.[49]

There was a wide range of relatively minor disagreements over such things as the tendency of the French drafts to omit the word "Allied" before references to the military command, while including provocative phrases such as "the centuries-old French mission in Lebanon." The two most significant differences centered on a reference in the French text to the 1936 Franco–Lebanese treaty as providing the general guidelines for Free French policy in the country and on an assertion of Lebanese territorial indivisibility (a clause identical to that which had been included in the Syrian declaration without causing any eyebrows to be raised in London). The British objection to both of these phrases was quite telling, for in the first case, it was clearly implied that Whitehall considered the 1936 treaty (which had in fact been modeled on Britain's 1932 treaty with Iraq) as too advantageous for the French; the opposition to the second clause stemmed directly from the Eastern Department's hope that the predominantly Muslim territories that France had annexed to the Maronite stronghold of Mount Lebanon in 1922 (forming Greater Lebanon) might yet be absorbed by Syria.[50]

The Anglo–French disagreement over this last point epitomized the polar contrast between each country's perception of its interests in the Middle East. In a rather ingenuous effort to convince Lyttelton of the importance of retaining the reference to territorial integrity, Catroux wrote him that Lebanon constituted a Western beachhead in the midst of a hostile Muslim world.[51] This letter alarmed Cairo. For years, Britain's Middle Eastern policy had

promoted close ties with majoritarian, Sunni Muslim governments at the
expense of minority interests. Now Catroux seemed to be trying to associate
Britain with France's traditional cultivation of political support among religious minorities in the Middle East and its hostility to all forms of Arab
nationalism.

Lyttelton also felt uneasy about Catroux's continued insistence on the
retention of the reference to the 1936 treaty, "which was concluded in quite
different circumstances and is unacceptable to the bulk of Lebanese opinion
to-day." In fact, Lyttelton was troubled by the whole prospect of imminent
Franco–Lebanese treaty negotiations:

> The moment we entered the country it became obvious that no section of the
> community wanted a treaty. It was therefore necessary for us to try to ensure
> that the Free French should carry out their promises of independence without
> still further antagonising public opinion. This has been successfully accom-
> plished by means of the Syrian proclamation, and we hope, impending Leba-
> nese proclamation. But if this is followed up by treaty negotiations, the
> inhabitants both of Syria and Lebanon will feel their hands are being tied in
> advance of a general settlement of Middle Eastern problems at the Peace
> Conference. . . . Therefore I hope that without explicitly denying the right of
> the Free French to embark on treaty negotiations, every effort will be made
> to dissuade General de Gaulle and General Catroux from this course.[52]

The Foreign Office agreed with this assessment, cautioning only that:

> We must however be careful not to act in apparent contradiction to our public
> statements and . . . best course would be that General Spears should take a
> suitable opportunity . . . to sound General Catroux about Free French inten-
> tions, and if necessary, to speak to him frankly.[53]

In view of Lyttelton's outrage over his note's reference to the Muslim
world as hostile, Catroux officially withdrew the communication. In London,
however, the whole issue was regarded with much less concern and there was
considerable willingness to let de Gaulle have his way over the text of the
proclamation.[54] When de Gaulle failed to communicate agreed-on textual
amendments to Catroux, Spears and Lyttelton became convinced the Free
French leader was exploiting the distance separating London from Beirut to
make a mockery of the negotiation process and wear down British patience
until he had his way. Although the Foreign Office tried to bring de Gaulle into
line,[55] in internal minutes doubt was cast on the ultimate significance of the
whole issue:

> The present regime in Syria and the Lebanon is purely temporary. What will
> happen after the war will not depend on the wording of this declaration, but
> on facts—amongst others what part France will be in a position to play in the
> Levant.[56]

The contrast between London's easygoing approach to the issue and the
zeal with which Spears and Lyttelton contested fine legal points with the Free
French seems to have been a reflection of the radically different political

environments in which the different sets of negotiations took place. The Foreign Office staff could look at the Levant from a distance and see its troubles in the context of the overall war effort and the wider scope of Anglo–Free French relations; however, the members of the Spears Mission and Lyttelton's staff in Cairo were confronted on a daily basis with a whole range of irksome conflicts spawned by the overlapping of British and Gaullist authority in Syria and Lebanon. Thus, in the desert region around Deir al-Zor in eastern Syria, a brief tribal revolt had broken out when the Free French had tried to collect taxes at gunpoint.[57] The British blamed the trouble on French heavy-handedness and on the forced termination of the friendly contact that had existed between Glubb Pasha and the Bedouin tribes. The Free French accused British political officers of having encouraged the tribes to resist the tax-collection effort. When Catroux sought to send reinforcements to the region, General Wilson forbade it and Lyttelton prepared (with the Foreign Office's approval) to declare British martial law in the troubled region. An unpleasant confrontation was averted at the last moment when the tribal revolt subsided at the end of October.[58]

Other nasty disputes continued to seethe over British efforts to recruit soldiers from among the local populace and over the never-ending problem of suspicious ex-Vichyites working in the Levant administration.[59] The British liaison officer in Beirut reported that anti-British sentiment had become the overriding criterion determining the selection of administrative personnel at all levels. Cooperative and efficient officials such as Lépissier (the secretary-general of the General Delegation), Ehrhardt, Gennardi, and Cuinat (the last three of whom, it will be recalled, had been active on behalf of Britain and/or Free France under the Vichy administration) were either being dismissed or deprived of any real influence.

> This regrettable and dangerous phenomenon is probably more due to an ultra-nationalistic attempt to run before they can walk plus an acute inferiority complex than to any conscious desire to sabotage our relations and consequently the war effort. The results, however, are none the less dangerous for that. To quote one French official in reduction [sic] ad absurdum, they would almost rather place an enemy agent than to have recourse to a pro-British Frenchman. To take a very long shot, the danger exists—and enlightened Frenchmen openly discuss it—that the ultranationalism of certain Free French opinion might well become anti-British to the point of hostility or even sympathy with Vichy.[60]

Echoing the tone of this report, Lyttelton telegraphed to London that, while the situation in Syria was under control due to the effective administration of the delegate in Damascus (Collet), Lebanon presented a different picture. In addition to the disproportionately high number of former Vichy officials who had remained in Beirut, the French were also much more defensive about their position in their traditional Lebanese stronghold than they were about their control over Syria. The population's disquiet over French rule was quite unsettling, and the country's stability could not be taken for granted in the event of a German invasion of the Levant via Turkey in the following spring. Lyttelton recommended that provision be made for the imposition of British martial law in Lebanon should the need arise.[61] In a letter written to the minister of state one week earlier, Spears expressed himself much more bluntly:

> I am sure it is difficult for you, even in Cairo to realize the horrible feelings engendered in those of us who have responsible positions here at seeing the Lebanon handed over more and more by us to the tender mercies of the Free French.
>
> It is impossible to have a serious conversation with anyone without being told that the people knowing Great Britain to have the power, hold her ultimately responsible for all that may befall the country. We know the French administration to be weak and corrupt, and yet we have to stand by and see it all happening, unable to do anything. It is increasingly difficult to condone the farce of the Free French holding the country, the only real white troops they have got being the Foreign Legion, all the others varying in hue from café-au-lait to the darkest café turc. This we are told is France when, under the eyes of the whole of Lebanon, 32,000 able-bodied Frenchmen sailed for Vichy France from Beirut.
>
> I have in particular had conversations with John Hamilton, and we both have a growing feeling that our personal integrity is becoming more and more involved. To use John Hamilton's own phrase "One feels as if we were holding down the Lebanon to be raped by Free France." I might add that this friendly service is only rewarded by a kick in the pants.[62]

In their representations to London, Spears and Lyttelton demanded that, at the very least, the scene of all negotiations with the Gaullists be transferred to the Middle East. As matters stood, Lyttelton reported, "owing to de Gaulle's presence in London, Spears and I are ceasing to have any local influence."[63] Spears likewise warned

> that if it is an established fact that De Gaulle is permitted to overrule all his subordinates including Catroux and to disregard agreements come to by them it must inevitably follow that no one in the Middle East can negotiate effectively on matters concerning Syria and the Lebanese. We are getting into the position whereby De Gaulle is ruling the Levant from London in complete disregard of his own representatives and of all British authorities on the spot.[64]

This attitude was regarded as absurd by the Foreign Office. Eden dismissed as nonsense Spears' comment to the effect that "since . . . [Catroux] has observed that the Free French Führer carries all his points at home, he has given up the struggle." As for the whole litany of complaints from the Middle East over the lack of support from London in the struggle with the Free French, Eden added, "I don't pretend to understand a word of this."[65] The Eastern Department staff pointed out that Whitehall could not issue orders to de Gaulle on how to run his movement and that part of the problem lay in the inadequacy of the liaison service between Whitehall and Carlton Gardens (Free French headquarters) now that Spears was no longer there to run it. Besides, one official pointed out, the British case over some of the points in dispute with de Gaulle was rather weak. Certainly "General Spears has, not for the first time, gone to extremes, and in his handling of General Catroux and the Free French in Syria has definitely nailed the Union Jack to the mast."[66] Rather than create a full-blown crisis over what seemed to be a series of petty disputes and misunderstandings, the Foreign Office thought it best to agree to the issuing of the declaration of Lebanese independence on November 26 with most of the amendments Whitehall had originally pressed for left out.[67] The other subjects of dispute could be dealt with during Spears' imminent visit to London.[68] Pending Spears' departure for England, tensions in the Middle East were alleviated by Catroux's visit to Cairo in early December, during which he assured Lyttelton that he fully intended to make Syrian and Lebanese independence a reality, while postponing the negotiation of treaties with those countries. The idea was even broached of demonstrating Anglo–French solidarity by issuing a joint declaration of policy on the Middle East, but this was discarded as soon as differences began to arise over the actual wording of the text.[69]

Spears' Appointment as Minister to the Levant States

Spears' visit to London in January–March 1942 came against a background of War Cabinet-level discussions concerning the nature of his role in the Levant following the declarations of Syrian and Lebanese independence. As an expression of Britain's recognition of Levant independence it was considered appropriate to invest Spears with ambassadorial status. Unlike de Gaulle's original proposal to that effect, the War Cabinet meant to leave the liaison mission under Spears' control as well; his political officers and he would merely lose their formal military ranks. A new head was also to be appointed to the central Spears Mission in London and its overseas branches outside of the Levant would be replaced with ordinary military liaison missions.[70]

Despite the increased prestige and continued power this arrangement would apparently give Spears in his dealings with the Gaullists in the Levant, Churchill initially expressed doubts about the proposal. In a note that seemed to reflect a greater concern for his protégé's psyche than for the proper conduct of foreign policy, the prime minister wrote that Spears might well feel hurt by the loss of his military rank and the dissolution of the network of liaison missions he had built up.[71] Indeed, Spears did become angry when presented with the proposal. His initial reaction was to connect it with de Gaulle's attempts to have him discreetly silenced.[72] If the London-based Spears Missions were done away with, he feared, it could serve as a precedent for his mission in the Levant.[73]

It is not surprising that Spears was defensive about his mission in the Levant. Within a few months of its formation, he had managed to convert it from a mere liaison office into what amounted to a British shadow administration in Syria and Lebanon. Certainly its staff and resources far exceeded that of the London Spears Mission. It grew to include a military section overseeing matters relating to press, propaganda, censorship, and cipher, not to speak of its naval, air force, economic, and financial sections. The cost of maintaining the mission (along with the British legations in Beirut and Damascus that were set up in 1942) amounted to approximately 300,000 pounds sterling a year.[74] By 1944, Spears' political officers would number nearly 100, only slightly fewer than the number of officers in charge of the Free French administration. Officially responsible for maintaining liaison with the French and native authorities at the local level, their actual powers were as wide as they were ill-defined, and their responsibilities included the reporting of political intelligence. In practice, there was little to hinder them from exercising executive functions as well.[75] When the weight of Britain's economic and financial influence in the Levant, combined with its military predominance, was also taken into account, Free French control was beginning to appear more like a legal fiction than a political reality.

In response, therefore, to the talk of an ambassadorial appointment, Spears demanded that the power wielded by the Spears Mission be legitimized by the rewriting of its charter. In particular, he complained, the clause restricting the mission to a liaison role without any executive powers was a thorn in his side:

> The word liaison should be avoided or qualified. It has only a precise sense when applied to illicit relations between the sexes. If liaison means cupid in the sentimental world, it only denotes some sort of a postman in the military one.[76]

His initial suspicions of a Gaullist–Foreign Office plot against his mission notwithstanding, Spears was quite pleasantly surprised to see that things went his way during his stay in London. No doubt owing to Churchill's influence, most of the features of his new appointment which Spears had objected to were eliminated. It was clarified that the political and economic sections of his mission would not be transferred to the new embassy and that his political officers and he would retain their military status. His appointment as minister to Syria and Lebanon would thus in no way detract from the power of the Spears Mission in the Levant. Although the London-based mission was to be replaced with a Foreign Office liaison service, Spears remained formally in charge of liaison with the Free French throughout the Middle Eastern theater of operations. He would also be allowed to retain his business directorships in Britain despite the general rule in the diplomatic service against such potential conflict of interest. Spears was even allowed to have a hand in the writing of his own instructions. These described his official mission in the Levant as providing support for the growth of Syrian and Lebanese independence while leaving the French in a position of privilege; he was to encourage the French to hand over as much administrative responsibility as possible to the Levant states pending the final negotiation of treaties. Lip service was paid to the technical continuation of the French mandatory regime in the absence of such treaties.[77] As Spears saw it, the gist of his instructions was "to foster the independence of the Republics while maintaining the Free French shop front."[78]

6

The Development of the
Power Struggle

The Creation of the Wheat Office

The tension created in Syria and Lebanon by the overlapping of British and Free French political authority was heightened by the wartime economic problems afflicting the region. The shortage of goods which had been created by the British blockade was compounded by the sudden influx of Allied military forces, resulting in an inflationary spiral. This was only partially alleviated by the resumption of trade relations between the Levant and its neighbors and by the integration of Syria and Lebanon into the sterling bloc.

The fragility of the economic situation and the danger it posed to military security by its potential for sparking off public unrest, created a need for close governmental oversight of all imports and exports as well as of the distribution of foreign currency. To this end, the *Commission Supérieure du Ravitaillement* was set up to regulate all foreign trade. Although a Frenchman (Ehrhardt) headed it and Lebanese and Syrian representatives sat on the board, it was the British representative (Walsh) who really wielded the most clout. This was because all vital decisions concerning the distribution of supplies in the Middle East were made by the British-run Middle East Supply Centre (MESC) in Cairo. In and of itself, this administrative framework did not immediately give rise to much friction. It was on a more specific supply problem that Franco–British economic rivalry came to focus, and that was the wheat shortage.[1]

As has been seen, bread riots had already afflicted Syria while it was under Vichy's control, and the unrest had immediately been exploited by the National Bloc and Axis agents to further their political ends. The key to preventing a recurrence of this phenomenon was to ensure that wheat stocks were raised to a level adequate to meet the rate of public consumption. That this should have been a problem at all seems surprising, for before the war Syria had been a net exporter of grain.[2] The wheat shortage was in fact largely the artificial result of speculative hoarding by landowners and merchants who counted on wartime conditions to force the price of grain up in the future.[3] Spears initially thought the hindrance to wheat sales was the concern among hoarders that the Syrian government would purchase large quantities at below-market prices, driving the overall price level down. The solution he proposed was to declare a free market for wheat sales combined with an announcement of severe penalties for anyone caught hoarding:

> Probably nothing less than hanging a few of them will do. I, however, hope to be able to arrange that the Free French will make themselves responsible for this.[4]

Before long, Spears realized that such measures were inadequate to deal with the tight-fisted stubbornness of the wheat hoarders. He accordingly put forward a scheme for the wholesale import of grain into the Levant by the United Kingdom Commercial Corporation (the executive arm of the MESC). He calculated that the accumulation of a massive reserve of grain, to be sold at prices lower than those on the black market, would force the hoarders to disgorge their own stockpiles. Whereas Spears had hoped to let the Free French take the credit for whatever executions took place, he had no intention of letting them take charge of distributing British-supplied wheat. This was a task that would be handled by fifteen British officers who would be appointed to the *Commission Supérieure du Ravitaillement* and who would be answerable to Walsh while Ehrhardt continued to run the commission in name only.[5] As Catroux was later to argue, "this was, for General Spears, the occasion to demonstrate to the [native] populations Free France's inability to resolve these problems and to fulfill one of its essential obligations as the tutelary power."[6] At the time, however, Catroux raised no objection to the scheme, expressing concern only about de Gaulle's likely reaction. This problem was avoided by simply presenting him with a fait accompli.[7]

Unfortunately, Spears' attempt to flood Syria with grain under free market conditions failed because he completely underestimated the capacity of hoarders to buy up supplies as soon as they became available. Despite the import of approximately 80,000 tons of wheat (most of it from Australia), stocks were immediately depleted and prices remained high.[8] Widespread hunger may have been averted, but the results were hardly commensurate with the resources that had been expended on the scheme (this at a time when low rainfall was causing an acute grain shortage throughout the Middle East).[9]

Although a limited amount of wheat continued to be imported into the Levant in early 1942, it was clear that a more sophisticated remedy would have to be found for the hoarding problem. In London, de Gaulle advocated the renewal of massive grain imports while eliminating the free market conditions under which earlier stocks had been snapped up. Above all, he emphasized to Catroux that the Free French should assume sole and direct responsibility for wheat distribution:

> I have lately regretted that you agreed to introduce the English, and to introduce them with a preponderant voice, into the distribution commissions. That was to attribute to them on the spot a power to which they have no right and, besides, to bring into this serious affair certain Britons whose personal disinterest is doubtful.[10]

After Anglo–Free French discussions in London and Beirut in spring 1942, the outlines of a new approach to the problem began to emerge. It was suggested that the General Delegation create a commission that would monopolize the wholesale purchase of grain in the Levant, using force when necessary to persuade hoarders to release their stocks. The project would be financed by loans from the Free French *Caisse Centrale* which would be guaranteed indirectly by the British Treasury. The Wheat Office could then take the risk of buying up wheat wholesale at relatively high prices, without worrying about staying in the black when the grain was resold at the retail level. Accordingly, on April 21, Catroux issued a decree creating a Wheat Office that was to be run by a Free French supervisory committee, with a representative of the Spears Mission sitting on the board.[11] Much to Catroux's surprise and shock, the hitherto pliable Syrian government under Taj al-Din balked at this scheme. Sheikh Taj was both unwilling to grant exclusive power to the French and afraid of alienating the big Syrian landowners on whose political support his regime depended. In what Catroux was bitterly to describe as "a seraglio maneuver," the Syrians turned to Spears for support.[12]

Spears immediately seized on this opportunity to make it clear to Catroux that he would not accept French control of a wheat scheme that would ultimately be financed by the British Treasury. The Syrian government should be given a chance to handle collection itself; if it proved incapable of this, Wilson's Ninth Army would assume responsibility for the operation. Faced with such an encroachment on Free French power, Catroux decided that a compromise would be the only way he could salvage a portion of his control over the enterprise. Casey, the new minister of state in Cairo, was asked to mediate the dispute.[13] During mid-May 1942, a series of meetings including Catroux, Spears, General Wilson, and Casey was held in Cairo, the conclusion of which was an agreement that the Wheat Office (in French, Office des Céréales Panifiables or OCP) would consist of a four-member commission including representatives of the Levant government as well as of the French and British. Ultimate decisionmaking power was reserved for a two-man supervisory team consisting of Catroux and Spears. Catroux made a last attempt to retain personal veto power over the commission's decisions, but was forced to back down when General Wilson began to hint about the continued possibility of unilateral action by the Ninth Army. Moreover, the delegate-general was forced to agree that, in the event combined Franco–British pressure was not sufficient to secure the Syrian government's cooperation, Wilson would indeed be authorized to put his troops into action.[14]

In London the FNC accepted, "bon gré, mal gré," the principle of equal Anglo-French responsibility for the wheat plan, but was dismayed at Catroux's agreement to a British army takeover of the operation in the event the existing plan did not work.[15] Catroux tried to justify his concession by arguing that he would in any case have to rely on the British army to suppress any disturbances arising from a wheat shortage. Besides, he reported, relations between Wilson and Spears had become tense and Wilson had recently shown himself to be much more cooperative with the Free French authorities than he had been in the past.[16] Catroux saw the final arrangement as

> a semi-defeat. I had obviously succeeded in blocking Spears' grab [mainmise] for [the control of] the Damascus Government and that of the British Army for the administration of wheat, two eventualities which would have been equivalent to our virtual eviction from Syria. . . . But I had been forced to accept that they enter on an equal basis with us into the conduct of an affair which appertained to us through our mandatory prerogatives and through the force of the [de Gaulle–Lyttelton] accords.[17]

In the months and years that followed, it was indeed Spears' political clout and the zeal of his political and economic officers that ensured that the wheat plan succeeded. When lack of cooperation from the Syrian authorities led to the General Delegation's demand in August 1942 for the outright use of force in grain collection by the French-commanded native levies, Spears rescued his system by threatening to hold the Syrian prime minister, Husni Barazi— himself a landowner with a large stake in the price of wheat—personally responsible for a failure of the wheat plan.[18] Abandoning his short-term financial interests, Barazi lent a hand to the task of convincing Syrian landowners to release their stocks. Enough grain was forced onto the market to allow Spears to emerge triumphant, having demonstrated that it was the British, and not the French, who could determine the outcome of the most vital issues affecting the Levant.[19]

The Debate over Elections

Concurrently with the wheat plan controversy, a separate contest was under way over the issue of whether or not to hold elections in the Levant during wartime. This was in part precipitated by the accession to power in February 1942 of the nationalist Wafd party in Egypt, and the announcement that elections would be held there under the auspices of the new cabinet. This development had been directly engineered by the British, who saw it as the best available means of checking the pro-Axis inclinations of King Farouk.[20] The Syrian National Bloc leaders took their cue from the events in Egypt and began formenting strikes and demonstrations during late February and early March in the apparent hope of inducing the British to bring them into power in Damascus.[21]

The British were not at all of one mind over how to deal with the Syrian nationalists. Although it was generally agreed that channels of communication should be kept open, the staff of the Spears Mission was opposed to facilitating their accession to power under existing circumstances. Hamilton, in charge of the mission during Spears' protracted stay in England, pointed out that the National Bloc enjoyed less popular support than did the Wafd in Egypt, and suffered from internal factionalization. Moreover, it was precisely the National Bloc that had been most closely linked with the Axis powers, toward which its leaders were still said to harbor sympathies. Influential members of the National Bloc also numbered among the most notorious wheat hoarders in Syria:

> We feel therefore that there is little to be gained in swapping horses at the present delicate juncture especially when the proposed new mount has a bad record for vice, has been proved unsound and is quite likely to try and throw its new rider at the first fence.[22]

In Hamilton's opinion, abstention from support of the National Bloc would not suffice. In view of the nationalists' success in propagating the notion that they enjoyed the backing of His Majesty's government, the British attitude ought to be clarified by the adoption of a clear stance *against* the National Bloc.[23]

Hamilton's view was not shared by everyone. Ambassador Cornwallis reported from Baghdad, where Shukri al-Quwatli was ostensibly engaged in the mediation of a dispute between the Iraqi and Saudi regimes, that he had met with the National Bloc leader and felt one could do business with the man: "He evidently distrusts the French and despises Skeikh Taj al-Din but I formed the impression that he would be willing to throw his lot in with us if he were convinced by Free French action that joint declaration [of Syrian independence] would be fully implemented as soon as military situation permitted."[24] When Catroux expressed the intention of barring al-Quwatli from reentry into Syria, the Foreign Office came down hard against such a move and Catroux was forced to back down. (The Foreign Office did instruct Cornwallis to warn al-Quwatli against stirring up trouble on his return.)[25] Meanwhile, Lebanon was also suffering from political instability as the opposition leader Bishara al-Khoury, backed by the Maronite Patriarch, issued a call for national elections and did all he could to make life difficult for President Naccache.[26]

On his return to Beirut in late March, Spears made it clear that he did not share Hamilton's hesitant approach to political change in the Levant. He immediately reported to London that no progress had been made toward the implementation of Levantine independence during his absence. The only way to rectify the situation was to force the Free French to hand over control of the common interests (the major sources of state income) to the Syrian and Lebanese governments and to fix a date no later than August for elections. This aggressive approach was discouraged by the Foreign Office, which did, in principle, support the holding of elections, but considered the idea impractical at that juncture in view of the difficult military situation in the Western Desert.[27]

Indifferent to the Foreign Office's doubts, Spears proceeded to launch a concerted pressure campaign designed to threaten and/or cajole the existing governments in Damascus and Beirut into demanding elections from the French. Not surprisingly, both Taj al-Din and Naccache were reluctant to press for a development that would undoubtedly force them from office. Spears quickly concluded that they might have to be replaced with interim heads of state if any progress was to be made.[28] As he put it, "it has been shown conclusively that Naccache is no more capable than the Sheikh Taj of being used as a lever for bringing Catroux into line with our policy."[29] At the same time, Spears obtained the full support of the Middle East War Council (MEWC)—consisting of the main figures of the British military and political establishment in Cairo—for his policy. Casey reported to the Foreign Office that the MEWC had resolved that elections should be held in the Levant before the end of the year and that the role of the Free French administration should be transformed from an executive to an advisory one. Faced with such a united front, the ever waffling Foreign Office approved these objectives and asked Casey to broach the topic with Catroux.[30]

Spears, however, was not about to rely on Casey's powers of persuasion to achieve his objectives. His approach was to try and create facts by supporting nationalist opposition figures in their quest to gain power in the Levant states. These politicians, in turn, were eager to draw Spears into the fray by playing on his anti-French feelings and making much of their own pro-British sentiments. As so often in Middle Eastern politics, it was never quite clear who was actually manipulating whom.

It was on Lebanon that Spears first set his sights, both because the complexity of its confessional and political makeup provided an inviting arena for intrigue and because it was on Lebanon that the French relied as the stronghold of their power in the region. Spears helped politically undermine President Naccache by encouraging the growth of factionalism within the Maronite community (from which the Lebanese president was customarily selected). Naccache was associated with the Jesuit order that was seen as a rival of the Maronite clerical hierarchy, while the head of the opposition Constitutional Bloc, Bishara al-Khoury, was related to a bishop in the Maronite church and consequently enjoyed the favor of Patriarch Arida.[31] Arida himself was not averse to cooperating with militant Muslim elements when it suited his purpose, while al-Khoury helped draw the Spears Mission into the game by telling its officials that the ultimate political goal he pursued was the achievement of an independent status for Lebanon under British protection.[32] Spears encouraged Arida and al-Khoury to make trouble for Naccache and to press for early elections. At the same time, the Egyptian and Iraqi governments also raised a hue and cry over the issue. Catroux saw this as more than just a coincidence:

> With a unanimity which would be surprising if one did not suspect it of being concerted, Spears, Nahas Pasha and Nuri Pasha Said [the Egyptian and Iraqi premiers, respectively] declare that Lebanon and Syria cannot be considered legitimately independent until they enjoy a democratic, parliamentary regime.[33]

Catroux was opposed to holding elections in the Levant states because he was convinced the British would exploit the occasion to increase their power. Instead, he suggested to de Gaulle that the crisis might be defused by restoring the assemblies and constitutions that had been suspended in 1939 as well as by regarding the unratified 1936 treaties as effectively operative.[34] Although de Gaulle agreed with the general tenor of Catroux's proposal, the Free French became bogged down in disagreements over who should head the Lebanese government and whether the implementation of the treaties should be included in the package.[35] In any case, the British were no longer willing to accept anything less than elections, and were, in fact, seeking American backing for their position. The United States had refrained from recognizing the proclamations of Syrian and Lebanese independence, both in order to avoid antagonizing Vichy and because Washington was reluctant to bestow its seal of approval on so dubious a form of self rule.[36] The American government decided to remain somewhat aloof from the current conflict as well, merely offering to mediate the dispute. Engert, the American consul-general in Beirut, took the view that the roots of the crisis lay in a personal clash between Catroux and Spears which was driving each side to positions more extreme than those it would adopt under normal circumstances.[37]

With de Gaulle and the FNC vociferously protesting Spears' pressure campaign, Whitehall decided that another showdown with the Free French leader would be counterproductive. Given the right circumstances it would be easier to arrive at an accommodation with Catroux in the Middle East.[38] Casey was therefore instructed to address the election issue at the same series of meetings in Cairo that dealt with the wheat problem. As in the case of the wheat plan, Catroux found it very difficult to stick to his original position when left alone in a room full of British officers and diplomats, as hard-nosed as they were high-ranking. At the May 11 meeting, the delegate-general found himself confronted with the vigorous insistence of Casey and Spears on the need to satisfy popular sentiment in Syria and Lebanon by announcing that elections would be held before the end of the year. His own proposal to restore the status quo ante 1939 was deemed insufficient. He then tried to stall by suggesting a private understanding with the British about the date of elections with no public announcement to be made until the last moment, but the British remained firm. When the issue came up again at the meeting of May 13, Catroux finally agreed that—subject to de Gaulle's approval—an announcement promising elections before the end of the year would be made within six weeks. The British promised in return to do their best to persuade Iraq and Egypt to establish diplomatic relations with the existing Syrian and Lebanese governments and to recognize the FNC. Lastly, the British were satisfied with a vague assurance that the transformation of the executive role played by the General Delegation in the Levant was already under way and that all important decrees (arrêtés) issued by Catroux would be submitted to Spears beforehand.[39] Catroux's readiness for compromise provoked de Gaulle's ire but there was little that he could do as word of the agreement was prematurely reported in the American press.[40] Free French attempts in London to postpone the announcement of elections were of no avail.

At the last moment, the Gaullists were granted a respite by a deus ex machina who cast his gigantic shadow across the tiny stage of the Levant. In June–July 1942, General Rommel's army plunged deep into Egypt once again, raising renewed fears that the entire Middle East might fall to the Germans. Under these circumstances, even Spears was willing to admit that an immediate announcement of Levant elections would be impractical.[41] (Catroux was later to claim rather unconvincingly that his concessions at Cairo had been based on the anticipation of this very eventuality.[42]) Spears, however, had no intention of easing the pressure on Catroux in its other forms during this period of limbo; instead, he vigorously pursued his anti-French intrigues.

An inviting opportunity for fomenting divisions within the Naccache government was soon provided by de Gaulle, who delivered a speech in Britain in mid-June reaffirming the importance of France's role as the mandatory power in the Levant. The Lebanese opposition launched a protest campaign over this speech and Spears and his staff contributed to the tension by actually helping Foreign Minister Franjieh draft a note to Naccache demanding that he call on the Free French to repudiate de Gaulle's statement.[43] Naccache rejected Franjieh's note and when the Foreign Office was informed by Spears of the incident, it decided in favor of Naccache: "I [Eden] trust that Lebanese President's rejection of his Foreign Minister's proposals is due to his wishing to put an end to this senseless agitation. You should tell Monsieur F[ranjieh] that His Majesty's Government have no sympathy with his attitude over this question."[44]

This placed Spears in a very awkward position, since it was he who had put Franjieh up to the action in the first place. He pointed this out to the Foreign Office, arguing that, in any case, Naccache's rejection of the note "was due solely to his moral cowardice." He went on to inform London that "what you describe as a 'senseless agitation' is in fact in the course of natural and inevitable reaction of patriots" to the Free French grip on political power.[45] While the Foreign Office agreed not to reprimand Spears, it viewed his attitude as completely unacceptable. In internal minutes, Sir Maurice Peterson, the undersecretary in charge of the Eastern Department, noted:

> A member of his [Spears'] staff, writing home recently, said that he had never known what was meant by animals eating their young until he had seen Sir E. Spears devouring the Free French Movement.[46]

The Syrian and Lebanese nationalists were not sitting idly by during this period. Encouraged by the obvious antagonism between the British and the Free French, they were becoming increasingly vocal in their own demands for real independence from France. On his return from a visit to Cairo, on which he had been accompanied by Bishara al-Khoury, Jamil Mardam let it be known that the Wafdist premier Nahas Pasha had endorsed the idea of creating an Arab federation that would include a Syria led by the National Bloc and a Lebanon under the presidency of Bishara al-Khoury. Mardam claimed this plan enjoyed Iraqi backing and, more importantly, the support of the British. The latter, however, were disturbed by Mardam's exaggerated claims, seeing in them an attempt to whip up the Anglo–French feud over the Levant. Ambassador Lampson also cautioned that, from the point of view of Britain's postwar interests, it would be dangerous to allow Egypt to assume the leadership of the Arab nationalist movement. Accordingly, it was decided that Mardam should be asked to retire to Lebanon for a while to prevent him from any further troublemaking. Spears and Catroux also managed to put on a rare show of public solidarity by issuing a joint communiqué assuring the Levantine public that they were working fully in tandem and were not at cross purposes with each other.[47]

Whitehall Moves against the Spears Mission

That this outward display of cooperation was devoid of substantive significance was made abundantly clear a few weeks later. When the continuing bread shortage in Lebanon resulted in a general strike and public demonstrations in mid-July, President Naccache was forced to accept the resignation of his ministers and Spears immediately claimed the right to a major say in determining the makeup of the new cabinet.[48] In a conversation with Boegner, Catroux's chief political aide (who had recently rallied to the Free French from the Vichy embassy in Turkey), Spears warned that if Catroux refused to consult with him over the distribution of cabinet portfolios, he would allow their dispute to become public. He also suggested openly that Naccache be replaced as president. Outraged, the delegate-general responded with a letter announcing his refusal to have any further direct contact with Spears. The latter then threatened to exclude the French from the administration of the wheat scheme in Lebanon unless Catroux withdrew his letter. On July 28, Vichy radio triumphantly broadcast news of the rupture between Spears and Catroux, which had been obtained by its embassy in Ankara.[49]

Doubtless aware that he had pushed things too far, Spears began sending defensive telegrams to London. He claimed that the main motive for his attempt to intervene in the formation of the cabinet was his concern over Catroux's intention of giving a portfolio to Ahmed al-Assad, the main political figure from predominantly Shiite southern Lebanon, who was also notorious for his involvement in smuggling operations and for his local sabotaging of the wheat plan. Despite Spears' objections, Catroux was still refusing (in communications made through third parties) to reconsider this selection. It was therefore crucial that Spears have a direct role in the matter.[50]

Rising, as always, to the defense of his protégé, Churchill remarked that "surely Spears is in the right with this fellow [Catroux] and his pompous letter."[51] The Foreign Office was far less sympathetic. As far as it was concerned, it was not British policy to push for an immediate replacement of Naccache, and Spears had had no business making such a suggestion to Boegner:

> What is clear . . . is that Sir E. Spears has reached the position where he is unable to have personal relations with the President [of Lebanon] or with General Catroux. This . . . is a complete negation of the essential character of a diplomatic representative. It is also dangerous.[52]

Bowing before the Foreign Office's judgment, Churchill approved the dispatch of a formal rebuke to the wayward Spears.[53] Catroux's victory was short-lived, however, for the new Lebanese premier, Sami al-Solh, insisted on submitting his list of proposed cabinet members to the Spears Mission for approval. Four men the British minister objected to were duly excluded from the government, including the controversial Ahmed al-Assad.[54] Spears gleefully telegraphed that "Catroux's move [cutting off relations with Spears] was therefore a mistaken one since it is we, and not he, who control the situation should we wish to do so."[55] At the beginning of August, in separate meetings held with Spears and Catroux, respectively, Minister of State Casey managed to put an end to the impasse between them by having Spears assure the delegate-general in writing that he had not implied any threat when warning of the publicity a quarrel over cabinet formation might generate. For his part, Catroux effectively withdrew his letter and promised to keep Spears closely informed of all future political developments.[56]

Spears' openly aggressive policy toward the Free French could leave little doubt over the true nature of his intentions in the Levant. Every move he made seemed to reflect an overwhelming desire to push the Gaullists out of the region, regardless of what the cost might be to overall Anglo–French relations both during and after the war. There seems to have been no aspect of the administration of the territories that was not colored by the Franco–British struggle for political control. The construction by the British military of a railroad from Haifa to Tripoli became the source of considerable tension both because the Free French were denied wartime access to it and because there was uncertainty over whether it was the French or the Lebanese who would have the first option to purchase the line after the war.[57] A more telling issue was that surrounding an agreement reached in June by Generals Wilson and Catroux on the nature of the measures that would be taken in the event of a military emergency in the region. The final text was viewed by the Foreign Office and the War Office as an improvement on earlier drafts, but Spears objected because the agreement provided for the retention of Free French administrative autonomy in the event a state of siege was declared; the British military would assume control only of the Syrian and Lebanese administrations. The text also spoke of the British military commander as exercising his authority in a state of siege only through the intermediary of General Catroux. Spears claimed that these provisions would enable the Free French to destroy what little independence Syria and Lebanon enjoyed, and suggested that Whitehall model itself on de Gaulle's own past behavior by changing the terms of the agreement unilaterally. The Foreign Office, after consultations with the War Office, dismissed Spears' complaints as totally out of line with Britain's continued recognition of Free French authority in the Levant. As W. E. Beckett of the Eastern Department remarked:

> General Spears is inspired by an extreme distrust of the Free French . . . and we are in the position where our Minister in the Levant, who should be a useful intermediary to smooth things over between our military authorities

and the local powers. . . . is far more extreme against the Free French than are the military authorities.[58]

In fact, it is apparent that if Spears had had his way, the exercising of state of siege powers would have meant the eradication of French authority in Syria and Lebanon. Whether this would have spurred him on to provoke a crisis that would result in the declaration of a state of seige can only be speculated.[59]

Spears' conduct during the summer of 1942 was the occasion of raised eyebrows in many quarters. The American State Department received a barrage of alarming reports from Acting Consul Gwynn in July, decrying Spears' policy as a brazen attempt to supplant French influence in the region. Gwynn reported that in private conversation, Spears laughed at the notion of Lebanese independence, about which he spoke with such conviction in public. Clearly, what he sought was exclusive British control of the territories. The consul reported that Generals Wilson and Catroux got along very well with each other and that Wilson resented the way Spears was creating an atmosphere of ill will between the two powers.[60] The State Department responded by asking Ambassador Winant in London to make discreet inquiries into the possibility of a replacement being found for Spears. Winant was told this was problematic in view of Churchill's personal involvement in the matter.[61]

While realizing that the outright removal of Spears from the Levant was impossible, the Foreign Office had come to the conclusion that his powers would have to be severely curtailed. The commanders-in-chief of the Middle East and Casey had already suggested that all military issues in Syria and Lebanon be dealt with by the Ninth Army's own liaison office rather than by the military branches of the Spears Mission. The other sections of the mission could be amalgamated with the British Legations in Beirut and Damascus (leaving Spears in charge in his role as ambassador).[62] At an interdepartmental meeting of Foreign Office and War Office officials held in London on July 21, 1942, it was discovered that:

> Nobody really knows how many sections the Mission is composed of, but we have at least established the existence of five—political, economic, financial, propaganda and military—of which it may be said with some confidence that the financial alone is in satisfactory rapport with London. . . .
>
> I think it would be useless to disguise from ourselves that the raising of this question is pretty certain in one quarter or another to bring up the allied question of General Spears' conduct of his diplomatic mission.[63]

In the eyes of Eden's private secretary, Oliver Harvey, Spears "is a hopeless misfit but he is a protégé of the P.M. Any professional diplomat would have been sacked, and rightly, for a third of what he has done."[64]

Churchill's approval was obtained, however, for the proposed integration of the Spears Mission into the Levant legations, and Casey was instructed to begin implementing the plan immediately. It is clear that this was viewed by the Foreign Office as a poor substitute for the complete elimination of Spears' influence in the Levant. Sir Maurice Peterson saw Spears as an uncontrollable figure whose conduct in the Levant completely hindered the implementation of British foreign policy in the region:

> I know of no instance in which . . . [Spears] may be said to have helped [the Free French] . . . except when his assistance could be used to boost his own position, his solicitude for which is based either on personal egotism or on Empire-building proclivities which are some two hundred years out of date. Or on both. . . .
>
> . . . Meanwhile we have had the interesting comment from an American source [doubtless Gwynn] that Sir E. Spears' real objective is, through the instrumentality of his over-elaborate Mission, to duplicate the French administrative system and squeeze them out much as Clive squeezed the French out of India.[65]

Whereas the Foreign Office placed the blame for the tension in the Levant squarely on Spears' shoulders, the Free French did not find it so easy to make a distinction between Whitehall's policy and the actions of its representative in Beirut. From de Gaulle's perspective, Spears' conduct fit neatly into the wider pattern of British and American policy toward his movement. When the Free French had acted unilaterally to liberate St. Pierre and Miquelon from Vichy rule in December 1941, Washington had protested. When Admiral Muselier had sought to withdraw from the Free French movement along with the fleet under his command, powerful elements in the British admiralty had tried to lend him support. Gaullist forces had been excluded from the battle for Madagascar and repeated ceasefires had been arranged there between British and Vichy forces with no mention being made of eventual Free French involvement in the administration of the island. It was only after his representatives in Equatorial Africa had declared their determination to maintain allegiance to de Gaulle even if he broke all ties with England, that the Free French leader was able to obtain Churchill's assurance that Britain would act in good faith over Madagascar as well as the rest of the French Empire once it had been liberated. Given this background of intrigue and suspicion, de Gaulle was bound to view Spears' latest escapades in the worst possible light. No amount of reassurance from the Foreign Office could convince him that Syria and Lebanon were not in danger of slipping from French control. He therefore decided to return to the Levant himself in order to reverse the course of events there.[66]

De Gaulle's Second Visit to the Levant

In August 1942, Rommel's forces still held a line less than 100 miles west of Alexandria, but his offensive had lost its momentum and the immediate danger posed to the Fertile Crescent had passed.[67] Arriving in Cairo in the second week of the month, de Gaulle found that the topic of Levant elections was back on the British agenda. When Casey broached the question at their first meeting, de Gaulle immediately reverted to the role he had played with Lyttelton the previous year. Adopting a harsh and uncompromising tone, de Gaulle bluntly stated that elections were out of the question after the recent setbacks in the Western Desert and that, in any case, this was an exclusively French concern that he had no intention of discussing with the British. Casey then asked whether there were any questions he *would* be willing to talk about, to which de Gaulle responded by saying that the conduct of General Spears was the only subject he considered suitable for discussion. Casey retaliated by declining to accept this as a legitimate topic, and the meeting ended shortly thereafter.

The rest of the plot unwound more or less along the lines of the script that had been written one year earlier. Catroux met with Casey on the following day and tried to assure him that de Gaulle's bark was worse than his bite, while Michael Wright of the British embassy met with the Free French leader and politely sought to convince him that his blustering approach could easily backfire. (Wright had filled the same conciliatory function during de Gaulle's row with Lyttelton.) On August 10, the general met with the minister of state again, but in a friendly spirit this time. He also met briefly with Churchill, who was passing through Cairo on his way to Moscow. Though nothing of substance was agreed on, the atmosphere of deadlock and crisis had temporarily dissipated.[68]

De Gaulle then proceeded to the Levant, where he began touring the country and meeting with Syrian and Lebanese politicians in a general effort to create a sense that Free France was fully in control of the region. He restricted his contact with British officials to a minimum and avoided any reference to the British in his speeches. De Gaulle was making an impressive attempt to compensate with imagery for what Free France lacked in material power. Encouraged by the friendly reception of the crowds, he reported to the FNC that the French position in the Levant could still be salvaged.[69]

De Gaulle saw his worst fears concerning Spears' activity confirmed, however. He had no doubt that his objective was to oust the French entirely from the region by actively undermining their control over all sectors of public life there. The decision on how to respond to this threat hinged on whether or not the local conduct of the Spears Mission was a genuine expression of British policy:

> For the English, the first matter is to create a condominium here. Then, having at its disposal money, supplies, force and considerable means of propaganda, England would transform the condominium into British domination. . . .
>
> The question is to find out whether this policy is and will remain that of the British Government as such. If so, I do not see any means of further pursuing the cooperation with England.

He added ominously that "I have begun to take certain measures with a view to all possible consequences."[70]

Handicapped by his lack of any real power and by the dependence of his movement on British support for its continued existence, de Gaulle nevertheless sought to force the British to pay Free France the deference due a sovereign government. His complaints were detailed in a lengthy memorandum sent to Casey, in which the Spears Mission was accused of a wide variety of violations of the de Gaulle–Lyttelton agreements. Apart from the flagrant intervention of Spears himself in the political life of Syria and Lebanon, the memo charged that, at the local level, Spears' political officers were energetically following their chief's example throughout the territories. In addition, the Spears Mission was attempting to take over the supervision of state finances in Syria and Lebanon, while the United Kingdom Commercial Corporation was monopolizing the control of practically all of the Levant's external trade. Spears was also seeking to gain control of the Tripoli oil refinery. In addition, de Gaulle complained, there was no justification for continued British participation in the wheat plan, now that it no longer entailed the import of grain into the region.[71]

The Free French leader resorted to a variety of pressure tactics in his attempt to have Spears reined in. He began by writing to Churchill during the latter's stay in Cairo on his way back from Moscow in late August, demanding that the de Gaulle–Lyttelton agreements be enforced both in letter and in spirit. The prime minister rejected de Gaulle's charges of British noncompliance, insisting that local British conduct was justified by military security considerations and by Britain's role as guarantor of Syrian and Lebanese independence.[72] This attitude doubtless reflected the influence of Spears, who had flown to Cairo to seek Churchill's support against de Gaulle. In his attempt to urge restraint on his friend, the prime minister expressed himself in words so honeyed as to give Spears the impression that they signified little short of encouragement.[73] Before leaving Cairo, Churchill made it clear to Casey that he backed Spears' demand that the holding of elections in the Levant be announced before the end of the year.[74]

Given their earlier experience, the British realized that it would be impossible to deal to their satisfaction with any substantive issues in the Levant until de Gaulle had left the area. Casey at first tried to coax him out by inviting him to return to Cairo for a discussion of the outstanding Anglo–French differences over Syria and Lebanon. De Gaulle responded characteristically by insisting that it was Casey who would have to come to Beirut. The minister of state accordingly transmitted a message from Churchill that had been held in reserve until then, requesting that de Gaulle return to London as soon as possible.[75] The general telegraphed to the prime minister that this was impossible at the moment: "I hope you will realise that the maintenance of independent position of France in Syria and Lebanon is for me and for the French National Committee an absolute duty and of first [urgency?]."[76]

De Gaulle appears to have been emboldened by the sympathetic hearing he received from Gwynn, the U.S. acting consul in Beirut. Gwynn, who had spent much of his life in France, shared de Gaulle's resentment of local British conduct and led de Gaulle to believe that his sympathy was a reflection of official American policy.[77] Tangible proof of this seemed to be offered by a telegram from the State Department to Ambassador Winant in London, a copy of which was apparently shown to de Gaulle by Gwynn. This instructed Winant to express interest in the Levant dispute with a possible view to U.S. mediation.[78] In fact, the State Department did consider Spears' continued presence in Beirut a liability for Allied interests, but it was no more pleased by the evident reluctance of the Free French to hand over substantial power to the Syrian and Lebanese governments.[79]

In the last week of August, de Gaulle raised tensions higher by threatening a complete breach with Britain unless the local British policy was fundamentally changed and Spears permanently recalled. When asked by Gwynn what such a rupture would involve, he responded that the British would be asked to leave the territory "and if they refused to leave he would take measures to force them out."[80] A week later, Casey was presented with a formal request for the transfer of the Levant military command to the Free French. This demand was based on a clause in the de Gaulle–Lyttelton agreements providing for the exercise of command by the power with the greatest number of troops in any given territory. Casey rejected the note out of hand, denying that French troops outnumbered British (which they did, apparently, only in Lebanon, and then only if the native levies were counted as French).[81]

Hoping to gain leverage over Whitehall, de Gaulle had earlier instructed Dejean to approach both the U.S. and the Soviet embassies in London with a view to winning their active support in the Levant dispute. At the same time, de Gaulle began emphasizing the importance of U.S. power in his own talks with the political leadership in Syria and Lebanon, as well as pressing for the accreditation of a Soviet diplomatic representative to the Levant states.[82] Dejean accepted his instructions with considerable reluctance, pointing out that Washington had never shown much sympathy for Free France in the past and arguing that the best policy would be one of close cooperation with Britain.[83] In a meeting with Strang of the Foreign Office, Dejean confided to him that he considered U.S. intervention in the Levant dispute to be undesirable and that he thought de Gaulle was losing his sense of perspective in the Levant and ought to be recalled to London.[84]

De Gaulle would have none of Dejean's conciliatory attitude. Although unaware of what his subordinate was saying to the British behind his back, he found Dejean's cables to Beirut aggravating enough. The final straw was the telegram of September 3 which suggested that de Gaulle go to Cairo to discuss the Levant dispute with Casey so as to smooth the way for Free French participation in the anticipated Allied invasion of North Africa.[85] De Gaulle's response seemed to seethe with fury:

> Twenty-four years of a French policy of neglect have produced the results which we see. I am not prepared to pursue this policy. One thing alone hinders the stupid voracity of our allies here, and that thing is their fear of pushing us beyond the limit. It is absolutely normal for the U.S. and Russia to be kept informed of a dispute which the English do not hesitate to present to

them in their own manner. . . . We will not become great by humbling ourselves. I claim to be supported by the National Commissioner of Foreign
Affairs in a task which is even more difficult. If you do not consider yourself
up to doing this, your duty is to tell me so.[86]

De Gaulle's uncompromising approach was not without its effect in certain
quarters. Brigadier Clayton, the head of the Middle East Intelligence Centre
in Cairo, argued that a rupture with de Gaulle could create serious problems
for British strategic interests in Free French-controlled Equatorial Africa. In
view of this, he suggested that a compromise might be reached over the
Levant, with Britain dismissing Spears and eliminating the entire liaison mission in return for various concessions by the Free French in their own administrative sphere. The Foreign Office was thinking along similar lines in early
September, and Casey actually proposed that he be authorized to incline to de
Gaulle's wishes by coming to Beirut for discussions.[87]

In many quarters, however, de Gaulle's tactics backfired. Churchill in
particular was very antagonized and wrote a furious minute to Eden regarding
Casey's temporary lapse: "Please forbid Casey explicitly from going to see de
Gaulle. He showed unexpected weakness in making the proposal."[88] The
Spears Mission, of course, delivered a constant barrage of reports to Cairo
and London on the dangers de Gaulle was creating for British security interests in the Levant. Particular emphasis was laid on the general's meeting with
Suleiman Murshid, a French-backed strongman in the backward Alawite region of Syria, whom both Spears and the British army command accused of
persecuting and antagonizing the local Sunni population.[89] Military intelligence reported with concern on the growing domination of Catroux's administration by ex-Vichyites like Boegner, Baelen, and Blanchet at the expense of
those Gaullists of long standing who were viewed as pro-British. The report
drew the conclusion that this reflected a conscious policy on the part of
Catroux, who probably regarded

> Vichy and the Free French as two aspects of the same situation, both smoke
> screens to put up to try and protect a prostrate France from alien encroach-
> ments and to ensure that whichever side wins France is covered by an insur-
> ance policy.

The French, military intelligence reported, were only too eager to exploit any
dissension that might arise between the Ninth Army and the Spears Mission.
The best way to combat such intrigues was to uphold Britain's commitment to
Syrian and Lebanese independence and to minimize friction within the British
establishment in the Levant.[90] To make concessions to de Gaulle at the expense of the Spears Mission would simply be viewed by the Free French as a
sign of weakness.

As we have seen, before de Gaulle's descent on the Middle East, Whitehall had been preparing to dismantle the Spears Mission despite reports such
as these. Now everything had been transformed into a matter of prestige and
the British felt obliged to close ranks rather than lose face. Although the

Foreign Office blueprint for the termination of the mission was ready by October, its implementation was indefinitely postponed in view of the general uncertainty over the future of Anglo–French relations in the Levant.[91] The Francophile Oliver Harvey was convinced that de Gaulle had in fact saved the Spears Mission from oblivion:

> If only de Gaulle had controlled himself, we could have got Spears out by now thanks to the complaints we have received from all sides. But de G. has played into his hands and put more than enough rope round his own neck to hang himself with.[92]

The same principle was also applied to the issue of elections in the Levant. Prior to his temporary loss of nerve in September, Casey had expressed his full agreement with Spears' insistence on an immediate announcement of elections for the following reason: "I feel that the fact that General de Gaulle has made this issue a test of strength is an additional argument for pressing for the announcement to be made now."[93]

Thus, in spite of the concern raised by the possibility of a complete estrangement of the Gaullist movement, the balance of opinion in Whitehall swung in favor of a hard line. The first priority continued to be de Gaulle's return to London, failing which, no substantive talks could be contemplated. All direct approaches to de Gaulle having failed, it was decided to put pressure on the FNC in the hope that it could persuade de Gaulle to return. Although Dejean already seemed to be in the pocket of the Foreign Office, his tougher-minded colleague on the FNC, René Pleven, had just had his spirits buoyed by conversations with the sympathetic American journalist Walter Lippman, who gave him the impression that U.S. public opinion was solidly behind the Free French cause. Pleven accordingly urged de Gaulle to hold out.[94] In order to swing the balance of opinion in the FNC decisively in favor of Dejean's moderate approach, the Foreign Office decided to employ a subtler method of persuasion than had been tried so far. On September 9, Eden met with both Dejean and Pleven to inform them that in the wake of the breakdown of negotiations with Vichy forces on Madagascar, military operations were about to be resumed. Whereas it had been His Majesty's government's intention to entrust the administration of the island to Free France once it had been totally liberated, the situation had been complicated by de Gaulle's conduct in the Levant. The final decision on Madagascar would hinge on the general's immediate return to London and the early resolution of the dispute over Syria and Lebanon.[95]

Immediately after the meeting, the FNC convened to discuss how to respond, but failed to arrive at a consensus. Despite Dejean's pleas, the majority refused to put their names to a telegram calling on de Gaulle to return immediately to England. Accordingly, two separate cables were sent to Beirut: Pleven's was written in the name of the FNC and urged de Gaulle to ease the tension by meeting with Casey in Cairo and then proceeding to Brazzaville, but it made no mention of London; Dejean's telegram urged the general to come straight back to Britain, arguing that the control of Madagascar was of far greater significance than the dispute with Spears in Syria, especially in view of the potential importance of Madagascar as a precedent for the future administration of French North Africa.[96] At the same time, de Gaulle was informed of Churchill's intense personal displeasure over his failure to heed his call to leave the Levant. Eden was reported to be hard put to continue defending the Free French in an increasingly hostile War Cabinet.[97]

In playing the Madagascar card, the Foreign Office had calculated correctly. Having failed to move the British by threats and having come to realize that he could not drive a wedge between Washington and London over the Levant dispute, de Gaulle was faced with a choice between risking a complete break with Britain on the eve of Madagascar's liberation and the invasion of French North Africa, or cutting his losses by backing down. In effect, his bluff had been called. Despite his attempt to create an illusion of power by conducting himself as though the Free French movement were *aequus inter pares* in the Allied camp, his position was really one of utter dependence on his British sponsors for the fulfillment of any of his goals. He accordingly cabled the FNC that he was leaving Beirut promptly and would stop over in Brazzaville before making his way back to London.[98] On the eve of his departure, he made a point of publicly reaffirming his commitment to the alliance in a speech broadcast over the Levant radio.[99]

The general's sudden reversal of attitude seems to have surprised and frustrated Spears, coming as it did just at a time when he was beginning to hope a crisis might be unleashed in which de Gaulle would be replaced as Free French leader by the more pliable Catroux.[100] While de Gaulle made his way back to Britain, Spears sought to contain whatever gains the Free French might make as a result of their leader's new appeasing tone. He reported to Casey that de Gaulle's change of mind was due only to his realization that he had alienated the British without gaining any friends. On his return to London, warned Spears, he must not be allowed to achieve with smiles what he had failed to gain with frowns. He added that the current situation, in which the Free French enjoyed direct access to Whitehall while Spears and Casey could only wire reports from afar, was grossly unfair and ought to be rectified by the creation of a powerful office in London that would represent the minister of state Middle East.[101] While agreeing with Spears' evaluation of de Gaulle's attitude, the Foreign Office took a jaundiced view of the latter proposal:

> I take it that this means that Sir E. Spears is getting tired of Beirut and would like to be a "powerful" representative of Mr. Casey in London, where he could ride the F.O. with whip and spur, and, in his spare time, grind the faces of the Free French.[102]

Another Attempt at Reaching a Written Understanding

Pending de Gaulle's arrival in London, the British debated over what objective they should pursue in their forthcoming talks with him. Spears was joined by Churchill in continuing to press for the immediate announcement of Levant elections, while General Alexander, the new commander-in-chief in the Middle East, recommended a postponement of elections until after Rommel's army had been decisively defeated.[103] While it was generally agreed that a written agreement should result from the talks, Spears advocated drawing up a document that would lay down very specific guidelines for the division of power and responsibility between British and Free French, whereas the Foreign Office favored seeking a more general understanding, to be based on the de Gaulle–Lyttelton agreements. All agreed that the Free French should formally accept the legitimacy of Britain's interest in the fulfillment of the promise of independence and in all matters affecting military security and economic stability; however, the Foreign Office was willing to let the Free French take the forefront in implementing policies as long as they were in accord with these interests, while Spears seemed to insist on publicizing Britain's role as much as possible. The Eastern Department still hoped that this inconsistency in British policy could ultimately be resolved by the removal of Spears from his post.[104]

In any case, the first order of business on de Gaulle's return would be to smooth the way to productive negotiations by effecting a personal reconciliation between the prime minister and him. As matters stood, Oliver Harvey recorded, the embittered Churchill seemed loath to live up to the deal that had been offered by the Foreign Office to the FNC:

> P.M. still being very difficult about admitting de Gaulle to Madagascar. The General is arriving from Syria on Thursday and he is then to be seen by the P.M. We hope that after the usual explosion there will be the usual reconciliation. But P.M. is very scratchy about him, hotted up by Spears' telegrams.[105]

Harvey's worst fears over the Churchill–de Gaulle meeting were confirmed when it took place on September 30:

> It couldn't have gone worse. A. E[den] was there and de Gaulle brought Pleven. De Gaulle was stiff and arrogant, the P.M. was frank but patient. . . . A. E. said afterwards he had never seen anything like it in the way of rudeness since Ribbentrop. Blank refusal to budge over Syrian questions, insistence on our evil motives as proved by Madagascar. Behind all this stands the evil influence of that charlatan Spears who has said "he is out to smash de Gaulle."[106]

Indeed, the entire episode of de Gaulle's Levant trip appears to have left a powerful, negative impression on Churchill's mind. Speaking before a secret session of the House of Commons on December 10, 1942, the prime minister expressed himself in words that reflected his sense of personal grievance toward de Gaulle:

> Now we are in Secret Session the House must not be led to believe that General de Gaulle is an unfaltering friend of Britain. On the contrary, I think he is one of those good Frenchmen who have a traditional antagonism engrained in French hearts by centuries of war against the English. On his

way back from Syria in the summer of 1941 . . . he left a trail of anglophobia behind him. . . .

All this and much more was very ungrateful talk, but we have allowed no complaint of ours to appear in public.

Again this year in July General de Gaulle wished to visit Syria. He promised me before I agreed to facilitate his journey, which I was very able to stop, that he would behave in a helpful and friendly manner, but no sooner did he get to Cairo than he adopted a most hectoring attitude and in Syria his whole object seemed to be to foment ill-will.[107]

Eden instructed Sir Orme Sargent of the Foreign Office to tell Dejean how shocked Churchill and he had been by de Gaulle's apparent hostility toward them and to propose that the negotiation of a settlement over the Levant be handled at the foreign ministry level. This the Free French readily agreed to.[108] As Harvey optimistically put it, "if once the professionals can get hold of this again and the prima donnas are kept out of the ring, we should soon reach agreement."[109]

Within a week, Dejean and the Foreign Office were able to draw up a draft agreement based on an interpretation of the de Gaulle–Lyttelton agreements. By the terms of this text, which largely followed the outline laid out in the Eastern Department minutes of September 23–25, the Free French would recognize Britain's right to be involved in major political decisions regarding the Levant and the FNC would formally renounce de Gaulle's demand for the handing over of the Allied military command in the territories. The agreement also provided for the creation of a mixed Anglo–French commission in London to help arbitrate disputes arising over Syria and Lebanon. As a concession to Gaullist pride, a reciprocity clause was included, giving the Free French a formal say in the running of affairs in British-controlled sectors of the Middle East. (This was seen by the Foreign Office as primarily directed toward the protection of French cultural and educational interests.) It was also understood that an announcement of elections to be held by spring 1943 would be made before the end of the year.[110]

What seemed like a reasonable compromise to the "professionals" did not sit well at all with the "prima donnas." Casey cabled his strenuous objections from the Middle East, arguing that the principle of reciprocity could be used by the Free French to justify a demand for a seat on the MESC. Instead of a reinterpretation of the 1941 Cairo accords, the minister of state demanded the negotiation of a totally new basis for Anglo–French relations in the Levant, placing the British on an equal footing with their partners in both the juridical and the practical spheres.[111] At the same time, Catroux telegraphed from Beirut urging de Gaulle not to approve the agreement precisely because he saw in it the elements that Casey complained it lacked. He viewed the draft text as effectively conceding the principle of joint rule in the Levant under cover of creating a theoretical Franco–British condominium throughout the Middle East.[112] De Gaulle indicated his concurrence with Catroux by immediately dismissing Dejean from his post and replacing him with the tougher Pleven.[113]

While the interpretive agreement itself fell by the wayside, letters that had been exchanged with Dejean over the announcement of elections and the creation of a mixed commission in London were not withdrawn by the FNC. The Foreign Office accordingly suggested that this commission could serve as the forum for a discussion of substantive issues such as the future control of the Haifa–Tripoli railway and the organization of elections. The Free French readily agreed to this.[114]

In the meantime, however, the Allied invasion of French North Africa (Operation "Torch") diverted the energy and attention of both sides away from the Levant. De Gaulle called Catroux to London for consultations as it became apparent that the Free French would have to struggle hard to gain a foothold in liberated Algeria. At the beginning of December, the acting delegate-general in Beirut, Jean Helleu, submitted a letter to Casey promising that elections would be held in April 1943 and reaffirming the intention of creating a mixed commission in London. (It was never actually formed.) This letter was regarded as replacing the unratified interpretive agreement. On December 14, a joint Anglo–Free French communiqué was issued in London announcing the signature by Eden and de Gaulle of an agreement over the administration of Madagascar, with General Legentilhomme named as the new high commissioner.[115]

The year 1942 had seen a steady, irreversible erosion of the Free French position in the Levant. Rallying the British Middle Eastern establishment behind him, Spears had taken advantage of every available opportunity to create institutions or precipitate developments that would enhance the importance of his mission's role in administering the territories. By dominating the administration of the wheat scheme, Spears placed British personnel at the center of the highest-profile form of state intervention in the Levant economy. By pressing for early elections, he undermined the Gaullists' potential bargaining power with the Arab nationalists, and hastened the replacement of French-appointed cabinets with governments that would derive their power from popular support, and owe their thanks—or so he thought—to his own intervention. The nationalists themselves were only too happy to play their assigned role for the time being, demanding full independence from the French while assuring the British of their sympathy for the Allied cause and their eagerness for British protection.

Confronted with so aggressive and resourceful an opponent as Spears, the Free French were divided over the appropriate way to respond. Catroux was painfully aware of the movement's complete dependence on London for its very existence, and considered it best to beat a strategic retreat in the face of British demands. This would allow the French to gain time without giving up their formal privileges as the mandatory authorities in the Levant. If they could manage to hold on until the end of the war and the evacuation of British troops from Syria and Lebanon, the French could still hope to retain an influential position in the Levant states by negotiating treaties of independence with them on the model of the 1936 agreements. But such prudence was not de Gaulle's way. As far as he was concerned, it was precisely the vulnerability of his movement that necessitated a confrontatory and provocative approach on his part. Otherwise, Free France would degenerate into little more than a British front organization and propaganda tool. In their overall effect, these tactics were quite successful: it can almost be said that de Gaulle singlehandedly preserved, nay embodied, the principle of French sovereignty through the war years. But within the context of the Levant, de Gaulle's calculated arrogance tended to backfire. Although the Syrians and Lebanese may have been temporarily cowed by de Gaulle's tough stance during his tour of the region, Winston Churchill was antagonized by what he saw as an unbridled display of ingratitude, and became all the more loath to acquiesce in Foreign Office suggestions that his friend Spears be dismissed.

7

The Electoral Campaigns

The Interplay of Personalities

The shift of attention to North African affairs brought about a change of actors on the Levant stage that was to leave its mark on the political evolution of the region during 1943. Free French politics during this period were dominated by the rivalry between General de Gaulle and General Giraud, whom the Americans and British had placed in charge of the civil administration in liberated French North Africa. After his trip to London in November 1942, Catroux joined de Gaulle on his visit to Washington in January and from then on most of his time was spent away from the Levant, dealing with the negotiation of a power-sharing agreement between de Gaulle and Giraud. (These talks ultimately led to the replacement of the FNC with the broader-based French Committee of National Liberation [FCNL], which, in turn, was to form the basis for the provisional government that assumed power in France following liberation in 1944.)[1] Of increasing importance in Levant affairs, therefore, was the role played by Jean Helleu, the acting delegate-general in Catroux's absence. At the same time, the U.S. government raised its profile in the region in November 1942 by appointing George Wadsworth, who had in the past taught at the American University in Beirut, as the diplomatic agent and consul-general in Beirut and Damascus. By accrediting him to the Lebanese and Syrian governments, Washington granted those regimes a measure of recognition that had been denied them before, although formal American recognition of the states' independence continued to be withheld.[2]

Jean Helleu was a professional diplomat who had served as Vichy's ambassador to Turkey before defecting to the Free French in 1942. Despite this background, Spears initially had a fairly positive attitude toward him, which stemmed in part from the British minister's antagonism toward Catroux. Spears reported that Lépissier, the pro-British secretary-general of the General Delegation, was greatly concerned that Catroux might try to maintain control over the Levant as a personal power base while he maneuvered in Algeria for a position of leadership in postwar French politics by playing off de Gaulle against Giraud as well as by maintaining contact with Vichy. Spears further reported to Churchill that Boegner, another recent defector from the Vichy camp who served as chief of the General Delegation's political cabinet, had been discovered by British intelligence to be corresponding with a Vichy agent in Ankara, raising the suspicion that he himself might be a planted agent. This, Spears asserted, could not have been going on without Catroux's knowledge and he therefore backed Lépissier's request that the British government press for the formal and permanent replacement of Catroux by Helleu as delegate-general.[3]

In fact, however, Lépissier was a less than objective source of information on the political infighting within the Free French movement. He bore Catroux a personal grievance for having allowed Boegner to emerge as the chief administrative officer and executor of policy, despite the formal primacy of the secretary-general in the mandatory setup. Lépissier was also closely associated with a growing number of left-wing republicans and members of masonic organizations who were becoming increasingly disillusioned by what they saw as the rightward drift of de Gaulle's politics and ascribed the phenomenon to the pernicious influence of various figures surrounding the general (in particular, his chief of intelligence, "Passy"). They feared that by coming to an agreement with Giraud in North Africa, the Free French movement would fall completely under the influence of Vichyite elements that would use it as a springboard for gaining political power in liberated France. Within the context of the Levant, the situation was aggravated by the continued influence wielded by those elements of the administration that had stayed on in July 1941 not so much out of enthusiasm for de Gaulle as for the various personal factors that bound them to the Levant. Many had also been swayed by the offers of easy promotion within the bureaucracy that the Gaullists had made in an effort to retain as much personnel as possible. These elements, best described as *attentistes* (and also bitingly nicknamed "les ralliés alimentaires"[4]) had a vested interest in maintaining the status quo and were resented by the progressive, republican ideologues who wanted the French community in the Levant to contribute actively to the creation of a new France. (Even more pernicious in the eyes of the left was the Jesuit order, most of the members of which did little to hide their Pétainist sympathies.)[5]

Lépissier's own perceptions came to border on the paranoid following his dismissal in April 1943, at which time he wrote a desperate letter to Professor Cassin of the FNC claiming that his life was in danger and begging Cassin to warn de Gaulle that fascists were taking over the French administration in Beirut.[6] In Cassin's view, the trouble probably stemmed from

> the personality of Madame Catroux, who surrounds herself with the rich, bourgeois elements in Beirut and created a non-democratic atmosphere around the Residency, which resulted in the false impression of a reactionary policy that was being attributed (quite wrongly no doubt) to General Catroux himself.[7]

Of course, no one was better informed than Spears about political intrigue in the Levant, and the question arises, why did he choose to pass on Lépissier's warnings in so uncritical a manner? The strongest possibility seems to be that he saw in Helleu, whose experience in the region was limited and who was an alcoholic, a malleable figure whom he could dominate far more easily than he could Catroux. With electoral campaigns impending in which the political future of the Levant states could well be determined, the British minister would want to assure himself of as free a hand as possible. Given this context, his eagerness to present London with derogatory reports about Catroux becomes more readily understandable.

Creating the Framework for Elections

Catroux's return to the Levant in late February signaled the start of serious preparations for the restoration of constitutional life in Syria and Lebanon. Spears had already leaked word of the impending elections to the Beirut and Damascus governments, but the Free French used this as an excuse for delaying their own official announcement of the decision.[8] This gave them some extra time in which to lay the groundwork for their political strategy in the trying period ahead of them. Their basic aim was to turn the elections to their advantage by ensuring that the governments that emerged would sign treaties on the model of the unratified 1936 accords. To negotiate such treaties with the existing Levant regimes would be an exercise in futility, since they had next to no legitimacy in anyone's eyes.[9] The best approach, Catroux thought, would be to set up interim governments that would themselves announce and organize the elections. This would prevent the loss of face the Free French might suffer if the current regimes, which they had appointed, attempted to take part in the elections themselves (they would inevitably be swept away). In the case of Syria, an interim regime could be created through the restoration of the 1936, National Bloc-controlled government and Parliament, which Catroux hoped would still be willing to put the 1936 treaty into effect even before elections were held. As for Lebanon, he thought a postelectoral coalition between supporters of Bishara al-Khoury and his Francophile rival Emile Edde would be the best option the Free French could hope for.[10]

The delegate-general's thinking on this question represented a major shift in approach to Levant politics. Before 1943, Free French policy had been to postpone any substantive changes in the political framework until after the war, while mollifying the Syrians and Lebanese (not to speak of the British) with cosmetic alterations in the structure of government. Over the past two years, however, it had become increasingly apparent that time was on Spears' side and that the longer a definitive settlement of Franco–Levantine relations was delayed, the more French power in the territories would erode. This consideration had convinced Catroux that it would be preferable to determine the precise nature of French privileges in the Levant as soon as possible; if elected governments were to come to power in Beirut and Damascus without recognizing postwar French rights in the region, the game would be all but lost.

Catroux was also innovative in his approach to Arab nationalism. In the past, the French had been consistently opposed to the inclusion of Syria in any pan-Arab federation, the proposals for which they had seen as British ploys for extending their own power into the Levant. After Britain's final victory at al-Alamein and the Allied landings in North Africa, both the Iraqi and the Egyptian governments had renewed the campaign for such a federation and Eden had seemed to give it an official nod of approval in his February 24, 1943 response to a question in Parliament.[11] Although Catroux was no less opposed than his predecessors to the idea of a British-dominated federation, the tactic with which he proposed to resist it was comparatively subtle. Rather than being frightened into ordering a suppression of nationalist activity in Syria and cultivating the support of minority groups at the expense of the Sunni Muslim majority, he recommended that Free France go along with the pan-Arab impulses of the National Bloc. The trick would lie in playing off the Arab regimes against each other by exploiting each one's ambition to lead the pan-Arab movement itself. The centrality of Syria to any larger regional federation ought to be emphasized, while attention was drawn to the importance of continued French protection of Syria against potential threats from British-sponsored Zionism as well as Turkish territorial ambitions. Similarly in Lebanon, the elections should be made to focus on the positive theme of Lebanon's special identity ("le Libanisme") rather than on the danger of pan-Arabism. Catroux recognized the difficulties entailed in such a major shift of policy, but felt there was no other choice:

> I do not with to conceal that the action to be undertaken in this spirit will be delicate and could be frustrated by the nature of my interlocutors, by the current weak international position of France and by the certain opposition which the British and Americans will raise to the project of a treaty.
>
> However, it is the only policy available to us; it must be liberal; at the present moment liberalism can benefit us morally—it must also be persevered in and not be allowed to be discouraged.[12]

Spears was initially relieved by Catroux's positive attitude toward the elections and effectively renounced his earlier warnings about the delegate-general's pernicious influence on the local political situation. He reported having had a friendly conversation with Catroux in which the latter declared his intention of formally resigning his post once the elections were over.

> It is clear to me that Catroux has largely lost interest in the affairs of these countries and is thinking in the main of North Africa and of his schemes there. For instance, talking of the elections, he told me that he was fed up with the whole question and wanted it out of the way.[13]

This unexpected spirit of cooperation between Catroux and Spears facilitated a relatively smooth transition to an interim government in Lebanon. The only twist to an otherwise straightforward development was President Naccache's stubborn attempt to hold on to his office. He was backed in this effort by George Wadsworth, who had been actively intervening in Levant politics from the beginning of his tenure as diplomatic agent. In lending behind-the-scenes support to Naccache in his refusal to resign, Wadsworth seemed to think he was aiding the cause of Lebanese nationalism, since Catroux was hoping to use the elections to secure French treaty rights in the country. Despite a brief groundswell of popular support for Naccache, the delegate-general decided to dissolve his government unilaterally, replacing it with a preelectoral caretaker regime headed by Dr. Ayub Tabet, a Protestant who was, ostensibly, politically neutral and who was also Spears' first choice for the post. Catroux was strongly backed in this action by the British minister, who issued a public statement of support for his proclamation of Lebanon's return to constitutional life.[14] Spears happily reported:

> Catroux's proclamation not only contains every one of the points I have contended were either essential or important if Lebanese independence was to be real, but both in his appeal to the people and in his references to the freedom they will achieve he expresses the views which we can wholeheartedly support. He has in fact been extremely responsive to my suggestions. This result justifies the very hard and prolonged struggle I have had in the past.[15]

When it came to Syria, Catroux had a trickier task to perform since his aim was to come to an understanding with the National Bloc on future French privileges in the country in return for reconvening the 1936 government as the preelectoral caretaker regime. (Being entrusted with organizing the elections would naturally mean being assured of winning them.) For Shukri al-Quwatli, this presented a painful dilemma: on the one hand, the National Bloc's electoral prospects depended on, to a large extent, the attitude adopted by the French; on the other hand, he was passionately committed to ridding Syria of all French influence once the war was over. Clearly, the role played by the British would be crucial, but he could not take British support for granted, and it would not do to become overly dependent on British support in any case. Al-Quwatli accordingly spent the spring of 1943 exploring what his range of options was and trying to juggle his relations with the French and British in such a way as to gain the maximal assurance of an electoral victory while keeping his political debts down to a minimum.

In his attempt to reach an understanding with the National Bloc, Catroux was mainly in contact with the former president, Hashem al-Atasi, who seems essentially to have acted as a frontman for al-Quwatli. These talks were held in March, when al-Quwatli let word reach the British to the effect that he was contemplating a preelectoral understanding with the French that would commit the National Bloc to the restoration of the 1936 Franco–Syrian treaty in exchange for French support in the party's electoral bid. It seems likely that his main purpose in leaking this information was to stir the Spears Mission into offering its own support to the National Bloc. In any case, Catroux was led to believe that a bargain could indeed be struck with al-Atasi. The latter initially told Catroux he was willing to agree to establish relations with the French on the basis of the 1936 treaty, but that he could not commit himself beyond the period of the war. A week later, Atasi went so far as to agree that postwar Franco–Syrian relations could be modeled on the terms of Britain's treaty rights in Iraq, but he argued that the preelectoral restoration of the 1936 government would represent a departure from the norm that Catroux had just set in Lebanon; it would therefore be better to appoint a politically neutral interim regime in Syria as well. Catroux was given to understand that, once the nationalists had won the elections, his agreement with Atasi would be operative. The advantage of this deal for the National Bloc is readily apparent: had they agreed to head the interim government, the French would have expected an immediate quid pro quo in the form of a treaty. As matters stood, Atasi had managed to secure a French policy of noninterference with the nationalist electoral bid on the promise of being open to a treaty once the elections had been won. Payment before delivery was to prove a fatal mistake for the French, although their alternatives were certainly limited.[16]

During this time, however, al-Quwatli was busy safeguarding his position by bringing the British into the game. His tactic of letting them know of the ongoing contacts with the French had already produced the desired alarm in the Spears Mission. On March 13, al-Quwatli met with Daniel Lascelles, a professional diplomat whose enthusiasm for this political game as a form of intellectual diversion neatly complemented his chief's passionate personal involvement in the struggle for influence.[17] Lascelles tried to discourage al-Quwatli from making any commitments to the French regarding treaty talks,[18] and al-Quwatli soon let the British know what he expected of them in exchange: active support for the National Bloc's effort to carry the vote on election day. This was too much even for the staff of the Spears Mission, who resented the obvious effort to play them off against the French and were antagonized by the arrogant tone the National Bloc's leader had adopted at a meeting with a representative of the British consulate in Damascus. Lascelles angrily commented as follows:

> It is doubtless too late in the day to cure Shukri Quwatli of being a pompous ass, but we hope it is not too late to convince him that we are not impressed by his Berchtesgaden manner.[19]

Apart from resenting the presumptious tone of this native chief, Lascelles also despised what he saw as an unwillingness by al-Quwatli to take his chances in the "fair play" of free elections:

> It is time someone said to these Nationalists: "For God's sake stop whining for foreign support and show a little of that courage which one is entitled to expect from an Arab. If you get in at the polls on the shoulders of a foreign power, we will have nothing to do with you. . . . If on the other hand you get in by fair means . . . then we will play ball with you. . . . Meanwhile we will not favour you or any other party: you may not understand what fair play means, but we can't help that."[20]

As it turned out, the wily al-Quwatli proved quite capable of adapting to circumstances. Moderating his tone and his demands during a 90-minute meeting with Lascelles, he gained the counselor's assurance that the British would not allow the French to intimidate the Syrian government into accepting a treaty if a duly elected parliament refused to ratify it.[21] This was all al-Quwatli had to hear. He could now rest assured that even if the French tried to hold the National Bloc to Atasi's personal word after the elections, the British would step in to save the day.[22]

Once Catroux had secured al-Atasi's promise of cooperation in the last week of March, he appointed a caretaker government under Ata Ayubi, issued a declaration (to take effect as soon as a president had been elected) rescinding Puaux's 1939 suspension of the Syrian constitution, and flew to Algeria.[23]

Spears' Falling Out with Helleu

As soon as Catroux had left, relations in the Levant reverted to their normal state of tension. In a letter he sent to Dr. Tabet, General de Gaulle assumed the patronizing tone that had offended so often in the past, referring to the "centuries-old link . . . which unites Lebanon and France." Spears reported:

> It is known from reliable secret sources that many influential Fighting French officials in Beirut were horrified at what they regarded as a dangerously liberal solution of the problem [Catroux's preelectoral political settlement]; these officials will doubtless welcome de Gaulle's language.[24]

The sudden tangibility of the approaching electoral campaigns seemed to act as a catalyst for an intensified Anglo–French struggle for control; this was especially the case in Lebanon, where the complexity of the confessional and political structure lent itself readily to suspicion and intrigue.

During his November visit to London, Catroux had already indicated to Maurice Peterson that "the results of the elections would not be left to chance" and an Eastern Department official had suggested that "in the circ[umstance]s the most practical plan may be to agree with the French authorities, if we can, on the persons to be favoured."[25] By February, the Spears Mission had been reporting that the Free French were drawing up lists of candidates regarded as pro-British or strongly nationalist, whose electoral bids were to be blocked. These included prominent Maronites such as Hamid Franjieh and Camille Chamoun as well as Sunni leaders like Riad al-Solh.[26] Despite Spears' and Catroux's agreement on the makeup of the interim government in Beirut, mutual suspicions began to mount again in April regarding possible preparations for electoral rigging. A proposal by Spears that a tripartite commission consisting of British, French, and American officials be set up to monitor the fairness of the Levant elections was viewed by Helleu as a ploy designed to "substitute a condominium for the particular responsibilities of France."[27]

Of much greater significance was an episode involving a political figure in Tripoli by the name of Rashid Mukaddam. Apart from being a protégé of the French and their preferred candidate for the local parliamentary seat, Mukaddam also ran a drug-smuggling operation with the help of some British officers who were paid to transport hashish to Egypt in their military trucks. The discovery of this operation led to Mukaddam's arrest by the British military, which handed him over to the French for trial. The latter, who were themselves notoriously lax about the drug trade, were convinced that the arrest was politically motivated, for it had removed "their man" from the political scene in Tripoli, leaving Abdul Hamid Karami as the only viable candidate. This was a figure associated with Riad al-Solh's pan-Arab grouping, who was suspected by the French of seeking a seat in the Chamber of Deputies only in order to call for Lebanon's absorption into a Greater Syrian state. The picture was rounded off by allegations that Karami was receiving money from the British.[28]

A plethora of other issues also served to exacerbate tensions during the spring of 1943. When disturbances occurred in Hama and Aleppo over allegations of land purchases in Syria by Jews from Palestine, Spears sought to establish British monitoring of the Syrian government's management of all land sales. Since this was one of the administrative responsibilities that the French had recently turned over to the Syrians, the former were understandably antagonized by what they saw as a cynical attempt to exploit their good will.[29] The French were also galled by Spears' direct approach to the Syrian government over the question of enlisting troops for the Middle East theater from among the native population; the MESC was accused of severely restricting the supply of paper to the French authorities in the Levant as a means of limiting their ability to influence public opinion through the written word. For his part, Spears insisted it was the French who were responsible for the tension by persisting in their obstructive policies: the tough police force known as the *Gardes Mobiles* (under the command of the *Services Spéciaux*) was terrorizing the native population throughout the land, he claimed. He also criticized the General Delegation for maintaining complete control over the common interests, which represented the main source of revenue for the Levant states. In general, Spears argued, the French placed their own narrow political interests first, and basic considerations of regional security and efficient administration second.[30]

The spring of 1943 also witnessed an attempt by the French to assert greater control over the OCP. Apart from its general concern with preserving stability in Syria and Lebanon, His Majesty's government felt it had a certain moral claim to joint control of the Wheat Office by virtue of the Treasury's guarantee of the OCP against whatever financial liabilities it might incur in the course of its transactions. This was a claim that the FNC hoped to undermine by terminating the effective subsidization of the OCP's wheat purchases. The issue came to the fore in May 1943, when the Free French *Caisse Centrale* refused to provide the Wheat Office with credit to cover the difference between the price which it had paid for the wheat harvest and the price at which the grain had been resold to the public by the Syrian government. The FNC insisted that the Syrians would have to pay back the difference themselves by raising taxes if need be.[31]

Of course, this move was immediately recognized by the British as an attempt to do away effectively with the wheat plan so as to secure exclusive French control of grain collection and distribution. Since, in the event of a

renewed bread shortage, it was the British who would once again be responsible for the import of wheat into Syria, they were completely unwilling to
indulge the French over this issue. To complicate matters even further, Helleu
himself proved most reluctant to follow his instructions. He appears to have
sympathized entirely with the Syrian government's reluctance to impose unpopular economic measures before the elections, even though it was only
supposed to be an interim administration with no political ambition of its own.
Appealing to Catroux for support, Helleu argued that the FNC was exaggerating the significance of the Wheat Office's deficit and that the matter should be
dropped. After a threat from the British military command that it would take
over the wheat scheme unless the OCP was refinanced, the French gave in
and agreed to issue a long-term credit guaranteed by the British Treasury.[32]

Helleu's willfullness over this matter was typical of a pattern of behavior
on his part that was causing increasing concern in many quarters of the Free
French movement. The manner in which he carried out his functions appeared to reflect a degree of insouciance and negligence that would have been
less alarming in some obscure colonial backwater than it was in the politically
central Levant. The delegate-general's apathy was particularly worrisome in
this preelectoral period, when the situation was in flux and the future of
French political control in the region could well hinge on a few vital decisions.
At the end of May 1943, the FNC wired Helleu to complain that he had not
sent any information on the local political situation since March. In an indig-
nant reply, Helleu insisted that the monthly reports he sent by diplomatic bag
were entirely sufficient. Ostensibly giving in to the demand for more information, he went on to report that not much was happening apart from personal
intrigues among the various parliamentary candidates, intrigues which the
British seemed eager to exploit for their own interests. In and of themselves,
these intrigues were of no real importance, and the British interference had
already been reported on in other cables.[33]

From Cairo, Admiral Auboyneau of the Free French mission sent a very
delicately phrased message recommending that Catroux return immediately
to the Levant to take charge of affairs before the elections took place:

> Helleu is esteemed by all and lacks neither tact nor firmness, but I fear that
> he may overestimate the strength of our position and underestimate the
> danger of English intrigues. Even if he were not handicapped by his position
> as Catroux's lieutenant and deputy, he would not, in my judgment, have the
> authority and prestige necessary in order effectively to defend the interests of
> France under these difficult circumstances.[34]

Spears' later evaluation of the man was more succinct, if less kind:

> Helleu himself was very undistinguished and a typical alcoholic. He was of
> lower middle height and had a slight shake. He made me think of an anteater
> because of his long nose, which, unlike that of the animal, was red at the tip,
> but seemed to be forever sniffing for something. His voice was plaintive and
> he wore a continuous simper. . . . In times of crisis he would disappear to a
> shed at the bottom of his garden armed with a large bottle of whisky.[35]

Auboyneau's warning notwithstanding, developments at Algiers continued to overshadow decisions concerning the Levant. The signing of an accord between de Gaulle and Giraud at the beginning of June meant that Catroux would stay on as a member of the new FCNL. Helleu was duly appointed delegate-general of Syria and Lebannon, with elections scheduled to take place around July 10. Spears reported that, although the conclusion of the Algiers accord had, unfortunately, strengthened the general French position in the Levant, Catroux's formal replacement as delegate-general had "greatly disconcerted [pro-French] politicians such as Jawad Boulos, the Lebanese M[inister] [of] F[oreign] A[ffairs], who were counting on the General's strong arm to hoist them into Parliament."[36]

The British Policy Debate

While Helleu was busy reporting on the absence of any developments worth reporting, a sharp debate was in fact under way between the Foreign Office and the British Middle Eastern establishment over the nature of the goals to be pursued in the region. This clash of views took place within the context of a wider discussion of the pros and cons of an Arab federation as a solution to the problems attending British rule in the Middle East.

A new round of sharp dissension had arisen between the Foreign Office and Spears over the narrower issue of Anglo–French relations in the Levant during the winter and spring of 1943. The trouble had started with ministerial consultations during Casey's visit to London in December 1942, which had resulted in what Spears viewed as a soft policy toward the Free French. He was particularly outraged by the Treasury's acquiescence in continued French control of the common interests in the Levant and the Foreign Office's acceptance of Catroux's avowed intention of using this control as a bargaining counter in future treaty negotiations with the Syrians and Lebanese. His ire was also provoked by the apparent refusal of the Foreign Office to force the French to allow British military enlistment among the local population. As Spears portrayed it, the ministries were sacrificing vital British military interests for the sake of a cozy relationship with the French in London.[37] After being warned not to go over the heads of the French authorities in seeking the acquiescence of the Levant governments in a British enlistment drive, Spears wrote a bitter letter to Eden decrying Foreign Office policy as one of appeasement:

> We who are quite close to the more direct and simple problems of the war feel sometimes galled beyond endurance when the French, who have done nothing but oppose us (until Catroux's change of heart), are constantly supported in London. . . . What I am quite certain of is that the obstructive attitude of the [French] National Committee . . . in regard to the Levant States has been due more than anything else to the knowledge that if they do take up a disputed question in London they will generally find the Foreign Office only too anxious to take their side. . . .
>
> You know I have a great affection for you . . . and I cannot bear to think that the belief should be allowed to grow that some people under your orders

do not hesitate to thwart the Army and the war effort because of a pusillanimous attitude and an ingrained desire to appease.[38]

With the Eastern Department in an uproar over Spears' provocative language, Eden wrote him a response rejecting the distinction between his
(Eden's) attitude and the policy of his ministry. He pointed out that the
substance of Spears' complaint over the enlistment effort had in fact been
resolved to British satisfaction as the result of no small effort on the part of
the Foreign Office. Spears, Eden complained, seemed to regard the ministry
as damned if it did and damned if it did not intervene in issues affecting the
Levant:

> If we see the French here over Levantine questions we are allowing the
> French to intrigue with us: if we do not see them, we are being insufficiently
> firm. What do you expect a poor Department to do?[39]

Although Spears desisted from direct confrontation with the Foreign Office at this point, he increased indirect pressure for a revision of British policy
toward the Gaullist movement. A major opportunity for this was provided by
Casey's decision to convene the MEWC in May in order to review the major
questions affecting British interests in the Middle East such as the Palestine
problem and the possibility of creating an Arab federation. Despite Eden's
public expressions of sympathy for the federation movement, Whitehall was
not enthusiastic about the idea, fearing that Arab unity could easily be turned
into a weapon in the hands of those elements most hostile to Britain's Palestine policy. The War Cabinet's Subcommittee on Palestine had recommended
in January 1942 that Britain restrict itself to the encouragement of cultural and
economic association among the Arab states, leaving the question of closer
political cooperation to be reexamined in the postwar period. Nonetheless,
there remained a strong current of opinion within the British establishment,
both in London and in the Middle East, which held that a solution to the
Palestine problem would in fact be facilitated by the inclusion of Arab Palestine in a larger regional political framework; however, even the most modest
federation plan would have to encompass not only Transjordan and Palestine
but also Syria and Lebanon, in view of the cultural and economic bonds
linking these four domains together. Any proposal for the creation of an Arab
federation under British auspices therefore immediately begged the question
of how this was to be reconciled with a continued French presence in the
Levant states.[40]

In the view of many British officials of long standing in the Middle East,
the best way to deal with the obstacle of French rule in the Levant states was
simply to remove it. As Glubb Pasha, the commander of Transjordan's Arab
Legion, saw it, Britain's tutelary role in the Arab world would have to be
redefined within the context of some form of international supervision and
with allowance made for the growing appeal of the federation movement. In
his view, the Arab countries were not yet ready for full independence, however, and Britain was also obliged to protect its strategic interests in the

region. In order to facilitate the continuation of British influence in the Middle East during the inevitable instability of the postwar period, it was vital that the number of potentially disruptive factors be reduced to a minimum. Continued French rule in the Levant numbered high on Glubb's list of such factors. The patterns of French and English colonial government were far too different from each other to permit any coordination of policy, let alone a joint fostering of Arab federation. Moreover, Glubb warned, a postwar renewal of the Anglo-French alliance was not to be counted on, given the hostility that already characterized relations with de Gaulle:

> Now France in Syria is the only Great Power in a position to threaten our Middle East life line. The eviction of Italy from Libya and Abyssinia leaves no other potential rival anywhere near the field. . . .
>
> The possible hostility of independent Egypt, Iraq or Syria is, in a serious crisis, of altogether minor importance *as long as no foreign power has a foot in these countries.* It is at least possible, if not probable, that France will be resentful and hostile to Britain after this war. An elementary knowledge of human nature is enough to convince us that, if we freely restore her independence and her empire to France, she will loathe us for it. In view of this fact, it is surely tempting fate to allow her to maintain herself in Syria, or even the Lebanon, in a splendid strategic position to cut our life line to the East by invasion of Palestine, by submarine activities in the Mediterranean from Beyrout, or by air activity all over the Middle East [italics in original].

Although he did not propose a direct, physical expulsion of the French from Syria, Glubb strongly recommended that they be "maneuvered" out of the region, possibly with the aid of an offer of territorial compensation in another part of the world. Administrative responsibility for the territory could then be assumed either by the United States or Britain.[41]

This approach to the Levant question was shared by Harold MacMichael, high commissioner of Palestine,[42] and with such a firm basis of support, Spears found it easy to win Casey over to an avowedly anti-French line. At the conclusion of its May 1943 conference, the MEWC formally recommended that

> The continued presence of France in the Levant is incompatible with our political and military interests in the Middle East as well as with the peaceful development and well being of the Arab countries.
>
> From the long-term stragegic angle the presence of an unco-operative and unreliable foreign power in the Levant States represents a permanent danger. . . .
>
> Any form of closer political association between the Arab States or even between the States of "Greater Syria" . . . a development to which His Majesty's Government have declared themselves sympathetic, is hardly possible as long as the French maintain any direct influence, political or military, in Syria and Lebanon.[43]

Although it paid lip service to the constraints imposed by Britain's formal obligations to the Free French, the MEWC argued that their removal from the scene could be achieved through indirect means, such as the further encouragement of the independence movements in Syria and Lebanon, the obstruction of Franco–Levantine treaty talks and a broader interpretation of the British military command's rights under the terms of the de Gaulle–Lyttelton agreements.

The Foreign Office was greatly perturbed by this blatant challenge to established policy, Peterson remarking that: "On Syria Mr. Casey has sold himself to Sir E. Spears much in the manner of Dr. Faustus."[44] Cadogan and Eden both agreed that the MEWC had gotten its priorities wrong and a note to this effect was sent to Churchill with the suggestion that Casey might be recalled to London for a refresher course on British foreign policy.[45] The Foreign Office was, however, well aware that Casey's outlook was merely a reflection of the underlying sentiment among British officialdom in the region, and that Whitehall's ability to shape events would remain limited as long as such views remained prevalent in the Middle Eastern establishment:

> Although His Majesty's Government have promised General de Gaulle that France shall have the predominant place among European powers in the Levant, this idea has never found acceptance among British subjects in the Middle East. Virtually every British officer and a large proportion of British officials everywhere in the Middle East, as the French must know perfectly well, *hope* to see the French turned out of Syria. . . . The MEWC resolutions of 10th May last are the most authoritative exposition of this view which has reached London. This much upsets the French who think we are playing a double game (though they presumably do not know of MEWC resolutions) [italics in original].[46]

The French certainly did see Arab federation schemes as posing a direct threat to their position in the Levant. Although they were not indeed privy to the deliberations of the MEWC, their worst fears concerning British intentions seemed to be confirmed by a variety of indirect sources and indications. The 1942 appointment of Lord Moyne, known as a proponent of Arab federation, to the number-two position under Casey in Cairo was taken as a potentially ominous sign. The French took a similar view of the favor with which the mandatory authorities in Palestine seemed to look on Dr. Judah Magnes' *Ichud* ("Unity") movement, which advocated the creation of a binational state in Palestine within the context of a wider Arab federation.[47] The British press was regularly scanned for articles on the movement for a Greater Syria, plenty of which were to be found.[48] As has already been seen, the efforts exerted by Iraqi, Egyptian, and Transjordanian leaders on behalf of various unification schemes were almost invariably perceived by the French as being prompted, if not actively coordinated, by the British (although in fact the latter usually discouraged such independent Arab initiatives). It was feared that institutions such as the MESC were intended to serve as the foundation for an economic and political union of the Arab world under British auspices.[49]

The London Talks

Given the gap in perspective between London and Cairo, the Foreign Office felt it would be impossible to arrive at a coherent and well-coordinated Middle Eastern policy unless differences were thoroughly hashed out in face-to-face discussions in London. Casey was accordingly summoned to the capital at the end of June, joined at the last minute by Spears.[50] René Massigli, in charge of foreign affairs for the FCNL, also arrived to take part in talks on the Levant. It was hoped that in the coolness of England tensions would ease, perspectives would change and understanding would be reached.

As far as Spears was concerned, his visit to Britain simply presented another opportunity for conveying his views on the Levant directly to the sources of political authority. In a lengthy memorandum written at the beginning of July, he not only recapitulated his list of complaints against Free French conduct in Syria, but he also called for a radical change in Britain's overall policy toward France. The establishment of a provisional government in liberated France by Generals de Gaulle and Giraud, he warned, would lead to the creation of a right-wing, undemocratic and imperialistic regime that would soon come into conflict with Anglo–American interests in the Middle East and elsewhere. It would be far more prudent to foster the creation of a popularly elected, left-wing government. Spears reminded his readers that it was Leon Blum's Popular Front government that had negotiated the 1936 treaties with Syria and Lebanon. In effect, what Spears seemed to be saying was that a left-wing government in France was likely to be far more pusillanimous and easy to influence than one led by de Gaulle:

> A government elected by the free will of the people, Left-wing in tendency, is most likely to suit our purpose since it would be most likely to collaborate with us and to carry out the promises of independence given to the Levant States.

The sincerity of Spears' respect for the democratic process was further reflected in the following:

> It may be argued that de Gaulle is the hero of France and that popular clamour will hail him as leader. His participation in the Committee of National Liberation will tend in time to dim his glory, our disapproval voiced no doubt by discreet propaganda will create doubt as to his position, which fundamentally depends upon our backing, and contact between this megalomaniac and popular leaders must inevitably lead to a clash which will in time destroy him in the minds of the masses.

As for the immediate problems in the Levant, Spears recommended that the French be asked to recognize what amounted to full British partnership in the running of the Levant states; failing that, the Ninth Army would unilaterally assume the exclusive control of all economic and financial affairs in Syria and Lebanon.[51]

Although Spears had originally prepared this report at the request of the

Foreign Office, he took the liberty of sending it directly to the prime minister's office as well, and Churchill's immediate reaction was enthusiastically positive. In a note to Eden, he wrote, "this is a very powerful and able paper, and I think it should certainly be printed and circulated to the Cabinet. . . . I had no idea the French were behaving so tyrannically." He urged that the Syrian question be taken up for consideration at a special cabinet meeting.[52] Indeed, the tenor of Spears' argument corresponded perfectly to the prime minister's hostile attitude toward de Gaulle during this period. Both Britain and the United States had yet to extend formal recognition to the FCNL, and in late May, during his visit to Washington where the anti-Gaullist spirit prevailed, Churchill had actually telegraphed to London calling for a complete break with the Free French.[53] On July 6, Oliver Harvey had observed:

> P.M. is being unbelievably tiresome over the French. He is now seeking to prevent early recognition of the combined [Giraud–de Gaulle] Committee as untimely. He is getting crazy on the subject. There is no alternative committee in sight. . . . Spears is here on leave, intriguing and spreading poison, A. E[den] is fed up with the way French policy is taken out of his hands.[54]

According to Harvey, after receiving Churchill's minute in praise of Spears' paper, Eden found it difficult to contain his anger at a dinner with the premier: "The paper is in flat disagreement with our Syrian policy. A.E. was so furious that I feared an explosion at the dinner."[55]

As is apparent from Harvey's diary entries, the Foreign Office did not take a favorable view of Spears' memorandum. While accepting his indictment of Free French policy in the Levant, both Eden and the Eastern Department staff rejected the radical solutions he proposed and the wider implications of his anti-French outlook. In a note for cabinet circulation drafted by Maurice Peterson and signed by Eden, both the premises and the conclusions of Spears' argument were forcefully challenged:

> Most of the validity which Sir E. Spears' arguments possess disappears with the recognition that the French hold a position in the Eastern Mediterranean which cannot be wholly jettisoned unless it is our intention to limit the postwar role of France and, incidentally, to create a vacuum in the Middle East which may not be easy to fill.

Peterson went on to lay partial responsibility for the tension in the Levant on Spears' shoulders and to argue that his paper exaggerated both the importance of British interests in Syria and the significance of the local nationalist movement. As for Spears' call for the establishment of a new Popular Front government in postwar France as a means of securing Anglo–American interests, the Foreign Office questioned the assumption that British and American interests would be identical. The implication seems to have been that it might be wiser for Britain to keep the French Empire alive as a partner in the face of possible American expansionism. The memorandum concluded with an optimistic assertion that the difficulties over the Levant could be largely overcome in the course of the forthcoming talks with Massigli, which would provide a much more productive forum for negotiation than the heady atmosphere of Beirut.[56]

In response to this angry rebuttal, Churchill agreed to cancel plans for a cabinet meeting on the subject and leave the matter to be dealt with through negotiation; however, he reiterated his conviction that:

> We are being knocked about unduly and unfairly by the French and that stiffer line should be taken against them in Syria. I should like to feel that our Officers there will be supported against ill-usage by the French, and that our Commander-in-Chief will not have to make ignominious compromises when he has overwhelming force at his disposal.[57]

The prime minister's passionate resentment of the Free French at this juncture and his reference to ignominious compromises can be understood against the background of events in Lebanon, where new developments in the Mukaddam affair had taken place just after Spears' departure toward the end of June. Convinced that the whole case represented nothing but a preelectoral ploy by the British, Helleu held a perfunctory trial for Mukaddam before a military tribunal which listened to the damning testimony of several British witnesses and then acquitted the accused. When the outraged General Holmes threatened to rearrest Mukaddam if the French did not expel him from the Levant themselves, Helleu ordered that he be placed under protective custody. Reluctant to provoke an armed clash between British and French soldiers, Holmes then backed down and agreed that Mukaddam could be allowed to stand for election in Tripoli provided he remained under house arrest. The case could be reopened after the elections.[58]

Helleu saw this agreement as a great victory, crowing that:

> This success will not fail to produce a considerable repercussion throughout the country and [public] opinion will interpret it as bearing witness to our resolution and firmness in the face of British demands.[59]

He also reported with satisfaction on the scheduling of the Lebanese elections for late September, despite British pressure for an earlier date.[60] In fact, the delegate-general's victory proved to be Pyrrhic, for its only lasting effect was to antagonize the British and reinforce the image they already had of the French colonial administration as narrow-minded and corrupt. Daniel Lascelles, in charge of the Spears Mission during his chief's absence, described the acquittal of Mukaddam as indicative of the French determination to rig the Lebanese elections. He thought it better to postpone the vote indefinitely rather than allow this to happen, and then went on to call the continued existence of Greater Lebanon into question in view of the sense of alienation that prevailed among the Muslim population. Alarmed by this bitter tone, the Eastern Department rejected the notion of playing around with political boundaries during wartime and recommended that the French should be restrained from going too far in their attempts at influencing the outcome of elections, "without making too much of it if we fail."[61]

The prime minister was not about to let the Foreign Office get away with such a lax attitude. As had been the case ten months earlier when Casey had been ready to accede to de Gaulle's demand for talks to be held in Beirut instead of Cairo, Churchill's spleen was provoked by the thought of Britain suffering public humiliation at the hands of the Free French:

> There is no doubt that the Army Commander gave in because he was doubt-ful of support from home. It seems also certain that de Gaulle is revenging himself upon us in Syria. In my opinion we should have a complete show-down about Syria, both with the Committee of National Liberation in Algiers and on the spot [in London].[62]

When the matter was brought up in the cabinet at Churchill's demand, it was decided to leave it for Eden to deal with in his discussions with Massigli.[63]

As far as Massigli and other professional diplomats in the leading circles of the Free French movement were concerned, Helleu's handling of the Mukad-dam case was an unmitigated embarrassment. They let the Foreign Office know that they had been on the verge of ordering Helleu to back down when word had come of the compromise with General Holmes. Now, in the face of British pressure for an abrogation of the agreement, the Free French appara-tus still in London began sending recriminating telegrams to Helleu. There was no doubt in the minds of Massigli and his colleagues that Mukaddam was indeed guilty as charged and they also decried Helleu's inconsistency in agree-ing to a reopening of the case after the elections. This, they pointed out, was naturally taken by the British as a tacit admission of Mukaddam's guilt, while at the same time it could safely be assumed that, once elected, he would claim parliamentary immunity from prosecution. It was foolish, Massigli argued, to associate French prestige and influence with a drug smuggler. Why not let him be deported and replace him with a more likely candidate for the Tripoli district?[64] In an internal memorandum, Helleu's judgment was called into question: "Although it is difficult to find honest candidates in the Levant, it is regrettable that our choice fell upon Makaddam." While it was true that the British political officers seemed to be promoting nationalist and pan-Arab candidates in the electoral campaigns, "a certain nervousness is nevertheless being displayed by our authorities, who tend to ascribe a political character to local incidents."[65] As a result of Helleu's repeated protests and complaints to FCNL headquarters in Algiers claiming that Massigli was selling out to the English, the matter was left open until the very eve of the Lebanese elections, at which point Spears finally induced Helleu to have Mukaddam's name with-drawn from the Tripoli list. The British then deported him to Cyprus, whence he returned only to die.[66]

Although it cast a long shadow over the London talks, the Mukaddam case was certainly not the only subject of discussion. Unfortunately, the results of the talks were as inconclusive as ever. As usual, there was an utter lack of clarity over who was really in charge on either side, let alone what each party's authoritative position was on any given issue. Thus, Spears and Casey were in favor of pressing for a change in Helleu's status from delegate-general to ambassador (an idea originally promoted by George Wadsworth). The Foreign Office rejected this as unnecessarily provocative, but since Spears had Churchill's ear, the latter brought the topic up at his July 7 meeting with Massigli.[67] Although one of the main issues Massigli wished to raise with the British was the disruptive nature of Spears' role in the Levant, he found that Spears himself was among his main interlocutors. At the July 7 meeting, Massigli found Spears at Churchill's side, leaving him with no choice but to smile and nod as the prime minister repeatedly assured him that Britain had no colonial ambitions in Syria. The Foreign Office was reduced to relying on Spears for an account of the meetings.[68]

For his part, Massigli was handicapped by his own embarrassment over Helleu's sometimes bizarre conduct. He seemed to agree with Spears' opinion that the delegate-general was lazy, indecisive, and reluctant to assume responsibility, and that his ex-Vichyite subordinates, Boegner and Blanchet, were exploiting his vulnerability to make trouble.[69] At the same time, Massigli's freedom of maneuver was undercut by a telegram from de Gaulle, who was concerned by indications of undue moderation on his part and called into question the whole point of his mission:

> It does not seem that you are in a very good position to negotiate in London over this very grave matter, distant as you are from the Committee of Liberation and without sufficient information. You must certainly find it vexing that General Catroux, who has an exceptional knowledge of the subject and who just returned from Syria yesterday cannot be consulted in the course of negotiation, a practical impossibility if it takes place in London. Finally, it seems awkward for us to enter important talks concerning the States of the Levant under French mandate as long as the London Government has not recognized the Committee of Liberation.[70]

In the end, the only concrete agreement reached in London was one concerning the integration of Syria and Lebanon into a new franc bloc as part of a wider arrangement affecting all the colonies under Free French control. This came over the vociferous objections of Spears and Casey, who would have liked to see the Levant kept within the sterling zone. It was agreed, however, that the relationship between the Levant currencies and sterling would remain fixed at existing rates.[71]

Closely linked to its hope of settling differences with the French had been the Foreign Office's intention of curbing Spears' provocative behavior. Before his visit to London, the idea of doing away with the Spears Mission had once again been floated by the Eastern Department, only to meet with objections from Casey, who was opposed to any administrative reorganization as long as the elections had not actually been held. Eden continued to believe that a smooth start to relations with the just-formed FCNL would be facilitated by finding "something [in London] for Sir E. Spears to do." Not surprisingly, however, after making discreet inquiries at both the General Staff and the Ministry of Information, Alexander Cadogan (the permanent undersecretary at the Foreign Office) reported that both were less than eager to find a post for Spears.[72]

The most the Foreign Office could hope for, accordingly, was that it might manage to bridle its wayward minister. In view of the state of personal relations between Spears and the policymakers at Whitehall, this too seemed like a long shot. He was well aware of the hostility the Eastern Department staff bore him, and he returned the sentiment in full. After his first meeting with the supervising undersecretary and the head of the Eastern Department, he set the following impressions down in his journal:

> Peterson is not at all what I had expected, big, flabby, with sunken eyes, cloaked with a hostility that will I feel never disappear. Baxter is the wettest thing I have ever come across. He just drips as he trots behind his chief, mindful only of following faithfully in his chief's steps. There was no question of even attempting to discuss the general situation in Syria.[73]

All else having failed, the Foreign Office was reduced to issuing Spears with a revised set of instructions emphasizing the importance of respecting French rights in the Levant. Whereas on the previous occasion it had been Spears himself who had the main say in defining his official order of business, this time the text contained the unmistakable stamp of Peterson's outlook:

> We can claim partnership with the French in all matters affecting the war effort, but we do not seek equal status, or claim partnership with them in the Levant. This last principle must determine the attitude we should adopt towards the forthcoming elections. . . . We should take steps to combat any suggestion that the election is in any way a trial of strength between the French and ourselves.

Reference was made in the instructions to Spears' frequently implied assertion that Free French rights in Syria and Lebanon were derived from the British military conquest of the territories and could therefore be revoked at will:

> This is not the view of His Majesty's Government. . . . The 9th Army cannot be regarded as an army of occupation, nor can His Majesty's Government claim to be an occupying Power in the Levant States. Our relations with the French are based on the Lyttelton–de Gaulle agreements . . . and on the public statements by the Prime Minister quoted in your original instructions.

The crux of Foreign Office policy toward the French was expressed in the following terms:

> Now that the French representatives in Beirut are to be controlled from Algiers, . . . it is more than ever necessary that our policy in Syria should be considered in relation, not only to our policy in the Middle East as a whole, but also to the French as a whole. It is essential that our interventions in Levant affairs should be so framed as not to give legitimate grounds to the French, either in the Levant or outside, to consider them to be part of a plan to oust them from the Levant altogether . . . or to whittle away and encroach upon this position for reasons of our own. The French are all too prone to suspicions of this sort. I shall, therefore, count on you to see that everything is done to allay such suspicion locally so that Levant questions may not

undesirably complicate our relations with the French and United States authorities in North Africa.[74]

In fact, however, Maurice Peterson entertained few illusions concerning the effectiveness of these words:

> In truth the leopard cannot change his spots and I have very little confidence in Sir E. Spears' ability either to understand or to carry out our intentions. At present he has been brought to pay lip service to the ruling that we are not to aim at turning the French out of the Levant. But it is no more than lip service and nobody who heard him at our recent discussions with M. Massigli . . . can fail to be conscious how Sir E. Spears is certain to rub the French up the wrong way on every possible occasion.

Peterson also expressed reservations about Casey's role, indicating that the current anti-Gaullist press campaign in the United States was at least in part due to his indiscreet criticism of the Free French in his discussions with U.S. government officials during a visit to Washington half a year earlier. Peterson hoped it would be possible to relieve the minister of state of his responsibility for Anglo–French relations in the Middle East once the FCNL had acquired the status of a provisional government.[75]

Had Peterson had access to Spears' private diary, he would have found his worst fears confirmed:

> Casey and I both came to the conclusion independently that the new set of instructions were an attempt by the department to handcuff me. They are full of loop-holes anyhow.[76]

The Levant Elections

During Spears' absence, life in the Levant was far from dull, but he could rest assured that his line of action vis-à-vis the French was being loyally maintained by his deputy, Lascelles. The main focus of political dynamics during this period, apart from the Mukaddam affair, was a constitutional crisis set off in Lebanon by Helleu's decision to authorize an increase in the proportion of seats to be occupied by Christians in the soon-to-be-elected Chamber of Deputies. The initiative for this disruptive move came from President Tabet, head of the interim government, who seemed intent on gaining as much political capital as possible from his brief stint in office. Before giving Tabet the green light, Helleu did secure the approval of Catroux, who was now in overall charge of Muslim Affairs for the FCNL. It is unclear, however, whether the latter understood the implications of Helleu's telegram, which simply referred to an increase in the number of parliamentary seats without specifying that ten of the twelve new seats were to go to Christian deputies.[77] The total number of seats was thus to increase from forty-two (twenty-two Christian and twenty Muslim) to fifty-four (thirty-two Christian and twenty-two Muslim). The formal justification for the move was that the old proportion was based on the

1932 census, which had failed to take into account those Lebanese living abroad, most of whom were Christian. Within two days of Spears' departure on June 22, the Lebanese government issued decrees that formally instituted the new arrangement, prompting the Muslim political leadership to threaten to boycott the elections. The French intention of setting an identical polling date in late July for both Syria and Lebanon accordingly had to be abandoned. Curiously, both Helleu and Lascelles hoped to use the extra time to undermine the other's influence over the final outcome of the voting.[78]

Matters were further complicated by Catroux's two-week tour of the Levant in mid-July. Meeting with Lebanese political leaders, Catroux sought to foster a compromise along the lines of a proposal made by Egyptian premier Nahas Pasha for a 29:25 Christian–Muslim ratio in the Chamber of Deputies.[79] However, Helleu felt his own position threatened by Catroux's presence in the region and resented the commissioner's personal attempt to defuse the political crisis. Claiming unconvincingly that he had been on the verge of resolving the problem himself before Catroux's visit, Helleu argued that French authority had been seriously undermined by the acceptance of Nahas Pasha's mediation effort. He sought to win Massigli's support by writing him that Catroux was claiming that the Levant fell under his jurisdiction as commissioner for Muslim Affairs rather than under that of the Ministry of Foreign Affairs.[80] Lascelles actually gained a similar impression of Catroux's motives, reporting to Eden that he was trying to establish himself as the real power broker in the Levant while undermining Helleu's position. He also repeated a conjecture that Spears had made some months earlier, that Catroux's recent adoption of an accommodating stance on Levant issues reflected his hope of gaining British support in the power struggle with de Gaulle that was sure to develop in the newly expanded Free French executive committee. This is not to say that Lascelles was an admirer of Helleu, whom he described as utterly incompetent and completely subject to the influence of the ex-Vichyite clique in the Grand Serail (the building housing the General Delegation in Beirut).[81]

Helleu did go so far as to follow Catroux's recommendation that the Lebanese government be reshuffled and Ayub Tabet replaced as president and prime minister (both posts which he had held) by the Greek Orthodox Petro Trad and Abdullah Beyhum (a member of the Muslim political committee that had threatened the boycott), respectively. Pending Spears' return, however, the political deadlock remained unresolved as the influential Maronite Patriarch continued to hold out for a 35:28 parliamentary ratio in favor of the Christians.[82]

In the meantime, the electoral process went ahead on schedule in Syria, where reports were widespread of the understanding between al-Atasi and Catroux over the conclusion of a treaty after a National Bloc victory.[83] The delegate in Damascus, General Collet, who had been closely associated with Taj al-Din, became conveniently ill and stayed out of sight throughout July before leaving for Morocco.[84] In primary elections held in mid-July, the nationalists wielded their influence effectively with little or no interference from the

French, except in the Alawite territory, where they refused to dismiss the antinationalist *muhafiz* ("governor"), Shawqat Abbas.[85] The results boded well for a National Bloc victory at the end of the month, and Shukri al-Quwatli was reported to be "confident that everything had been 'nicely arranged' in advance (by himself)" everywhere except for Homs and Latakia. The Eastern Department's Hankey commented that "elections are a travesty of democracy in the East anyway. This looks none too bad."[86] On July 26, the National Bloc swept the secondary elections, and two weeks later, the new Parliament elected Shukri al-Quwatli as president of the republic by an overwhelming majority.[87]

While the political progress of the National Bloc went ahead according to plans, the French found their ambitions being rapidly thwarted. Hashem al-Atasi had withdrawn from the electoral race at the last minute, effectively voiding the personal understanding Catroux had reached with him over the early conclusion of a Franco–Syrian treaty. The desirability of such a treaty being concluded in wartime also remained the subject of uncertainty and controversy among the British. Soon after his return to the region, Spears was told by al-Quwatli that he did not feel bound by Atasi's word and that he had no intention of allowing the French to retain any privileges in his country even if the fomenting of popular unrest proved to be the only means of dislodging them. Both Spears and Lascelles supported his stand. At the same time, however, the Foreign Office was reconsidering its position on the subject. In July, it had still held that the FCNL could not commit itself to a treaty in the name of France, but in August, the head of the Eastern Department sent a dispatch to Campbell, the ambassador in Washington, D.C., asking him to find out what the American position would be on the possibility of FCNL–Levantine treaties being negotiated immediately after the Levantine elections. (Perhaps Peterson saw in this a way of hindering Spears' future maneuverability in the Levant.) It was emphasized that such a treaty would have to allow for the possibility of Syria's inclusion in an Arab federation as well as for the institution of English-language instruction in the country so as to facilitate its integration into a British-dominated federation.[88] When a copy of this dispatch reached Spears he protested that both the Syrians and the Lebanese hoped that the end of the war would bring with it the end of French influence in their countries; he himself had told them Britain was opposed to wartime treaty talks. The Foreign Office responded by warning belatedly that "we are not anxious that Syrian and Lebanese politicians should be given any ground for representing us to the French as constituting the only barrier in the way of immediate negotiations." Yet, the telegram went on to point out that the dispatch to Campbell had merely contemplated the possibility of such talks and that no final decision had yet been made.[89]

In Lebanon, Spears' return brought about a rapid resolution of the political crisis that had plagued Helleu. During a brief stopover in Algiers on his return trip, he had conferred with Catroux, who had agreed that Helleu was botching the elections arrangements. In Beirut, Spears found the frustrated delegate-general to be on the verge of unilaterally issuing a decree setting a

30:25 Christian–Muslim ratio without gaining the prior agreement of the communities concerned. Spears easily obtained Helleu's approval to intervene personally with the communal and political leaders and rapidly gained Muslim consent to and grudging Christian acquiescence in the proposed deal. After radio messages from both Helleu and Spears, the former published a decree on July 31 providing for a new apportionment of seats as well as for a census to be held within two years (a condition that the Muslims had set but was never to be met); the election date was now set for August 29.[90] Helleu's ineptness had thus furnished Spears with a perfect opportunity for demonstrating his effectiveness as the ultimate arbiter in the volatile environment of Lebanese politics.

The combination of the outcome of the Syrian elections and the increase in Spears' political clout in Lebanon had a major impact on both the conduct and the results of the Lebanese elections. The National Bloc victory in Syria gave a moral boost to the similarly inclined political groups in Lebanon; Spears' central role in resolving the political crisis enhanced his ability to support their electoral bids. Conversely, the loss of face that the French suffered as a result of Atasi's last-minute escape act induced the General Delegation to abandon Catroux's policy of enlightened restraint and push for an all-out victory by pro-French candidates in Lebanon.

Although Lebanon's political institutions, including the presidency, were to remain under the domination of the Maronite Christian community, the French were by no means assured of continued local support for their position of predominance in the country. As had become clear in 1942, the political and ideological divisions within the Maronite community itself were growing, and Spears was encouraging this process. The two main political groups were the National Bloc (diametrically oposed in outlook to its Syrian namesake), and the Constitutional Bloc, headed by Bishara al-Khoury. Both men had served in high office in the past (Edde as president and al-Khoury as minister of the interior and premier) and had been regarded by the French as trustworthy collaborators in the running of the country. As has been shown, however, al-Khoury had proved eager to win Spears' support in his 1942 opposition campaign against Naccache, in the course of which he had cultivated closer cooperation with the Sunni Muslim community as well. Edde, by contrast, was culturally and politically oriented toward Europe generally and France specifically: his mother was Italian, he had been educated in French and he was even accustomed to addressing the Lebanese Chamber of Deputies in that language (his knowledge of Classical Arabic being inadequate for the purpose). Given the rising tide of pan-Arab nationalism among the Lebanese Muslims, al-Khoury seemed to be in a better position to reach an understanding with the Muslim leadership than Edde, who conceived of Lebanon as a non-Arab, European-oriented country.[91]

Disregarding Catroux's earlier recommendation in favor of seeking the creation of a coalition government between these two rivals, Helleu decided to throw all his weight behind the candidates associated with Edde's National Bloc. He persisted in this course despite the advice of the French Delegation in Beirut, which warned that Edde was bound to lose and therefore did not merit a heavy investment of French effort and prestige.[92] The secretary-general of the General Delegation, Chataigneau, was critical of Helleu's approach, but found himself in the shoes of his predecessor, Lépissier—unable to exert any meaningful influence on policy in the face of Boegner's political dominance.[93] Naturally, Helleu's hostility merely served to reinforce al-Khoury's reliance on British support. The stage was set for a dirty campaign.

As early as April, U.S. military intelligence had reported:

> Information from Baalbek and Zahle tends to show that the forthcoming elections will be anything but free and democratic. It seems evident that the situation is actually one of political struggle between Anglo-philes and Franco-philes, and that both Britain and France are taking active parts. It is a matter of common knowledge that both are canvassing the regions in attempts to find the most powerful candidates definitely favorable to their designs. It is evident that financial as well as moral support will be furnished.[94]

This prediction was fulfilled, as combined Franco–British spending attained a level of approximately one Palestine pound per voter. The governments of Egypt, Iraq, and Syria threw what political and financial weight they had behind al-Khoury's list. British political officers and French *conseillers* alike met with local notables in attempts to win their support for this or that candidate. The *Sûreté Générale* harassed and even arrested candidates from al-Khoury's camp while the Spears Mission did its best to publicize such incidents and reassure pro-British figures that they would not be left in the lurch. Although Spears and Helleu managed to conclude an agreement to exclude the troops of either side from being posted at polling stations, when election day came the British deployed their military police in the vicinity of the polls in order to enforce this ban. The French naturally saw this as a devious perversion of the agreed-on arrangement. Nevertheless, French-organized ballot stuffing seems to have been extensive in Beirut and the Mount Lebanon area. Spears sent the British vice-consul in Damascus, Richard Beaumont, to Tripoli with orders to falsify the election results in that hotly contested district. (As it turned out, the British candidate won handsdown without any recourse to fraud on Beaumont's part.)[95] The worst nightmares of the Foreign Office and Catroux were thus fulfilled, as the Lebanese elections, which had been intended to stabilize political relations, turned instead into a no-holds-barred, Franco–British struggle for ascendancy.[96]

The results of the voting on August 29 gave al-Khoury's backers an edge over their opponents, although the outcome was by no means decisive. Only in the Maronite stronghold of Mount Lebanon did Edde do well, gaining eleven of eighteen seats. The French lists fared poorly in North and South Lebanon as well as in the Bekaa region. Most notably, the British-backed Abdul-Hamid Karami gained an easy victory in Tripoli after the removal of Mukaddam from the scene and the pan-Arab nationalist Riad al-Solh won election from his district in the south (both these men were from the Sunni community). Even more galling to the French was the election of Camille

Chamoun, an Anglophile Maronite who was suspected of having ties to British intelligence, to represent a district in the vicinity of Beirut.[97]

Nevertheless, the new Chamber of Deputies contained a large pool of deputies who were either uncommitted to any action or whose political leanings were unclear. The composition of the new government remained to be determined, and Spears certainly was not assured of entirely excluding pro-French elements from power:

> It is generally agreed that [due to British efforts] the results, though far from satisfactory, represent a definite advance over past elections, where lists were merely imposed before hand by the French authorities through the Government in power. Nevertheless, the new Chamber will not contain more than a dozen Deputies with any strength of character or of purpose, and these dozen, Moslem and Christian, are far from united in their aims; so that it is too much to hope that anything like a strong Government can be formed amongst them.[98]

For his part, Helleu remained true to his habit of maintaining telegraph silence. For more than one month, the FCNL did not hear a word from him concerning the significance of the electoral results. After two weeks, fearing the worst, Free French headquarters summoned Chataigneau to Algiers to report personally on the situation. Although highly critical of Helleu's role, he reassured the committee that the election results had not been a complete disaster. In a dispatch to Helleu, Massigli urged him to associate his secretary-general a little more closely in the running of affairs in the future (the obvious implication being that he should reduce his dependence on Boegner and Baelen).[99] The two weeks after the final vote tally on September 5 were a period of intensive bargaining, maneuvering, and intrigue, as al-Khoury and Edde each strove to secure his election as president when the Chamber of Deputies was convened. Al-Khoury's supporters raised constitutional objections to the election of Edde to the post, while Spears reportedly passed information to the Egyptian and Iraqi consulates regarding election-rigging techniques that the French had employed on behalf of "their" candidate. Most importantly, Spears let it be known in Lebanese political circles that he would not be ready to maintain close ties with the presidency if that office were held by Helleu's man. Realizing that Edde stood no chance of heading the government himself, the French sought to mediate between him and al-Khoury in the hope that they could at least agree on a compromise candidate who would then lead a government including members of both factions; however, Spears managed to insinuate himself into the negotiation process and pressed al-Khoury to insist on Chamoun as the only other possible man for the job. Edde agreed, but from the French perspective, of course, Chamoun was unacceptable.[100] Helleu thus found himself in the absurd position of insisting on al-Khoury as by far the lesser of two evils. Edde was furious, threatening to mount disturbances in his home territory, but he soon found his base of support disintegrating. When the Chamber of Deputies was finally convened on September 21, with a smug-looking Spears and an anxious Helleu observ-

The

ing, it elected al-Khoury to the presidency by a vote of 40—0 (with eleven deputies either failing to show up or abstaining). Riad al-Solh was named prime minister, heading a strongly nationalist and anti-French cabinet, with Camille Chamoun as minister of the interior and the Druze Sheikh Majid Arslan in charge of defense. Edde was completely cut out of the leadership.[101]

Having been thoroughly outfoxed and beaten by Spears and al-Khoury, Helleu sought to put the best possible face on the situation in the reports that he finally saw fit to send Algiers. He suddenly asserted that al-Khoury was, after all, worthy of French confidence and that Riad al-Solh seemed to have moderated his anti-French proclivities. He even claimed (without specifying any names) that the new Lebanese cabinet contained strong Francophile elements.[102] Other observers did not see matters in the same light. Wadsworth reported that Spears was the "clear winner"[103] while the Jewish Agency's Eliahu Sasson saw the formation of the new government as a watershed in Lebanese history. He took note of al-Khoury's apparent adherence to the idea of Arab federation as indicated by his past talks with Nahas Pasha in Cairo. Great significance was also attached to the promptness with which Iraq and Egypt now recognized Syrian and Lebanese independence and to Nahas Pasha's extension of a formal invitation to the leaders of both countries to return to Egypt for talks intended to lead to the actual convening of an Arab League. The days of Maronite dependence on French protection seemed over as Bishara al-Khoury prepared to integrate Lebanon into the Arab world.[104]

The policy debates within both British and Free French camps regarding the Levant during 1943, reveal the emergence of some interesting patterns that were to play an increasingly important role in the following two years.

In its approach to the Levant problem, the attitude of the MEWC was conditioned by its vision of the postwar years as a period during which Britain would consolidate its position in the Middle East through an alliance with the forces of pan-Arab nationalism. Britain was to support the creation of an Arab federation on the assumption that, in return, such a federation would gratefully accept the protective umbrella of a Pax Britannica. It was also hoped that the Palestine problem could be more readily solved within the context of such an arrangement. Clearly, though, a continued French presence in Syria and Lebanon would present an annoying hindrance to the accomplishment of a regional settlement of this sort. The British Middle Eastern establishment therefore endorsed Spears' policy of driving the French out of the Levant.

The Foreign Office, in its concern to maintain good relations with postwar France in the European sphere, sought to rein in Spears and his backers, but was, as usual, hampered by the attitude of the prime minister. Not only did Churchill feel personally committed to Spears, he also felt a personal grievance against de Gaulle for his insolent behavior and apparent ingratitude for Britain's support of his movement. He was therefore sorely tempted to join the Americans in their resistance to de Gaulle's assumption of control over the North African administration, and responded with enthusiasm to Spears' memorandum suggesting that Britain should work for the establishment of a pusillanimous, anticolonialist, left-wing regime in postwar France. It was all the Foreign Office could do to prevent a complete rift with de Gaulle from occurring.

For their part, the Free French were also becoming increasingly divided over their Levant policy. Within the mandatory administration, the strings of power lay mostly in the hands of an ex-Vichyite clique that pursued a rigid, unimaginative policy and committed repeated blunders both in its relations with the British and in its handling of the Syrians and Lebanese. The polarizing effect of this approach met with increasing criticism from Massigli, Catroux, and other professional diplomats and administrators with long experience in the Middle East. On the other hand, Catroux's attempt to reach an understanding with the Syrian National Bloc bore little promise, in view of the nationalists' confidence of being able to play their British card in the event of a crisis. De Gaulle held himself somewhat aloof from the policy debate for the time being, but it had been made clear repeatedly that his main concern was to guard against the inclination of professional diplomats to compromise. All the factors were in place for the unhappy sequence of events that was to follow.

8

The November Crisis

The Slide toward Confrontation

It did not take long for the practical ramifications of the Lebanese political transformation to manifest themselves. The day after the election of the new government, Helleu reported that Syria and Lebanon intended jointly to raise demands for the transfer of the common interests to their control. Helleu was opposed to this pending the negotiation of treaties, arguing that: "If we had no pledge at our disposal, we would not be able to obtain satisfactory guarantees in the course of the negotiation."[1] Catroux supported this position and the delegate-general was instructed to propose the formal linking of the two issues in talks with the Levant states.[2]

Both Syria and Lebanon refused to accept any such linkage, however, knowing full well that the power of the Spears Mission stood behind them on this issue. Spears gleefully reported that the Lebanese leaders had told the French they would rather have their right hands cut off than sign a treaty with the FCLN, which, they insisted, had no right to enter into any commitments on behalf of France. For the first time ever, the minister noted, Lebanon was taking the initiative in confronting France instead of acting as a brake on Syrian nationalism.[3]

In the absence of any common ground for discussion with the French, the Lebanese proceeded to take unilateral steps to secure their independence. The achievement of full national solidarity was embodied in the oral agreement between al-Khoury and al-Solh known as the National Pact.[4] This reconciled the differing Christian and Muslim conceptions of the nature of the Lebanese state by defining it as "a homeland with an Arab face seeking the beneficial good from the culture of the West." The National Pact also formalized the confessional division of political power among Lebanon's religious communities.[5] On October 7, Riad al-Solh delivered a landmark address to the Chamber of Deputies announcing an ambitious political program according to which control of the common interests would be assumed by the Lebanese government, close collaboration would be established with the rest of the Arab world, French would be abolished as an official language, and constitutional reform would be undertaken to provide for Lebanon's full independence and national sovereignty (a thinly veiled euphemism for the abolition of the French mandate).[6] Spears reported that this speech marked a climax in the development of Lebanese national consciousness:

> Scenes of great enthusiasm took place outside the Parliament during and after the session. As a result of these developments the Lebanese population has been profoundly stirred and has become really conscious, for the first time, of its national entity. This result, which has dismayed the French, is attributable to the general realisation that they attempted blatantly to rig the elections and failed in the attempt.[7]

When Helleu sent President al-Khoury a letter rejecting his government's program as incompatible with the provisions of the French mandate, the Lebanese government took a page out of Spears' book by threatening to bring the letter up for public debate in the Chamber of Deputies unless it was withdrawn. When Helleu refused to back down, the Lebanese government added insult to injury by presenting the General Delegation with a formal demand for the transfer to it of all attributes of sovereignty and the transformation of the General Delegation itself into an embassy.[8]

The serious crisis into which Lebanon was thus once again plunged raised suspicions in the Foreign Office over the nature of Spears' role in the affair. When Spears was informed of the repeated accusations made against him by Viénot (the FCNL's representative in London), he protested his innocence, insisting that the mess the French found themselves in was entirely of their own making.[9] Yet when the Foreign Office made so bold as to suggest that the Lebanese had been acting in a needlessly provocative manner,[10] he rose to their defense as naturally as though it were his own program under attack. Not to proclaim Arabic as the only official language in Lebanon would, he argued, merely serve to antagonize the neighboring states, while the threat of publicly airing the dispute with the French was the only weapon available to the Lebanese goverment. As for the French mandate, although it was true that it existed in the legal sense, the least Britain could do was to contribute toward the fulfillment of Lebanese independence "by treating mandate as a dead letter in practice."[11] When instructed by London to do what he could to restrain the Lebanese, he simply refused on the grounds that to do so would violate his intellectual honesty:

> The only way of getting them to do what we want is to convince them by objective reasoning that the case [for the unilateral establishment of Lebanese independence] is *not* sound [italics in original]. For the present I must frankly say I do not see how.
>
> . . . I feel that unless we show sympathy to legitimate Lebanese claims, not only will we . . . lose such influence as we now possess, but that the quarrel may well spread to other countries in a way harmful to us since no one in the Middle East will agree that we have not got a major responsibility in the Levant.[12]

Powerless to influence Spears, the Foreign Office weakly tried to shore up the French position by making a statement in Parliament to the effect that it was "technically impossible now to terminate the mandate."[13] In response, Spears angrily warned that the Lebanese government "have no intention of allowing the French to fob them off with trifling concessions on unimportant points."[14] The chief British official on the OCP sought to reassure the General Delegation by privately informing the French that Spears' conduct was in fact completely out of line with Foreign Office instructions, but they must have found little comfort in this knowledge.[15] Much more telling, as far as they were concerned, were the visits to Syria at the end of October by experienced Arab hands based in Cairo, General Iltyd Clayton and Colonel Newcombe.[16] Though assured by the British that the visits were of a purely private nature, the French understandably attached greater signifcance than that to the series of meetings these officers held with Syrian and Lebanese cabinet members as well as Egyptian consuls. The General Delegation was reliably informed that Clayton and Newcombe had urged on their interlocutors, and offered their assistance to, the immediate realization of the Greater Syria federation scheme.[17]

Confronted by an increasingly overt challenge to their authority in Lebanon, the French were divided over how to respond. This disagreement reflected the wider divergence in approaches to the colonial question that had begun to emerge as a result, in part, of the weakening of de Gaulle's previously unquestioned authority over his movement. Although the minutes of FCNL meetings remain closed to researchers, the events of November 1943 indicate that de Gaulle could no longer expect to have his way with the committee as a matter of course. Despite the progressive eclipsing of General Giraud's power, the committee contained a wider array of forceful figures, such as Massigli and Catroux, than had its predecessor. As of September 1943, the FCNL also reported on its decisions to a consultative assembly formed of representatives of the various resistance organizations.[18] Given the broader political base of the FCNL, Catroux and Massigli seem to have been able to challenge de Gaulle's views a little more audaciously and with greater hope of success than would have been possible in the FNC. As will be seen, this trend grew even more marked after the expansion of the FCNL on November 9, 1943.

Within the FCNL, Pleven appears to have been closest to de Gaulle on the colonial issue, viewing with suspicion U.S. proposals for a postwar trusteeship system as well as British Colonial Secretary Cranbourne's attempt to appease the Americans by proposing a system of intergovernmental regional councils that would oversee the administration of colonial territories.[19] De Gaulle and Pleven saw the French Empire and the French state as essentially one and the same thing. Rather than moving toward international control or colonial independence, the native populations should be made to feel a part of French civilization. (This was essentially the idea behind de Gaulle's later, quixotic experiment with the French Union.)[20]

Catroux's view, by contrast, largely reflected the influence of one of his key advisors on Middle Eastern affairs, the orientalist Robert Montagne. The latter had for years been a severe critic of the heavy-handed style of French colonial rule, and was keenly aware of the potential threat which the rise of

Arab nationalism posed to continued French control of the Levant and Algeria. He argued that France could learn a thing or two from Britain's subtler, more indirect methods of political control.[21]

Within the Levant, the traditional, hard-line approach to Arab nationalism was supported by the bulk of the French bureaucracy and officer corps, in view of the vested interest the members of the colonial administration had in the maintenance of direct French control. A more enlightened group of 1940-vintage Gaullists and left-wing intellectuals was highly critical of Helleu's policies but powerless to change them. Within the General Delegation itself, only Chataigneau was closely associated with Catroux; however, the latter's progressive approach to Middle Eastern affairs was also supported by Benoist, the Free French representative in Cairo, and his deputy, Filliol.

This doctrinal schism was clearly reflected in the various recommendations made in regard to the mounting crisis in Lebanon. Boegner saw a violent showdown with the Lebanese as inevitable, and warned that if the British were left to put down an uprising, they would never restore the French to power. He therefore urged Helleu to ask Algiers for more troops so as to ensure French military self-reliance. Once an adequate force had been assembled, he argued, the administration would be able to afford to make some concessions to the Lebanese, leaving the implementation of a full-fledged treaty to the postwar period, when a legitimate French government would be in a position to ratify such a pact. Helleu, as usual, followed his subordinate's advice and cabled Algiers asking for military reinforcements.[22]

Helleu's approach alarmed Catroux's supporters, who saw in it a recipe for certain disaster. Casey reported that, in a frank discussion with Hamilton in Cairo on October 14, Filliol had said

> that the result of Lebanese election had been severe blow to the French position in the Levant. . . . The blow . . . had been so severe that they had to make up their minds whether to sit down under it (which would mean, he stated, elimination of French influence from the Levant) or else react violently. Filliol was certain that they would choose the latter course . . . [in] the form of a visit from De Gaulle to Beirut where he would make clear in truculent tones that they had no intention of being ousted.

Casey concluded that "Filliol is generally well informed and has been quite well disposed to us in the past. It looks as though we should be prepared for trouble ahead."[23] Around the same time, Riad al-Solh told Spears "that Boegner had informed one of the Prime Minister's colleagues 'that the French were tired of this comedy and would now resort to force.' "[24]

While agreeing that it was crucial to adopt a very firm line against Lebanese demands for the complete elimination of French influence in their country,[25] Catroux and his supporters also felt that substantial concessions were urgently needed. To allow a violent confrontation to take place was to ensure the destruction of the French position. Helleu's recommendation of a military show of force made no sense in Catroux's opinion, because to send in French troops from North Africa would place an intolerable strain on the FCNL's meager resources, whereas the use of the hated Senegalese units already posted in the Levant would, past experience indicated, only serve to antagonize the Arabs even further.[26]

From Cairo, Benoist sent de Gaulle a telegram which was almost desperate in tone, charging that

> one would have to regard the moral and intellectual insufficiency of our functionaries in the mandated territories as the ultimate cause of the setbacks we have just suffered there.

He decried what he described as "the glaring dishonesty and incompetence of so many others among them."[27] Benoist insisted that the French position in the Levant could be saved only by immediately adopting the following three measures:

1. Appointment of a clearsighted and energetic delegate-general.
2. The radical suppression of all that is corrupt in the French administrations in the Levant states, civil as well as military.
3. Change in our policy, taking into account the result of the elections and the new ideas which are seeing the light of day among the peoples of the Middle East, ideas from which France would have but little to fear if she wished to exploit them in her own favor.[28]

Endorsing Benoist's views, Catroux urged the FCNL to issue a definitive declaration regarding its policy on Levant independence. His idea was that the Syrians and Lebanese would be assured control over the common interests and all other attributes of independence once they had signed treaties modeled on those of 1936. He also reiterated his earlier suggestion for an official endorsement of pan-Arab unity as a desirable goal provided Damascus stood at the center of any federation. Such a declaration, Catroux felt, would give clear expression to French resolve in the Levant while leaving the door open to the fulfillment of Arab nationalist aspirations.[29]

Helleu's Coup

Catroux's proposals soon proved to be too little, too late. From the beginning of November, events moved much too rapidly to be accommodated by the slow-moving process of general policy reformulation. Besides, the deadlock in the FCNL between reformists and traditionalists seems to have been much too tight to permit the adoption of any clear-cut decision on the issue.

It remains impossible to reconstruct the developments of November 1943 in full and accurate detail both because of incomplete documentation (particularly on the French side) and because unrecorded oral exchanges may have played a decisive role at certain crucial junctures. The sequence of events began with Helleu's trip to Algiers on October 29 to present in person his view of the situation to the FCNL and to reiterate his request for military reinforcements. The substance of his discussions with de Gaulle, Massigli, and Catroux remains unknown because the Quai d'Orsay archives have never made the minutes of the FCNL meetings available.[30] The only public outcome of the consultations was a communiqué issued on November 5, warning the Lebanese government not to undertake any unilateral revisions of the country's constitution. Helleu was given instructions in the same vein, to the effect that no handover of powers to the Lebanese could be undertaken pending the negotiation of a treaty.[31]

The effect of the French communiqué was the opposite of that which had been intended. On November 6, the Lebanese government issued a defiant communiqué of its own announcing its intention of proceeding immediately to the revision of the constitution along the lines envisaged in the political program of October 7. Helleu, who heard of this development during a stopover in Cairo on his way back from Algiers, contacted Beirut, requesting the Lebanese not to proceed with the vote on the reform bill until he had returned. When this request was turned down, the French tried to convince Edde's supporters to boycott the session of the Chamber of Deputies set for November 8, in the hope that the two-thirds' attendance necessary for a quorum would be lacking. It was a telling sign of the disintegration of French authority that only Edde himself and one follower boycotted the session; the Chamber of Deputies passed the constitutional bill into law by a unanimous vote.[32] The French promptly seized all newspapers containing accounts of the parliamentary proceedings and the chief of the *Sûreté Générale* was "reliably quoted as saying 'All is prepared for effective reprisals.' "[33] This tough line appears to have represented the approach of Boegner's staff rather than of Chataigneau, even though the latter was formally in charge during Helleu's absence. Significantly, the French military commander, General de Lavalade, was opposed to this confrontational policy, promising the British military command that he would do all he could to avoid needless provocation.[34]

Helleu himself returned to Beirut on November 9, in time for the scheduled celebration of Armistice Day two days later. On November 10, the members of the Lebanese cabinet were informed that their invitations to the military parade on the following day had been cancelled. President al-Khoury accordingly declared that he would not attend and, at Wadsworth's suggestion, Spears then assembled the entire Diplomatic Corps (of which he was the ranking member) which decided collectively to boycott the event as well. Despite this unpleasantness, Spears and Helleu had a friendly conversation after a reception for the visiting king of Yugoslavia that evening, with Helleu assuring Spears that he had no intention of taking any disruptive measures. That same night, French troops arrested al-Khoury, al-Solh, and most of the cabinet. The following morning, Helleu announced that the Chamber of Deputies had been dissolved, the constitution suspended, and a new government appointed under the leadership of Emile Edde.[35]

The precise nature of the roles played by Spears, Helleu, and de Gaulle in these developments is unclear. Although the French suspected Spears of putting the Lebanese up to their provocatively defiant behavior, there does not seem to exist any written evidence directly proving this. As has been demonstrated, however, there had been a growing pattern of interference by Spears in Franco–Levantine relations over the course of the previous two years, leaving no doubt in the minds of the Lebanese that they would be supported by him in whatever claims they made against the French. Whether or not Spears had explicitly urged the Lebanese to abolish the mandate unilaterally seems almost inconsequential. From the telegrams he sent to London during October 1943, it is clear that he saw himself as the champion of Lebanese nationalism and took delight in watching the rapid erosion of French power. It was Spears who had created the atmosphere in which the Lebanese government dared to throw the gauntlet down before the French, knowing that if it were taken up, their duel would be fought for them by the British minister. It is certainly difficult to imagine that, during wartime and with their country under British military occupation, al-Khoury and al-Solh would have proceeded as they did, had Spears warned them not to.[36]

A more ambiguous question concerns the background to Helleu's coup. It seemed unthinkable at the time, as it does today, that such an irresolute character should have suddenly resorted to so harsh a measure entirely on his own initiative. Yet it is clear that the FCNL had not authorized such action and he himself was later to accept sole responsibility for what proved to be a catastrophic decision.[37] Certainly both Catroux and Massigli were aghast at what Helleu had done. But de Gaulle adopted a much more understanding attitude toward the delegate-general and, at the time, Helleu claimed that his actions reflected de Gaulle's wishes.[38] Was this in fact the case? As with the issue of Spears' role, the answer probably cannot be clear-cut. On the one hand, the Lebanese government's crucial decision to go ahead with the constitutional revision did not take place until after Helleu's departure from Algiers. On the other hand, Helleu may well have been unofficially instructed by de Gaulle to adopt tough measures in the event the Lebanese maintained their defiant stance. This hypothesis appears to be borne out by a cable sent to de Gaulle by Catroux from Beirut on November 17, in which he reported that Helleu "appears to have returned from Algiers with the impression that you wished to see him act vigorously if the need arose."[39]

Within the General Delegation itself, Helleu was reported by Catroux to have "consulted with only a very small number of collaborators" before making his decision.[40] This presumably refers to Boegner and Baelen, who had been in favor of the use of force all along. Whatever doubt there may have been in the delegate-general's mind over the precise nature of the action de Gaulle would expect him to take, it was quickly dispelled by the advice of his political cabinet. Chataigneau appears to have been left out of the decision-making process as usual. More remarkably, General de Lavalade was later to issue a general circular to all French officers in the Levant disclaiming any foreknowledge on his part of the events of November 11:

> Some persons trying to compromise the Army by seeking to impute to it part of the responsibility for the events which just took place in Beirut are going about spreading the rumor that the Army Chiefs . . . had been informed in advance by the General Delegation of the measures which were to be executed on 11 November. . . .

I respond to these tendentious and malevolent rumors with the most formal denial.[41]

De Lavalade went on to report that the *Sûreté Générale* had been in charge of the arrests. He himself had been told on November 10 only that there was fear of popular unrest taking place the next day and that military precautions should be taken and reinforcements provided for the use of the *Sûreté Générale*.[42]

Immediate Repercussions

The impact of the November 11 coup was as great as the group of men who had embarked on it was small. The arrest of the political leadership of Lebanon and the sometimes violent popular demonstrations and confrontations with French troops that ensued, plunged the country into a siegelike atmosphere which Spears skillfully exploited for his own political ends. His task was made easier by the ineptness with which Helleu and his associates had planned their action. The arrests themselves were badly handled, with the hated Senegalese troops doing the arresting and little effort made to respect the dignity of those being apprehended. Moreover, two ministers, Majid Arslan and Habib Abu Shahla, managed to escape arrest and fled to a village in the Shuf mountains overlooking Beirut. There they declared themselves acting prime minister and vice-premier, respectively, an action which was endorsed by a secretly convened meeting of the Chamber of Deputies. The isolated Emile Edde was condemned as a traitor and found it impossible to get anyone to join his government. On the propaganda front, the French seemed completely unprepared, as for the first three days they issued nothing but reprints of Helleu's and Edde's original communiqués, while their Lebanese opponents printed a wide range of tracts that vigorously assailed the legality of the French actions. By their crude tactics, the French had ensured that no sector of Lebanese society would support them. Even the Phalangist party was driven into the arms of the Muslims by the arrest of its top leadership.[43] Needless to say, Spears and Wadsworth refused to have anything to do with Edde, while the British minister remained in close contact with members of the rump legislature and the Shuf government.[44]

The General Delegation's handling of information for the outside world was also hopelessly bungled. The French sought to impose a news blackout by preventing all foreign correspondents from mailing any reports for the first four days of the crisis. Spears adeptly turned this to his advantage by having whole teams of journalists flown from Cairo to Beirut, where their only source of official information was the Spears Mission itself. As soon as they were able to get their stories out they sent their papers the exaggerated accounts (which Spears fed to them) of French violence against Lebanese demonstrators. Using the Reuters news agency as his main conduit for the dissemination of information, Spears thus gained an almost complete monopoly of influence over public opinion in Britain and the United States.[45] In Cairo, the local branch of the British Ministry of Information also

> pushed the stories of the trouble to an undo [sic] degree. Immediately upon receiving reports from Lebanon, the Ministry phoned all agencies and independent reporters, to give them a lurid, circumstantial account of what had taken place.[46]

No less an authority than the political warfare executive (PWE), in charge of Britain's wartime propaganda effort, was stunned by the effectiveness of Spears' tactics: "As if at a single command, the entire British press had launched a large-scale campaign against the Committee on National Liberation in connection with the arrest [of the Lebanese government]." The PWE viewed this as a dangerously counterproductive campaign that would not only sour overall Anglo–Free French relations, but would also adversely effect public opinion in occupied France.[47]

Spears' chief goal during the November crisis appears to have been its exploitation as a means of eradicating French influence in the Levant once and for all. His immediate recommendation to Cairo was that he be authorized to declare martial law and the assumption by the British of full governmental powers in Lebanon. As usual, he argued for his position on the basis of military security requirements.[48] The military itself, however, seems to have seen things in quite a different light. General Holmes told Wadsworth that he was most reluctant to take the drastic step Spears proposed because it would, in fact, disrupt the overall war effort:

> Let us be frank about this. The man most responsible for jeopardizing our common war effort in this theatre of operations is Spears. He can't see it in his overriding belief that the French must be ousted to support that effort.[49]

After conferring with the commanders-in-chief Middle East, Casey turned down Spears' request, reserving martial law for a situation in which the disorders became so grave as to really endanger British military operations.[50] The Foreign Office was even more cautious in its attitude, informing Casey that the "Cabinet sincerely hope that it will not be necessary to employ British troops at the present stage."[51] As Maurice Peterson pointed out, the de Gaulle–Lyttelton agreements provided only for the declaration of a state of siege in the event of military emergency, and that only at the formal request of the Free French. To impose martial law would be a unilateral and arbitrary act that would entail a complete break with the Gaullist movement.[52]

Within the Lebanese political scene, Spears stayed in close touch with the rump government in the Shuf, around which a group of several hundred armed supporters had rapidly congregated. Spears wished to fly Arslan and Abu Shahla to a safe haven in Cairo, thus effectively turning them into a government-in-exile under British protection. London objected to this and the ministers were forced to stay put. Their requests for additional arms were politely turned down by the British, who referred them to the black market instead. Spears also claimed to have restrained them from launching attacks against the French. Nonetheless, the friendly contact with the local British authorities must have given a considerable boost to the morale of the Lebanese resistance.[53]

Although the Foreign Office angered Spears by the evenhanded view it took of the Lebanese situation, accusing the al-Khoury government of having acted in an unnecessarily provocative manner, London certainly was not prepared to sit idly by while Helleu destroyed all hope for a political dialogue in the country. With the entire Arab world in a furor over the events in Beirut, it was clear that British prestige lay on the line.[54] The French had to be forced to retreat. The question was how much they should be made to concede and what sort of pressure should be applied. In the immediate aftermath of the coup, the Foreign Office instructed Harold Macmillan, the resident minister in Algiers, to demand the immediate release of the Lebanese ministers as well as the replacement of Helleu. At the November 12 meeting of the War Cabinet (held in Churchill's absence), it was suggested that the FCNL should also have been asked to reinstate the al-Khoury/al-Solh government in full. Since no response to the first two demands had yet been received, it was deemed inappropriate to add on yet another one. The War Cabinet reached the curious decision that this was to be done only in the event the French refused to comply with the original pair of British desiderata. His Majesty's government was most reluctant to contemplate the use of direct force in the form of martial law, although it recognized that it might ultimately be left with no alternative. For the time being, Macmillan was to let the FCNL know that Britain might withdraw its recognition of the committee unless the Lebanese crisis was satisfactorily resolved.[55] A few days later, the War Cabinet reaffirmed its cautious approach, ordering the dispatch of a telegram to Spears

> to make it clear that at the present stage, and without further reference to the War Cabinet, no threat of the imposition of British martial law should be made use of, or referred to, in the course of the negotiations.[56]

Throughout this period, the British took care to keep the U.S. government fully informed of their actions and even sought a certain amount of coordination with the Americans. The War Cabinet approved the dispatch by Churchill of a cable to Roosevelt requesting that the United States join Britain in withdrawing recognition from the FCNL if the Lebanese ministers were not released and the Chamber of Deputies not allowed to reassemble. The prime minister expressed his fear that the Lebanese crisis was merely a foretaste of the things to come if and when de Gaulle assumed the leadership of France. He also hinted at the possibility of resorting to armed force if all else failed:

> Meanwhile I am enquiring carefully into the state of our forces in the Levant. At the same time should action be taken it would be necessary to take precautions in North Africa, for I assure you there is nothing this man will not do if he has armed forces at his disposal.[57]

Whitehall's eagerness to involve the United States in pressuring the French arose not only from its general policy of close cooperation with the

Americans in all aspects of the war effort, but also out of concern lest a unilateral British crackdown against the Gaullists provoke a hostile reaction in Washington. Ambassador Halifax warned that the American press and public opinion tended to suspect the British of expansionist designs in the Middle East and that, no matter how odious Helleu's action might seem, Britain's criticism of it could be seen as hypocritical in view of the arrest of the Congress Party leadership in India.[58]

In fact, though, both the White House and the State Department were so antagonized by the conduct of the French in Lebanon that it is questionable whether the imposition of martial law by the British would have provoked an adverse reaction in Washington. President Roosevelt was reported to have curtailed plans for expanding cooperation with the FCNL as a result of Helleu's coup,[59] and Paul Alling of the Near Eastern and African Affairs Department (NEA) wrote a memorandum in which French policy was vilified in the harshest of terms:

> The Free French authorities in Syria and Lebanon have followed a course of unbridled and unjustified imperialism ever since they entered the [Levant] States on British heels in 1941, bearing promises of independence.
>
> Their present brutally repressive action in Lebanon is worthy of Hitler, but certainly not of "la France civilisatrice."[60]

George Wadsworth was ordered not to establish any contact with the Edde regime and, in Algiers, U.S. Consul-General Wiley was instructed to threaten the FCNL with a public breach of relations unless the status quo was restored.[61]

The Search for a Diplomatic Way Out

French policy was in considerable disarray in the immediate aftermath of November 11. The French press in Algiers unabashedly supported Helleu's policy and blamed the Lebanese for the crisis. At Catroux's request, however, the commissariat of information issued a statement asserting that the delegate-general's action had not received prior authorization from the FCNL. The favorable impression this communiqué made on His Majesty's government was offset by a declaration Helleu issued, claiming his policy was endorsed by de Gaulle.[62]

Despite this confusion, there were important factors already in place that made a conciliatory attitude on the part of the French very likely. The political disaster which Helleu had precipitated in Lebanon came at a time when a major reorganization of the FCNL had just taken place. The resignation of General Giraud represented a major political victory for de Gaulle; but at the same time, the FCNL had been expanded to include prominent Resistance leaders like André Diethelm and Henri Frenay, representatives of the moderate Left such as Pierre Mendès-France, and notable personalities like Jean Monnet, who had long maintained a critical distance from de Gaulle's movement.[63] While enhancing the legitimacy and broadening the popular appeal of the FCNL, this expansion also served to reduce de Gaulle's sway over it. The events in Beirut two days later naturally created scepticism over the wisdom of his uncompromising approach to the Levant question and to relations with the British. After the receipt of the American and British governments' official demands, the FCNL decided to send Catroux on a special assignment to Lebanon, whence he was to send recommendations on what could be done to stabilize the situation. On leaving for Cairo, Catroux must have felt he had a strong hand within the FCNL, although the options available to him in Lebanon were painfully limited. As early as November 13, Massigli was able to assure Robert Murphy, President Roosevelt's special representative in French North Africa, that Catroux's purpose was to negotiate a peaceful settlement and "that Helleu, whose judgment apparently he [Massigli] does not rate highly, would be quietly shelved and that the political prisoners would be released."[64]

After arriving in Cairo, Catroux's trip to Beirut was delayed by a day or two because he had a fever, and he took this opportunity to confer with Casey, who had just been on a brief visit to Lebanon. Fresh from his discussion with Spears and with Lebanese notables, the minister of state had adopted a tough line toward the French, suggesting to the Foreign Office that Catroux was playing for time and urging Whitehall to set November 17 as a deadline for French compliance with Britain's demands.[65] Catroux sought to appease Casey by assuring him of his reasonable intentions while pointing out the difficulty engendered by the rapid transformation of the Lebanese crisis into a Franco–British confrontation. French prestige was on the line and there was a danger that the release of the ministers and their reinstatement in office might be perceived as a French surrender to British pressure. In that event, Catroux warned, the FCNL would have no choice but to order a unilateral French withdrawal from the Levant, leaving the British in the role of the nasty imperialists. Unnerved, Casey expressed his willingness to go so far as to cast all the blame for the affair on Helleu, but insisted that security considerations demanded immediate action to defuse the crisis no matter what the circumstances.[66]

Meanwhile, His Majesty's government was no more certain over what sanctions it was ready to impose than Catroux was over what concessions he was willing to make. From Beirut, Spears sounded positively eager to see Catroux fulfill his threat of unilateral withdrawal, assuring London that the native administration was perfectly capable of assuming control over all vital services.[67] This attitude was a source of concern for Harold Macmillan, who had returned to Algiers in the hope of finding a diplomatic solution to the problem before it completely poisoned overall relations with the French:

> The Lebanon crisis is running absolutely full out. Meanwhile, it worries me greatly; because I feel that Spears is out for trouble and personal glory, and Casey is so weak as to be completely in his pocket.[68]

In Macmillan's view, the presentation of an ultimatum to the French was the most counterproductive action that could be taken; the moment national prestige vis-à-vis Britain was involved, de Gaulle would rally the FCNL behind him in a haughty rejection of foreign intervention. What was required was a subtler approach that would play on the divisions within the FCNL. Meeting with Churchill (who was recuperating from pneumonia in North Africa following the Teheran and Cairo conferences), Macmillan told him that, despite Giraud's removal, the new members of the FCNL were much more willing to challenge de Gaulle's authority than in the past:

> This interested the P.M. enormously. What he fears is a sort of de Gaulle dictatorship, hostile to Britain and mischievous if not dangerous. This led on naturally to the Lebanon. I told him that I regarded this as rather a test case. If we handled the affair with some tact, as well as energy, we would get the support:
>
> a) of Catroux,
> b) of Massigli,
> c) of quite half if not two-thirds of the Committee, and we could put de Gaulle in a minority of three or four.
>
> But this required avoidance of ultimatums, except if absolutely necessary. I am afraid I also said that I thought as long as *Spears* [italics in original] was in Beirut there would be open and bitter warfare between us and the French. P.M. did not much like this.[69]

Macmillan was convinced that he could

> get *all* [italics in original] that H.M.G. requires from the French if I am given a chance. But I want to get it in such a way as preserves and does not destroy the work of nearly a year here and that carries with us the reasonable French-men who are our friends. Spears wants a Fashoda; and I do not.[70]

In typical fashion, the War Cabinet opted for the middle ground when confronted with these diametrically opposed recommendations. While accept-ing Casey's and Spears' insistence on the need for a firm deadline, the cabinet remained unwilling to demand the reinstatement of the Lebanese ministers immediately on their release. Casey was instructed to fly to Beirut on Novem-ber 19 and present Catroux with a forty-eight hour deadline (expiring at 10 A.M. on November 21) for dismissing Helleu and releasing the ministers. If it was not met, British martial law would be imposed. Once the Lebanese political leadership was out of jail, it was anticipated, Franco–Lebanese talks aimed at reaching a modus vivendi could begin, a process in which Britain could act as arbiter.[71] At the same time, Maurice Peterson and R. M. A. Hankey met with an official of the War Office and agreed that in the event Britain was left with no other choice but to impose martial law, this would be exploited as an occasion for removing Spears from his mission. Command of the organization would be assumed by General Holmes, leaving Spears in charge of a powerless embassy.[72] Anticipating this development with evident relish, Hankey warned:

> I think we'd better keep this up our sleeves for the moment. It will be useful if we declare martial law, and we must in that case consult M[iddle] E[ast] as suggested. Meanwhile, let's lie doggo![73]

Although he knew nothing of Peterson's latest plot against his mission, Spears found sufficient cause for outrage in London's formal instructions to Casey. Anything less than the full reinstatement of the Lebanese government as it had been constituted before the coup would create a completely unworkable situation, he argued. In addition, he contended that the negotiation of a modus vivendi should be predicated on the complete restoration of political authority to the Lebanese government rather than centering on what degree of authority it would wield.[74] Concurrently, Casey complained that in his discussions with Catroux on November 15 he had acted on the mistaken assumption that His Majesty's government was indeed demanding the reinstatement of the ministers.[75] This revelation placed the War Cabinet in a quandary. If the Lebanese government was placed back in charge without any prior negotiation of a modus vivendi, Eden argued, the situation would return to the deadlock that had preceded the coup. In any case, the French were not likely to comply with this demand. On the other hand, if Casey were instructed to withdraw his demand, this would be seen as a sign of indecision and weakness on the part of Britain. The War Cabinet therefore concluded that Casey should stick to the line he had already adopted, with the proviso that, during the proposed Franco–Lebanese talks on a modus vivendi, "neither party should take action to vary the position, and the Lebanese Parliament should not meet." In other words, the British government refused to recognize the unilateral changes in the Lebanese Constitution that had originally precipitated the crisis:

> In this connection it must be remembered that the Lebanese Government were not without blame, and that if the French had not taken such precipitate and unjustified action, we might well have thought it right to support the French against the attitude adopted by the Lebanese.[76]

Meeting with Catroux in Beirut on November 19, Casey presented him with an aide-mémoire formally threatening a British military takeover of Lebanon unless British demands were met by the twenty-second (a twenty-four-hour extension of the original deadline having been granted by the War Cabinet in view of the confusion over the precise nature of the demands). Although the discussion was reported to be friendly, Catroux remarked before they parted that "this is another Fashoda."[77]

Catroux's task was not an easy one. He had to try and preserve a modicum of French influence in Lebanon while simultaneously resisting British pressure on the one hand and de Gaulle's hard-line stance on the other. The Free French leader was making repeated threats to withdraw from the Levant and even to resign from the FCNL rather than suffer any humiliation at the hands of the British.[78] In a cable sent to Helleu on the thirteenth, de Gaulle had assured him that Catroux's mission was to lend him support rather than to disavow him:

> The forceful measures which you believed you had to take were perhaps necessary. In any case, I must consider that they were since you took them. You are covered in this regard and we will not disavow you.[79]

Hoping to tap de Gaulle's sympathy for his approach, Helleu sent him a continual stream of telegrams accusing Catroux of exceeding his authority and selling out to the demands of the British. In his increasingly desperate attempts to save his position, the tone of his cables became more strident and their content increasingly divorced from reality. He warned that a restoration of the Lebanese government would be disastrous because Bishara al-Khoury was nothing less than a British agent. The delegate-general also sent Massigli a copy of a memorandum that, he claimed, had been presented to him by the consul of a friendly country and that purported to provide details of a secret British plan to gain control of French North Africa as well as other French colonial possessions.[80]

Trying to keep calm and reach a satisfactory solution before the weekend was over, Catroux sent an emissary to the Shuf government and he himself met with Bishara al-Khoury in the prison where he was being held; however, all suggestions of substantive talks with the French were rejected by the Lebanese as long as the status quo had not been completely restored.[81]

In the interim, the FCNL had approved Catroux's request for authorization to dismiss Helleu and release the Lebanese ministers as the prelude to the formation of a new government under the continued presidency of Bishara al-Khoury. This came over the objections of de Gaulle, who had advocated the adoption of a completely inflexible stance, in the hope of calling what he took to be Britain's bluff.[82] It was clearly too late for even a compromise solution, however, and in Whitehall Eden came down firmly in favor of full reinstatement as the only acceptable course of action and "the absolute minimum required to preserve our good name throughout the Middle East."[83] Macmillan was outraged by what he saw as London's spineless submission to the initiatives of Spears and Casey, especially in view of the fact that the French had now acceded to the demands originally made of them:

> Historians will not fail to observe that the solution now proposed [by the FCNL] is an acceptance of the only formal demand made on the French Committee.
>
> The solution proposed does not necessarily concede the French point of view about the change in the personnel of the Government. It merely allows it to be discussed among other questions at a conference.
>
> We are it seems endangering Anglo–French relationship and undoing the work of many months toil for a difference which is now much reduced. Moroever the vote at this morning's French Committee shows a development of independence and judgement [vis-à-vis de Gaulle] which needs to be fostered.[84]

The Foreign Office stuck to its hardened position, however, reasoning that, once released, the Lebanese ministers would in any case reconstitute themselves as a government, and that this would create renewed conflict unless the French agreed beforehand to accept the reinstatement. The only concession the British government was prepared to make was the extension of the deadline by another forty-eight hours to November 24. It was also reemphasized that the scope of the al-Solh government's authority (including the question of the Constitutional Reform Bill) would be the subject of negotiation with the French.[83]

In practice, after the release of the ministers amid scenes of public jubilation on November 22,[86] the British War Cabinet decided that martial law could no longer be imposed automatically on the twenty-fourth if the French had not taken the final step of reinstatement by then. Military takeover was, however, to be retained as an option independent of any fixed deadlines until a final solution had been reached.[87]

Catroux himself had no doubt that the full reinstatement of the Lebanese government was France's best option under the circumstances. Whlie French dignity would indeed be preserved by a unilateral withdrawal from the region, as de Gaulle advocated, nothing substantive would be gained. Britain would receive full credit for having liberated the Lebanese and Syrians while the empire would have lost one of its more important colonies. In Catroux's view, the British ultimatum was not even the central factor to be considered, for no viable alternatives to reinstatement existed in any case. If prevented from reinstating themselves as a government, the released ministers would join the rebel group in the Shuf mountains, where the British would help them organize an armed insurrection. Given the recent growth in national consciousness among the native population, the exclusive reliance on direct military force was an anachronistic means of preserving political authority in the Levant.[88]

De Gaulle remained set in his views, refusing to regard the issue in any light other than that of the Franco–British confrontation. To give in completely to British demands represented a humiliation that the general appeared to conceive of in almost personal terms. His outlook was reinforced by the stream of telegrams sent to him by Helleu and his subordinates in their struggle to save their positions along with their policies by playing on de Gaulle's Anglophobia.[89] Helleu refused to accept the FCNL's decision to recall him as transmitted by Catroux, insisting that he would recognize an order to that effect only if it came directly from de Gaulle. The latter did confirm the committee's decision, albeit in a very friendly and sympathetic tone.[90] He simultaneously warned Catroux to take care to present Helleu's departure as a routine matter of consultations rather than a "brutal disavowal."[91] As for the issue of reinstatement, he reiterated that, while approving the reappointment of al-Khoury to the presidency, the FCNL was opposed to the return of the al-Solh cabinet to office.[92]

Al-Khoury absolutely refused to consider any such compromise, however, and Catroux then decided to take matters into his own hands. He reported to the FCNL that its instructions were designed to resist British demands without taking into account the psychological and human factors that were playing so great a role on the local scene. Since he could not carry out his formal instructions and since resigning on the spot would be playing into the hands of the British, Catroux announced his intention of proceeding with the full reinstatement of the Lebanese government on his own authority and in the face of the explicit order not to do so.[93] He justified his position in a lengthy and impassioned telegram sent to de Gaulle on November 23, in which he forcefully presented his conception of the Lebanese crisis. He repeated that Spears had merely exploited a phenomenon that had been developing on its own: the growth of political consciousness among the Lebanese. Helleu's suspension of the constitution and imprisonment of the government were acts that

> were resented as an affront to national dignity and as a sign of the decline of France. . . . It is important to be aware that the coup of 10 November [sic] produced what amounts to a crystallization of the national idea and, more than the defeat of 1940, weakened the faith in and admiration for France among the Lebanese.
>
> We are no longer recognized as the spiritual descendants of the French revolution. That is the reproach voiced to me by the visitors whom I receive and by the letters which are addressed to me. This is why our recovery must be effected on the moral plane, there where we have sinned against the spirit by employing force. This is why we will not restore our image unless we make total amends for our errors. This is why we must adapt our political behavior to the susceptibilities of the Lebanese national sentiment, this is why, finally, . . . I cannot execute the decision of the Commiteee without doing harm to France.

Catroux went on to present a bitter indictment of Helleu, from whom de Gaulle seemed so reluctant to dissociate himself:

> May I speak to you of Mr. Helleu? I consider it unnecessary to assure you that I am guarding against lending his departure the character of a brutal disgrace. I must nonetheless tell you that he had completely lost prestige among the Syrians and Lebanese, even before he was discredited by his latest decisions. It was known only too well that old age had worn away his ability to work, that he did not follow affairs and that, at certain hours of the day, he ceased being lucid, a point which I have personally ascertained on two recent occasions. This is to explain to you how painful it was for me to follow your personal recommendation and display personal solidarity and the solidarity of France with Mr. Helleu on the occasion of an act of force which he persists in regarding as an act of high political opportuneness. . . . This is why it is not fitting, in my opinion, that the Committee should appear to cover for him, for the Levant and the World would not understand why.[94]

Catroux was temporarily deterred from carrying out his act of defiance by a personal telegram (#450) from de Gaulle, which he received on the morning of November 23. Unfortunately, this cable appears to have been pulled from the relevant Quai d'Orsay file and its content can only be guessed at from references in other communications. The telegram was apparently written prior to the receipt of Catroux's announcement of his unilateral decision on reinstatement, but seems to have contained a warning that the FCNL would not recognize a reconstituted al-Solh government and possibly even an order to use force if need be to prevent the Lebanese ministers from returning to power. In any case, Catroux responded by backing down from his stand, but he did insist that, if presented by al-Solh and his colleagues with a fait accompli, he would not resort to force to undo it. He then informed al-Khoury that this was his position, thus effectively giving the Lebanese a green light to proceed with their own reinstatement.[95]

During this time, however, Massigli had received Catroux's earlier telegram announcing his unilateral initiative. Unaware that de Gaulle had sent a personal cable to Catroux, Massigli assumed that the latter had already gone ahead with the reinstatement. He read Catroux's telegram to the FCNL in light of that assumption, thus blocking de Gaulle's intransigent approach. The only question was whether or not the committee would rubber stamp an action that it assumed already to have been taken. What ensued was described by Massigli a few days later as having been

> a scene in the grand tradition, in the course of which I [Massigli] offered my resignation. But it is important that you [Catroux] know this: the great majority of the Committee was with me and notably the men of the Resistance—Le Trocquer, who is excellent, Frenay, d'Astier and even the Resistance group in the Assembly.[96]

The result was a defeat for de Gaulle, as the FCNL decided to authorize the dispatch of a curtly worded telegram to Catroux, informing him that: "The Committee, meeting this morning, has taken note of your initiative."[97] Whatever doubt this cryptic message may have left in Catroux's mind was dispelled when Spears showed him a cable from Macmillan reporting in greater detail on the committee's meeting as described to him by Massigli. Catroux accordingly went ahead with his original decision, informing al-Khoury on November 24 that he had his formal approval for the return to power of the al-Solh cabinet.[98] Soon afterwards, he received a personal telegram from Massigli warmly endorsing his decision:

> The conditions under which the Committee's examination of your telegrams of the 22nd was concluded obliged me to telegraph you simply that note had been taken of your initiative. *Personally* I wish to express to you my complete solidarity. The decision which you took was that which, given the state of affairs, best served the French interest. Most of our colleagues shared this point of view [italics in original].[99]

While the triumphant Lebanese ministers were being wildly acclaimed by huge crowds in Beirut, Boegner and Baelen quietly left for Algiers, and Chataigneau, who had been designated as the acting delegate-general, formally took the reins of power from Helleu.[100] Catroux also stayed behind to oversee the transition to what he was determined would be a new chapter in Franco–Lebanese relations.

9

The Lull between the Storms

The Search for a Modus Vivendi

The events of November 1943 left the French in a very tenuous position in the Levant. The unconditional victory that had been won by the Lebanese had sent them into a state of euphoria, in the face of which it would be very difficult to proceed with any measures intended to preserve French influence in the country. As American military intelligence saw it:

> Intense Lebanese nationalism has been aroused by the French coup. All group antagonism seems to be broken for the time being, and the Lebanese have been almost miraculously fused into an undivided nation, determined to win independence.[1]

No less importantly, the outcome of the crisis had made it clear that the British would not allow the French to employ coercion in their attempt to retain influence in the region. This left the French with little bargaining power, and emboldened the Levant states to secure their independence before the end of the war and the departure of the protective glacis of British troops.[2]

The Syrians, who had maintained a cautious wait-and-see attitude during the crisis itself, were now eager to reap the fruits of the Lebanese victory. Before the end of November, they were already preparing to remove the article in their constitution that recognized the authority of the French mandate. In his meetings with the two Levant governments, Catroux found both of them equally unwilling to consider the negotiation of treaties with the French either during or after the war. The most they were willing to discuss was the settlement of various outstanding differences as part of a wartime modus vivendi, and this only if the French were prepared to be forthcoming over such matters as handing over control of the common interests.[3]

Catroux was acutely aware of the weakened condition of French power, yet persisted in the belief that the rapid implementation of a liberal program in the Levant could help salvage some degree of political influence for France in the future. For the time being, the British military presence clearly deprived the FCNL of the leverage necessary to induce the Levant states to negotiate treaties. The commissioner hoped gradually to win the confidence of the Syrians and Lebanese by making substantive concessions to them in the modus vivendi

167

talks and then tye together the resulting agreements in a package that could serve as the basis for postwar treaties. The idea was to play for time while concurrently convincing the Syrians and Lebanese of French good faith.[4]

To carry off such a plan was easier said than done. Apart from the obvious problem of Arab hostility and Spears' obstructiveness, Catroux continued to encounter resistance from the right wing within the local French administration. This problem became apparent when Catroux prepared to rescind the last of Helleu's November 11 decrees, namely the one that canceled the Lebanese Parliament's constitutional reform bill. To accept the reform bill was to accept the termination of the mandate for all practical purposes, and this prospect sparked off widespread disaffection among French officers and officials. When rumors began to spread of an impending right-wing Putsch, Catroux decided not to act on the issue until he had secured the official sanction of the FCNL.[5]

Catroux's liberalism in this respect actually went beyond what the British Foreign Office considered to be the limits of prudence. Perplexed at the commissioner's proposal, the Foreign Office pointed out that it had considered that the issue of constitutional reform was a subject to be discussed in the talks on a modus vivendi. The ultimate objective for Whitehall remained the negotiation of Franco–Levantine treaties (to be ratified after the war) modeled on the Anglo–Iraqi treaty. Only after the signature of such treaties would the mandate be terminated:

> Recent events will have worsened French chances of negotiating such a treaty but having regard to our own position elsewhere it is not in our interest that the Levant States should by unilateral action succeed in breaking all political ties with France. Flouting of French authority in the Levant might . . . have inconvenient reactions upon our own interest in Egypt, Iraq, Palestine and elsewhere.[4]

This pro-French position was, in part, the result of a meeting between Eden and Macmillan in Cairo at the end of November, at which it had been agreed that the prime minister's approval should be sought for a policy that would shift the burden of British pressure to the Levantines:

> Both the Syrians and (especially) the Lebanese must be deflated. They must be told that they cannot rely on us to help them eject the French, only to get a fair arrangement.[7]

Both men also agreed that the British should not force themselves on the French as arbitrators in the negotiations; this was a role that they could assume once both sides considered it desirable.[8]

When Eden returned to London, he secured the prime minister's approval of this approach, but both Macmillan and the Foreign Office staff were understandably pessimistic over the prospects for the implementation of this policy as long as Spears remained the man in charge:

> I particularly doubt whether Louis Spears will or can address himself to the uncongenial task of "deflating" the Lebanese. I cannot help thinking that

being a popular hero in the Levant has rather gone to his head. I cannot believe he was ever so cheered and applauded in Carlisle [Spears' constituency in his role as M.P., 1931–1945]![9]

In fact, the resident minister feared that his own job was at risk in the wake of his recent criticism of Spears. He noted that Churchill

does not like opposition as much as he did, and I may have made trouble over this last incident, since Louis Spears is an old friend, and Winston is very loyal (too loyal, sometimes) to old friends.[10]

Spears did indeed prove true to form. In an angry and impassioned telegram, he effectively refused to accept London's instructions, claiming that they were completely incompatible with political conditions in the Levant. The Syrians and Lebanese regarded the mandate as dead in all but letter and were, he felt, justified in this attitude. The Anglo–Iraqi accord did not represent a suitable model for the Levant states, since their independence had already been proclaimed in 1941, whereas in Iraq's case a declaration of independence had only been issued in tandem with the conclusion of a treaty with Britain. The only sort of modus vivendi the Levant governments were ready to contemplate was one based on "the limitations imposed on their sovereignty by the needs of the Allied armies while the war lasts. They would also be prepared to take into account the French cultural position in the Levant."[11] The nature of Spears' personal feelings on the issue became readily apparent, as he stated that

the Levant Governments have never had the least intention of negotiating with the French. To suggest that they should do so now, is to show how little the depth of feeling aroused by recent events has been understood. Restraint of the Lebanese has been remarkable, but this does not mean that they have forgotten the outrages perpetrated upon their leaders or the murder of their children. For us to press them to discuss a treaty now with the perpetrators of those crimes would strike them as callous and unseemly.[12]

In another cable, Spears reiterated his old claim that French power in the region was derived from British military occupation rights rather than from the mandate.[13]

During this time, Catroux was in Algiers presenting his case for a new look for French policy in the Levant. In the wake of his earlier victory over de Gaulle, he now found it relatively easy to win the FCNL's support for his program. Although the decree abolishing the Lebanese constitutional reform was not officially repealed, it was not enforced either. Catroux also won approval for his recommendation that the next delegate-general should jointly head both the civil and military administrations, so as to avoid the conflict of authority and rancor that had characterized relations between Helleu and de Lavalade.[14] The idea was even considered of changing the delegate-general's status to that of ambassador, but this was dropped when it appeared the British would not or could not reciprocate by removing Spears from the scene.[15] Most importantly, it was agreed that the common interests were to be turned over to the control of the Levant states, while the native levies (*troupes spéciales*) remained under French command as the last important gage that could be used to secure postwar treaties.[16]

The new line of action in the Levant was formulated in a lengthy memorandum issued in the name of the FCNL, but clearly bearing the mark of Catroux's authorship. The desired modus vivendi, it was clarified, would bring a practical end to the mandate and thereby facilitate the maintenance of a less provocative French presence in the region in the form of counselors attached to the Levant states' governments, the French judges still present on many of the courts, the French educational institutions, the *Services Spéciaux* officers, and the military. This is what provided the French with an opportunity to win new influence in Syria and Lebanon through the pursuit of an enlightened policy. A basis would thus be created for a healthy and cooperative relationship between the tutelary power and its Middle Eastern protégés once metropolitan France had been liberated and the Levant states had reverted to their age-old sectarian tension and political infighting:

> France will become France once again and this resurrection will have its extension in the Levant. Lebanon, which we so inopportunely incited against us, will disunite and will once again witness clan and confessional antagonisms and, for its Christians, the obsessive fear of absorption by the lands of Islam. Syria will inevitably see the rebirth of the particularisms of its compact minorities and it will feel the menace of dismemberment at its southern, northern and northeastern frontiers. And in both countries, the functioning of the constitutional regime will disrupt the momentary solidarity of the parties. . . .
>
> To wait, to remain in place, to adapt ourselves to the conditions of the moment, to avoid the psychological errors of the past, to reconstruct our moral credit on its liberal and intellectual foundation; strictly to reserve our rights, to seek an entente with Great Britain—such are the lineaments of the policy of conservation and recovery which we must attempt in the Levant.[17]

Returning to the Levant after his week in Algiers, Catroux met jointly with the Syrian and Lebanese leaderships over the following weeks and settled the arrangements for the transfer to their control of the common interests as of the beginning of January. Many other administrative functions, as well as certain aspects of internal security, were also made the responsibility of the local governments, and the French *Sûreté Générale* was renamed the *Sûreté aux Armées* to indicate the narrowing of its formal jurisdiction to matters relating to military security. Catroux proceeded with this transfer of authority despite clear indications by the Syrians that they had no intention of modifying their opposition to treaty talks with the French in the future. On December 22, 1943, the main agreement regulating the handover of power was signed by French, Syrian, and Lebanese representatives meeting in Damascus.[18]

Catroux's only reward was the conciliatory attitude displayed by the British. Eden and Macmillan had met with Spears in Cairo at the beginning of December, during Catroux's visit to Algiers, and impressed on him that it was now British policy to help bring about the initialing of treaties on the Anglo–Iraqi model between the FCNL and the Levant governments. Spears appeared temporarily cowed as well as genuinely pleased to find on his return to Beirut that Catroux was actually making major concessions. For the rest of the month, the minister sent London telegrams dutifully reporting on his efforts to convince the Syrians and Lebanese to deal with the French in a spirit of compromise.[19] His fundamental attitude had not changed, however, for Spears was happy only when he had the French on the run.[20]

The Continuing Undercurrent of Rivalry

When Catroux left the Levant for the last time in early February, he had ostensibly laid the foundation for the new policy of indirect influence that he had been advocating over the course of the previous year. In the acting delegate-general, Chataigneau, he had a man who could be relied on to carry out his instructions and keep to the spirit of the new guidelines. The appearance that all was set for a peaceful transition was quite misleading, however. Even if the Syrian and Lebanese governments had been willing to forget past grievances and deal with the French in good faith, underlying structural factors would still have made the development of Anglo–French–Levantine symbiosis impossible.

Some of the memos and instructions Catroux himself left behind before his departure betrayed his own doubts about the chances for a successful implementation of his policy. He argued that a complete change of personnel in the General Delegation would be necessary before the French could begin to recultivate the friendship and support among the Lebanese on which their continued position in that country now depended.[21] He issued General de Lavalade with a set of guidelines for his officers to follow in their future relations with the Syrians and Lebanese. They were to avoid associating themselves with any of the local political factions and they were to desist from questioning or seeking to obstruct the new FCNL policy. Catroux was also keenly aware of the need to avoid any unnecessary provocation of the British and he warned that officers should not be permitted to express their resentment of the FCNL's ally in public.[22]

The type of sentiment Catroux was trying to curb is well exemplified by an editiorial published in December by *En Route,* an organ of the French general staff in the Levant. Although not referring specifically to the recent events in Lebanon, the article was suffused with bitterness and resentment at the British and Americans for not treating the Free French as equals in the councils of war. Arguing that Britain had made selfish use of France as a buffer against German attack in 1940, the editorial insisted that France should be considered the first among equals in the war effort. The fact that the FCNL was being denied such a role was condemned as an expression of the narrow self-interest that actuated the British and American governments:

> What goal do they thus pursue? The bestial satisfaction of their national egoism? . . . We can tell them that they are taking the wrong path if they believe they can reserve the great principles for their personal use while adopting towards others methods of which the Nazis would not disapprove, for although iniquities do perhaps facilitate the achievement of temporary advantages, they most certainly always receive their chastisement.[23]

Chataigneau personally apologized to Spears for this xenophobic outburst and cabled to Algiers complaining about the obstreperousness of the military.[24] Even if it were possible to silence the open expression of resentment, however, this would hardly serve to remove it as a determining factor in the outlook and conduct of the officers and administrators whom Catroux had left behind in the Levant. Even as high an official as the delegate in Damascus, Oliva-Roget, inveighed against the Syrians for their ingratitude and the British for their perfidy, without being able to offer any constructive suggestions for bringing about the recovery of France's position in the region.[25]

French hostility toward the British was heightened by the effectiveness with which the latter continued to cultivate contact with the political leadership in Syria and Lebanon. Many of the British officials and officers were experienced Middle Eastern hands who combined in-depth knowledge of the region with a degree of personal initiative that was uncommon among their French counterparts. The French were convinced that a huge proportion of Spears' personnel actually worked for British intelligence.[26] Indeed, many of the British political officers and OCP representatives did periodically provide information for use by intelligence even when they were not directly affiliated with the secret services. In May 1945, the OSS office in Cairo was to draw up what it described as an incomplete list of fifteen "men maintained by Britain in Syria as specialists in national and regional affairs." This included names such as Altounyan of the Ninth Army intelligence, who had been a close friend of T. E. Lawrence, and Colonel Stirling, also a former associate of Lawrence's as well as a friend of the Hashemite royal family, who dealt with Bedouin affairs in Syria. Others on the list included members of the OCP staff, officers with the British Security Mission (BSM) and civilians not formally associated with the British government, but called on regularly to provide information on the local political scene.[27]

Apart from the various suspicious characters associated with the Spears Mission or the Ninth Army staff, the French were greatly concerned by the proliferation of British organizations explicitly devoted to intelligence-related activities. To begin with, there was the BSM, a security and counterintelligence organization reporting to General Headquaters in Cairo and responsible for tracking down Axis agents as well as vetting visa applications for the Levant and assisting in frontier security. Under the terms of the de Gaulle–Lyttleton agreements, such functions were supposed to be in the exclusive domain of the *Sûreté Générale,* but in practice, the head of the BSM from 1942 on, Lieutenant-Colonel Patrick Coghill, established a healthy working relationship with his French counterpart, Marcel Gautier, and security work was carried out jointly. Nonetheless, latent tension persisted between these parallel organizations, and, after Gautier's replacement in the wake of the November crisis, relations deteriorated precipitously. Coghill was then instructed "to obtain unobtrusive control of the Sûreté Générale aux Armées," a suggestion he himself claims to have regarded as laughably unrealistic.[28]

The SOE also remained active in the Levant throughout this period. It maintained a badly run intelligence-gathering operation of sorts[29] and, more importantly, built up a network of operatives whose job it was to perform sabotage and intelligence-gathering missions in the event of a military occupation of the region by German forces. (The *Haganah* agents who had originally run this network were replaced largely by locally recruited Armenians in 1942 after it was discovered that *Haganah* men at a British-run training center in Haifa had stolen equipment for the use of the Jewish underground.)[30]

Given the presence of such an intricate network of British security and intelligence organizations, it was easy for the French to continue to attribute the provocativeness of Syrian and Lebanese behavior solely to the incitement of the British. Wherever they were posted, British personnel seemed able to manipulate and dominate local politics with as great a facility as Spears displayed on the national scene.[31] Even appointments to Syrian administrative posts were said to be made in accordance with British recommendations and desires.[32] During Spears' temporary absence from the Levant in August 1944, Beynet reported that the nefarious activities of his underlings and of British military officers continued unabated:

> In Syria, as in Lebanon, the absence of the British Minister gives us the advantage of not having to battle against an active, tenacious and unscrupulous adversary, coordinating against us the efforts of his agents and causing them to undertake maneuvers on a broad scale. But this relative truce does not signify that we are at peace. Each in his own sphere, these collaborators continue to battle against French influence in the Levant. Whether it is Captain Lawson in Tripoli, Captain Nairn in Sidon, these so-called 9th Army liaison officers Colonel Stirling or Major Altounyan, each one does his best to implement his absent chief's thinking, to our detriment.[33]

Oliva-Roget reported that the Syrian government, which had remained quiescent during the height of the Lebanese crisis, had virtually been coerced by Major Beaumont, the British vice-consul in Damascus, into issuing anti-French statements and demands after the crisis had subsided.[34] The encouragement and advice offered to the Syrians by emissaries from other Arab countries was also seen as an integral facet of British policy.

In addition to the large measure of truth in these charges, it is also apparent that the Syrians and Lebanese did their best to play off the French and British against one another.[35] (Most of the information on which Oliva-Roget based his accusations was obtained from sources within the Syrian government.) But even an official who took this factor into account and who was genuinely committed to Catroux's program of reform would have hesitated to embark on it while the British political/military machine remained intact and seemed poised to exploit any false move on the part of the French.[36]

Thus, the zeal with which Spears pursued his ends combined with the semimythical reputation of British intelligence as an omnipresent fomenter of subversion, to produce an image of a sinister English octopus slowly enveloping the Levant in its embrace while a prostrate France lay helpless. Painfully aware of their inability to confront British power directly, the French finally resorted to the same underhanded methods that they accused their rivals of employing. The easiest tactic was the passive sabotage of British interests. Thus, the authorities turned a blind eye to Zionist arms-smuggling operations across the Lebanese–Palestinian border. When the British raised the issue with them, the French suggested that British political officers might first try showing a little more respect for French interests in southern Lebanon; *then* perhaps the border control could be tightened.[37]

More ominous in British eyes was the establishment of a secret office known as the *Bureau Noir,* designed to disseminate inflammatory, anti-British propaganda in the Middle East. Palestine was specially targeted in the apparent hope that both Arab and Jewish extremists could be incited to create unrest. The *Bureau Noir* was reported to have been set up by Lieutenant-Colonels Neuhauser and Boisseau of French military intelligence. It was headed by Lieutenant-Colonel Alessandri, who had served as Vichy's military attaché in Teheran during Helleu's tenure as ambassador there. Described as violently anti-British, Alessandri had later been in charge of the volatile district of Deir al-Zor, where he had immediately clashed with his British counterpart and was ultimately removed. The short-sighted vindictiveness of Alessandri's efforts is of interest only as a measure of French bitterness and frustration over the decline of their power in the region, in the face of which they were fundamentally impotent. The only discernible effect of the *Bureau Noir*'s activities was to deepen the suspicion and resentment with which the British regarded French policy in the Levant.[38]

The superficial appearance of an improvement in relations engendered by the Franco–Levantine transfer of powers in January 1944 was thus belied by the persistence of deep undercurrents of suspicion, intrigue, and hostility among the major players. The British suspected the French of undermining the purpose of the power transfers by carrying them out in a deliberately precipitate and ill-coordinated fashion. During February and early March, Spears reported a sudden influx of Vichy diplomatic officials from Turkey into the Levant, warning that many of them could well be plants rather than genuine defectors. Concurrently, reports were rife of a right-wing coup plot by the disaffected elements in the officer corps, purportedly led by General Monclar of the foreign legion. Security Intelligence Middle East (SIME) in Cairo warned of the possibility of a concerted French effort to undermine the Levant governments by playing on internal factionalization and regional disaffection. SIME also feared the possibility of Franco–Zionist political collusion in the Middle East. Tensions were exacerbated by a rumor campaign mounted by some French officers to the effect that 40,000 troops were about to be sent in from Algiers to reimpose the mandate.[39]

The left wing also was not above the use of intrigue to further its ends. In

December 1943, a number of *anciens ralliés* formed themselves into a "Groupe de Resistance du Levant," which aimed at a purge of Vichyite elements from the Levant administration. Lépissier continued his alarmist talk of the threat from Cagoulard elements and those around him expressed the hope that he would return to a position of influence once Catroux's man Chataigneau was replaced by the newly selected delegate-general, General Beynet.[40]

Further Sources of Conflict

As in the past, a variety of nettling issues continued to create friction among the various authorities in the Levant during early 1944. No change of personnel was without its political implications and no administrative measure could be taken without its causing a dispute.

During late February and early March, controversy centered around the nature of General Beynet's appointment. At issue was not the choice of person, but rather his scope of power. In the hope of improving the coordination of political and military affairs, the FCNL had accepted Catroux's recommendations that supreme civil and military powers be wielded by one and the same man, as had been the case with Catroux himself as well as with a number of high commissioners before the war. When this became known, the Levant governments protested the arrangement as incompatible with the independent status of their countries. The Syrians and Lebanese went even further by demanding that Beynet be appointed as an ambassador only and that their formal *agrément* be obtained in advance.[41]

Although the French naturally suspected Spears of being behind this move, it became increasingly apparent that it was Wadsworth who had seized the initiative on this occasion.[42] In fact, he had for weeks been warning the Lebanese to beware of possible saboteurs among the French personnel retained in the administration of the Common Interests and had been encouraging the authorities in Beirut to reduce all ties with the French while bringing Lebanon into closer cooperation with the other Arab states.[43] The General Delegation also managed to obtain the text of communications sent by the Egyptian consul in Beirut to his government, reporting on meetings in which the Iraqi and Egyptian representatives had threatened the Lebanese leaders with a withdrawal of recognition unless the nature of the Beynet appointment were protested.[44]

Coming as it did in the midst of the scare over a possible right-wing coup against the General Delegation, the Beynet issue sharpened the tension of the political atmosphere in a manner that both Spears and Chataigneau found counterproductive. The latter feared that the Lebanese and Syrian move would play right into the hands of the reactionary officers opposed to the new political arrangement. At the same time, the French realized that the Levant governments—and al-Solh's patchwork coalition in particular—could ill afford the loss of face that a retreat from their positions would entail.[45]

Chataigneau's top aide, Count Ostorog, criticized the nonchalant manner in which the terms of the appointment had been decided on without even pro forma consultations with the Syrian and Lebanese governments. Chataigneau accordingly advocated that Beynet be appointed as chief of the civil administration alone, leaving the acting commander-in-chief, General Humblot, in charge of the military for the time being. In Algiers, of course, this met with opposition from de Gaulle, but a compromise was finally worked out under which Beynet was appointed as delegate-general only, while secretly reserving the option of assuming full military command should he find it necessary at any time. For their part, the Levant governments effectively dropped their demand for the reduction of the French representative's status to the ambassadorial level and Beynet was greeted on his arrival in Beirut in mid-March by Lebanese officials acting in an unofficial capacity. This little drama, as complicated as it seemed pointless, thus ended with no one's honor permanently damaged and the fragile structure of relations among the various parties preserved.[46]

Although Spears appears to have been careful not to provoke the French right wing over the Beynet issue, he continued to press ahead with his general effort to undercut French influence throughout this period. This was most immediately noticeable in the economic sphere, where, as has been seen, French presidency of the *Commission Supérieure du Ravitaillement* had been offset by French exclusion from the MESC.[47] In January 1944, Spears and Wadsworth moved to diminish the French role in economic affairs even further by creating a number of advisory boards, each of which would administer the supply and distribution of a separate group of products, and which would function as branches of the MESC. The latter, of course, was now jointly administered by the British and the Americans, and it was intended that the Levant advisory boards would be supervised by a new supervisory council on which French, British, and U.S. representatives would carry equal weight. Chataigneau objected that this would leave the French outvoted, but it rapidly became apparent that they had no real say in the matter. When a representative of the MESC visited the Levant to arrange the provision of Lend-Lease aid to Lebanon and Syria, Wadsworth saw to it that he bypassed the French and dealt directly with the Beirut and Damascus governments instead. Presented with this fait accompli, Chataigneau could only be satisfied that the General Delegation would be represented at all on the supervisory council. In April, Spears was to take the next logical step of demanding that British economic specialists be regularly consulted by the Syrian and Lebanese authorities. With customs income in the hands of the Levant governments and supply questions dealt with by the British and Americans, the French were left with practically no economic influence in the region.[48]

The one major form of leverage retained by the French was provided by their continued control over the native military levies, the *troupes spéciales*. While most bureaucratic functions as well as many internal security responsibilities were being handed over to the Syrians and Lebanese subject to the British commander-in-chief's review and approval,[49] the French held on to the approximately 20,000 *troupes spéciales* as the last bargaining chip with which they hoped to extract postwar treaties from the local governments.[50] In January, the Syrians issued a formal demand for the immediate transfer of the levies to their control (this after having been assured by General Holmes that he had no objections to such a development). The point was reinforced by public agitation and demonstrations that broke out over the issue in Damascus.[51]

Before departing for Algiers at the end of February, Catroux had stalled for time over the issue by suggesting that command over the *troupes spéciales* be theoretically transferred to the Syrians while effectively leaving it under French territorial command for the duration of the war.[52] The Syrians rejected this, demanding that they exercise the territorial command, leaving operational control in British hands as was already the case.[53] Spears sought to find a solution by suggesting various convoluted, legalistic compromises, but there was no getting around the fact that the Syrians wanted an army of their own right away, and the French would not give it to them.[54] This was to remain the major bone of contention between the two sides during the course of the next year, and it did not take Spears long before he tried to use the issue as a means of destroying the last vestiges of French influence in the country.

Internal Political Dynamics

As the immediate impact of the November crisis receded, the fractured structure of Levantine politics gradually reemerged, providing fertile ground for the intrigues of the French and British. In Syria, the French began to find opportunities for renewing their traditional support for the various minority groups against the centralizing power of Damascus. A bulletin issued by the headquarters of the *Services Spéciaux* in September restated the traditional French policy of *divide et impera* as follows:

> The Alawite separatist movement can serve the same function as Kurdish nationalism, the defence of Armenian rights and in general of other minorities, as a point of support which will enable France to retain a platform of activity in the Middle East and to arrive at the conclusion of a Franco–Syrian treaty acceptable to both parties and to the minorities.[55]

The British backed the Syrian government in its attempts to crack down on regional autonomy. The French-supported, Alawite, religiopolitical figure Suleiman Murshid, decried by the British as nothing more than a ruthless brigand, was arrested by the Syrian authorities and brought to Damascus to be held in detention. The Jebel Druze, which had been formally incorporated into Syria in 1942, now became fully integrated into the state.[56] Hardly an incident occurred that was not attributed by one party to the machinations of the other. In May, antigovernmental demonstrations in the Midan quarter of Damascus were put down by the government at the cost of several casualties. Although ostensibly instigated by a Muslim fundamentalist group, French intelligence connected the outbreak to attempts by pro-Hashemite groups to create a consolidated opposition bloc in the country. (As usual, the ultimate initiative in the matter was attributed to British intelligence.)[57]

In Lebanon, the French *Sûreté* appears to have supported antigovernment elements in the Maronite community in the hope of reviving the Christian–Muslim antagonism on which their power as arbiters had depended in the past. In the wake of indications that Emile Edde was involved in these plots, Spears and Furlonge (the British consul in Beirut) encouraged a number of members of the Lebanese Parliament to introduce a motion to expel Edde from the Chamber of Deputies in retribution for his role in the November crisis and before he could reorganize an effective opposition party. The motion was passed overwhelmingly on March 31 despite Beynet's efforts to intervene and Edde was forced to leave in disgrace.[58] In Spears' view, there was a real danger that the Maronite community could drift back into dependence on the French unless active measures were taken to assert British interest in playing a long-term role on the Lebanese political scene.[59]

Political tensions were raised to a higher level by the April 1944 victory in a Tripoli byelection of one Joseph Karam, whose nineteenth-century ancestor and namesake had been a renowned Maronite leader and symbol of Lebanese Christian nationalism.[60] Karam was affiliated with Edde, and Beynet saw his election as a great success for the French in view of what he described as Spears' and the Lebanese government's attempts to maniuplate the voting to their own advantage. The pro-French opposition elements within the Maronite community planned to use Karam's entry into Parliament on April 27 as the occasion for mounting a demonstration of their political strength. Spears was not about to let this happen, however, and he actually sat in on the meeting of the Lebanese Cabinet on April 26 which decided what measures to employ in the event of trouble the next day. On April 27, when the crowd triumphantly escorting Karam to the Chamber of Deputies sought to gain entry into the building itself, they were confronted with police barricades and a riot ensued. Shots rang out from various directions and one of the demonstrators, a Lebanese-born, French noncommissioned officer, was killed in the act of hoisting the tricolor in front of the Parliament building.[61]

The Karam incident immediately became the source of suspicion and fear, charges and countercharges for all the parties concerned. Beynet was convinced Spears had deliberately provoked the violence in order to further his own political ends, while Spears presented the incident as the result of a plot by Edde's supporters and right-wing French elements beyond Beynet's control. The al-Solh government sought to make the most of the affair by arresting eighty to ninety prominent Francophiles while accusing the French of once more conspiring against Lebanese independence. From Algiers, Duff Cooper (newly appointed as British representative to the FCNL) reported that Massigli had told him Beynet had been authorized at his own request to adopt retaliatory measures against the Lebanese should the need arise. This reminded the British of the November crisis and in response to the uproar from the Foreign Office, Beynet insisted that all he had asked for was permission to prevent the Lebanese from taking any precipitate action. In any case, the

French ended by exercising self-restraint while the Lebanese, realizing that they had overplayed their hand, released most of the arrested men. The entire incident was finally buried through the consignment of its investigation to a joint Anglo–French board of inquiry.[62]

Spears Oversteps the Mark

In the months that had elapsed since the November crisis, Spears' popularity had not risen in Whitehall. Even Churchill appeared to have less confidence in his friend. At the time when the French were still suspicious about Spears' role in the clash over Beynet's dual appointment, Duff Cooper had transmitted Massigli's concerns to London and the prime minister had, in turn, admonished his friend. He pointed out that relations with de Gaulle had been improving as his power within the FCNL had been reduced, and that there was therefore no reason to seek renewed confrontation:

> I told you in Cairo [in December 1943] that I had no wish to destroy French influence in Syria and the Lebanon. . . . You are however going further than I wish and anyone can see you have become bitterly anti-French. . . . Admire efficiency and vigilance in your work but "surtout pas trop de zèle."[63]

But when Eden took heart from this and recommended Spears' transfer to a new assignment,[64] Churchill responded as follows:

> I am not prepared to throw over Spears at the present time. I hope he will take my warning seriously. Duff Cooper has set himself to discredit him in every way, and runs some risk himself in the line he takes.[65]

Nonetheless Cooper persisted, pointing out in one letter:

> There has recently been some discussion in the House of Commons about those members of Parliament who are engaged in work which prevents them from attending the House. . . .
>
> . . . If it were thought that those members of the House of Commons who have been longest absent from their parliamentary duties should be the first to return, perhaps consideration could be given to the three years' disfranchisement that has befallen the burghers of Carlisle [Spears' constituency].

Churchill responded concisely: "Nothing doing about the burghers of Carlisle."[66] In May 1944, a dispatch from Spears addressed to the ambassador in Algiers and enclosing a report on one of Lépissier's paranoid diatribes, was mistakenly delivered to Massigli instead of Cooper, allowing the French to see at firsthand in what sort of light the British minister was portraying them. Cooper wrote Eden that Massigli and de Gaulle saw the contents of the report as proof of Spears' inveterate hostility toward their movement.[67] When confronted with this by Eden, Churchill conceded only that Spears had been careless to send the report by ordinary post, insisting that Cooper's attitude was nonetheless uncalled for. The political significance of the issue seemed to pale in comparison to its personal dimension as far as the prime minister was concerned:

Both these men are friends of mine, but I should certainly not allow my friendship for Spears to be affected by the activities of . . . Cooper.[68]

In the summer of 1944 Spears finally pushed his luck too far. In the second half of June, at a time when the Franco–Syrian talks on the *troupes spéciales* were being kept alive only through Spears' mediation, the British military command suddenly made public a plan to transfer 7,000 rifles and other equipment to the Syrian-controlled gendarmerie.[69] The French, who had only around 3,000 troops—mostly Senegalese—in the region, immediately raised an uproar. The political ramifications of this move were glaringly apparent to them:

Be it for the sake of openly forming the first elements of a national army, or under the pretext of facilitating the reinforcement of the gendarmerie, any supply of arms, materiel and military equipment would lead to the same result.[70]

In addition to its significance in the context of the Franco–Syrian negotiations, Massigli saw the move as aimed at disrupting the forthcoming, high-level Anglo–French talks in London concerning the Gaullist role in liberated France after D-Day.[71]

Whitehall was outraged by what it correctly identified as Spears' initiative regarding the gendarmerie. The Foreign Office placed a high priority on the establishment of good postwar relations with the French and did not want to see this policy sabotaged by yet another petty dispute in the Levant. Indeed, Duff Cooper recommended abandoning Syria and Lebanon to the French as the price for a cooperative relationship with them within the European sphere.[72] Moreover, the Gaullists were hinting at the possible consequences of an estrangement by encouraging the Soviets to establish diplomatic ties with the Levant states. (In the event, the Soviet Union recognized Syria and Lebanon as unconditionally independent, further undercutting the legitimacy of the French presence there).[73] After joint consultations, the Foreign Office and War Office sent Spears and Commander-in-Chief Middle East General Paget, respectively, telegrams ordering them to form an ad hoc committee with the French that would iron out the gendarmerie issue. After a brief attempt to flout London's authority, Spears and Paget gave in, but the Ninth Army command then used the committee as a forum for notifying the French of its decisions rather than seeking to adjust outstanding differences with them. It became clear to Whitehall that another attempt would have to be made to reach an agreement with the French over the Levant at the foreign ministry level.[74] Eden also urged the prime minister to recall Spears for consultations "in the hope that you and I may once more be able to make our policy clear to him, which is not to undermine the French in the Levant."[75]

Despite his temporary setback over the ad hoc committee, Spears relentlessly pursued his provocative policies. Using the Beirut diplomatic corps as a weapon in his struggle, Spears organized a boycott by foreign representatives of the French military review in Beirut scheduled for July 14. In a move obviously coordinated with Spears' effort, the Syrian and Lebanese governments issued nationwide orders barring all native officials from attending any of the French ceremonies. In the wake of the successful boycott, the Syrian government launched a virulent press campaign against the French, in the apparent hope of provoking them into an ill-considered reaction that would lead to their downfall.[76] Finally, Spears once again tried to present the Foreign Office with a fait accompli by letting it know that he had taken the liberty of informing the Levant governments that they would shortly be presented with deliveries of arms and supplies for their gendarmeries: "If therefore there is any hold up in deliveries a new and serious problem will be introduced."[77] In another cable sent on the same day, Spears argued, "The French do not wish the gendarmerie to be adequately armed so that there should be no local force capable of resisting a coup if and when it suits the French to attempt another one."[78] R. M. A. Hankey saw Spears as guilty of "absolute insubordination" and the Foreign Office categorically ordered him to make no arms deliveries pending authorization.[79] More importantly, Churchill had finally been convinced that things were not as they should be in the Spears Mission, and a cable recalling the wayward representative for consultations was sent off on July 19.[80]

The French were alarmed over the state of the affairs in the Levant and Beynet had flown to Algiers to confer with the FCNL in early July. He painted a sinister picture of British duplicity and underhandedness in the region. The breakdown of the *troupes spéciales* talks in June had come just after a trip by Spears to Damascus and it was only his personal arbitration that had kept the negotiations going. Beynet was convinced that this was no coincidence; in other words the British minister was instigating the very disputes which he would then help to mediate.[81] Oliva-Roget was reporting that a sympathetic, high-ranking British officer had spoken of a British plan to reorganize and modernize the transportation and communications systems in Syria. The MESC had taken over all effective responsibility for problems of supply in the Levant and Wadsworth was apparently on the verge of arranging for direct Lend-Lease aid to the region as soon as Beirut and Damascus had declared war on Germany (this step was not to take place until the following year).[82] The British military command was also preventing the French from increasing their troop strength in the region. Beynet was personally convinced, as Catroux had been before him, that Spears could not be undertaking such consistently aggressive actions on his own initiative, but rather that his conduct must represent the policy of the British government.[83] The FCNL decided that the best way to ascertain the truth of the matter was to gauge London's attitude by raising two specific issues as test cases. When Massigli went to London in August, he would adopt firm stands (1) against the provision of arms to the gendarmerie and (2) on behalf of the FCNL's intention of stationing in the Levant 500 Alsatian troops recently released from Soviet prisoner-of-war camps:

> The solutions which will be found for these problems . . . will enable us to see to what degree the London Government supports a policy in the Levant which gravely hampers Franco–British relations.[84]

The results of Massigli's talks in London were ambiguous. A temporary compromise was reached on the gendarmerie issue whereby the French and British were jointly to issue 2,000 new rifles, the question of additional arms deliveries being relegated to discussions between the military commands in the Levant. Massigli's demands for French inclusion in the MESC were again turned down and no French troop reinforcements in Syria and Lebanon were approved; however, this setback was more than compensated for by indications on the part of the Foreign Office that Britain intended to take active measures in support of the conclusion of Franco–Levantine treaties and that Spears' days in Beirut were numbered.[85]

The month of August 1944 did indeed prove to be a fatal one for the Spears Mission. As soon as Spears had left for London, what seemed like a prearranged plan to destroy his power base went into effect. In his absence, the embassy came under the direction of his deputy Gilbert MacKereth, who had replaced the loyal Lascelles only in June. MacKereth was a regional expert who had served as consul in Damascus during the 1930s and who had a reputation as one of the most Francophile members of the British Middle Eastern diplomatic service.[86] Nonetheless, during his brief association with Spears that summer, he had helped him draft numerous telegrams defending his controversial positions on Levant affairs.[87] Yet as soon as Spears was gone, MacKereth began to supervise the wholesale dismantling of the Spears Mission along the lines of the Foreign Office's suspended 1942 blueprint.[88] The British military command moved to assume responsibility for all liaison functions that had until then been exercised by the Spears Mission's military section; the MESC prepared to absorb the mission's economic section; and the War Establishment Board Middle East began discussions with the Beirut Legation aimed at the severe reduction in numbers, amounting almost to elimination, of the political officers under Spears' command (this last move never really got off the ground). The Beirut Chancery reported on this with the telegraphic equivalent of a poker face:

> All these events seem to point to a dissolution of the Spears Mission, although the question has not been presented in this form. You may care to raise this question with Sir. E. Spears whilst he is in London.[89]

Hankey gleefully noted: "The cat being away, the rats are at his mission. I think we should leave this quite alone. It's all for the best."[90]

In addition to facilitating this sort of organizational sabotage, MacKereth also let loose a flurry of cables that painted a sharply critical picture of Spears' entire policy and served as ammunition for the Foreign Office in its talks with Spears in London. MacKereth called into question the Syrian and Lebanese capacity for effective self-government and suggested that Spears' efforts to undermine French authority were so energetic as to raise suspicions among the native political leadership that he might simply be trying to supplant the French rather than genuinely striving for local independence. Furthermore, argued MacKereth, the minister's aggressiveness was causing the French to harden their position over questions such as the *troupes spéciales*. If they became less worried about British designs to profit from their losses, they would be more willing to make concessions gracefully.[91]

Spears reacted with the bitter outrage of a Shakespearean tragic hero who has discovered, all too late, the vile and treacherous plot that has been hatched against him. On his return to Beirut in September he accused MacKereth of concealing from him some of the telegrams he had written during his absence and charged that he was nothing less than a "planted consul," an *agent provocateur* sent by the Foreign Office to destroy his mission. MacKereth refused to leave his post at Spears' demand and only departed in October at Eden's explicit behest.[92]

Of course, MacKereth was not the main source of trouble for Spears. His real problem lay with the Foreign Office, which had long chafed under the restraint which Churchill's personal loyalty to his friend had imposed upon it. With Paris about to be liberated and de Gaulle established as the head of the French provisional government, it was imperative that Spears' efforts to disrupt Anglo–Gaullist relations be terminated. It had also become apparent that the prime minister himself had begun to entertain doubts about his protégé's conduct and Eden took advantage of this to press the official line on Spears with renewed vigor. The balance had swung too far against the French in the wake of the November crisis, he argued:

> While we must continue to urge the French to make gradual progress, it is perhaps even more necessary to exercise some restraint on the two States lest they should be tempted to think that all is over now bar the shouting and that there is no need for them to make some constructive and permanent effort to regularise their future relations with the French.[93]

In a meeting on September 1, Eden handed Spears a formal directive instructing him on his return actively to encourage the Levant governments to conclude treaties with the French, as well as to proceed with the absorption of his mission's various sections into the military establishment and the embassy. Spears objected to everything in the paper, pointing out heatedly that it was the French who had let the Germans into the Levant in the current war and that there was nothing to keep them from repeating their performance the next time. When Eden then asked him point-blank whether this meant he wished to supplant the French, Spears beat a wary retreat and finally "promised to go away and to consider his directive."[94]

More ominous from Spears' point of view was Eden's suggestion that he could expect a successor to his post to be appointed within approximately two months. Spears immediately turned to Churchill for succor:

> I am . . . writing to ask you, if you will, to ensure that I am not asked to leave my post until the end of the war with Germany, and that I be allowed to ask to be relieved when the time comes.
>
> . . . I hope . . . you will prevent action being taken which would be interpreted by the outside world as a sign that you considered I had failed.
>
> . . . I hope you will send me word, in due course, as to how matters stand. You will readily understand the state of suspense involved is most unpleasant.[95]

This time, however, Spears' craven importunities did him no good, as Churchill felt obliged to support his foreign minister's stand:

> I had great difficulty in securing your return to your post. You did not take my advice to try to keep your Franco-phobia within reasonable bounds and there is no doubt that great irritation is felt by the French. . . . I think you must take it that two or three months will be the limit of your tenure out there. . . .
>
> I will however arrange that when the time comes, you will be given the opportunity of asking to be relieved instead of being abruptly superseded. This is the best I can do.[96]

The Fall of Spears

Spears returned to Beirut bearing the Foreign Office's directive he had objected to, regarding the active encouragement of Franco–Levantine treaty talks. He proceeded to inform the Syrians and Lebanese of Britain's official stand on the subject, and then promptly cabled to London that the local governments had been outraged and were categorically refusing to pay any serious consideration to the matter.[97] The Foreign Office was not surprised. One Eastern Department official observed:

> I don't suppose that anyone in this office is very optimistic about the chances of Sir E. Spears getting the Syrians to negotiate for a treaty. This telegram may read as if he was sticking to instructions, but he doesn't want to succeed and much can be done with intonation and eyelids.[98]

George Wadsworth did his best to encourage the local governments' resistance to the new British line and the United States' unconditional recognition of Syrian and Lebanese independence on September 19, with Wadsworth promoted to the rank of ambassador, lent weight to his support. Possibly at Wadsworth's suggestion, the Syrian government sent official notes to Eden, Churchill, Roosevelt, and Stalin, protesting against British pressure and invoking the Atlantic Charter in defense of the Syrian right to national self-determination.[99] In the Foreign Office it was speculated that Spears must have put Wadsworth up to assuming his role as defender of Levant independence.[100] With the Syrians threatening to bring the whole altercation into the public arena unless the *troupes spéciales* were transferred to their control before the convening of the Syrian Chamber on October 5, London sought to stabilize the situation before it got out of control:

> We shall have to tidy this up a bit before October 5th.
>
> I feel bound to record a doubt whether we can do so with Sir E. Spears there. He's created this row absolutely deliberately, in my opinion, in order to show that he was right in wanting to turf the French out neck and crop, and that F.O. were wrong. If this is so (and I'm sure it is) he will want things worse and not better.[101]

The Foreign Office's suspicions regarding Spears' conduct appear to be borne out by the observations he was to record in his diary a few months later:

> I had felt convinced that as since I returned from England early in September all my prognostications had proved to be so accurate, and the refusal of the locals to sign treaties was so unanimous and so well backed by the other Arab states, that Winston and Anthony would feel it was necessary I should stay on. Things had worked out exactly as I thought and I had the satisfaction of finding that the proposals to sign a treaty which I had been ordered to make were not only not acceptable but that it was only the fact that I had made them that prevented the States going off the deep end.[102]

Spears' calculations were all wrong. When he urged the Foreign Office to support the transfer of the *troupes spéciales* as part of a temporary modus vivendi, London rebuffed him by arguing that the French should not be expected to sacrifice their last, remaining bargaining counter.[103] Spears' single-minded pursuit of his anti-French policy also reinforced Churchill's realization that he was no longer suited for his job. Although the Prime Minister did not care for the idea of actively helping the French secure a privileged position in the Levant,[104] he was alarmed by the Damascus government's indirect threats of public unrest over the troop-transfer issue and cabled to Spears ordering him to restrain the Syrians.[105] "I do not like the way Spears is handling this business," he wrote, adding, "We had better get him to meet us [in Egypt]."[106]

As it turned out, Spears was not able to get to Cairo during Churchill's and Eden's stopover there on their way to and from Moscow in October. In any case, the prime minister continued to resist Eden's demands for Spears' immediate dismissal, pointing out that the two or three months' grace period promised him had not yet expired;[107] however, in meetings held with General Paget and Lord Moyne, the new minister of state in Cairo, it was agreed that, what with a conference between de Gaulle and Churchill scheduled for the following month in Paris, Spears would have to take leave of his mission very soon. It was also agreed by all that General Paget should continue to veto the French attempts at reinforcing their military forces in the Levant as long as a final settlement had not been reached.[108]

Despite the agreement on specific details, the Cairo talks left the overall thrust of British policy ill-defined. Whereas Paget and Moyne insisted that Britain should not withdraw its forces from Syria and Lebanon before the French, Eden distanced himself from the implications of such a policy. He also seemed to sympathize with the French over the issue of further arms deliveries to the Syrian gendarmerie:

> Eden said that the French naturally objected to automatics [machine guns for the gendarmerie] as they might well be used against them. He seems to take the view that the French have every right to occupy the [Levant] States. He compared French claims in the Levant with ours in Egypt. When I told him of the deep hatred of the French [on the part of the native population] . . . he

replied that there was just the same dislike for us in Egypt where however we had every intention of remaining.[109]

In Eden's view, a blow struck against French colonial privileges was ultimately a blow against British regional predominance as well.

In Paris, the talks in early November between the British and French leaders went well. The French were gratified by the British offer to create an occupation zone for them in Germany once the war was over. Their outstanding differences regarding the Levant were glossed over in a manner typical of summit meetings: the French agreed to further discussions concerning the gendarmerie issue, but refused to budge over any of its substantive aspects. As for the question of the *troupes spéciales,* they agreed to take under consideration a new British formula that would provide for a partial initial transfer, to be completed on the successful conclusion of Franco–Levantine treaties. Needless to say, nothing came of this in the end.[110]

Having heard from Moyne that his imminent removal had been reconfirmed at the Cairo conferences, Spears wrote Churchill once again, desperately imploring him to change his mind. He portrayed the Levant states' rejection of treaty talks as a vindication of his position and warned that the political stability of the region depended largely on his own good offices. Considerations of policy apart, Spears tried to make his dismissal as painful as possible a decision for Churchill, presenting it as little less than an act of personal betrayal:

> I do not believe *you* wish me to be a burnt offering to de Gaulle. All I am asking for is to be given time to prevent the work I have done being destroyed, and that when I go the world will have no reason to say that I have failed, or that the French have obtained my recall [italics in original].[111]

The prime minister held firm, and on November 23, Spears received a telegram from him suggesting that he resign as of December 15. Spears' reaction was less than sportsmanlike: "I concluded that this was the direct result of his [Churchill's] visit to Paris where he had been extremely well received, and that this had made him sell me to the French."[112] In an effort to spare him the personal embarrassment he dreaded, the Foreign Office presented his resignation as being due simply to his wish to resume his duties in Parliament.[113] When several leading papers published pieces referring to his removal as his "recall" instead of his "resignation," Spears reacted like a slighted prima donna, threatening to sue and forcing them to print retractions.[114]

In the final weeks before his departure, Spears did his best to boost the morale of the Syrians and Lebanese and assure them of his continued support from afar for their resistance to French demands. With nothing left to lose, he dropped all pretences and freely made his feelings known in public:

> From that time on I considered myself a free man and began to make very open speeches. They were really very good speeches and made a profound impression. . . . This counter-acted the French propaganda that it was owing to their efforts that I had been recalled. The speeches also served to give real confidence to the local people.[115]

In his private meetings with Syrian and Lebanese leaders, Spears warned them that his successor might well be ordered by the Foreign Office to lean toward the French in their dispute with the local governments. This could best be countered, he counseled, by looking to support from the Arab states and by counting on his influence in London. In the event a Franco–Syrian conflict broke out, he would use his position in Parliament and his friendship with Churchill to aid the Arab cause.[116]

In his final report to the Foreign Office, Spears elaborated at length on his conception of British interests in the Levant. He argued convincingly that the French experiment in the region had been a failure and that the French had missed their last chance to conclude preferential treaties in 1937. To associate British prestige with such a lost cause would tarnish Britain's image throughout the Arab world. It would be far better to exploit the situation in order to expand British influence into Syria and Lebanon:

> In this country [the Levant], the people as a whole regard the British as the ultimate arbiters of their destinies. The great majority look to us, firstly, to help them to get rid of the French, and secondly, to establish our influence over these States in the same manner as in the rest of the Arab world. . . .
>
> If . . . we are prepared to stand firm now and hereafter in support of these States, until their aspirations are satisfied, I am convinced that we shall be able to build . . . a solid position for ourselves which would buttress the whole structure of our influence in the Middle East.[117]

Curiously, many members of the Eastern Department staff seemed to approve wholeheartedly of the views expressed in this memorandum, now that its troublesome author was on his way out.[118]

10

The Unseemly Dénouement

The Foreign Office had little occasion to celebrate its victory over Spears. His departure from the scene came at a time when it could no longer contribute to the peaceful resolution of differences in the Levant. The French and Syrians were already locked in a stalemate over the related issues of the *troupes spéciales* and the negotiation of treaties. Both sides became more unyielding in reaction to Spears' fall—the French because they interpreted the development as a green light for a more aggressive stance on their part and the Syrians because they realized that, with the end of the war imminent, time was no longer on their side and they had to get rid of the French before the British withdrew the protective buffer of their forces. Whitehall quickly came to realize that in the absence of a Spears on whom all the blame for British difficulties could be pinned, it was not so easy to determine which of Britain's many conflicting interests should assume top priority, let alone how they should be secured.

The Situation in the Wake
of Spears' Departure

Spears' replacement as minister to Syria and Lebanon was Terence Shone, a professional diplomat who had served most recently in the Cairo embassy. Given the fanatical single-mindedness and personal tenacity of his predecessor, Shone was almost bound to impress those he came into contact with on his new assignment as being somewhat weak-willed and colorless. Coghill wrote of him as "full of charm but lacking in personality and decision."[1]

Eden's instructions to Shone were ostensibly identical to those given to Spears: complete the dismantling of the Spears Mission and press for the early conclusion of Franco–Levantine treaties. But whereas in Spears' case the Foreign Office had a tendency to compensate for his Francophobia by writing such orders in categorical terms, an element of ambiguity now entered Eden's cable. He impressed on Shone the importance of getting treaties signed before the end of the war with Japan so as to prevent Britain from later being placed in a false position:

Both Russia and the United States of America have recognized the independence of the Levant States without any qualification and have shown no disposition to accord France a privileged position. I am anxious to avoid a situation in which we should find ourselves left alone with the French in opposition to the two nascent Arab States and to our two major partners in the war.[2]

The British authorities in the Middle East were not slow in making their own views known. Although Spears may not have been the darling of the regional British establishment, his policy had certainly struck a responsive chord among the mixture of Arabophiles and old-fashioned imperialists who dominated it. Ambassador Lampson (now Lord Killearn) in Cairo sent London a forceful telegram in this vein which was immediately backed up by the ministers in Baghdad and Jedda as well as General Paget and Grigg (the new minister of state in Cairo). He argued that what he referred to as London's policy of "promoting Zionism in Palestine and French predominance in Syria" was incompatible with British support for the formation of an Arab federation. The rising tide of Arab nationalism would soon turn against Britain if the French were allowed to impose treaties in the Levant. Killearn questioned Britain's ability to deal with such a challenge given the limitations on its resources: "Can we while involved in repressive action in liberated territories such as Greece undertake in the near future repressive action in Egypt–Arab world?"[3]

From Beirut, Shone concurred with this view. His first impression on arrival in the region had been the intensity of emotion and bitterness with which the local governments rejected the notion of accommodating any French demands. His immediate reaction had been to assure the governments that no fundamental change had taken place in British policy. Indeed, Shone even proved reluctant to do away entirely with the Spears Mission. Although the mission was formally renamed the "Military Staff of His Majesty's Legation," it was reduced in size at a very gradual pace, so that at the end of 1945 its personnel still numbered 60 people out of an original 100. Given such administrative continuity, the reluctance of the British Legation to pursue a policy of active pressure in favor of treaty talks became painfully apparent.[4]

The Foreign Office failed to find an effective means of reconciling the conflicting interests that were at stake for Britain in the Levant. Its overall inclination continued to be in the direction of Franco–Levantine treaties, not only out of concern for future Anglo–French relations in the European sphere, but also because it was feared that a French collapse in Syria and Lebanon would undermine Britain's own claim to continued authority in the parts of the Middle East under its control.[5] Eden and Cadogan therefore favored an attempt to break the Franco–Levantine deadlock by means of active British mediation. On the other hand, the fear was expressed that if London became directly involved in the negotiation process, it would ultimately be forced to take clear-cut stands on various points of dispute and thus risk the permanent alienation of one party or another. Moreover, pressure on the Levant governments would probably prove ineffective unless it were backed up by the United States, and there was considerable reluctance to facilitate the expansion of American influence in the region.[6]

For his part, Churchill saw no reason at all to work for the restoration of France's prewar position in the Levant. In January 1945, the prime minister went so far as to warn Eden that "de Gaulle will be a great danger to peace and to Britain in the future." He went on to inquire whether due progress was being made on the dismantling of German-built fortifications on the portion of the French coast facing Britain![7]

It is clear in retrospect that Franco–Levantine antagonism had become too intense by 1945 to be overcome by any mediation efforts. Catroux's attempts to instill a new spirit of liberalism and a sense of mission among the French administrators in the Levant had failed to produce any tangible results, both because of the ingrained cynicism that suffused the General Delegation and because of the obvious unwillingness of the Syrians and Lebanese to make any reciprocal concessions now that they seemed to have the French on the run. The organized boycott of the Bastille Day celebrations and the anti-French propaganda campaign that ensued in Syria, had reinforced the back-to-the-wall mentality of men such as General Oliva-Roget, the delegate in Damascus. The Syrian government had subsequently asserted its authority in Latakia by arresting Suleiman Murshid, the leader of the French-backed, Alawite autonomy movement.[8] The French had thus come to feel that they had best salvage what they could before it was too late. The degree of anxiety in the General Delegation is indicated by the fact that it actively considered the reconstitution of a pro-French Maronite stronghold in Mount Lebanon, with the Muslim areas of the country to go to Syria, possibly in exchange for a French treaty with Damascus.[9] This came in the wake of Lebanon's participation in the October 1944 Alexandria Conference which had laid the foundation for the creation of the Arab League and which the French saw as a further step toward the region's integration into the British sphere of influence. (Significantly, although the French denounced the Alexandria program as an infringement on Lebanon's independence, Syria's participation in the conference was not specifically condemned.)[10] Their efforts to deal with Lebanon on a separate basis came to nought, however, as the majority of the Maronite community remained committed to the concept of a Greater Lebanon held together by the October 1943 National Pact. French objections notwithstanding, the Lebanese government insisted on taking part in the Franco–Syrian talks on the *troupes spéciales* and the two Levant states continued to coordinate the conduct of their relations with the French authorities.[11]

Spears' departure combined with the exhilarating aftereffect of the liberation of France to produce a bolder, more aggressive French stance in the Levant. The French began to pressure the local governments to accept the *Convention Universitaire* which would give French schools a virtual monopoly over foreign-language instruction in the region. In Lebanon, they sought to impose the French baccalaureate as the only certificate of education to be recognized by the government when hiring employees, to the exclusion of those graduating from the English and American schools.[12] At the end of

December, a French cruiser sailed into Beirut harbor on an ostensibly innocent call, and tanks and armored cars were sent to Damascus in response to the Syrian government's latest veiled threats of unleashing popular unrest as an anti-French pressure tactic. The Syrians, in turn, pushed through an educational law of their own which abolished French-language instruction in primary schools and ended the monopoly of French-language instruction in institutions of higher education. They also spoke to Shone of the possibility of suborning the *troupes spéciales* as well as getting arms from Iraq.[13] A Foreign Office clerk noted that the situation had all the makings of an armed confrontation, and in Cairo Grigg and Paget discussed military contingencies in the event a conflict did break out.[14]

French Procrastination and British Indecision

In the course of the late winter and early spring of 1945, it became increasingly apparent that the French intended to delay any serious discussion of treaty terms with the Levant states until the war was over and the approximately 40,000 British troops had left. In Lebanon, the new cabinet formed in January under Abdul-Hamid Karami was seen as less nationalistic than Riad al-Solh's, but for their part the Syrians remained determined to gain control of the *troupes spéciales* before a British evacuation left them vulnerable to French pressure tactics. Faced with this insoluble dilemma, the British continued to expend the bulk of their energy on their internal policy debate, as articulate in expression as it was crippling in effect.

In the Levant, an attempt was made to maintain an impression of movement toward treaty talks; however, Count Ostorog, Beynet's ex-Vichyite aide who had returned from a stay in France with the title of Minister Plenipotentiary on Mission, was not in fact authorized to discuss anything of substance apart from the issue of the *Convention Universitaire,* regarding which the French were prepared to make some concessions.[15] When London sought to elicit a note from the French detailing the treaty terms they would seek, the Quai d'Orsay refused to commit itself in writing. In conversation with Cooper and during a brief visit to London, Foreign Minister Bidault indicated orally that the general headings of a treaty should include military bases, safeguards for French economic and cultural interests, and a preeminent position for the French ambassador. Bidault did present the British with a note reiterating the French position on the questions of the *troupes spéciales* and gendarmeries and suggesting the possibility of sending military reinforcements to the Levant. The French also proposed the initiation of a general Franco–British discussion of policy in the Middle East.[16]

Whitehall's reaction was simply not to respond to the note. His Majesty's government could not tolerate French troop reinforcements in the Levant prior to the conclusion of treaties, but there was no point in saying so unless the French actually tried to send in additional units. The Foreign Office was prepared to consider the idea of offering the withdrawal of some British troops in exchange for a partial transfer of *troupes spéciales,* but this idea was rejected by the War Office, which claimed it needed the Levant as a military reserve until the war with Japan was over and that a premature pullout would make it appear as though Britain were abandoning the Levant States to their fate. Moreover,

> The military authorities have fairly recently spent something like 1,000,000 [pounds sterling] on camp accommodation in Syria, and have only done this after convincing themselves (and H.M. Minister) of the need for this, so I think there must really be something in it.[17]

A general discussion of Middle Eastern policy and the French role in protecting the Levant was to be avoided. Given the uncertainty of France's future in the region, it made no sense for Britain to enter into any further engagements of the sort that had crippled its policy in the past:

> Unless the French are able to reach an amicable agreement with the Levant States, they will never be anything but a very disturbing factor in the Middle East, for which we shall be blamed. We have been extremely embarrassed by the existing commitments which we have given to the French and from every point of view it would be better for us to remain uncommitted to them.[18]

While seeking some sort of general accommodation with the British, the French persisted in their attempts to strengthen their grip on the Levant. These took such provocative forms as an official communiqué by the French Council of Ministers asserting that France retained full responsibility for security in the Levant and that force would be used if necessary to maintain order. Syria and Lebanon responded predictably with countercommuniqués of their own and large anti-French demonstrations broke out in the major Syrian cities with the apparent encouragement of the Damascus government.[19] There was also a resurgence of trouble in the Alawite territory, where French-armed supporters of Suleiman Murshid clashed with his opponents, demanding their leader's release from detention in Damascus and challenging the Syrian government's authority in the region. When the Syrian gendarmerie proved ineffective in handling the situation, the French used the occasion as an excuse to send troops (from the ranks of the *troupes spéciales*) into the area over the objections of Damascus. It was also reported that Shiites in the Bekaa Valley of Lebanon were being provided with arms by the French in the hope of creating trouble for the Lebanese government.[20] The overall thrust of French policy as seen by the British was best described by one officer as follows:

> The sum total of my impressions of the French amounts to this: their intention is to maintain the status quo here until the end of hostilities in Europe or, more important to them, until France is really re-established as a European power. Their method is to obstruct the equipping of the Gendarmeries with much needed machine guns and transport, to oppose the transfer of the Troupes Spéciales, to weaken the authority of the Local Governments by all possible means and at the same time keep them sweet by continuing conversations with them, off and on.[21]

Given the absence of any substantive Franco–Syrian talks and the lack of any sense of direction on Britain's part during this period, a sort of diplomatic vacuum was formed, within which various events seemed to form a patternless sequence leading nowhere. In mid-February, Richard Law of the Foreign Office responded to the provocative questions put to him in Parliament by Spears and his associates by stating that Britain's endorsement of Levant independence did not constitute a guarantee. This fed fears in Damascus and Beirut that Britain and France might have concluded a secret agreement at Syria and Lebanon's expense.[22] On the other hand, when Churchill and Eden stopped in Cairo a few days later on their way back from the Yalta Conference and met with Shukri al-Quwatli, the latter was assured by the prime minister that no second Sykes–Picot agreement was in the works and that, while he was in favor of a privileged position for France in Syria, he realized that the Anglo–Iraqi precedent was no longer acceptable to the Syrians. Al-Quwatli came away from the meeting much relieved and with the clear sense that Britain would not take active measures to impose a treaty with the French on Syria.[23]

In early March, Beynet was recalled to Paris for instructions regarding proposed treaty terms, but he did not return for weeks and in his absence, the meaningless charade of diplomatic activity was carried on by Ostorog.[24] The legitimacy of Levantine independence was enhanced at the end of March when an unwilling French government was forced to agree to the invitation of Syria and Lebanon to the United Nations Conference in San Francisco. Paris tried to turn the occasion into an opportunity for treaty talks, but the Levant states would have none of it. A slight and brief thaw in the relations between the antagonists did ensue.[25] Underlying tensions remained high, though, and were kept alive by disputes regarding the issue of jurisdiction over the Alawite territory and occasional statements by French ministers hinting at the possibility of using force to settle the Levant question.

Whitehall Takes another Crack at Policymaking

As has been made clear, at the end of February, Britain's policy toward the Levant remained as indecisive as ever. While continuing to mouth support for French rights to a privileged position, Whitehall no longer considered it as even remotely possible that the French could succeed without bloodshed in securing a position for themselves analogous to that of Britain in Egypt or Iraq. Indeed, when seeking American support for Franco–Levantine treaty talks, the British argued that the content of the final accords could be restricted to guarantees of minimal cultural (that is, educational) and financial privileges of the sort that might be granted any friendly power.[26]

Within His Majesty's government, sharp controversy continued to rage over what role should be played by Britain in this long drawnout affair. Although the debate proved inconclusive, it reflected the difficulty that the British continued to encounter in attempting to set priorities among their many different, and frequently conflicting, interests, as well as in coming to grips with the growing limitations on their power.

Throughout the war years, the British had been toying with a variety of schemes for reworking the political framework of the Middle East with a view to maintaining their influence in the region under the changed conditions that would undoubtedly prevail after the termination of the conflict. No matter what the plan, a continued French presence in the Levant seemed to present an obstacle to its implementation. This was most obviously apparent in the case of proposals for a postwar Arab federation. The most detailed version of this idea was elaborated by the secret Cabinet Subcommittee on Palestine created in 1943 by Churchill, who had his doubts concerning the wisdom of implementing the controversial 1939 White Paper. The committee (which included the pro-Zionist Leo Amery, secretary of state for India and Burma, as well as Lord Moyne, Casey's deputy in Cairo) recommended the partition of Palestine between the Jews and Arabs, but argued that such a solution would be acceptable to the Arabs of the territory only if they were included in a larger Arab political entity that would alleviate their fear of being inundated by Jewish immigration. This Greater Syrian state would include the Arab section of Palestine, all of Syria and Transjordan, and a portion of Muslim Lebanon. Jewish Palestine, Christian-dominated Lebanon, and a Jerusalem state under a British high commissioner would form separate political entities.[27]

French acquiescence was most unlikely. As Leo Amery put it, the prospects for Arab union would be "greatly helped by the removal of direct French control in Syria."[28] It was agreed that "the Foreign Office should endeavor to ensure that the French should not acquire rights in Syria and Lebanon which would be incompatible with the creation of the Greater Syria."[29] Unwilling to advocate the actual expulsion of the French, the committee comforted itself with the assumption that, given their existing difficulties, the French would ultimately be grateful for whatever British support they received in their quest for strategic access to the Levant. The solution envisioned would have made Britain, France, and possibly the United States, coguarantors of the new states. Britain would assume overall responsibility for defense, while the French would be allowed to retain access to some of the military bases in the Levant. In effect, the French would have been reduced to depending on Britain's hospitality for their continued presence in the region.[30]

The practical ramifications for the French of the committee's plan became readily apparent when the Post-Hostilities Planning Subcommittee (PHP) of the Chiefs of Staff was asked to project Britain's strategic needs in the Middle East within the context of a Greater Syria. The PHP immediately saw in the proposed confederation a wonderful opportunity for solving the problem presented by the treaty restrictions on Britain's peacetime stationing of troops in Egypt: "The Levant States will provide an important further area for the location of our strategic reserves."[31] Ideally, British forces would enjoy unrestricted access to all harbors, airfields, and means of communication in Greater Syria in addition to military bases and training grounds. Oil from Iraq (and possibly Kuwait and Iran) passing through Greater Syrian pipelines on its way to Europe would be exempt from any taxation. In response to a Foreign Office note, however, the PHP reluctantly conceded that it might not be practicable to station British garrisons in the Levant itself.[32]

In the course of 1944, the Palestine Committee continually revised its recommendations in view of changing circumstances. In the fall of that year, Lord Moyne, now minister of state in Cairo, recommended initially restricting the proposed new Arab state to Transjordan and Arab Palestine; this, he argued, would allow Britain to fulfill its obligations toward the Emir Abdullah as well as prevent the spread of French influence to areas then under British control! The Palestine Committee adopted this scaled-down plan, but after Moyne's assassination in November at the hands of Jewish extremists, it was shelved. In any case, the Foreign Office remained consistently opposed to the partition of Palestine. (Eden argued at one point that it would antagonize the Arab world and facilitate the expansion of American influence in the region.)[33]

While the plan for a Greater Syria fell by the wayside, the military had no intention of abandoning the goals it had originally set itself within the framework of that plan. In the spring of 1945, the PHP reiterated that British forces should have complete access to all necessary facilities in Syria and Lebanon in the event of a military emergency as well as peacetime use of airfields and radar installations.[34] Within the Middle East Command itself there was a growing determination in 1944–1945 to maintain a British presence in the region after the war as long as the French remained there and possibly even after they had withdrawn. General Holmes was quoted as having told George Wadsworth that "since British cannot rely on Anglo–French Entente as a basis for fundamental policy because of the French performance in the war it was undesirable to have bridge of Empire in the Middle East under French domination."[35] Whereas Eden advocated a British troop reduction as a means of facilitating French flexibility toward the Syrians, the Joint Planning Staff of the Chiefs of Staff objected that troop strength had already been reduced to the point where continued French control over the *troupes spéciales* gave them a numerical advantage. This had not, of course, been brought to their attention, but if they did become aware of it, they might claim the right to control over the operational command under the terms of the de Gaulle–Lyttelton agreements. This would of course deprive the British of the right to invoke general security needs as an excuse for intervening in any Franco–Levantine conflict.[36]

Without any formal authorization from London, the army had begun to take measures clearly indicative of its intention of retaining a foothold in the region. The construction of stone military barracks for British troops, which had begun in 1943, proceeded apace under General Paget, with the army responding to French objections by insisting that the quarters were purely temporary. After a tour of the region in February 1945, Hankey returned to London quite won over to the views of the British officials in Cairo and the Levant and evidently persuaded of the need to maintain a British military presence in the region for some time to come. In what seems like an attempt to still his own doubts as well as those of others, Hankey began to resort to rather convoluted arguments and transparent excuses in his advocacy of the military establishment's views. Regarding the issue of barracks construction, he wrote:

> The War Office deny absolutely that the barracks can be regarded as "permanent." It is true that they are made of stone, but the reason for that is that in the whole Middle East there is hardly any wood. It is therefore cheaper to use stone. Apparently, it is intended to keep quite a considerable British Empire strategic reserve in the Middle East until at any rate the end of the war with Japan. The relatively cool climate of Syria and Palestine is the reason why it is desired to be able to send a certain number of troops there, who would otherwise have to stay all the time in the much hotter areas (Iraq, Canal Zone, etc.).[37]

In the following paragraph, Hankey admitted:

> At the back of the War Office mind, and the Chiefs of Staff have also referred to this, is the idea that as the Syrian frontier is only twenty miles from Haifa, the principal source of oil for the British forces in the Mediterranean, we ought to be able to establish air defenses and use the communications of Syria and the Lebanon in the event of another war.[38]

In Hankey's opinion, the likeliest solution for the Levant problem would be the integration of the region into the area of British strategic responsibility, with the French to be restricted to a couple of bases far removed from any centers of population. If Syria and Lebanon were left to themselves, a dangerous vacuum would be created and the French alone would never be accepted by the native population. The tone of his comments almost made it seem as though the permanent extension of British power to the region would be an act of magnanimous self-sacrifice.[39] Hankey's outlook reflected that of the Eastern Department (which was no longer under Peterson's supervision) and represented a significant shift away from the line it had adopted in Spears' time. It was almost as though Spears had personally driven the department into a pro-French line that did not come naturally. With Churchill's provocative friend gone, Hankey and his associates occupied his doctrinal niche, as it were, by assuming responsibility for defending the principle that British influence ought never be withdrawn from a region once it had been introduced there.

Hankey's arguments seemed to baffle and distress the branches of the Foreign Office dealing directly with European affairs, which upheld the view, evidently shared by Eden himself, that the prospect of postwar cooperation with France should not be sacrificed on the altar of imperial adventurism. J. G. Ward of the Postwar Reconstruction department wrote:

> Is it wise to suggest that we should seek peace-time bases and military facilities in the Levant States? . . . I am not clear whether the Eastern Department feel themselves that this is the right solution or whether they feel bound to try to give effect to the views of the P.H.P. Staff as endorsed by the Chiefs of Staff. If the latter, I do not think the Foreign Office ought to be influenced against their better judgment by pronouncements of P.H.P. Staff. This Staff is composed of quite junior officers whose opinion really counts for very little

even though the Chiefs of Staff may sometimes endorse their reports. Their natural tendency is to open their mouths as wide as possible and claim every conceivable guarantee which the British Empire might require. . . .

Personally, I feel grave doubts of the effect of our putting forward a request for facilities in the Levant States. However pure our motives, they would certainly be misunderstood by the Americans and other Allies.

Ward suggested that the whole question be postponed until after the convening of the United Nations Conference in San Francisco, after which some international framework could be created to accommodate British security needs in the Levant.[40] Hankey objected that time was running short as the French prepared to present concrete treaty proposals to the Syrians, but the officials of the Western Department echoed Ward's skeptical views:

The present scheme seems to amount to reducing the strength of the French position in Syria and replacing them ourselves.[41]

Hankey's line seemed temporarily to prevail, and Cadogan authorized him to redraft a note to the Chiefs of Staff discussing the specifics of the proposed joint Anglo–French defense responsibility in the Levant, when a sudden rush of political developments rendered the whole question irrelevant.[42]

The Reinforcement Issue

In the last week of April 1945, it had become known that Beynet's protracted sojourn in Paris was nearly over and that he would return to Beirut with full-fledged proposals in hand for treaties with the Levant states. At the same time, de Gaulle issued orders for the dispatch of three battalions via French naval cruisers to relieve and reinforce the French military presence in the Levant, with only one batallion to be withdrawn in turn. De Gaulle's readiness to resort to such blatant pressure tactics probably stemmed from the assumption that the imminent termination of hostilities in Europe would put an end to Britain's ability to use military security requirements as an excuse for intervention in any Franco–Levantine conflict.

From Beirut, Shone warned that British failure to prevent French reinforcements could result in widespread nationalist violence in the Levant.[43] The Chiefs of Staff pointed out that the French must not be permitted to use increased troop strength as the basis for a claim to the operational command.[44] In Paris, Duff Cooper remonstrated with the French leader, but to no avail. De Gaulle simply reiterated his conviction that the British were trying to ease the French out of their rightful position in Syria. Only if British troops were withdrawn would the French be willing to hand over the *troupes spéciales* and withdraw their own forces.[45] Meanwhile, the general sent a telegram to General Mast in Tunisia, whence the first troop detachment was to be sent to the Levant aboard the cruiser *Montcalm:*

The objections, and even eventually the opposition, of the British command must be held as null and void. The mission of the *Montcalm* is categorical and must be executed.[46]

With V-E Day rapidly approaching and the United Nations Conference under way in San Francisco, His Majesty's government was in no mood to engage in yet another unpleasant confrontation with the French over the Levant. The cabinet approved the dispatch of a telegram from Churchill to de Gaulle requesting cancellation of the reinforcement order and offering the complete withdrawal of British forces from the region as soon as Franco–Levantine treaties had been put into effect. The internal debate over British postwar desiderata in the Levant was thus abruptly suspended. Unfortunately, the credibility of Churchill's offer was undermined by the nearly simultaneous introduction into Lebanon of a brigade of Palestinian Arab troops under British command, ostensibly as part of a routine training exercise.[47]

De Gaulle's response to Churchill's overture was noncommittal. It promised that the formal announcement of Beynet's return to the Levant with treaty proposals would be issued shortly. The note also reaffirmed French willingness to turn over the *troupes spéciales* and terminate all intervention in the internal political affairs of the Levant states once basic French cultural, economic, and strategic privileges (including the use of military bases) had been guaranteed by treaties. Once again, however, de Gaulle did not hesitate to make it perfectly clear that he owed Britain no explanations and no concessions:

> I believe this affair could already have been resolved had the rulers in Damascus and Beirut not been able to believe that they would be able to avoid any engagement by using your support against us.[48]

On the same day, May 6, 850 troops (most of them Senegalese) disembarked from the *Montcalm* at Beirut harbor, and an approximately equal number of soldiers were taken aboard. This took place without incident, but British concern remained intense, for the French were sticking to their plan of sending the next shipment of troops as a reinforcement, rather than relief, of their forces.[49]

Even before the arrival on May 17 of the *Jeanne d'Arc* with 500 more troops, the atmosphere in the Levant had taken a dramatic turn for the worse in the aftermath of disturbances on V-E Day (May 8). French celebrants in Beirut and Damascus behaved in a provocatively assertive manner, setting off two days of violent nationalist demonstrations in Beirut. Many members of the Palestinian brigade that the British had just introduced into the country took part in this unrest and ended up brawling with French-led Lebanese troops. A temporary lull was introduced after both British- and French-commanded troops were withdrawn from the city's streets and the British military authorities formally apologized to the French, but the fatal damage had been done. The French were now convinced that the British were prepared to instigate unrest to secure their aims and de Gaulle was reinforced in his determination to maintain an unbending attitude.[50]

On the diplomatic stage, efforts to work out a solution at the highest level came to nothing. De Gaulle was prepared to come to London to discuss the Levant with Churchill, but by the time the latter could spare the time for such a meeting, the *Jeanne d'Arc* had arrived with its reinforcements, sparking off disturbances in Damascus and other Syrian cities and prompting the Syrian and Lebanese governments to announce publicly that they were breaking off all talks with the French until the reinforcements were withdrawn.[51]

For his part, Churchill was frustrated by his inability to halt the slide toward confrontation with the French. The prime minister directed the main thrust of his anger at General Paget, whom he accused of irresponsible behavior in first proceeding with the construction of the stone barracks and then introducing the Palestinian brigade onto the scene precisely at the moment when de Gaulle was being offered joint withdrawal as a solution to the Levant problem: "Why should such steps, of great political consequence, be taken at this time without my being advised?"[52] The War Office lamely sought to reassure him by insisting that the brigade's training mission was entirely routine.[53]

The French decision to push ahead with the troop reinforcements despite British and Levantine protests appears to have been made personally by de Gaulle, acting alone and against most of the advice offered by his subordinates. Beynet himself appealed for a reversal of the decision and the Quai d'Orsay was at a loss to clarify French intentions when Cooper sought to remonstrate with its officials. He reported to London that "there seems to be at present a lack of liaison between General de Gaulle's entourage and the Quai d'Orsay."[54] At one point, a member of the French cabinet actually sent his deputy to the British embassy for information regarding the state of affairs in Syria. The embarrassed official explained that the minister

> was unable to judge the position from what transpired at meetings of the Council of Ministers. Apart from the Ministry [sic] of Foreign Affairs, who was himself sometimes not very clearly informed, Members of the Cabinet had only the French press as guidance. . . . General de Gaulle was thus able to swing decisions with little discussions [sic] and to state that communiqués would be issued without Ministers being able to express an opinion.[55]

The British Foreign Office concluded as follows:

> All our evidence goes to show that it is on General de Gaulle's own initiative that reinforcements are being sent to the Levant, and that he has either not consulted, or ignored the advice of those French officials who are best able to judge the local situation.
>
> This will presumably make anything savoring of a climb-down all the more difficult for the General.[56]

De Gaulle seems to have been convinced, as he had been in November 1943, that if only the French remained resolute they would be able to call Britain's bluff. His exclusion of the Quay d'Orsai from the decisionmaking process over the Levant appears to have been due to fear of seeing his firm stand undercut by his compromise-prone subordinates:

> Although I wished to avoid any direct collisions with our allies, I did not intend to renounce our intentions under any circumstances. This refusal would be sufficient to oblige the London Government finally to come to

terms with the situation—on condition, however, that I was supported by my own country. If it appeared resolved, as I was, not to give in to formal demands, there would be every chance that Great Britain would not push things to an extreme, for the unmasking of its ambitions and the eventuality of a rupture with France would have soon placed it in an impossible position. I therefore hoped that, as the crisis broke out, opinion would back me up. Conversely, the English, particularly Churchill, counted on the fears and calculations of the French ruling circles to restrain de Gaulle, and, perhaps, cut him down to size. In fact, I was to find, in political and diplomatic circles and the press, a very uncertain source of support, if not recrimination.[57]

The general saw in himself the embodiment of French national will. If his country was ready to back him in a showdown with the British, he would be able to transcend the limitations apparently imposed on him by geopolitical circumstances; his failure, on the other hand, would signify nothing but France's unwillingness to live up to the standards he expected of it.

De Gaulle appears to have been bent on using the Levant issue as a means of demonstrating France's resolve to return to the status of a great power in the postwar world. The crisis was unfolding at just the time when plans were under way for the first postwar meeting of the Big Three, from which the French leader was to be excluded. His predisposition to Anglophobia having been reinforced by the conduct of the Palestinian brigade in Beirut, the general was convinced that Churchill was seeking to orchestrate events with a view to isolating France and keeping it dependent on British good will, much as the Free French movement had been during the war. In a message to the French ambassador in Washington regarding the possibility of arranging a meeting with President Truman, de Gaulle warned that the British would seek to obstruct such an encounter and drive a wedge between Paris and Washington:

> The English—and above all Mr. Churchill—will do all they can to obstruct the plan. It is with this in mind that Churchill is publicizing our absence from the future meeting of the Three and, for another thing, throwing oil on the Syrian flames in order to excite the United States.[58]

De Gaulle's perception of British policy was not far wrong when it came to the Middle Eastern establishment, but he was mistaken in attributing such sinister, anti-French motives to Churchill. As has been seen, the prime minister was himself frustrated by his inability to get a grip on the situation and, throughout May, he was most reluctant to commit himself to any course of action that might lead once more to British embroilment in a Levantine crisis. The logic of events was a compelling force, however, and the internal pressure for British action mounted as it became increasingly clear that the French were bent on forcing a decisive confrontation with the Syrians. Grigg, the minister of state in the Middle East, had been warning London for weeks that such a confrontation would necessarily put British prestige on the line:

> With Palestine in the balance, to say nothing of our need in other vital matters for the goodwill of the Arab League, we cannot afford to be dilatory

or weak. The eternal fear of the small states is that they will be [exposed] to mutual exigencies of the great. It is hardly possible to suppose that this issue between ourselves and France will not be regarded throughout the Middle East as a test case.

Grigg recommended warning the French of British preparedness to take whatever measures necessary to ensure security—the customary euphemism for a threat of military action.[59] In the Eastern Department, Hankey recommended the threat of far-reaching diplomatic sanctions as a means of reining in de Gaulle. The French should be warned that Britain was prepared to stop restraining the Arab League over the Algerian question and withdraw its recognition of French predominance in the Levant. He even went so far as to suggest that the Middle East Command be authorized forcefully to prevent French reinforcements from reaching the Levant, although his superior, Baxter, rejected this as too extreme a step.[60]

When nothing came of the plans for a Churchill–de Gaulle meeting, the focus of diplomatic expectations turned to Washington. The Foreign Office hoped that involving the Americans in talks with the French and the Levant states would introduce the sort of leverage necessary to bring the parties together in a new modus vivendi, to be followed after the end of the Pacific war by a general agreement on French rights in Syria and Lebanon. The State Department had recently indicated its willingness to consider the possibility of the French controlling a military base in the Levant on behalf of the United Nations and this seemed to afford hope of a successful American mediation.[61] In the event such mediation ran aground on French obstinacy, it could be hoped that Britain would gain U.S. backing for a more forceful approach to the problem.

The State Department did not reject the Foreign Office proposal out of hand, but it seemed more interested in settling the long-term issue of French military prerogatives in the Levant than in dealing with the messy business of the crisis then under way. British Ambassador Halifax reported that the Americans were willing to enter into three-way talks with the British and French in London, with the Syrians and Lebanese to be brought in later, once the basic framework of a long-term settlement had been agreed on by the Western powers. The Foreign Office accepted the notion of trilateral discussions excluding the Levant governments (a somewhat remarkable suggestion for the United States to have made in view of its earlier pronouncements regarding the principle of self-determination), but insisted that the issue of base rights be dealt with at a later stage, once the immediate dilemma created by the French troop shipments had been resolved.[62]

Given the rate at which Franco–Syrian relations were declining, these hopes for a diplomatic solution were completely misplaced. In any case, it is clear that the State Department would have made a less than dispassionate arbiter, given its own intense resentment of French conduct:

While we in San Francisco are talking about world security and are devising methods for combating aggression, France is openly pursuing tactics which are similar to those used by the Japanese in Manchukuo and by the Italians in Ethiopia."[63]

As for the French, they were willing to engage in talks with the British on the Middle East in general and the Levant in particular, but balked at the idea of American participation, which de Gaulle saw as a means of placing France in the dock, with Britain and the United States acting as judge and jury.[64]

While pursuing the increasingly unlikely possibility of a diplomatic solution, His Majesty's government was also bound to consider its options in the event the worst came true. For months, General Paget had been pressing, with Grigg's support, for authorization to respond to a French-provoked crisis by confining all French troops to barracks and using the occasion to arm the native gendarmeries with the automatic weapons and transport that would allow them to take an active part in quelling disturbances. These desiderata, reflecting as they did an obvious eagerness to help the Levantines expel the French from the region, were resisted by the Foreign Office.[65] In mid-May, however, Grigg used his wide discretionary powers to authorize Paget to take such steps in the event disorder broke out. The Foreign Office promptly intervened, urging Grigg to avoid any action likely to lead to an armed clash with the French and explicitly warning him against arming the gendarmeries.[66] In Eden's view, the whole issue need not have arisen had British troops been withdrawn unilaterally a few months earlier. It was clearly impossible to pull out in the midst of the current crisis, but a tight rein had to be imposed on the military, which was probably still indulging in expansionist fantasies.[67] As the Levant crisis approached its final phase, the fixing of British military contingency plans remained the subject of controversy.

Within the Levant itself, Shone continued his desultory efforts at mediation while both the French and the Syrians prepared for a violent confrontation. (For his part, Wadsworth encouraged the Syrian and Lebanese governments to draw up proposals for treaties granting equal cultural and commercial rights to all four major powers, and sought to sway the State Department in the direction of supporting the sort of armed British intervention Paget had in mind.[68]) It is difficult, and probably pointless, to say which side was responsible for the outbreak of conflict. While Lebanon remained relatively quiet, riots in towns all over Syria quickly degenerated into armed attacks on French installations by both the populace and the gendarmerie. The Syrian government (which was effectively run by Foreign Minister Jamil Mardam at this point, Shukri al-Quwatli being ill) clearly had an interest in provoking a decisive clash while British troops still occupied the country. There also seems to have been some hope of Iraqi intervention against the French.[69] By May 28, Homs, Hama, and Aleppo had reached a state of full-scale, armed revolt and Jamil Mardam informed Shone that he was unable to control the situation or to prevent the defection of members of the *troupes spéciales* to the Syrian side. Only if the native levies were transferred to formal Syrian control and all French troops withdrawn from urban areas could stability be restored.[70]

If Jamil Mardam seemed overly complacent about his inability to prevent violence, the French certainly were not innocent victims either. Whatever de Gaulle's implicit or explicit instructions to Beynet may have been, it is clear that the General Delegation, and Oliva-Roget in particular, was eager for a violent showdown with the Syrians.[71] In the last week of May, French tanks, armored cars, and low-flying military aircraft engaged in a provocative display of force in Damascus despite Shone's and Paget's appeals to Beynet for restraint. In Hama, where some of the earliest clashes took place, the French commander ordered his troops to fire on a British party attempting to set up a radio transmitter.[72] In Paget's admittedly biased view, "French are deliberately courting clash with Levant states."[73] The Syrian authorities also claimed that the delegation in Damascus had printed pamphlets for distribution to French residents of the city, promising that a decisive blow would soon be struck against the Syrians. The French initially denied this story, but Oliva-Roget's deputy, de la Garde, changed his attitude at a meeting with a British official:

> After his third whisky he came clean, and said Oliva Roget prepared these pamphlets. He, de la Garde, had personally burnt the lot that afternoon after the Syrian protest.[74]

While the Eastern Department and War Office backed Paget and Grigg in their demand for advance authorization to intervene directly in the event full-scale fighting broke out in Syria, Churchill remained extremely reluctant to commit himself irrevocably to such a course of action. Only if American troops were to join in such a thankless task would he be prepared to change his mind. As matters stood, Paget was ordered to halt the routine supply of ammunition to French troops and Syrian gendarmerie alike and to maintain a strictly neutral stance while French and Syrians fought it out. He was, however, authorized to bring an additional British infantry division into Syria as a reinforcement.[75]

The Pot Boils Over

The climax came on May 28, when French forces went on the offensive in Homs and Hama, directing mortar and artillery fire at the towns and causing extensive casualties. On May 29, fighting broke out in Damascus between French forces and the local populace and gendarmerie, and by nightfall the French were hitting portions of the city with shellfire and even from the air.[76] Despite an order from Beynet to desist, Oliva-Roget resumed the bombardment on the night of May 30, inflicting hundreds of civilian casualties.[78] In one particularly gruesome incident, machete-wielding Senegalese soldiers seized the Parliament building, cutting down twenty-three Syrian gendarmes in the process. (The Syrians claimed, and the method of killing strongly suggested, that the gendarmes had been murdered following their surrender.)[78]

Although the precise purpose of all this violence remains unclear, it appears that the French were keeping a group of Syrian opposition politicians in the wings with the intention of appointing them to a pro-French provisional government once a ceasefire had been arranged.[79] The members of the Syrian government in Damascus were forced to flee from quarter to quarter in an effort to find a bombardment-free refuge where they could discuss the options available to them. The ferocity of the French offensive had taken them by surprise, and with Shukri al-Quwatli being sick, the ministers' morale sank rapidly; indeed, a number of them advocated handing the reins of power over to a French-backed puppet government. Only Jamil Mardam is said to have retained his poise.[80]

Beside themselves with fury over the audacity of the French, the leading members of Britain's Middle Eastern establishment issued strident demands for immediate authorization to intervene. From Cairo, Lord Killearn warned that the unrest could easily spread to Egypt, where the British were being blamed for not having prevented the arrival of French reinforcements in the first place.[81] Grigg assessed the situation as follows:

> The French have now put their hands to a German process of butchery and blind destruction in Syrian towns. Recent telegrams from all over Missions in this region have also shown that continuation of the process will rouse all of the Arab States. What remained of French influence in the Levant is now completely lost. Nothing we can do will help the French to recover it. The only question is whether we are to sacrifice all we have gained of trust and admiration during the last five years for the sake of France.[82]

From the scene of violence in the Syrian capital, Shone sent a personal telegram to Eden along the following lines:

> The French have instituted nothing short of a reign of terror in Damascus. Apart from indiscriminate shelling their troops, black and white, are behaving like madmen, spraying the streets with machine-gun fire from vehicles and buildings. . . .
>
> I can only put this to you and implore His Majesty's Government to allow the Commander-in-Chief to intervene without delay.[83]

Visiting President al-Quwatli at his sickbed, Shone told him: "I could but hope that my reports would bring home to His Majesty's Government the vital necessity of intervening in order to put an end to this intolerable situation."[84]

With British prestige now clearly on the line, Churchill had no choice but to relent. On May 30, the cabinet decided to authorize intervention by Paget as soon as American endorsement for the move had been obtained. Although there was a strong inclination to request token participation by U.S. troops, the idea was dropped at the last minute for fear of creating a backlash in American public opinion that would undermine future prospects of American participation in Middle East defense responsibilities. (The idea was also resented by General Paget.) On May 31, it was decided that there was no point in awaiting Truman's response to Churchill's request for support, and Paget was instructed unilaterally to assume the territorial command, confine all French troops to their barracks, and adopt whatever measures he deemed necessary to restore order. (The expression of support from Washington arrived shortly thereafter.)[85]

In taking these steps, the British government was violating the various accords that had regulated Anglo–French relations in the Levant over the previous four years and, more significantly, it was risking a bloody military confrontation with the French that would undoubtedly end in victory for Britain's military forces, but would also result in a severe setback for its postwar European policy. The officials of the Western Department sought to comfort themselves with the rather naïve hope that this would not necessarily be the consequence:

> I think that . . . we should take the line that Syria is something quite apart from the general run of Anglo–French relations and that, even if bloodshed occurs between British and French troops there, we do not intend to relax our efforts for closer relations between the two countries nearer home. . . . *In fact we should continue to behave as if nothing had happened in the Levant,* unless or until the French themselves refuse to follow this line [italics added].[86]

The British accordingly tried to present their decision to the French in as conciliatory a fashion as possible under the circumstances. Massigli, who was now serving as the French ambassador to the Court of St. James, was actually consulted about the wording of Churchill's message to de Gaulle. On his advice, the demand for a unilateral ceasefire and withdrawal of French troops to barracks was placed within the context of the need to ensure the security of the lines of communication to the war against Japan. A reference was also made once again to the possibility of tripartite talks in London, an idea that Massigli personally favored.[87]

Although the packaging of the message could have done little to mitigate the significance of its content, matters were made even worse by Eden's premature announcement in Parliament of the British decision to intervene; by the time Churchill's communication reached de Gaulle's desk, London's move had already become a matter of public knowledge.[88] Realizing that he had no practical alternatives, de Gaulle instructed Beynet to withdraw French troops to barracks, allowing British soldiers to take over their positions.[89] The situation was then complicated by the lack of diplomatic nicety with which Paget set forth his demands to Beynet. He informed him that he was assuming direct military command in Syria and Lebanon and required that:

> Instructions will be issued by French military, naval and air headquarters that all orders and instructions issued by me or on my behalf as Supreme Commander will be obeyed without question by all ranks of the French Military, Naval and Air Forces.[90]

When de Gaulle learned of this message, he warned Beynet that under no circumstances were French troops to be placed under British command:

> We hope that it does not become necessary to use force against the British forces. But this does not mean we should allow ourselves to be deprived of

the possibility of eventually employing our weapons, which English behavior
may render necessary. If they threaten to fire upon us, under no matter what
circumstances, we must threaten to fire upon them. If they shoot, we must
shoot.[91]

In response, Beynet pointed out that he had already complied with all of
Paget's demands and that French dependence on the British for supplies made
any sort of resistance to them impracticable.[92]

De Gaulle's exasperation had been further intensified by the news that the
British had taken advantage of their intervention by seizing complete control
of the OCP and imposing miltary censorship on French radio broadcasts. In
apparent response, he ordered the *Jeanne d'Arc* to leave Oran and sail back to
Beirut. Fearing that more reinforcements were aboard, His Majesty's government requested that the ship's destination be altered. De Gaulle's cabinet
prevailed on him to relent and Bidault informed Cooper that the *Jeanne
d'Arc*'s destination had been altered, violating his chief's order to keep the
decision a secret.[93]

These combative gestures notwithstanding, de Gaulle fundamentally realized that provoking a military clash with Britain would be pointless. The main
thrust of his response came in the public arena. Responding to Eden's premature parliamentary announcement of May 31, the French leader held a press
conference on June 2 at which he rehashed the entire history of Anglo–French
relations in the Levant, placing full blame for the deterioration of the situation on Britain. As for London's suggestion of a tripartite conference to
resolve the crisis, de Gaulle suggested that a five-power conference including
the Soviet Union and China, and dealing with the Middle East as a whole,
would be more appropriate.[94] This was intended not so much as a serious
counterproposal as an attempt to throw "a stone into [Britain's] diplomatic
pool."[95] De Gaulle also tried to strengthen the image he was projecting of
Britain as the aggressor by claiming that orders for a ceasefire had been issued
to Beynet on the evening of May 30, in response to an initial British appeal. In
other words, Paget's assumption of the local command was a wanton arroga-
tion of power, the proclaimed object of which had already been accomplished
one day beforehand. Attempting to put a bold face on a bad situation, de
Gaulle insisted that the withdrawal of French troops to barracks was also the
result of an independent French decision that had been made before Britain
undertook coercive measures.[96] In private, however, Massigli assured the
Foreign Office that, to the best of his knowledge, no ceasefire order had been
issued on May 30. The only grain of truth in the claim was that, after warning
his government that British intervention was imminent, Massigli had received
a message from de Gaulle by telephone around midnight of May 30/31
"which, on this point, was vaguely worded, but in view of M. Massigli's earlier
recommendations seemed clearly to apply to orders to the French military
authorities in Syria to avoid firing on British troops."[97]

In Syria, relative calm was restored as soon as the French troops were
withdrawn. The attitude of the French authorities in the area mirrored that of
de Gaulle. The immediate reaction of men such as Beynet and Oliva-Roget to

the British intervention was a bitter feeling that France had been robbed of a victory that would have assured her of her rightful position in the region. In fact, the British were seen as having engineered the crisis from the very beginning with a view to achieving just that result. As early as May 28, Beynet had written to de Gaulle that the whole uproar over the reinforcement issue

> was, in my opinion, coordinated in advance and they were just searching for a pretext; I anticipated this and that is why I tarried in Paris trying to gain some time.
>
> All this is naturally orchestrated by our English friends. If we suffered a setback, they would be the arbiters of the situation. . . .
>
> The attitude of the English is quite simple: Shone claims to preach calmness. . . . Stirling and Marsac [British political officers] arm the people and tell them not to give up.[98]

The British intervention, Beynet argued, constituted a wanton seizure of power that took place after French forces had basically mastered the situation:

> At the moment when the British ultimatum produced its effect, the sitation in Syria had been almost completely restored. Aleppo, Homs, Hama, Latakia were calm. Damascus and Deir al-Zor were well in hand and the majority of the Druze squadrons [which had earlier defected] had made it known to General Oliva-Roget that they wished to return to his command. . . .
>
> The British action transformed us from victors to vanquished.[99]

Oliva-Roget, who was to be sent back to France within days of the fiasco in Syria, went even further in his accusation, charging that a detailed scenario for the crisis had been planned far in advance by the British:

> The recent events in Syria were the culmination of a concerted plot between the Syrian Government and the British agents, to expel the French from the Levant.
>
> What took place in Syria before 31 May—including the aggression against French establishments—had been planned in advance and was carefully implemented.
>
> What took place on 31 May—the British intervention—also formed part of the plan.[100]

And again, in a lengthy report apparently prepared by the Damascus delegation, it was concluded that

> As of the end of December [1944], the crisis was clearly inevitable. It did not break out until May because it was only at that moment that the British gave the Syrian leaders freedom of action against France. It could have broken out earlier had England wanted it to.[101]

The shock of the French setback seemed to reinforce the preexisting divisions within the French community of the Levant. The liberal and left-wing groups advocating political reform had renewed their critique of the conservative establishment in mid-May, peppering the General Delegation with protests and petitions calling for an end to what was seen as a policy of intimidation in Syria and Lebanon. These groups felt that their views had been vindicated by the events of May–June and hoped that the stage was now finally set for the implementation of a truly liberal policy. On the other hand, the conclusion drawn by Beynet and his associates was that the concessions that had been made over the past year had undermined French power without gaining France any respect, proving that Catroux's reform program had been ill-conceived in the first place. Some hard-line elements even continued to dream up coup plots.[102] The truth of the matter was that the options left to the French were as few as their sense of bitterness was deep. With French troops confined to their barracks and British soldiers patrolling the streets of all Syria's major towns, French power in the Levant was clearly at an end.

In the Aftermath of the French Defeat

With the situation in Syria remaining in limbo, the diplomatic charade concerning a conference on the Levant continued. While the Soviet Union appeared to support de Gaulle's anti-British charges, the United States and Britain resented his attempt to exploit incipient East-West rivalry, and accordingly rejected the French proposal for a five-power conference. Various formulas were floated for overlapping sets of discussions involving the Western powers and the Levant states, but no common basis for agreement on the format was ever found.[103] Shone reported from the Levant that no realistic prospect whatsoever remained for an accord between France and the two Levant states,[104] and as far as Churchill was concerned, there was no need to rush into a negotiated settlement:

> There can be no hurry about this. The French have no Army yet nor have they even the foundations of a democratic Government. The personality of de Gaulle stands as a shocking barrier. It always seems to me that so much of diplomacy consists of waiting. I am not supposing that business can be transacted every day and day after day. There should be intervals. I should not be in favor of making an alliance with France at the present time. I do not wish to see General de Gaulle over here or go to Paris to see him.[105]

The prime minister's comment came in reaction to a growing concern within the Foreign Office that the prospects for an Anglo–French alliance— regarded as the essential foundation for any Western European security system—could be irreparably damaged by the events in Syria. Oliver Harvey (who was now the supervising undersecretary in charge of the Western Department) expressed his concern:

> The Syrians have been allowed successfully to play us off against the French. . . . Foolish as de G[aulle] has been, we have been inexcusably foolish too. We have publicly humiliated the French in Arab eyes. We have temporarily taken over Syria. . . . The P.M., H.M.G. and the British people have no wish to take over Syria. Local pro-Arab officials in subordinate

positions are of course working for it. Spears certainly did so in spite of F.O. instructions while he remained there as the protege of the P.M. carrying out the opposite of the P.M.'s policy. The stupid military mind fell of course for this nonsense, supposing that we should always have troops to waste in this way.[106]

To prevent the British intervention in Syria from being transformed into an outright seizure of power was deemed crucial. The developments on the scene already seemed to point in that direction, with French troops being withdrawn altogether from urban centers, while the British military command assumed the main responsibility for security, took over the Wheat Office, and supplied the Levant gendarmeries with their long-awaited machine guns and reconnaissance cars.[107] Even Grigg recognized that a problem existed and suggested that if an American force were to take part in peacekeeping, the British would no longer be seen as supplanting the French. He also argued that if the United States assumed future responsibility for arming the gendarmerie, a joint Franco–British withdrawal could take place without immediately plunging the region into chaos. When Halifax floated the suggestion in a meeting with State Department officials, however, Loy Henderson of NEA expressed doubt whether the American government would be prepared to undertake such a task.[108] Washington preferred to use its economic leverage to elicit a more cooperative attitude from France on the Levant problem,[109] but Cadogan (temporarily in charge of the Foreign Office while Eden recuperated from an ulcer[110]) balked at this suggestion, pointing out:

> During the next six months France will need all the aid which we and the Americans can give her. If they do not receive it, there is danger of economic collapse followed by perhaps disorder and disturbances not only in France but in Belgium and Italy as well. Moreover, the French would be very quick to detect any change in our attitude, and our ability to settle the Syrian question without serious damage to Anglo–French or Franco–American relations, which is surely our objective, would be lessened. It seems to me, therefore, that both our short and long term interests require us to continue to do all we can to aid France to recover her economic stability.[111]

After seeing a copy of this cable, however, Churchill repudiated it and Halifax was instructed not to act on it.[112]

The Rift within the Foreign Office

In the confused circumstances of the time, the Foreign Office found itself pulled in different directions as it struggled to adopt a clear course of action with regard to the Levant. From Beirut, Shone was expressing the Middle Eastern establishment's collective sentiment by calling for the final liquidation of the French presence in the region.[113] At the same time, Massigli was appealing to the Foreign Office to curb General Paget's aggressive behavior if only as a means of strengthening Bidault's hand against de Gaulle.[114] As had happened so often in Spears' time, the actions of the men on the scene in the Levant were undermining the possibility of a diplomatic solution at the foreign ministry level. (Indeed, Paget's conduct was seen by some as a rather crude imitation of Spears' sophisticated anti-French maneuvers.)

In the wake of the events in Syria, it had become more obvious than ever that British ambitions in the Middle East were completely irreconcilable with the country's interests in Europe. Under the strain of that realization, the rift between Western and Eastern Departments of the Foreign Office grew even wider than it had been before. Concerned over the effect Levant tensions might have on the chances for an Anglo–French treaty, the Western Department echoed the French Foreign Ministry's appeal for restraint. Noting that the reaction of the French press to the crisis had been remarkably restrained so far, Hoyer Millar (head of the Western Department) urged that official British statements and BBC reports on the subject be moderately worded:

> There is, too, the point that so far the French policy in Syria has been largely the personal policy of General de Gaulle. We do not want, by attacking France more severely than can be avoided, to strengthen de Gaulle's position with his own public or to rally French opinion behind him.

Above all, a diplomatic solution had to be found as soon as possible.[115] Later in the same month, Oliver Harvey wrote in a similar vein. He perceived both French and British public opinion as moving in favor of an Anglo–French alliance that would act as a counterweight to the Franco–Soviet pact. The main obstacle was presented by de Gaulle himself, whereas the main chance for success lay in the possibility of the general's electoral defeat that fall. It was therefore crucial that Britain support French claims for a privileged position in the Levant so as to prevent de Gaulle from using the issue as a means of gaining victory at the polls.[116]

The Eastern Department addressed the issue from a far different perspective. Concerned first and foremost with Britain's standing in the Middle East, it wholeheartedly endorsed Shone's recommendation that the French position in Syria and Lebanon be effectively liquidated. This provoked an intense debate with the Western Department, which argued that foreign policy could not be compartmentalized and that clear priority had to be given to the country's European interests:

> The need for close and effective cooperation with the French (and through them with the Western Allies)—not only in European but in world matters and in economic, commercial and colonial matters—is so great and so important to us if the U.K. is to maintain its position vis-à-vis the U.S. and the U.S.S.R., that we cannot any longer justifiably regard this Levant problem as primarily a Middle Eastern one. Nor . . . can we afford to regard France and the Levant States as on a par and of equal importance to us. We must take our long term overall interests into account and try to rebuild our close Anglo–French relationship, even at the risk of some friction with the Arab States and some differences of opinion with the U.S. . . .

I hope therefore that this problem may be considered from this wider angle and not solely as a Near Eastern one. If this premise is accepted, then it would seem that the problem should be tackled from the angle of seeing how to solve it with the least possible damage to the French, rather than of how best to help the Levant States.[117]

In Oliver Harvey's opinion, the Eastern Department's approach was ultimately self-defeating from the point of view of Britain's Middle Eastern interests as well. Indeed, he seemed to cast doubt on the general inclination to appease Arab nationalism:

I feel we shall pay dearly for our present pro-Arab and anti-French policy in the Levant. The Syrian politicians—aided no doubt by de Gaulle—have succeeded in splitting the Anglo–French front. The Americans disapprove of us in Palestine and Egypy [sic] just as much as they disapprove of the French in Syria. We are allowing the Arabs a dress rehearsal in the Levant of what they hope for in Egypt, Iraq and Palestine. Our best friends in those lands, because their interests are identic, should be the French.

Because we cannot bring ourselves to fulfil the Balfour Declaration in Palestine but wobble backwards and forwards we have annoyed the Arabs without appeasing them and we have lost the confidence of the Jews and added American mistrust. If we had built up a strong Jewish Palestine, we should at least have had a real solid European base for our imperial communications now threatened by Arab nationalism. We now have to build literally on shifting sands. The Americans are levering us out of Arabia. We are levering the French out of the Levant. And tomorrow the Arabs, aided and abetted by the Americans, will lever us out of Egypt etc. in the name of San Francisco [U.N. conference].

. . . I cannot believe that we shall ever strengthen or prolong our own position in the Middle East by eliminating the French.[118]

R. M. A. Hankey rejected all of these arguments and remained firm:

It is not a matter of whether the Levant States are more important to us than the French; this is not the correct antithesis at all. It is much more that we cannot maintain our position in the Middle East as a whole if we continue to be committed to forcing on Syria and the Lebanon the granting of concessions which they regard as fatal to their independence when the French behave as they do.[119]

In any case, he argued, the termination of French influence in the Levant need not come at the expense of an Anglo–French alliance. De Gaulle's inability to inflame popular passions over the Syrian affair was to be taken as an encouraging indication of this for the British. Conversely, a failure to put a clear-cut end to the French role in the Middle East would be "the worst of both worlds" in so far as it would continue to complicate Britain's relations with both France and the Arab states.[120]

The Eastern Department's reluctance to support the French in the Levant was matched by the prime minister's scepticism over the wisdom of committing Britain to an alliance with western European powers. British security, in his view, would best be served by concentrating on building up the country's own military and economic capacity rather than by committing it to the defense of other powers.[121] The line finally adopted by the Foreign Office represented a rather substanceless compromise: Britain was to present itself in the role of honest broker between the French and the Levant states. The latter would be encouraged to grant France cultural rights and to retain some French advisors in government ministries. Once an agreement had been reached, a joint Anglo–French troop withdrawal could take place.[122]

This internal debate in Whitehall is of broad interest in so far as it encapsulates the long-standing tension in British foreign policy between colonial objectives and concern with the continental balance of power. Was Britain's power derived primarily from the possession of a strong empire and the control of strategic lines of communication (to be supported, in the postwar world, by the might of the United States) or did its security depend first and foremost on close cooperation with allied powers on the European mainland? This was the question faced by Whitehall's policymakers in 1945, much as it had been by their predecessors at the turn of the century.

The Disintegration of the French Position

In the Levant itself, events followed a course independent of the policy discussions in London and Paris. Throughout the summer of 1945, the Syrians kept the French on the run by provoking a spate of violent incidents wherever their isolated garrisons remained. Tensions ran particularly high in Aleppo and in the Alawite territory, which the French saw as their last stronghold in the country and where the Syrians accordingly concentrated their efforts.[123] The situation was made particularly volatile by the large-scale desertion of *troupes spéciales,* desertions that were occasionally marked by the murder of French commanding officers.[124] Entirely dependent now on the British for protection, the French were forced to impose increasingly stringent limitations on the movement of their troops, ultimately withdrawing to a restricted area of western Syria and into Lebanon. In a vain effort to turn the tide in France's favor, Count Ostorog returned to the Levant with an authorization to hand over formal control of the *troupes spéciales* to the Syrian and Lebanese governments in return for limited concessions in the cultural and economic spheres. Maintaining their joint stand, and supported by Arab League resolutions calling for the complete eradication of French influence in the region, the Levant states spurned the overture. In view of the fait accompli created by the mass desertions, the French were obliged unilaterally to hand over the *troupes spéciales* as of August 1945. Apparently hoping to win a measure of good will, they also prepared to surrender control over a variety of services including the Radio Levant and Radio Orient broadcasting stations, the French-run railways, and the telephone service. Ostorog also assured the governments that, in principle, French troops would withdraw from the Levant as soon as the British were prepared to follow suit.[125]

Both Beirut and Damascus nevertheless continued to maintain their hostile stance and proceeded to dismiss dozens of French advisors and employees from government ministries and services, in accordance with Arab League demands. Although the Maronite elements in the Lebanese ruling circle expressed private reservations over this rupture of all ties with France as well as over the increasingly intrusive role of the Arab League in Levant affairs, they felt it necessary to go along with the Syrians for fear of provoking an external as well as internal nationalist backlash.[126] While maintaining some hope of partially restoring their position in Lebanon, the French seemed to recognize that Syria was a lost cause:

> If we have some reason to hope to see Lebanon make its way yet further towards a comprehensive policy towards us, . . . this is not so in Syria, where the Government, constantly pressed by francophobe extremists, is, by contrast, in a rush to undermine our remaining interests before international politics force greater restraint upon it.[127]

Syrian aggressiveness reached such a degree that even British officials were taken aback and concerned. Shone complained that Spears' encouragement from afar of Syrian intransigence was not making his job any easier[128] and the Foreign Office expressed concern about Syria's systematic circumvention of the Franco–Syrian mixed courts that adjudicated cases affecting the interests of foreign (including British) nationals.[129] Even General Paget became worried by what he saw as the irresponsible demagoguery of the Syrian leadership, which was exploiting the relative defenselessness of the French to provoke incidents that could get out of control.[130] But when Shone and Paget met with Shukri al-Quwatli and his ministers and urged them to be a little more forthcoming toward the French, they were rebuffed.[131] It was becoming apparent that by helping rid the Syrians of their French yoke, the British had in fact reduced their own leverage over the Damascus government.

Bevin Presses for a Settlement

Throughout June and July, the Foreign Office continued its futile efforts at creating a format for a diplomatic conference that would be acceptable to the French without allowing them to dominate the proceedings. The French remained suspicious of the notion of a three-power conference and insisted that they could not accept London as the venue, whereas the Foreign Office feared that a French-chaired meeting in Paris would degenerate into a platform for anti-British propaganda.[132] In any case, Churchill had been extremely antagonized by de Gaulle's bellicose behavior during May–June and was hostile to the notion of an immediate diplomatic settlement with the French. The prime minister's resentment was aggravated by de Gaulle's unceremonious dissolution in late June of the Anglo–French field-hospital unit that Lady Spears had been running for the First Free French Division.[133] (Churchill appeared to suffer from a general sense of remorse during this period over his earlier dismissal of Spears, a sentiment that the latter doubtless did little to discourage.[134]) However, the Labour Party victory in Britain's July 1945 elections rendered Churchill's personal feelings irrelevant and opened the way to a new initiative in resolving the festering problem of the Levant and establishing a basis for closer cooperation between Britain and France.

After the assumption of power by the Attlee government on July 26, the Western Department quickly seized the initiative by pressing its views on the new secretary of state for foreign affairs, Ernest Bevin. Recapitulating the ideas it had developed earlier in the year, the department advocated the forging of an Anglo–French alliance that would serve as the foundation for a "Western Block" that was to include the Netherlands, Belgium, and possibly Scandinavia:

> The Foreign Office felt that British interests would clearly benefit from such an arrangement—strategically because we should be provided with a system of defence in depth, politically because in associating with the Western countries (and the Dominions) we should be better able to hold our own in comparison with the U.S. and the U.S.S.R., economically because close economic and commercial ties with Western Europe would greatly strengthen our own position.[135]

The memorandum presented the disputes over the future status of the Ruhr (the French wished to detach it from Germany) and the Levant as the two major obstacles to a rapprochement with Paris, and urged that the secretary of state act to settle them as soon as possible. If not, the Soviets, who had already made a half-hearted attempt to raise the Levant issue at Potsdam,[136] would seek to exploit these differences to their own advantage within the forum of the newly created Council of Foreign Ministers.[137]

Bevin, who, unlike Eden, dominated the shaping of Britain's foreign policy during his tenure in office, was in fact amenable to the Western Department's views (which were generally backed by Cadogan, the permanent undersecretary) and hoped to get the Levant issue out of the way before the first meeting of the Council of Foreign Ministers scheduled for mid-September.[138] He felt encouraged by a conversation with Massigli, "who told him that the atmosphere in France was now favourable to closer Anglo–French understanding."[139] In a subsequent meeting, Bevin presented the French ambassador with the outline of a proposal for a joint Franco–British troop withdrawal from the Levant. The question of access to military bases and general security questions were to be left for the United Nations to deal with, and Paris, London, and Washington were to consult jointly in the event of a threat to the Christian minorities in the Levant during the interim between military evacuation and the implementation of U.N.-administered security measures.[140] In a more detailed version of the plan that was tentatively approved by the cabinet, Bevin suggested that, during the interim period, France would be the power responsible for intervening on behalf of threatened minority groups whenever Washington, London, and

Paris agreed it was necessary. To provide a more solid basis for long-term security, the local gendarmeries would be trained by officers from disinterested countries such as Sweden or Denmark.[141]

Ostensibly, this plan should have been acceptable to the French, who were still telling the Lebanese that they were prepared to take part in a joint withdrawal. In fact, however, they seem to have been playing for time in the hope of securing some privileges for themselves, at least in Lebanon.[142] Massigli informed Bevin that a total French withdrawal was not possible under the circumstances—in order to fulfill its responsibility for the protection of the region's Christian minorities, France would need to retain a couple of aerodromes in Syria as well as the right to station ground forces in certain designated zones in Lebanon. Various commercial and financial privileges would also have to be granted to the French. The French also demanded that the American government promise not to replace French advisors in the Levant with its own personnel. In return for British backing for these desiderata, France was prepared to lend its support in the United Nations to British claims for bases in Iraq, Transjordan, and Palestine. Needless to say, Bevin turned down this proposal, while keeping the door to continued talks open.[143] A few days later, Duff Cooper reported from Paris that Bidault remained eager for an Anglo–French treaty once a number of problems—chief among them the Levant issue—had been resolved:

> The real difficulty in the Levant is the French mistrust of the British and their conviction that if we agree to withdraw together it is with the intention of returning alone. Nothing short of a categorical undertaking that in no circumstances we will send troops back into Syria or the Lebanon would convince them of our sincerity.[144]

When asked about de Gaulle's personal attitude toward the prospect of an alliance with Britain, Bidault answered ambiguously: "He hesitated before replying and then said there were two men in de Gaulle, one who was guided by his head and the other by his feelings."[145]

Bidault and his secretary-general, Chauvel, used the occasion of the mid-September convening in London of the Council of Foreign Ministers to approach His Majesty's government with a pair of new formulas for resolving the Levant problem. On the question of troop withdrawal itself, the French accepted joint evacuation in principle, but insisted that their forces must be authorized to remain in Lebanon until the United Nations was prepared to implement a security plan for the country. This the British were now prepared to accept.[146] However, this plan was linked to another proposal which the French outlined in a second memorandum and which was far more problematic from London's point of view. In effect, what the French seemed to have in mind was an updated version of the Sykes–Picot agreement. Arguing that French and British policies in the Middle East had been subject to each other's influence throughout the interwar period, the Quai d'Orsay suggested that in future the two parties should keep each other informed of their plans for their respective spheres of interest with a view to coordinating policies to their mutual advantage. More specifically, the French claimed the right to be responsible for Levant security under the auspices of the United Nations:

> The French Government, in fact, does not conceal its desire to assume the obligation, within the framework of the collective security organisation, for the arrangements to be made on the territory of the Levant States. The British Government has been willing to recognise the right of France to a privileged position in these States. The military sphere is, properly speaking, the only one in which France asks to be accorded a privilege. The French Government, therefore, relies on the British Government's support with the United Nations for this claim.
>
> . . . The establishment to be anticipated in the Levant must form part of a plan of regional security rationally conceived. It is thus important that this plan should be examined in concert by British and French military experts with a view to drawing up proposals to present to United Nations Organisation.
>
> The principle of this collaboration would in short consist of the mutual recognition by the two Governments of a special interest in what concerns the territories in which they bear, or have borne since 1920, special responsibilities. This interest would take the form of a preferential right which each of the two parties would maintain in its zone with respect to the other party, whether it is a question of military, financial, economic or technical matters.[147]

Written at a time when the French were being systematically hounded out of Syria, this bid for an equal partnership with Britain in the Middle East is stunning in its utter divorce from reality. It can be understood only within the context of de Gaulle's obsession with abstract conceptions of national prestige and honor.[148] It was precisely this obsession that had facilitated his success as leader of the Free French movement in the apocalyptic circumstances of the war years, and which now stood in the way of implementing a pragmatic foreign policy under the more prosaic conditions of the postwar world.

Although Bevin was not prepared to give serious consideration to the French proposal as it stood, he did not reject it out of hand. The foreign secretary was sensitive to the French fear of being supplanted in the Levant and understood their reluctance to evacuate the region without any face-saving quid pro quo. Above all, he remained eager to resolve this nettlesome problem quickly, so that he could turn his full attention to formulating a coherent policy regarding Britain's Middle Eastern interests in general and the Palestine problem in particular (not to mention the plans for a Western Block).[149] The question was therefore referred once again to the Eastern and Western Departments for their consideration.

Predictably, the Eastern Department took a very dim view of the French proposal, and was reluctant to countenance any gesture that could be taken as giving the French a say in Middle Eastern affairs. The most Baxter and Howe (the new supervising undersecretary overseeing the department) were prepared to do was to include a vague and meaningless clause in the as-yet-to-be-negotiatied Anglo–French treaty, to the effect that the two governments would keep each other informed regarding their common interests worldwide. The Western Department objected that this would actually lie beyond the scope of the projected treaty and argued that all the French really required was a self-denying ordinance on Britain's part regarding its intentions in the Levant. This would entail the exclusion of the minister in Beirut from the Middle Eastern Conference of British representatives due to be set up in Cairo to promote regional economic and political cooperation. It would also mean that Britain would not send any technical advisers to the Levant to fill the gap left by the French departure. Surely this was not too much to sacrifice for the sake of Britain's European interests?

Not so, according to the Eastern Department, which accused its counterpart of proposing a one-sided bargain. Why should Britain undertake to disengage itself entirely from Levant affairs in return for French reciprocity vis-à-vis the British sphere of influence? Clearly the French were in no position to intervene in any case, whereas for Britain such a promise would represent a very real concession. Indeed, Shone (who was in London at the time) warned that the exclusion of the Levant from consideration by the Middle East Conference might well induce Syria and Lebanon to turn to Moscow for assistance. The most that the Department was prepared to offer was not to send British advisors to the Levant in an official capacity for a period of two years.[150]

Given its different order of priorities, the Western Department was able to take the Eastern Department's argument and turn it around. Precisely because Britain *was* in a much stronger position than the French, it could afford to be generous:

> What is important is to devise a means of breaking the deadlock as soon as we can, because unless we do so the otherwise favourable conditions for the negotiation of a treaty will slip by and we may never have a treaty at all. The consequences of this would be more serious than any consequences that could follow from a concession and as we are in almost every sense stronger than the French it is easier for us to do so. The stubbornness of the French is in fact a reflection of their sense of weakness.[151]

If a vague British commitment to mutual consultations with the French regarding the Middle East proved insufficient to break the deadlock, argued the Western Department, then the only recourse left to Britain would be to withdraw its troops unilaterally from the Levant.[152]

Alarmed by the suggestion of a unilateral withdrawal and prodded by the impatient Bevin, the Eastern Department was finally forced to draft a general statement regarding the mutual recognition of interests in the Middle East, a draft which Bidault found acceptable and which even de Gaulle was reported willing to consider.[153] In the wake of the elections of October 21, however, the French spent most of November preoccupied with the political confrontation between de Gaulle and the Communists.[154] After de Gaulle's formation of a coalition government on November 21, rapid progress was finally made toward the settlement of the Levant question. On December

13, the French and British governments issued joint communiqués including the texts of the joint evacuation plan and the statement obliquely referring to spheres of influence. The British had insisted on watering the latter down even further under secret pressure from the American government, which remained hostile to the imperial pretensions of the European powers and which also feared that the Soviets might use the document as an excuse for maintaining their presence in northern Iran.[155] The crucial clause in the final version was worded as follows:

> The two Governments are agreed that it is in their mutual interest to promote, in collaboration with other Governments, the economic well-being of the peoples of this region in conditions of peace and security. They will exchange information as may be required regarding the best means by which this object may be attained. It is their desire that by such exchanges of information they will be able to avoid divergences of policy which might impair their mutual interests. Each Government affirms its intention of doing nothing to supplant the interests or responsibilities of the other in the Middle East, having full regard to the political status of the countries in question.
>
> It is in this spirit that they will examine any proposal submitted to the United Nations Organisation on the subject of collective security.[156]

As soon as the actual implementation of the evacuation plan was referred to a joint Anglo–French military committee in Beirut, a serious difference of interpretation arose.[157] The French clearly wished to retain their own troops in Lebanon for as long as possible in the hope of inducing some accommodation of their demands there. They understood the agreement to mean that their forces would remain on the scene after the British had left and until the United Nations was ready to implement a permanent security arrangement (in which, it was hoped, France would continue to play a vital role). For their part, the British assured the alarmed Syrians and Lebanese that the Ninth Army's withdrawal would not be completed until the French, too, had left. Indeed, the British military wished to retain numerical superiority in Lebanon to the very end, evacuating troops at a rate proportional to the French pace of withdrawal, in order to maintain its claim to the operational command.[158] De Gaulle's ire was aroused once again:

> The Foreign Ministry has engaged us in a so-called accord with the English which appears to be a deception.
>
> The stage is now being set for leading us to the objective pursued by the English, namely our total departure from Syria and Lebanon; the English, for their part, remain in force in Palestine, in Iraq, in Transjordan and in Egypt.[159]

After de Gaulle's sudden resignation on January 20, a compromise was reached providing for an equal ratio of French and British troops to be retained in Lebanon until the last soldiers had left the country; Paget's overall operational command was to be regarded as no longer in force. The final withdrawal from Syria was scheduled for the end of April, with the date for evacuation from Lebanon remaining contingent on the actions of the U.N. Security Council.[160]

Epilogue

In order to speed the implementation of the evacuation agreement, the Foreign Office hoped to see the Security Council take up the Levant question as soon as possible. The immediate goal was to induce the Security Council "to take a decision which will in fact authorise French and British troops to remain in the Lebanon until the Security Council have been able to consider the security problem in the Levant." It was decided, however, that Britain should leave the initiative in the matter to the Syrians and Lebanese, for fear that a British motion would be defeated and might, in any case, provide the Egyptians with an excuse for raising the issue of Britain's military presence in that country:

> The conclusion which we have reached, therefore, is that it might for tactical reasons be better for the United Kingdom *not* to take the initiative at present. . . . But it would suit us quite well if the Syrians and Lebanese took the initiative, as it would then be for them to get seven votes in the Security Council in favour of the [eventual] departure of the British and French troops and we should be in a stronger position.[161]

When the Levant States raised the issue of evacuation before the Security Council in February 1946, however, they did so in a manner that shocked the British government. Counting on tacit support from the United States, they challenged the validity of the bilateral agreements of December 13, 1945 between Britain and France, and presented the whole issue as a dispute with the occupying powers.[162] In a joint letter to the Security Council, the Syrian and Lebanese delegations treated the French and British as one, characterizing the presence of their troops on Levant soil as a "grave infringement of the sovereignty" of the states and calling for their simultaneous *and immediate* withdrawal.[163] Similar language was used in a resolution put forward by the Egyptian delegation in support of the Levant states. The British seemed genuinely outraged by this ungentlemanly display of ingratitude, and a dialogue of the deaf (and the inarticulate) ensued at the Security Council, where Bevin himself was leading the British delegation:

> Mr. BEVIN (United Kingdom): I do not want to be separated from my fellow-accused. (*Laughter.*) But as a matter of accuracy, in the Egyptian resolution [in support of the Levant states' demands] and in the [Syrian–Lebanese] letter it says that the presence of British and French troops constitutes a "grave infringement of the sovereignty" of the two States.
>
> The British Government is very much concerned about that; and in view of the fact that we are still there at the request of the Governments concerned, I wonder whether, apart from the point as to whether this is a dispute or not, this will lead to a declaration that the British troops there are infring-

ing the sovereignty of those two countries, because there is that charge made against us. . . .

Mr. AL-KHOURY (Syria): I wish to give an explanation in regard to what the honourable delegate for France said about our declaration that we did not want to take part in negotiations.

I said, in fact, that we prefer that the matter should be solved by them without consulting us. . . .

As to the dispute, we said in our first letter that there was a dispute, and then we said that the presence and the continuance of the presence of foreign troops might lead to a more serious dispute. That dispute may be in one form or it may be in another form, more or less serious; it may take different forms. So that a dispute existed, and it is possible that it may well exist also in a different form from the previous one.

Mr. BEVIN (United Kingdom): I did not hear your last words.

Mr. AL-KHOURY (Syria): I did not give any reply to your question, Mr. Bevin.

Mr. BEVIN (United Kingdom): But I want you to, so that I can make up my mind.

Mr. AL-KHOURY (Syria): You had better find it out yourself.[164]

Seeking to end the acrimonious debate, the United States introduced a compromise resolution that urged "that the foreign troops in Syria and the Lebanon will be withdrawn as soon as practicable."[165] Both France and Britain joined in a majority vote in favor of the resolution, which was vetoed by the Soviet Union (the first of many occasions on which the Soviets would exercise this prerogative).[166] Nonetheless, His Majesty's government decided to regard the resolution as legally binding. Piqued by what he saw as the unfairness and arrogance of the Levant states, and eager to wash his hands of the whole affair, Bevin decided to take matters one step further by regarding the Security Council resolution as superseding the Anglo–French agreements of December 13 as well as the subsequent assurances to the authorities in Beirut and Damascus that British forces would not leave before the French did. The crucial phrase in the resolution, as Bevin chose to interpret it, was "as soon as practicable." Accordingly, little more than a week afer having reached the final agreement with the French on the wording of the joint directive on evacuation, the British announced that they were fixing their own timetable for the complete withdrawal of their troops from Syria and Lebanon, regardless of what the French intended to do. Although Bevin hoped that the French could be induced to coordinate their own withdrawal with the British schedule, it is clear from Whitehall's internal correspondence that he seriously intended to carry out the evacuation as rapidly as possible in any event.[167]

Taken aback by this unexpected *volte-face,* both the French and the Levant states raised a hue and cry: given the tense and ill-defined situation in the region, each party feared that an abrupt and unilateral British withdrawal would leave it in a vulnerable position. The Foreign Office enjoyed a self-righteous sense of satisfaction at the discomfiture of Britain's critics—small comfort in view of the general antipathy toward Britain among Middle Eastern countries, which the Security Council debate had revealed. One Eastern Department official wrote:

> The Foreign Office decision to take urgent steps to withdraw British troops in the light of the proceedings at the Security Council has occasioned dismay on every side (the French Embassy and French Government have both complained, Mr. Shone expressed grave misgivings . . . and the [Levant] Governments themselves appear to have hardly believed we were in earnest). I think this is a measure of the impossible situation in which we had found ourselves and a sign that we should not be deterred from maintaining the position we have taken up. Both sides in this dispute have found our presence in the Levant States most convenient. The Levant States Governments have used us as a lever to remove the French, and the French Government have used us as a cushion against the hard facts of the situation. . . .
> I therefore suggest that both sides have received a salutary eye-opener.[168]

R. G. Howe wrote to Shone in a similarly gleeful vein:

> I do not think that the Levant States fully understood what would happen to them if they submitted this dispute to the Security Council, and they were slightly bewildered when they found themselves in the whirlpool of great power politics. . . . The French of course are equally resentful. . . . The fact of course is that we started as peacemakers but found the position untenable and our escape from this awkward situation has upset both parties.[169]

Spears' assumption that his interventionist policy would produce a profound sense of indebtedness to Britain in the Levant states had proved groundless. Now all the British could do was leave in a huff, consoling themselves with the notion that they had been morally vindicated.

Confronted with the prospect of being left with a few thousand troops facing a hostile Levant population, the French had little choice but to coordinate their own withdrawal with the British. A timetable was drawn up at military talks in Paris during March, and by mid-April, Syria was entirely free of foreign soldiers. By the end of August, the last French troops had sailed away from Lebanon as well.[170] Providing a foretaste of things to come, the United Press reported as follows:

BEIRUT, Lebanon, August 5

> Time bombs exploded simultaneously in the American Legation and the British Consulate last night, damaging the American building so badly that it was condemned today as uninhabitable. . . .

> All foreign legations were placed under the guard of Lebanonese [sic] troops today and police guards were posted at all consulates.[171]

The identity of the perpetrators remained unknown.

CONCLUSION

Regarded through the lens of hindsight, the wartime events in Syria and Lebanon seem like scenes from a low-budget stage production of a dusty, old period piece. While the future of mankind hinged on the outcome of the monumental struggle between the Axis powers and the Allies, the Levant witnessed an anachronistic game of colonial rivalry, quaintly reminiscent of the nineteenth-century imperial contest in Africa.

An unwillingness or an inability to confront the problem of Arab nationalism on its own terms was the most uniform characteristic of French policy in the Levant throughout the mandatory period. Instead, the French approach to the Levant problem was molded by a gnawing sense of national decline and an obsession with issues of prestige. The response to the nationalist challenge tended to be shaped more by the preoccupation with British behavior in the region, than by an examination of the political factors within Syria and Lebanon on their own merits. The nationalist movement was seen as inveterately hostile to France, and essentially a creature of British expansionist interests. In light of this assessment, and apart from a brief interlude under the Popular Front, it was considered that the best means of maintaining French control over the region was to encourage the self-assertion of local minority groups, while obstinately refusing to countenance the political demands of the Sunni, Arab majority.

The conditions created by the events of World War II caused these features of the French approach to stand out in bold relief, and what resulted was almost a caricature of traditional French colonial policy. During the period of Vichy's rule in the Levant, the narrowly Anglophobic outlook so common among the French officials in the mandated territories fit perfectly with the blinkered vision of the metropolitan government. With all prospects of an independent continental role for France apparently dead, Vichy looked to the empire as one of the few remaining spheres in which French honor could be preserved, and perhaps even glory recovered. The most immediate threat to Vichy control of the empire came from Britain, the country which in any case served as one of the Pétain regime's most convenient scapegoats for the disaster of 1940. The legacy of interwar tension between the two colonial powers in the Middle East combined with the corruption and apathy of the Levant administration made it very difficult for the Free French to seize control of the apparatus from within. Enthusiasm in the Levant for Pétain's National Revolution never ran very deep, but Bourget's purge in October 1940 and the subsequent replacement of Puaux with Dentz did ensure that basic discipline would be maintained and orders from Vichy accepted unquestioningly. Whatever remaining illusions the British and Gaullists may have retained concerning the attitude of the Levant administration were quickly dispelled during the invasion of June–July 1941, when the forces under Dentz's command threw themselves into the fray with a passion that had been missing in the face of the German onslaught against France one year earlier.

In assuming formal responsibility for the protection of French interests in Syria and Lebanon, the Free French were immediately confronted with the same geopolitical factor that had helped mold their predecessors' outlook: the main threat to French control over the region still seemed to come from the British, except that now they were effectively joint rulers of the territories rather than rivals on the other side of the border. The potentially explosive chemistry of this situation was aggravated on the Free French side by the high stake de Gaulle felt he had in preserving the French position in the Levant against any British encroachments. After all, for de Gaulle—just as for Vichy—control of the empire, or any part thereof, was one of the few available ways of establishing his movement's legitimacy as heir to the mantle of French national grandeur. Any substantive wartime concession on de Gaulle's part to the demands of Arab nationalists would, he felt, be seen as a knuckling under to British pressure and as an indication that France had indeed been irrevocably stripped of its pride and independence in June 1940. Thus, apart from the partial continuity in local personnel between the Vichy and Free French administrations in the Levant, there was a certain continuity of outlook that contrasted strangely with the overall clash between Gaullist and Vichy conceptions of France's role in the war.[1]

Clearly, Spears' conduct during this period only served to aggravate what would in any case have been a sensitive situation. His role was indeed a very curious one. Ever the odd man out, Spears was neither a professional diplomat nor a member of the top-level military establishment; his position in public affairs had always seemed to depend on his personal friendship with Churchill. He was always viewed—and frequently resented—as an outsider whose command of the French language was too perfect and affectation of continental manners too conspicuous to permit his acceptance as "one of the boys." Before the First World War, as the adjutant at Aldershot, Spears was already regarded with distaste by many of his fellow officers. As a sympathetic observer later recalled:

> The Adjutant of the time . . . had still the lingering cobwebs of unpopularity clinging to him, the reasons for it being that he was an unusually intelligent man, liked conversation and, worse yet, talked French as easily as he spoke English. Moreover he paid a great deal of attention to his hands, in the way a foreign officer might, and this made his brother officers more uneasy. I used to watch his shrewd, keen, rather thin face as he pared his nails, much in the way I have seen Italian officers do.[2]

His image was quite similar thirty years later; Patrick Coghill, head of the BSM in Beirut, described his first impression of Spears as follows:

> When he entered the room I saw a thick-set powerfully built man of 5'10"–5'11" with thinning blond hair with touches of gray, a strong nose and a rat-

trap gash for a mouth. Quie [Quite?] unaccountably my reaction was that he was a Jew—and I am not Jew conscious—it was only later that I heard the speculative gossip that his original name was Speier [it was actually Spiers] and that he was a Jew from Alsatia. I still do not know his origins. . . . He is certainly 100% bilingual in French and English and if anything I have a feeling that French comes the easier to him. . . .

A remarkable man of great gifts and power and some charm when he chose—but I never felt that I could trust him.[3]

Spears seems to have been acutely sensitive to this undercurrent of resentment against him, and this heightened his sense of attachment to and dependence on Churchill. It also combined with his long-standing Francophilism to turn him into a jealous guardian of Free French interests against the encroachments of the Foreign Office and War Office during 1940 and early 1941. He became increasingly embittered by de Gaulle's defiantly independent stance, however, and the general's bellicose outbursts over the terms of the St. Jean d'Acre armistice appear to have shocked Spears into the realization that he had helped create a Frankenstein that was now beyond his control. In his dismay, he turned into a bitter enemy of the Free French.

Perhaps even more important than the shift in his personal relations with de Gaulle were the political conditions created for Spears by the conquest of the Levant. In London and Cairo, Spears had confronted the diplomatic and military establishments in his role as patron of the Free French. In the Levant, he was suddenly presented with the opportunity of bringing the local British power structure under his own control. From that point on, any Free French loss became Louis Spears' gain. Here at last was an opportunity to carve out a niche for himself in public life as well as a place for himself in British history. What would his former detractors at Aldershot have to say when they saw the bilingual officer with delicate hands adding the jewel of Syria to the crown of the British Empire? Exploiting his friendship with Churchill to the full, Spears seemed bent on transforming the Levant into his personal satrapy. For all that he advocated Syrian and Lebanese independence, he must have expected to hold on to a role in the postwar Levant similar, if not to that of Clive in India, than at least to that which Lampson had for years played in Egypt—the maker and breaker of governments and effective viceroy of the country. What is remarkable is not so much the unrealistic nature of Spears' ambitions a mere decade before the final collapse of British influence in the Middle East, but how close he seemed to come to fulfilling this fantasy, if only for a little while. His successor enviously described Spears' apparent accomplishment in glowing terms:

His remarkable personality, his great talents—not least his aptitude for public speaking in French as well as English—his tireless energy, his gift of personal appeal to people in these countries in all walks of life and, above all, his championship of the cause which is closest to their hearts—their independence—had won him a position here which was altogether exceptional for a foreigner. The Governments turned to him for advice in a multitude of matters, great and small. The people often acclaimed him in the streets. The tributes paid to him and Lady Spears, who had also gained the esteem and affection of the States to a remarkable degree, when it was known that they were about to leave, were quite unusual. Streets in capital cities have no doubt often been named after distinguished soldiers or servants of the Crown; but it must be rare for one of His Majesty's representatives to be made an honorary citizen of the countries in which he served. Sir E. Spears had indeed set the prestige of Great Britain high in the Levant States. His place here was not easy to take.[4]

Spears' relative autonomy as minister and chief of mission in the Levant led to the development of an unusually wide gap between the theory and practice of British foreign policy in the region. The combination of Spears' personal animus against de Gaulle and his political ambition seems to have played a decisive role in molding his conception of British interests in Syria and Lebanon. His direct link with the head of the British government allowed him to circumvent the institution officially responsible for the formulation of policy, namely the Foreign Office.

Yet the collapse of French authority in the Levant cannot be attributed to such personal dynamics alone. The deterioration of Anglo–French relations in the region was also conditioned by powerful structural factors that would have been very difficult to overcome in any case. In the wake of Vichy's eviction from the territories, an anomalous situation was created in which juridical Free French control was exercised over a region effectively occupied by British forces and in which French prestige among the native population had sunk to an all-time low. The British Middle Eastern establishment did not relish the prospect of antagonizing Arab nationalists by turning the Levant over to the French for the second time in twenty years. Their outlook blinkered by their immersion in the Levantine sideshow, British officers and officials in Syria and Lebanon came to refer to the Free French as "the enemy" and to relish the games of rivalry and intrigue to which the situation so readily lent itself.[5] It seems most likely that, even in the absence of Spears, a profound difference in perspective would have been bound to develop between the policymakers in London and the British authorities on the spot.

Many of the principals were themselves aware of this fundamental problem and sought to convince each other to reorder priorities in accordance with their respective interpretations of the national interest. Thus John Rosa, the Treasury representative in the Levant, argued in October 1942 that the only chance for Anglo–Free French cooperation in the region had been lost when Catroux issued his promise of independence to Syria and Lebanon on the eve of the invasion:

This offer of June 1941 set in motion a chain of events which can neither be undone nor ignored. In the first place, the offer had to be implemented if both we and the French were to escape the charge of treachery. . . . To the Oriental mind, which is realist to the point of cynicism, it is inconceivable that we, as financial backers of the Fighting French, do not call the tune and it is, therefore, assumed, and nothing will dispel this belief, that all action

taken by the Fighting French has our approval. In these circumstances, failure to implement independence reacts on our prestige just as much as on that
of the French. We cannot, however much we might wish to, wash our hands
of Syria or give the French a completely free hand there, their privileged
position notwithstanding. . . .

   In view of the foregoing, it would seem a surrender of our most elemen-
tary rights and interests to permit the French to pursue in Syria a policy which
can only redound to our discredit.[6]

For its part, the Foreign Office long remained convinced that Britain could
maintain overall cooperation with the Gaullist movement by avoiding confrontation in the Levant, but that this need not entail any substantive concessions
to French demands:

   . . . Apart from limitations imposed on us by our legal commitments, there is
   the inescapable fact that our requirements in the Levant States have continually to be considered as a part of our policy to the French as a whole. The
   consequence is that in the general war interest we as the Cinderella of the
   party are apt to have to give way. For instance, if de Gaulle is behaving
   himself, we are told that it would be highly undesirable for us e.g. to impede
   French unity by staging a first-class row in the Levant States. *Per contra,* if we
   are already in the throes of one of our periodic rows with the General, we are
   told that we must not pour oil on the already burning fires. Even to those
   sitting in London who deal with the affairs of the Levant States, it is sometimes galling to be forced to play the minor role, and we fully understand that
   it must be even more irritating in its effect on those like you on the spot. But
   it is none the less necessary and it boils down to the fact that in our dealings
   we have to trust the French as allies. . . . It means in particular that there are
   certain lengths beyond which we cannot go. Consequently on certain subjects
   if we cannot reach agreement by negotiation, we eventually have to agree to
   differ, e.g. about the Haifa–Tripoli Railway. It does not mean that we concede the French point of view; for, to take that case, we are in possession of
   the railway and intend to run it as we like.[7]

Clearly, Britain's various interests were mutually incompatible and after December 1944, now that they no longer felt compelled to rally their forces
against Spears, the Foreign Office departments responsible respectively for
Middle Eastern and Western European affairs themselves began to fall out
over the ordering of priorities.

   Given these conditions, it appears as though French prospects for maintaining a privileged position in the Levant would have been very dim regardless of Spears' role. His policy could be taken simply as the manifestation of a
deep undercurrent of opinion in Britain's Middle Eastern establishment that
favored the integration of Syria and Lebanon into the British sphere of influence.[8] Moreover, the fact that it was largely British forces that had won the
Levant from Vichy as well as the continued numerical preponderance of
British troops in the region, made Free French power appear like an empty
façade to the Syrians and Lebanese. It could therefore strongly be argued that
French power in the region would have collapsed by the end of the war in any

case. Indeed, British influence in the Middle East was to prove quite short-lived itself.

The point is, however, that Spears' overtly hostile conduct made the French *perceive* their collapse as the direct result of a concerted and precon-ceived plan to oust them. Although it was clearly the intention of the Foreign Office to lend some measure of support to French influence in the Levant, the French found it hard to believe that Spears was acting largely on his own initiative and in disregard of his instructions from London. Their own govern-mental system was too highly centralized to permit such long-term dissidence and, indeed, it is difficult to imagine any ordinary British diplomat—be he Arabophile or Francophobe—being allowed to get away with such flagrantly insubordinate behavior.[9]

In the absence of Spears' constant incitement, it is unlikely that the Syrians and Lebanese would have been emboldened to challenge French authority so openly in the midst of the war. The French collapse would probably have come about more gradually and the Levant issue would not have been pro-pelled into the center of Anglo–French relations and would not have served to embitter de Gaulle's attitude toward Britain so deeply. The fact that the struggle for control over the Levant strikes one in retrospect as an anachronis-tic issue that bore little relevance to the real interests of Britain and France, does not diminish its importance as an obstacle to better relations between the two countries at the time.

Although the gap between the formulation and implementation of foreign policy on Britain's part is particularly striking, Free French foreign policy was no smooth-running operation either. But whereas the Foreign Office was frustrated by Spears' active defiance of its policy, those responsible for Free French foreign affairs were generally confronted with a combination of incom-petence and passive resistance on the part of the Levant administration. French personnel simply lacked the experience and expertise of their British counterparts. There was a strong tendency among them to report on the mood of the native population as they would have liked it to be rather than as it really was. During 1943, the contrast between Helleu's lethargic complacency and Spears' energetic enterprise was truly remarkable.

Indeed, the Vichy period's spirit of *attentisme* continued to prevail through-out the lower echelons of the French bureaucracy in Syria and Lebanon after the Allied invasion, given the large proportion of personnel in the General Delegation that had been retained from the pre-June 1941 High Commission. Just as Bourget had failed to instill much enthusiasm for the National Revolu-tion among these jaded bureaucrats, so too the idealism and progressive outlook of the committed Gaullists did not penetrate far beneath the surface of the administrative apparatus. This problem was compounded by the influ-ence wielded within the General Delegation by opportunistic defectors from Vichy's diplomatic service. During Helleu's tenure as delegate-general, all sense of purpose seems to have been drained out of the French administra-tion, and Catroux's calls for a remolding of French policy in the image of Britain's indirect method of colonial rule fell on deaf ears. Likewise, the efforts of the Commissariat for Foreign Affairs to reach a definitive under-standing on the Levant with the Foreign Office were repeatedly stymied by local clashes of authority such as the dispute over the arrest of the drug smuggler and parliamentary candidate, Mukaddam.

Just as the British and French foreign policymakers were frustrated by their inability to exert control over local developments in Syria and Lebanon, so did they find themselves repeatedly reined in by the men at the top of their respective governmental hierarchies—Churchill and de Gaulle. The signifi-cance of Churchill's personal support for Spears has been made abundantly clear. There is no question that the repeated Free French demands for Spears' removal provoked the prime minister's ire, as did de Gaulle's occasional outbursts of bellicose Anglophobia. For Churchill, personal relations could not be separated from issues of public policy, and he took de Gaulle's appar-ent ingratitude toward Britain as a personal affront.[10] His sense of loyalty to Spears and his increasing resentment of de Gaulle thus had a mutually re-inforcing effect.

De Gaulle, by contrast, drew a sharp distinction between considerations of personal obligation and the exigencies of public policy; the demands of raison d'état took precedence over the rules of common courtesy. Therefore, the fact that his movement was dependent on Britain for its material existence made it all the more important that he assert its independence on the ideal plane through striking displays of unbridled arrogance. Regarding himself as the embodiment of French national honor, a twentieth-century Joan of Arc, de Gaulle felt he could not afford to make concessions that would transform the Free French–British association into a client–patron relationship.[11] When practical considerations did render compromise necessary, he left the unpleas-ant task for his subordinates to manage. More often, Catroux's, Dejean's, or Massigli's efforts to resolve differences with the British were derailed by the haughty general's interventions. In the overall context of relations with the Allied powers, de Gaulle's provocative tactics and deliberate arrogance were indeed successful: almost singlehandedly, he managed to salvage a sense of French national dignity and unconditional sovereignty from the wreckage of wartime defeat and occupation. But within the framework of the Levant, his approach backfired. By repeatedly jumping into the fray with Spears and by preventing Catroux from making timely concessions to the demands of the Levant nationalists, the Free French leader both solidified Churchill's support for the British minister in Beirut and exacerbated the process of political polarization that was to hasten the demise of the French mandate in the Levant. When, in June 1945, he was at last forced to back down in Syria, de Gaulle blamed the fiasco not any lack of realism on his own part, but rather on the unwillingness of French public opinion, the press, and the foreign service to rally enthusiastically behind him. Internal divisions, he felt, had prevented the national will from rising to the occasion.

Thus, the structural tension caused by overlapping responsibilities in the Levant combined with a clash of personalities to form a potent brew of mutual Anglo–French suspicion and resentment. Although it was a marginal sideshow, the struggle over Syria and Lebanon continually stood in the way of cooperation between the British and French over the broad community of interests that they shared in the European sphere. Especially where France was concerned, issues of prestige were inextricably intertwined with questions of security or pragmatic self-interest. In the wake of the final debacle in Syria, one French observer wrote:

> In France the Levant question has had much deeper repercussions than in England, less perhaps on its own account than because it aroused in the French the painful feeling of having to suffer injustice because of their weakness. The average Frenchman, the man in the street, has got the impression that Great Britain is taking advantage of our temporary weakness in order to humiliate us, eliminate us from the Levant and take our place.[12]

D. W. Brogan pointed out similarly:

> There was a time when the only equivalent in the world to English self-satisfaction was French self-satisfaction, but those days are gone, possibly for ever. The French are very far from being self-satisfied today, and some of the odder and more deplorable aspects of French policy arise from a desperate need of reassurance . . . that France has still a role to play worthy of her past. . . .
>
> As an Imperial Power ourselves, we should have had more understanding of the role of prestige, *their* prestige. Syria was, in any case, the Achilles' heel of the French imperial system; our (and the Gaullist) intervention was a golden opportunity for the local Arab leaders to play off the stronger against the weaker.[13]

Indeed, the nationalist leaders in Syria and Lebanon had conducted a very skillful game of maneuver and deception during the war years. The French General Delegation played into the hands of Spears and the nationalists by repeatedly rising to their bait and overreacting to their provocations, while refusing to make the timely concessions advocated by Catroux. Even had Catroux's advice been more consistently taken, the situation, particularly that in Syria, would not have been greatly improved. Among the leaders of the National Bloc, only the slippery Jamil Mardam, whose political star was on the wane and who was eager to find a way of regaining a dominant political role, seemed willing to consider the permanent cession of treaty rights to the French.[14] The leading figure in the movement, Shukri al-Quwatli, gladly led Catroux on with false hopes, but was never really prepared to grant France any privileges in Syria as the price for the country's independence.

But Spears and his colleagues were themselves rather gullible in their belief that the Arab nationalists would feel themselves bound to Britain by a debt of gratitude once the French had been expelled from the region. Spears was particularly prone to make much of the flattery and apparent adulation with which he was showered by notables and masses alike.[15] And yet, the strength of his influence was ultimately derived, not from British power as such, but rather from the usefulness of his mission to the nationalists as a tool with which to rid themselves of the French. The nationalist leaders were acutely aware of the danger that the French yoke might be replaced by a British one at the end of the war, and the sudden change in tone that marked the Levant states' appeal to the Security Council in February 1946 made the British realize with a sudden shock just how little real credit they had gained in Beirut and Damascus over the preceding five years. Indeed, the forebodings that the officials of the Foreign Office's Western Department had expressed were borne out as Syrian and Lebanese attainment of unconditional independence from France set a precedent for Britain's own client states in the region.[16] Successive attempts at treaty revision with Egypt and Iraq came to nought and the outbreak of the Palestine conflict in 1947 spelled the beginning of the end for the British Empire in the Middle East.

In retrospect, the wartime episode in the Levant strikes the observer of the 1990s as a black farce in which two declining imperial powers became obsessed with undermining each other's influence in a colonial backwater while the German menace lurked in the background. The mental timelag that Schumpeter has described as crucial to the development of neomercantilistic imperialism in the Age of Capital is, perhaps, discernible in a different form during the period of imperial decline as well.[17] As the force of Arab nationalism grew, and as the burgeoning global influence of the United States began to make itself felt in the Middle East, the British and French displayed little awareness of their own fundamental weakness; they both operated on the assumption that the prewar constellation of forces in the world could be preserved in the future through relatively minor modifications of policy. This was indeed a dismal last hurrah for the Great Game of European colonial rivalry.

NOTES

Abbreviations

AN	Archives Nationales
BGA	Ben-Gurion Archive
BSM	British Security Mission
CAB	Cabinet
CFR	Cabinet's Committee on Foreign (Allied) Resistance
CO	Colonial Office
COS	Chiefs of Staff
CZA	Central Zionist Archive
DGFP	Documents on German Foreign Policy
FCNL	French Committee of National Liberation (1943–1944)
FNC	French National Committee (1940–1943)
FO	Foreign Office
FRUS	Foreign Relations of the United States
GFM	German Foreign Ministry
GHQ	General Headquarters
G.O.C.	General Officer Commanding
HMG	His [Britannic] Majesty's government
IPC	Iraq Petroleum Company
MEC	Middle East Centre
MESC	Middle East Supply Centre
MEWC	Middle East War Council
NA	National Archives and Records Service
NEA	Near Eastern and African Affairs Department
OCP	Office des Céréales Panifiables (Wheat Office)
OSS	Office of Strategic Services
PHP	Post-Hostilities Planning (subcommittee of the Chiefs of Staff)
P.M.	Prime Minister
PREM	Premier's Papers
PRO	Public Record Office
PWE	Political Warfare Executive
S. of S.	Secretary of State
SD	State Department
SHAT	Service Historique de l'Armée de Terre
SIME	Security Intelligence Middle East

SIS   Secret Intelligence Service
SOE   Special Operations Executive
TSMF   Territoires sous Mandat Français (Levant territory)
U.N.   United Nations
WJC   World Jewish Congress
WO   War Office

Preface

1. This is the picture presented by Charles de Gaulle in his memoirs (Charles de Gaulle, *Mémoires de Guerre*, 3 vols. [Paris, 1954–59) as well as by Georges Catroux (*Dans la bataille de Méditerranée* [Paris: 1949]).

2. George Kirk, *The Middle East in the War* (Oxford, 1953), pp. 104–29 (especially note 4 on p. 114); Stephen Longrigg, *Syria and Lebanon under French Mandate* (Oxford, 1958), pp. 317–33 and note 1 on p. 346; John Harvey, ed., *War Diaries of Oliver Harvey* (London, 1978).

Introduction

1. Kamal S. Salibi, *The Modern History of Lebanon* (New York, 1965), chapter 6.

2. Mathew Burrows, " 'Mission Civilisatrice': French Cultural Policy in the Middle East, 1860–1914," *The Historical Journal*, 29, no. 1 (1986): 109–35.

3. Stephen Longrigg, *Syria and Lebanon under French Mandate* (Oxford, 1958), chapter 3; Elie Kedourie, *England and the Middle East* (London, 1956), chapters 2, 5 and 6; Henry H. Cumming, *Franco–British Rivalry in the Post-War Near East* (Oxford, 1938), chapter 9. These mandates had originally been granted at the 1920 San Remo conference; the League defined their provisions in detail and formally confirmed them.

4. Elizabeth Monroe, *The Mediterranean in Politics* (Oxford, 1938), chapter 2.

5. Howard Sachar notes that, as of 1938, the ratio of French trade with the Levant to expenditure on the mandate was 300 million to 5 billion francs (Howard Sachar, *Europe Leaves the Middle East, 1936–1956* [New York, 1972], p. 10.) See also Monroe, *The Mediterranean*, chapter 3.

6. It has been argued, however, that the increased cultural, economic, and political activity of France in the Levant during the decade before the First World War had already antagonized important elements among the Syrian population (William I. Shorrock, *French Imperialism in the Middle East* [Madison, 1976]).

7. Asher Susser, "Western Power Rivalry and its Interaction with Local Politics in the Levant, 1941–1946" (Ph.D. diss., Tel-Aviv University, 1986), pp. 18–19.

8. Pierre Rondot, "L'expérience du mandat français en Syrie et au Liban (1918–45)," *Revue des droits internationals publiques* 52 (1948): 387–409; Albert Hourani, *Syria and Lebanon, A Political Essay* (Oxford, 1946), chapter 9; Itamar Rabinovich, "The Compact Minorities and the Syrian State, 1918–1945," *The Journal of Contemporary History*, 14, no. 4 (October 1979), pp. 693–712. For a sketchy, but critical, first-hand account of early French mandatory policy in the Levant, see the reminiscences written by the first delegate in Damascus (later the first Free French delegate-general

in the Levant): General Georges Catroux, *Deux Missions en Moyen-Orient* (*1919–1922*) (Paris, 1958).

9. Longrigg, *Syria and Lebanon,* chapter 8; Hourani, *Syria and Lebanon,* p. 153; author's interview with Professor Maxime Rodinson (Paris, 2 May 1985).

10. See Philip S. Khoury, *Syria and the French Mandate* (Princeton, 1987), chapter 2.

11. Sachar, *Europe Leaves the Middle East,* chapter 1.

12. Khoury, *Syria,* chapters 9 and 10; conversation with Dr. Asher Susser (Tel-Aviv, 27 December 1987).

13. Longrigg, *Syria and Lebanon,* chapter 6; Pierre Rondot, "Les mouvements nationalistes au Levant durant la deuxième guerre mondiale," *La guerre en méditerranée 1939–1945* (Paris, 1971), pp. 643–65.

14. Hourani, *Syria and Lebanon,* chapters 10 and 11; Khoury, *Syria,* chapter 22; Michael G. Fry and Itamar Rabinovich, *Despatches from Damascus: Gilbert Mac-Kereth and British Policy in the Levant, 1933–1939* (Tel-Aviv University and University of Southern California, 1985), pp. 28–41.

15. Puaux personally believed, as did many French officials, that the Syrians' concern for their mercantile and material interests was more deeply rooted than their nationalistic or pan-Arab impulses (letter from Puaux to Robert Montagne [Paris], 1 June 1940, Papiers d'Agents: Puaux–36).

16. High commissioner of Palestine to CO #267, 19 August 1925, FO 371/10851–E 5276/357/89; Smart (consul in Damascus) to FO #153, 3 September 1925, E5273; dispatch from Smart to FO, 9 November 1925, FO 371/10852–E 7290/357/89.

17. Reports by Cox (Amman) and Symes (Jerusalem), 9 and 13 August 1925, FO 371/10851–E 5329/367/89; dispatch from Duport (Beirut) to Foreign Ministry, 10 November 1925 and dispatch from Maugras (Jerusalem) to Foreign Ministry, 16 November 1925, E–Levant: Syrie–Liban, 2ème partie, 1922–1929, vol. 163.

18. Dispatch from MacKereth (consul in Damascus) to Macpherson (Jerusalem), undated (fall 1939), FO 371/23280–E 6879/2143/89.

19. Dispatch from MacKereth to Eden, 5 February 1938, FO 371/21873–E 862/10/31; "Summary of Jewish Agency's relations with Arab States," 19 July 1939, CZA, S25/4549.

20. MacKereth to Eden, 19 October 1937, as cited in Joan Peters, *From Time Immemorial* (New York, 1984), p. 284.

21. Elizabeth Monroe, *The Mediterranean,* chapter 4; Lukasz Hirszovicz, *The Third Reich and the Arab East* (London, 1966), chapters 1–3; Khoury, *Syria,* chapter 16. The National Bloc's youth movement was popularly known as the Steel Shirts.

22. Report by Bouvier (French military commander in Jebel Druze), 9 July 1939, E–Levant: Syrie–Liban 1930–1940, vol. 457; minute by Baggallay (Eastern Dept.), 17 January 1940, FO 371/24547–E 255/255/65; dispatch from MacMichael (high commissioner of Palestine) to Shuckburgh (CO), 3 March 1940, E 1588; extract from Bennett (Cairo) to Downie (CO), 26 April 1940, FO 371/24591–E 1138/103/89.

23. On Franco–British relations in Europe between the wars, see Arnold Wolfers, *Britain and France between Two World Wars* (New York, 1940). Wolfers argues that Britain's drift back toward its traditional role as arbiter of the European balance undermined French resolve toward Germany.

24. Dispatch from Smart (consul in Damascus) to Chamberlain (S. of S. for Foreign Affairs), 21 May 1925, FO 371/10850–E 3200/357/89.

25. Translated excerpt from a 1934 report written by the flag officer commanding

French naval forces in the Levant and found by British personnel among documents captured from Vichy army (forwarded to London on 21 October 1941), FO 371/27060–E 7667/7667/65.

26. Pierre Benoit, *La Châtelaine du Liban* (Paris, 1924), pp. 76–77.

Chapter 1

1. Gabriel Puaux, *Deux années au Levant* (Paris, 1952), p. 209.
2. Ibid., p. 200.
3. Palmer (Beirut) to S. of S. #38, 23 June 1940, *FRUS* 3 (1940): 892–93.
3. Salisbury Jones to Wavell, 25 June 1940, FO 371/24592–E 2239/2160/89.
4. Puaux, *Deux années au Levant,* pp. 201–2.
5. Halifax to Stonehewer-Bird (Jedda) #69, 21 June 1940, FO 406/78–E 2170/2170/89.
6. Telegram from Noguès to Weygand, 25 June 1940, Guerre 1939–1945, Vichy–Levant 33.
7. Ibid.
8. Ibid., appended minute.
9. Puaux to Baudoin, 26 June 1940, as quoted in Jean-Baptiste Duroselle, *L'Abîme—1939–1945* (Paris, 1982), p. 221 and in Puaux, *Deux années au Levant,* p. 204.
10. Puaux, *Deux années au Levant,* pp. 201–3. The records actually indicate that the British government refused to entertain the notion of territorial concessions to the Turks at French expense as long as the Levant remained stable and out of reach of the Axis (ME [O] [40] 21, 26 June 1940, CAB 95 and Halifax to Knatchbull-Hugessen [Ankara] #522, 29 June 1940).
11. Gabriel Puaux, letter to *Le Figaro*, 1/2 October 1949. (I would like to thank Dr. Henri Lerner for drawing my attention to this letter.) It should be pointed out that this presentation of the events bears the distinct mark of historical hindsight.
12. Edgard de Larminat, *Chroniques irrévérencieuses* (Paris, 1962), p. 50.
13. Havard to Halifax #20, 27 June 1940, FO 406/78–E2200/2170/89.
14. De Larminat, *Chroniques,* pp. 55–56.
15. Puaux, *Deux années au Levant,* pp. 206–7.
16. Palmer to S. of S., 2 July 1940, *FRUS* 3 (1940): 894–96. The Pétain government was briefly located in Bordeaux, before establishing its seat in Vichy.
17. Puaux to Baudoin #684, 5 July 1940, Vichy–Levant 33.
18. Ibid.
19. Puaux, *Deux années au Levant,* pp. 207–8. See also Duroselle, *L'Abîme,* p. 234.
20. Newton (Baghdad) to Halifax #94 and #295, 29 June 1940 and Stonehewer-Bird (Jedda) #108, 21 June 1940, FO 406/78–E 2170/2170/89.
21. Copy of telegram from High Commissioner MacMichael of Palestine, ME (0) (40) 24, 1 July 1940, CAB 95.
22. Gardener (Damascus) to Halifax #19, 28 June 1940, FO 406/78–E 2170/2170/89.
23. This included a cutoff of the oil flow to Tripoli by way of the IPC pipeline.
24. Eastern Department memorandum, ME (0) (40) 21, 26 June 1940, CAB 95.
25. Ibid.
26. WM (40) 187th meeting, minute 1, 29 June 1940, CAB 65/17; memorandum by Eden, WP (40) 231, 29 June 1940, CAB 66/9. See also the memorandum by the Chiefs

of Staff presented to the Middle East Committee, ME (0) (40) 26, 8 July 1940, CAB 95.

27. Text of 1 July 1940 declaration by His Majesty's government, FO 406/78–E 2200/2170/89.

28. Hailfax to Knatchbull-Hugessen #522, 29 June 1940, FO 406/78–E 2200/2170/89.

29. Wavell to WO #0/12794, 27 June 1940 and WO correspondence on liquidation of military mission in Beirut, FO 371/24592–E 2239/2170/89.

30. Ibid., WO to Wavell #74995, 75007–75010, 28 June 1940.

30. Personal message from P.M. to Wavell via WO #75263, 1 July 1940, PREM 3–422/14.

32. ME (0) (40) 6th meeting, 4 July 1940, CAB 95 and Havard to FO #49, 14 July 1940, FO 371/24593–E 2282/2170/89.

33. See R. T. Thomas, *Britain and Vichy* (London, 1979), chapter 4.

34. COS (40) 561, memorandum of 22 July 1940, CAB 80/15.

35. ME (0) (40) 22, 1 July 1940, CAB 95; Halifax to Havard #35, 6 July 1940, FO 406/78–E 2240/2170/89.

36. Halifax to Havard #53, 19 July 1940, FO 406/78–E 2240/2170/89.

37. Havard to FO #66, 31 July 1940, FO 406/78–E 2318/2170/89.

38. Puaux to Vichy #887, 9 August 1940 and #1066, 5 September 1940, Vichy–Levant 43.

39. Ibid., Puaux #690–691, 6 July 1940.

40. Ibid., Rochat to Puaux #74, 7 July 1940.

41. FO to high commissioner of Palestine #616, 19 July 1940 and #629, 22 July 1940, FO 371/24595–E 2264/2264/89.

42. MacMichael (high commissioner of Palestine) to CO #659, 13 July 1940, FO 371/24593–E 2240/2170/89.

43. Havard to FO #69, 31 July 1940, FO 371/24595–E 2264/2264/89.

44. Havard to FO #27, 1 August 1940, FO 371/24593–E 2333/2170/89.

45. Ibid., FO to Havard #63; Havard to FO #78, 8 August 1940 and minutes on latter by Eastern Department staff.

46. FO 371/24593–E 2318/2170/89 (minutes).

47. Puaux to Vichy #952–954, 20 August 1940 and #1066, 5 September 1940, Vichy–Levant 43; Havard to FO #86, 13 August 1940, FO to Havard #77, 16 August 1940 and Eastern Department minutes, FO 371/24593–E 2395/2170/89.

48. Puaux to Vichy #887, 9 August 1940, Vichy–Levant 43; FO to Havard #69, 10 August 1940, FO 371/24593–E 2351/2170/89; Havard to FO #82, 12 August 1940, FO to Havard #76, 15 August 1940 and Eastern Department minutes, E 2372/2170/89; Havard to FO #85, 12 August 1940, E 2377/2170/89.

49. P.M. to Eden, 10 August 1940, PREM 3, 422/14.

50. Gardener to Halifax #22, 3 July 1940, FO 406/78–E 2227/2170/89; Lampson to Halifax #720, 14 July 1940, E 2285/2170/89.

51. Halifax to Lampson (Cairo) #654, 21 July 1940, FO 406/78–E 2285/2170/89.

52. See Crosthwaite's minute in FO 371/24593–E 2455/2170/89.

53. Stonehewer-Bird to Halifax #186, 12 August 1940 and #189, 16 August 1940, Halifax to Stonehewer-Bird #131, 22 August 1940, FO 406/78–E 2396/2170/89.

54. Newton to FO #484, 25 August 1940 and minute by Crosthwaite, FO 371/24593–E 2518/2170/89.

55. Puaux to Vichy #692, 6 July 1940, Vichy–Levant 26.

56. The man who was British vice-consul in Damascus at the time is convinced that

Jamil Mardam was behind the assassination of his bitter political rival, Shahbandar (interview with Sir Richard Beaumont, London, 27 August 1987).

57. Ibid., Puaux to Vichy #891, 10 August 1940.

58. Ibid., Charles-Roux to Puaux #260, 11 August 1940.

59. Gardener's "Note on Political Parties in Damascus," October 1940, FO 406/78–E 2365/198/89.

60. Ibid., Puaux to Vichy #918–919, 13 August 1940.

61. Baudoin to Puaux, #279, 17 August 1940, Vichy–Levant 26.

62. Ibid., Puaux to Vichy #950–951, 19 August 1940.

63. Hautecloque to Puaux, 15 September 1940, Papiers d'Agents: Puaux.

64. Puaux to Vichy #1414, 19 October 1940, Vichy–Levant 26.

65. Havard to Halifax #186, 20 October 1940, FO 406/78–E 2814/2170/89.

66. Philip S. Khoury, *Syria and the French Mandate* (Princeton, 1987), chapter 23.

67. Copy of canceled telegram from Flandin that would have advised Dentz to commute the sentences. According to an explanatory minute, Flandin judged it better not to intervene in a case falling under the sole authority of the high commissioner. Found in Vichy–Levant 26.

68. Khoury, *Syria,* chapter 23.

69. Palmer to S. of S. #75, 12 August 1940, *FRUS* 3 (1940): 901.

70. Charles-Roux to French embassy in Washington #167, 23 July 1940, Vichy–Levant 47.

71. Ibid., note by Hencke, member of the Wiesbaden armistice commission, 20 August 1940.

72. As has been noted, it was actually a subcommission of the main commission at Turin, but for the sake of simplicity, it will be referred to henceforth as the Italian Control Commission.

73. See Lukasz Hirszowicz, *The Third Reich and the Arab East* (London, 1966), *passim*; Elizabeth Monroe, *The Mediterranean in World Politics* (New York, 1938), pp. 187–203; F. Charles-Roux, *Cinq mois tragiques aux affaires étrangères* (Paris, 1949), pp. 267–68.

Chapter 2

1. Gardener (Damascus) to Halifax #38, 5 September 1940 and Newton (Baghdad) to Halifax #545, 9 September 1940, FO 406/78–E 2604/2170/65; Gardener to Halifax #40, 27 September 1940, E 2709/2170/89. The Iraqi government was trying to exploit British concern over this activity to pressure the British into establishing contact with the exiled Syrian nationalist leadership. Ambassador Newton in Baghdad was actually authorized to do so a few months later (Gardener #38, 5 September 1940, FO 406/78–E 2604/2170/65; Newton #633, 22 October 1940, E 2814/2170/89; Gardener #46, 25 October 1940, FO 406/78–E 2814/2170/89; Newton #737, 2 December 1940, E 2829/2170/89).

2. Lampson (Cairo) to de Gaulle via #1026 to FO, 1 September 1940, FO 371/24593–E 2542/2170/89.

3. See, for example, Palmer to S. of S. #88, 9 September 1940, *FRUS* 3 (1940): 907–8.

4. Havard to Halifax #117, 3 September 1940, FO 406/78–E 2570/2170/89.

5. CFR (40) 48th meeting, item 3, 29 August 1940, CAB 85/22.

6. Edgard de Larminat, *Chroniques irrévérencieuses* (Paris, 1962), chapters 2–3; J.-B. Duroselle, *L'Abîme 1939–1945* (Paris, 1982), chapter 9.

7. I. S. O. Playfair et al., *The Mediterranean and the Middle East,* (London, 1954), 1: 197–201.

8. The CFR was an interdepartmental committee that made policy recommendations regarding Britain's support for resistance movements in Axis-occupied countries.

9. Summary of CFR conclusions, FO 371/24592–E 2567/2157/89.

10. ME (0) (40) 10th meeting, 3 September 1940, CAB 95.

11. Havard to Halifax #117, op. cit.

12. ME (0) (40) 10th meeting, 3 September 1940, CAB 95.

13. Ibid., Havard to Halifax #11.

14. Georges Catroux, *Dans la bataille de Méditerranée* (Paris, 1949), chapter 1.

15. Translated text of undated dispatch from Free French Headquarters to CFR, with attached note from Major Morton (committee chairman) dated 6 September 1940, COS (40) 718, CAB 80/18.

16. COS (40) 714, memorandum of 5 September 1940, CAB 80/18.

17. COS (40) 299th meeting, 7 September 1940, CAB 79/6.

18. Lampson to de Gaulle via #1026 to FO, 1 September 1940, FO 371/24593–E 2542/2170/89; Lampson to FO #1066, 10 September 1940 and FO minutes, E 2607/2170/89.

19. See chapter 1 (of this book).

20. COS (40) 293rd meeting, 3 September 1940, CAB 79/6; Havard's weekly political report 1/40, 10 September 1940, FO 371/24595–E 2707/2707/89.

21. Correspondence between FO and Havard about ship exchange and clearing agreement, September 1940, FO 371/24594–E 2621/2170/89.

22. MacMichael to CO #870, 6 September 1940 and CFR (40) 52nd meeting, 12 September 1940, FO 371/24592–E 2606/2157/89.

23. Ibid., Baggallay to Jebb (at the Ministry of Economic Warfare), 13 September 1940.

24. Lampson to FO #1116 reporting on Des Essars' views, 17 September 1940, FO 371/24592–E 2606/2157/89.

25. MacMichael to CO #84, 18 September 1940, FO 371/24592–E 2667/2157/89; for the prevailing attitude among the reservists see also MacMichael to CO #850 reporting on talk with Gilbert MacKereth, just back from Damascus, in FO 371/24593–E 2569/2170/89 and Palmer to S. of S. #82, 20 August 1940, *FRUS* 3 (1940): 903–5.

26. Interview with Professor Maxime Rodinson (who resided in Lebanon and was active in leftist circles there during 1940–1947), Paris, 2 May 1985.

27. Lampson to FO #1116, as cited above.

28. De Larminat to FO via consul-general in Leopoldville's #209, 17 September 1940, FO 371/24594–E 2649/2170/89.

29. Catroux, *Dans la bataille,* chapter 3; interview with Sir P. M. Crosthwaite (London, 5 January 1985). De Gaulle interpreted Churchill's apparent offer to Catroux as an attempt to strengthen British influence over the Free French movement by creating divisions within its ranks (Charles de Gaulle, *Mémoires de Guerre,* [Paris, 1954], 1:113).

30. De Gaulle, *Mémoires de Guerre,* 1:113 and 365 (telegram to Churchill, 21 September 1940; also found in FO 371/24594–E 2674/2170/89). Catroux (*Dans la bataille,* p. 33) claims de Gaulle was consulted about his assignment, but this clearly contradicts all other records.

31. De Gaulle, *Mémoires de Guerre,* 1:366 (telegrams from Churchill to de Gaulle and de Gaulle to Catroux, 22 September 1940; also found in FO 371/24594–E 2674/ 2170/89). The complete text of de Gaulle's telegram to Catroux is in Charles de Gaulle, *Lettres, notes et carnets, Juin 1940–Juillet 1941* (Paris, 1981), 1:119–20.

32. Catroux, *Dans la bataille,* chapter 6.

33. Zerubavel Gil'ad, ed., *Magen be-Seter* [Secret Defense] (Jerusalem, 1952), pp. 75–86. Some of the Hebrew source material on this subject refers to the British intelligence unit with which the Jewish Agency was cooperating as Section D. This was the sabotage branch of the Secret Intelligence Service (SIS) with which the contact had originally been made. As of July 1940, however, it was formally absorbed into the new Special Operations Executive (SOE) (see Christopher Andrew, *Her Majesty's Secret Service* [New York, 1986], pp. 475–76).

34. Havard to FO #16, 19 February 1941 enclosing copy of paper submitted by Lucien Ehrhardt, former financial counselor at the High Commission, as part of his own defense against charges of conspiracy, FO 371/27292–E 2038/39/89.

35. Catroux, *Dans la bataille,* chapter 1.

36. FO to Lampson #1011, 26 September 1940, FO 371/24594–E 2674/2170/89.

37. Puaux to Vichy #1125–1126, 14 September 1940, Guerre 1939–1945, Vichy–Levant 48.

38. Havard to FO #145, 19 September 1940, FO 371/24594–E 2649/2170/89; Havard to FO #137, 14 September 1940, FO 371/24592–E 2606/2157/89; Havard's weekly political report 7/40, 22 October 1940, FO 371/24595–E2707/2707/89. Haute-cloque was the nephew of General Leclerc of the Free French forces, a fact that can hardly have enhanced his image in the eyes of Vichy. (My thanks are due to Sir Richard Beaumont for pointing out this fact.)

39. Gennardi to de Gaulle, 8 September 1940 (letter confided to Havard), Vichy–Levant 43.

40. Ehrhardt's paper in Havard to FO #16, op. cit.

41. MacMichael to CO #76, 10 September 1940, FO 371/24593–E 2570/2170/89. According to Kirkbride, the British resident in Amman, Bouvier on one occasion misdirected the head of the Italian Control Commission while he was on an inspection tour, sending him into Transjordan and letting the British know of their opportunity to arrest him. Due to last-minute confusion, the British missed their chance (Sir A. S. Kirkbride, *A Crackle of Thorns* [London, 1956], chapter 19).

42. Havard to FO #132, 11 September 1940, FO 371/24592–E 2606/2157/89; report by Colombani, chief of *Sûreté Générale,* 8 October 1940, Vichy–Levant 33.

43. Havard to FO #137, 14 September 1940, FO 371/24592–E 2606/2157/89.

44. Ehrhardt's paper in Havard to FO #16, op. cit.

45. De Larminat, who seems to have remained unfamiliar with the details of the coup plot's undoing, was actually to write in 1962 that "Colombani . . . was for the resistance at heart . . ." (de Larminat, *Chroniques,* p. 51).

46. Havard's weekly political report 3/40, 24 September 1940, FO 371/24595–E 2707/2707/89; Havard's weekly report 12/40, 10 December 1940, FO 371/27327–E 104/ 104/89; report by Havard, 27 February 1941, FO 371/27292–E 1809/39/89; report by Colombani, 8 October 1940, Vichy–Levant 33; see also Ehrhardt's paper in Havard to FO #16, op. cit.

47. Palmer to S. of S. #93, 20 September 1940, *FRUS* 3 (1940): 909–11; Havard's weekly political report 2/40, 17 September 1940, FO 371/24595–E 2707/2707/89; Puaux to Vichy #1114, 13 September 1940, Vichy–Levant 48; Puaux to Vichy

#1139, 16 September 1940, Vichy–Levant 33; Bourget's report, 9 October 1940, Vichy–Levant 25.

48. Puaux to Vichy #1125–1126, 14 September 1940, Vichy–Levant 48.

49. Ibid.

50. Puaux, letter to *Le Figaro,* 1/2 October 1949.

51. The term "National Revolution" was used to describe Vichy's ill-defined, right-wing program of replacing what it saw as the corrupt values of the Republic with the supposed virtues of traditional French society. Parliamentary pluralism was to be replaced by the sort of patriarchal authoritarianism embodied by Marshal Pétain, and the Third Republic's democratic political institutions were to give way to corporatism. Above all, the agrarian life style was to be promoted as an ideal, and the integrity of the family stressed as the key to the recreation of a stable, healthy France. (The standard work on this topic is Robert Paxton's *Vichy France* [New York, 1972].)

52. See for example extract from letter sent by unnamed official in the Levant to unknown person in France, September 1940, Vichy–Levant 15.

53. Dispatch from Baudoin to Puaux, 20 September 1940, Vichy–Levant 15; memorandum from Puaux to Baudoin in response to note from Pétain, 5 October 1940, Vichy–Levant 32.

54. Interview with Prof. Maxime Rodinson (Paris, 2 May 1985); see also "Note sur l'activité 'Gaulliste' actuelle en TSMF (Territoires sous Mandat Français)," June 1941, Levant Military Command, 2ème Bureau, SHAT 4H 276, p. 7.

55. Puaux to Baudoin, 5 October 1940, Vichy–Levant 32.

56. "Ordre de Mission" for Colonel Bourget signed by Marshal Pétain, 18 September 1940, Vichy–Levant 41.

57. "Instruction pour le Colonel Bourget" by General Huntziger, 18 September 1940. The importance of this form of leverage is borne out by the example of Bouvier, who presented the main impediment to his defection as being his concern about the fate of his family and property in France. He also asked Kirkbride about the possibility of financial compensation from the Free French movement in the event of his defection to its cause (Kirkbride, *Crackle of Thorns,* chapter 19).

58. Baudoin to Puaux #475–476, 17 September 1940, Vichy–Levant 33.

59. Puaux to Baudoin #1169–1173, 19 September 1940, Vichy–Levant 33.

60. Baudoin to Puaux #492, 20 September 1940, Vichy–Levant 33.

61. Havard's weekly political reports 3/40, 24 September 1940 and 4/40, 1 October 1940, FO 371/24595–E 2707/2707/89.

62. Ibid. See also Puaux to Vichy #1389–1390, 16 October 1940, Vichy–Levant 16.

63. Lucien Ehrhardt's account of his prison conversation with Colombani included in his paper in Havard to FO #16, op. cit.

64. Report to Vichy by Colonel Bourget, 9 October 1940, Vichy–Levant.

65. Political report on Syria #17, 21 October 1940, FO 371/24591–E 2365/198/89.

66. Puaux to Vichy #1389–1390, 16 October 1940, Vichy–Levant 16.

67. Bourget report, 9 October 1940, Vichy–Levant 25.

68. Ibid. Indeed, Bourget described a Colonel Collet as one of the most loyal commanders in the Levant forces. He was to defect to the British along with a unit of Circassian cavalry only a few months later.

69. Political report #17 on Syria, op. cit.

70. Bourget report, op. cit. The Légion had been created by Vichy in August 1940 as a unified war veterans' organization, but it was rapidly transformed into an instrument of political coercion and ideological indoctrination, and the possibility of mem-

bership in it was accordingly thrown open to anyone with the appropriate political motivation. (See H. R. Kedward, *Resistance in Vichy France* [Oxford, 1978], pp. 84–89.)

71. Bourget report, op. cit.

72. TSMF intelligence report #206, 27 August 1940, Vichy–Levant 26.

73. General Pintor (head of Turin Armistice Commission) to Admiral Duplat, 26 September 1940, Vichy–Levant 33. Pintor called for the expulsion of Havard as well as the replacement of Puaux.

74. Bourget report, op. cit. The British records bear out the truth of the latter charge, although there is no evidence of direct involvement by Havard in propaganda activities.

75. Ibid.

76. Puaux to Vichy #1344–1346, 10 October 1940, Vichy–Levant 43.

77. Puaux to Vichy #1366–1367, 13 October 1940, Vichy–Levant 43.

78. Baudoin to Puaux #677–678, 17 October 1940, Vichy–Levant 43.

79. Note from Duplat to Pintor, 25 October 1940, Vichy–Levant 46.

80. Havard to FO #147, 21 September 1940, FO 371/24592–E 2667/2157/89; Havard to FO #153, 26 September 1940, FO 371/24594–E 2674/2170/89; anonymous report in English summarizing information provided by an Arab source recently departed from Damascus, 14 October 1940, Guerre 1939–1945, Londres C.N.F. 39; Palmer to S. of S. #97, 28 September 1940, *FRUS* 3 (1940):911–12.

81. Havard's weekly political report 8/40, 29 October 1940, FO 371/24595–E 2707/2707/89.

82. Catroux, *Dans la bataille,* pp. 63–67; see also Isaac Lipschits, *La politique de la France au Levant, 1939–1941* (Paris, 1963), pp. 63–67.

83. David Hacohen, *Et lesaper* [A Time to Tell] (Tel-Aviv, 1981), pp. 147–49; François Coulet, *Vertu des temps difficiles* (Paris, 1967), pp. 85–106.

84. Catroux–FO correspondence, 2–28 November 1940, FO 371/24594–E 2875/2170/89.

85. Puaux to Vichy #1613, 14 November 1940, intelligence summary #266 and secret report with no heading, Vichy–Levant 43.

86. FO to Havard #159, 2 November 1940, FO 371/24594–E 2848/2170/89; Havard to FO #204, 5 November 1940, E 2887/2170/89. The Levant authorities were finally to take the initiative in cutting off diplomatic ties altogether in the wake of British attacks on Syrian airfields in May 1941 (see chapter 4 of this book).

87. Havard's weekly political report 10/40, 20 November 1940, FO 371/24595–E 2707/2707/89.

88. Interview with Prof. Maxime Rodinson (Paris, 2 May 1985).

89. Dispatch from Dentz to Darlan, 2 April 1941, Vichy–Levant 37.

90. Havard's weekly political report 10/40, op. cit.

91. Havard's weekly political report 11/40, 27 November 1940, FO 371/27327–E 104/104/89.

92. Puaux, letter to *Le Figaro,* 1/2 October 1949. He was to rally to the Free French in 1943, in Tunis.

93. For a hilarious account of Colombani's hysterical reaction to his dismissal, see Havard's weekly political report 12/40, 10 December 1940, FO 371/27327–E 104/104/89.

94. See Lipschits, *La politique de la France,* chapter 4. There was no French or British archival material from the World War II period available for scholarly research at the time Lipschits wrote his book.

95. De Larminat, *Chroniques,* p. 50.

96. See for example Puaux to Vichy #1133–1136, 16 September 1940, Vichy–Levant 43. Longrigg describes Puaux's policy as "one of ostensibly correct but actually minimal obedience to Vichy" (Stephen Longrigg, *Syria and Lebanon under French Mandate* [Oxford, 1958], chapter 9).

97. Puaux to Vichy #1114, 13 September 1940, Vichy–Levant 48.

98. See for example the text of Puaux's 21 September 1940 speech at a military decoration ceremony, included in material sent to Vichy on 27 September 1940, Vichy–Levant 43.

99. Puaux to Laval #1547–1550, 4 November 1940, Vichy–Levant 43. In his memoirs (*Deux années au Levant*, p. 213), Puaux provides a slightly different text of this telegram, without significantly altering its substance.

100. Puaux, *Deux années au Levant,* p. 214.

Chapter 3

1. WM (40) 284th meeting, 7 November 1940, CAB 65/10; WP (40) 431, 1 November 1940, CAB 66/13.

2. ME (0) (40) 11th meeting, 18 October 1940, CAB 95 and appended Eastern Department minutes as found in FO 371/24594–E 2878/2170/89.

3. Havard to Halifax #172, 12 October 1940, FO 406/78–E 2774/2170/89.

4. ME (0) (40) 11th meeting, op. cit.

5. Newton (Baghdad) to FO #563 (20 September 1940), #574 (25 September 1940) and #589 (2 October 1940), FO 371/24594–E 2675/2170/89; Knatchbull-Hugessen (Ankara) to FO #328, 17 October 1940, E 2831/2170/89.

6. FO to Lampson #1310, 12 November 1940, FO 371/24595–E 2788/2264/89.

7. Havard to FO #203 (5 November 1940), Lampson to FO #1470 (6 November 1940) and Commander-in-chief East Indies to Admiralty #1216Z/14 (14 November 1940), FO 371/24594–E 2888/2170/89.

8. FO minute summarizing relations with Vichy since Dakar, 6 November 1940, FO 371/24303–C 11868/9/17; William L. Langer, *Our Vichy Gamble* (New York, 1947), pp. 87–97.

9. FO to MacMichael #1190, 27 November 1940, FO 371/24595–E 2991/2264/89.

10. Palmer to S. of S. #140, 4 December 1940, *FRUS* 3 (1941):668–70; see also series of minutes and draft telegrams about navicert system in FO 371/24594–E 2786/2170/89.

11. Havard to Halifax #252, 9 December 1940, FO 371/24595–E 3054/2170/89; Gardener (Damascus) to FO #28, 12 December 1940, FO 371/27290–E 102/34/89.

12. Gardener to FO, December 1940, FO 406/78—E 3082/2170/89.

13. Catroux to de Gaulle, 13 December 1940 and Catroux to FO via Lampson's #1794, 21 December 1940, FO 371/24595–E 3084/2170/89.

14. Gardener to Cairo (by bag), 21 November 1940, FO 371/24592–E 3103/2157/89; Lampson to FO #1851, 30 December 1940 and #1852, 31 December 1940, FO 371/27282–E 21/11/89.

15. Havard to FO #234, 27 November 1940 and #251, 8 December 1940, FO 371/24595–E 3013/2170/89; Havard's weekly political report 12/40, 10 December 1940, FO 371/27327–E 104/104/89.

16. André Laffargue, *Général Dentz, Paris–Syrie 1941* (Paris, 1954), p. 25.

17. Rendel (Sofia) to FO #6, 2 January 1941, and accompanying Eastern and French Department minutes, FO 371/27290–E 105/34/89.

18. Gardener to FO #3, 7 December 1940, FO 371/24595–E 3064/2264/89.

19. MacMichael to CO #20, 4 January 1941, FO 371/24595–E 3064/2264/89.

20. Eastern Department minutes, 26–31 December 1940, FO 371/24595–E 3130/2170/89; COS (41) 8th meeting, 4 January 1941, CAB 79/8; Wavell to WO #0/48964, 25 February 1941, FO 371/27282–E 775/11/89.

21. Langer, *Our Vichy Gamble,* pp. 118–35; William D. Leahy, *I Was There* (New York, 1950), pp. 13–14.

22. Havard to FO #13 (17 January 1941), #17 (21 January 1941) and #35 (11 February 1941), FO 371/27282–E 207/11/89; Havard to FO #37, 13 February 1941, E 478/11/89; S. of S. to Winant (London) #477, 13 February 1941, *FRUS* 3 (1941): 675–76. On 19 January, Otto von Hentig, a German Foreign Ministry official on mission in Syria, secured the adhesion in principle of the Levant to a Franco–German barter agreement, but export licenses had yet to be issued. (Syrian wool and cotton could be used to produce clothing for the *Wehrmacht,* and silk was important in parachute manufacture.)

23. Memorandum from British embassy to the Department of State, Washington, D.C., 17 January 1941, *FRUS* 3 (1941): 670–71.

24. Havard to FO #1 (4 January 1941), #7 (7 January 1941), #18 (21 January 1941), #20 (23 January 1941), #22 (27 January 1941), FO to Havard #19 (19 January 1941), #24 (27 January 1941) and FO minutes, FO 371/27292–E 39/39/89.

25. Dentz to Vichy #164–166, 28 January 1941, Guerre 1939–1945, Vichy–Levant 43.

26. Ibid.

27. Ibid., Dentz to Vichy #173–174, 29 January 1941. Dentz was not really in a position to know who or what went aboard the ship.

28. Flandin to Dentz #183–184, 5 February 1941; Vichy–Levant 43.

29. Havard to FO #24, 28 January 1941, FO 371/27292–E 304/34/89.

30. Correspondence about *Providence* between FO and Havard, 27 January–14 February 1941, FO 371/27292–E 304/39/89; Engert to S. of S. #38, 17 February 1941, *FRUS* 3 (1941): 676. Spears' consistent defense of Free French interests in CFR discussions is attested to by Sir P. M. Crosthwaite (interviewed by the author in London, 5 January 1985).

31. Spears to Cadogan, 17 February 1941, FO 371/27292–E 571/89/89.

32. Ibid., FO minutes. For de Gaulle's letters of protest over the *Providence* decision, see Charles de Gaulle, *Mémoires de Guerre* (Paris, 1954), 1:373–74.

33. Dentz to Vichy #230–231, 6 February 1941, Vichy–Levant 43.

34. Memorandum from Contre-Amiral Negadelle to Ministry of Foreign Affairs, 27 February 1941, Vichy–Levant 43.

35. Dentz to Vichy #358, 4 March 1941, Vichy–Levant 43.

36. FO to Havard #63, 6 March 1941, FO 371/27292–E 692/39/89.

37. Dentz to Vichy #379–381, 8 March 1941, Vichy–Levant 43.

38. Francis Nicosia, *The Third Reich and the Palestine Question* (Austin, 1985).

39. Lukasz Hirszovicz, *The Third Reich and the Arab East* (London, 1966), chapter 5. On political developments during this period in Iraq and the steady deterioration of relations between Baghdad and London, see Daniel Silverfarb, *Britain's Informal Empire in the Middle East. A Case Study of Iraq, 1929–1941* (Oxford, 1986), chapters 11–13.

40. Hirszovicz, *The Third Reich,* pp. 98–103; I. S. O. Playfair et al. *The Mediterranean and the Middle East* (London, 1956), 2: chapter 1.

41. Conversation with Prof. Albert Hourani (London, 5 August 1987).

42. Reports by French *Services Spéciaux* in Jezireh, 1939–1941, discovered by British military officials and forwarded to the Spears Mission in Beirut in 1944, FO 226/265.

43. Note from Hencke (member of the German armistice commission) to French representative at Wiesbaden, 29 Autust 1940, Vichy–Levant 47.

44. General Doyen (Wiesbaden) to Vichy, 20 November 1940, Vichy–Levant 47.

45. French delegation at Wiesbaden to Vichy #10403, 28 December 1940, Vichy–Levant 47.

46. Werner Otto von Hentig, *Mein Leben. Eine Dienstreise* (Goettingen, 1962), p. 337.

47. Weizsacker to Ankara embassy (von Hentig) #15, 8 January 1941, *DGFP* D XI, #626.

48. Summary of Stern Gang proposal, GFM T-120–4759/E234155-8; von Hentig, *Mein Leben,* pp. 338–39; Ya'acov Eliav, *Mevukash* [Wanted] (Jerusalem, 1983), pp. 187–91. Eliav claims his group's overture to von Hentig was the result of a British provocation. How this explains the group's eagerness to fall for the provocation is unclear.

49. Dispatch from Eliahu Epstein to Shertok, 16 March 1941, CZA S25/5630.

50. *Services Spéciaux* report from Jezireh found in FO 226/265. The *Services Spéciaux* were a corps of army officers who reported directly to the high commissioner on political conditions among the Arab population, and who in effect exercised considerable executive authority as well, particularly in the Bedouin territories (see Albert Hourani, *Syria and Lebanon, A Political Essay* [Oxford, 1946], p. 170).

51. Report on "Ha-matsav be-Suriyah" [the situation in Syria] by Jewish Agency operative just back from the Levant, 20 February 1941 and Epstein's dispatch to Shertok, 16 March 1941, CZA S25/5630; George Kirk, *The Middle East in the War* (Oxford, 1953), p. 87; W. K. Fraser-Tytler, *Afghanistan* (London, 1967), pp. 266–67.

52. Report on German activity in the Levant, March 1941, Vichy–Levant 47; Gardener to FO #23, 13 March 1941, FO 371/27281–E 946/10/89.

53. Report on the situation in Syria, 20 February 1941, CZA S25/5630.

54. See Abetz to Wörmann #684, 28 February 1941, *DGFP* D XII, #103.

55. Von Hentig, *Mein Leben,* pp. 336–37, 342.

56. Oberkommando der Wehrmacht (High Command of the [German] Armed Forces) (OKW) directives to Wiesbaden Commission, 8 February 1941 and memorandum by Wörmann, 7 March 1941, *DGFP* D XII, #50 and #133.

57. Report on the situation in Syria, op. cit.; see also chapter 1 of this book.

58. Dentz to Vichy #196, 3 February 1941, Vichy–Levant 47.

59. "Note" (apparently written by the *Services des Renseignements* in the Levant), late February 1941, Vichy–Levant 37.

60. Baudoin to Puaux #556–559, 27 September 1940, Vichy–Levant 37; Baudoin to Puaux #706–707 (21 October 1940), Puaux to Baudoin #1455 (23 October 1940) and Baudoin to Puaux #1456 (26 October 1940), Vichy–Levant 26.

61. Dentz to Vichy #62–69, 10 January 1941, Vichy–Levant 37.

62. Flandin to Dentz #125–130, 26 January 1941, Vichy–Levant 37.

63. Unsigned report recommending that Atasi be asked to form government, Beirut, 16 January 1941, Vichy–Levant 37.

64. Report on the situation in Syria, op. cit.

65. Dispatch from Catroux to Dentz, February 1941, FO 371/27293–E 754/62/89; Havard to FO #46, 20 February 1941, E 650/62/89; Havard to FO #47, 21 February 1941, E 625/407/89; FO to Havard #46, 15 February 1941, FO 371/27335–E 407/407/

89. See also Georges Catroux, *Dans la bataille de Méditerranée* (Paris, 1949), chapter 12. Catroux's overture to Dentz followed the policy line of the Foreign Office in offering a lifting of the blockade in return for a promise of greater cooperation; de Gaulle was kept in the dark about this.

66. Minute by Seymour, FO 371/27293–E 650/62/89.

67. Gardener to FO #17, 1 March 1941, FO 371/27281–E 778/10/89; Gardener to FO #19, 5 March 1941, E 854/10/89; Davis (Aleppo) to FO #5, 11 March 1941, E 892/10/89.

68. Engert to S. of S. #61, 6 March 1941, *FRUS* 3 (1941): 689–90; Havard to FO #72, 19 March 1941, FO 371/27290–E 1046/34/89; see also Dentz to Vichy #411–416, 13 March 1941, Vichy–Levant 37, reporting on German radio propaganda serving to inflame Syrian unrest.

69. COS (41) 96th meeting, 12 March 1941, CAB 79/9.

70. Wavell to WO #I/48819, 13 March 1941, FO 371/27283–E 945/11/89; Lampson to FO #533, 13 March 1941, E 955/11/89.

71. Gardener to FO #23, 13 March 1941, FO 371/27281–E 946/10/89; Gardener to FO #28, 18 March 1941, E 1039/10/89.

72. Report from Damascus, 12 March 1941, CZA S25/8908.

73. Gardener to FO #23 and #28, op. cit.

74. CO to MacMichael #395, 19 March 1941, FO 371/27283–E 989/11/89; Mac-Michael to FO #374, 20 March 1941, E 1107/11/89; Winant to S. of S. #1087, 20 March 1941, *FRUS* 3 (1941):681–82.

75. Account summarizing the *Yishuv*'s (Palestine Jewish community's) secret war effort, 30 August 1945, CZA S25/8883; Zerubavel Gil'ad, ed., *Magen be-Seter* [Secret Defense] (Jerusalem, 1952), pp. 75–86; David ha-Cohen, *Et lesaper,* [A Time to Tell] (Tel-Aviv, 1981), pp. 149–52; Yehudah Slutzki, ed., *Sefer Toledot ha-Haganah* [Official History of the *Haganah*] (Tel-Aviv, 1972), 3: chapter 20; Yig'al Allon, *Ma'arachot ha-Palmach* [Campaigns of the *Palmach*] (Tel-Aviv, 1965), pp. 15–18.

76. Dispatch from Gerard de Saint-André (director of Free French Press Information Service) to Pleven, 15 July 1940, Albert Cohen to Pleven, 2 April and 28 April 1941, J. Escarra to Free French representatives in New York and note from Escarra to Pleven, 5 May 1941, Guerre 1939–1945, Londres C.N.F. 207.

77. Copies of dispatch from Jewish Agency delegation in London to Shertok, 6 September 1940 and Shertok to London, 18 September 1940, Londres C.N.F. 207 (originals in CZA S25/8913); see S25/8912 for examples of Free French propaganda leaflets.

78. François Coulet, *Vertu des temps difficiles* (Paris, 1967), p. 98.

79. Passy to Catroux via FO to Lampson #1385, 24 November 1940, FO 371/24351–C 12688/7389/17 and Catroux to Passy via Lampson to FO #1653, 3 December 1940, C 13089/7389/17; Catroux, *Dans la bataille,* chapter 10. (The Foreign Office did not take note of this cryptic telegraphic exchange until months later.) Coulet (*Vertu des temps,* p. 98) refers to a similar overture by Passy in March 1941. It is unclear whether this represents a separate proposal or whether Coulet simply has his dates confused.

80. Catroux to de Gaulle #N/006, 3 January 1941, AN, Papiers de Larminat 72 AJ 1915 (no response found.)

81. Unsigned dispatch to Brigadier Clayton in Cairo, 8 January 1941, CZA, S25/8913.

82. Repiton-Preneuf to Catroux #150, 13 March 1941, AN, Papiers Catroux I/A, 72 AJ 428.

83. See Playfair, *The Mediterranean,* pp. 70–75.

84. Catroux to Eden, 19 March 1941, AN, Papiers Catroux I/A, 72 AJ 428.

85. Ibid.

86. MEC, Spears Papers I (Cairo Diary), 28 March 1941; see also Catroux to de Gaulle, 7 March 1941, de Gaulle, *Mémoires de Guerre*, 1:377–78.

87. COS (41) 116th meeting, 31 March 1941 (Churchill in Chair as Minister of Defense), CAB 79/10. See de Gaulle to Spears, 29 March 1941 in Charles de Gaulle, *Lettres, notes et carnets, Juin 1940–Juillet 1941* (Paris, 1981), pp. 283–84.

88. MEC, Spears Papers I, 4 April 1941.

89. Ibid., 15 April 1941.

90. Ibid., 5 May 1941. For an examination of the hindrances to well-informed decision making created by the "collegial" format prevalent in high-level British policy discussions, see Ernest R. May, "Cabinet, Tsar, Kaiser" pp. 11–36 in Ernest R. May, ed., *Knowing One's Enemies* (Princeton, 1984). It was to help coordinate the formulation of policy that the post of Minister of State in the Middle East was created in July 1941.

91. MEC, Killearn Diaries, 8 and 11 May 1941.

92. Repiton-Preneuf's report #210 to Catroux, 15 April 1941, AN, Papiers Catroux I/A, 72 AJ 428; also in FO 371/27322–E 2221/76/89. In the actual invasion two months later, the reverse proved to be the case, as the appearance of Gaullist troops awakened a particularly visceral hostility in Vichy ranks.

93. See Catroux, *Dans la bataille,* chapter 15, for his account of this period.

94. MEC, Spears Papers I, 15 April 1941.

95. MEC, Killearn Diaries, 15 April 1941.

96. Lampson to FO #1003, 18 April 1941, FO 371/27321–E 1571/76/89.

97. MEC, Killearn Diaries, 5 May 1941; Spears to P.M. via Lampson's #1259, 7 May 1941, FO 371/27322–E 2018/76/89.

98. Dentz to Vichy #421–422, 15 March 1941, Vichy–Levant 37.

99. De la Baume (Bern) to Darlan, 14 March 1941, Vichy–Levant 47.

100. Dentz to Vichy#526–527, 31 March 1941, Vichy–Levant 37; Reuter dispatch, 1 April 1941, FO 371/27290–E 1262/34/89; Gardener to FO #9, 9 April 1941, FO 371/27291–E 2837/34/89; Asher Susser, "Western Power Rivalry and its Interaction with Local Politics in the Levant, 1941–1946" (Ph.D. diss., Tel-Aviv University, 1986), pp. 98–99.

101. Dispatch from Dentz to Darlan, 12 April 1941, Vichy–Levant 37; Havard to FO #86, 2 April 1941, FO 371/27281–E 1268/10/89; Havard to FO #87, 5 April 1941, E 1324/10/89; Havard to FO #94, 10 April 1941, FO 371/27290–E 1468/34/89; Havard to FO #36, 18 April 1941, FO 371/27291–E 3022/34/89.

102. Dispatch from Dentz to Darlan, 2 April 1941, Vichy–Levant 37.

103. Memorandum by Wörmann (head of Political Department of German Foreign Ministry), 15 April 1941, *DGFP* D XII, #352; de Brinon (Paris) to Darlan, 15 April 1941 and *Verbalnote* from German embassy in Paris to Benoist-Méchin, 18 April 1941, Vichy–Levant 47. Free French and British records do actually indicate that a number of these men were working for the Gaullist cause.

104. Dispatch from Dentz to Lagarde, 21 April 1941, Vichy–Levant 16; Dentz to Vichy #683, 29 April 1941 and Darlan to Dentz #646, 16 May 1941, Vichy–Levant 47.

105. Havard to FO #123, 9 May 1941, FO 371/27322–E 2082/76/89.

106. B. H. Liddell Hart, *History of the Second World War* (New York, 1982), pp. 134–35; Playfair, *The Mediterranean,* chapters 2, 4–5.

107. MI 14, appreciation #56 A, 2 May 1941, WO 190/893; report by senior intelligence officer in RAF HQ Palestine and Transjordan summarizing intelligence reports

of May 1941, AIR 23/6409; WO to Wavell #0/60304, 28 April 1941, FO 371/27290–E 1791/34/89; FO to Beirut #107, 28 April 1941, FO 371/27333–E 1797/298/89; F. H. Hinsley et al., *British Intelligence in the Second World War* (London, 1979), 1: chapter 13. In fact, the timing of Rashid Ali's revolt was largely the result of local circumstances, and its outbreak was premature from Berlin's point of view.

108. CFR (41) 33rd meeting, 28 April 1941, CAB 85/24; FO to Lampson #1329, 1 May 1941, FO 371/27284–E 1846/11/89.

109. Crosthwaite's minutes on late April 1941 meeting between FO and WO personnel, FO 371/27290–E 1795/34/89; also COS (41) 153rd meeting, 30 April 1941 as recorded in FO 371/27322–E 1969/76/89.

110. Catroux to FO via Cairo #1002, 18 April 1941 and de Gaulle to Churchill, 19 April 1941, FO 371/27283–E 1601/11/89.

111. De Gaulle to Wavell, 10 May 1941, de Gaulle, *Mémoires de Guerre,* 1:397.

112. FO to Halifax #2430, 11 May 1941, FO 371/27283–E 968/11/89.

113. De Gaulle, *Mémoires de Guerre,* 1:398–99. See also p. 399, de Gaulle to Free French headquarters in London, 12 May 1941.

Chapter 4

1. See Robert L. Melka, "Darlan between Britain and Germany 1940–41," *Journal of Contemporary History,* 8, no. 2 (1973):57–80.

2. Lukasz Hirszovicz, *The Third Reich and the Arab East* (London, 1966), pp. 145 and 147.

3. Ibid., pp. 147–50; Eberhard Jäckel, *Frankreich in Hitlers Europa* (Stuttgart, 1966), p. 162.

4. Melka, "Darlan," pp. 66–68; Pierre Queuille, "La politique d'Hitler à l'egard de Vichy," *Revue d'histoire diplomatique* 3–4: 1983; see also Ribbentrop (via courier) to Abetz and latter's response, 11 February 1941 and memorandum by Wörmann, 11 March 1941, *DGFP* D XII, #44 and #152.

5. Ribbentrop to Keitel, 28 April 1941, *DGFP* D XII, #421; Melka, "Darlan," pp. 68–69; Jäckel, *Frankreich,* p. 163. Abetz was chosen as the medium of communication over this question because of suspicion that the content of discussions at the Wiesbaden commission was being leaked to the British or Americans (see Abetz to Ribbentrop #1376, 5 May 1941, *DGFP* D XII, #459).

6. Jacques Benoist-Méchin, *De la défaite au désastre* (Paris, 1984), 1:68–69.

7. Ibid.; Jean-Baptiste Duroselle (*L'Abîme—1939–1945* [Paris, 1982], p. 285) has described Darlan as so obsessed with the French fleet that he had built up over the past decade that he was willing to do anything that would facilitate its rearmament.

8. Benoist-Méchin, *De la défaite,* pp. 70–71; Robert Aron, *Histoire de Vichy* (Paris, 1954), pp. 427–30; Melka, "Darlan," pp. 68–69; Jäckel, *Frankreich,* p. 163.

9. Benoist-Méchin, *De la défaite,* pp. 71–72; Rudolf Rahn, *Ruheloses Leben* (Düsseldorf, 1949), p. 152. The Germans would have preferred to send von Hentig, but deferred to French objections (see memorandum by Wörmann, 8 May 1941, GFM T-120–70/50259).

10. Benoist-Méchin, *De la défaite,* chapter 7; Duroselle, *L'Abîme,* p. 286; Robert Paxton, *Vichy France* (New York, 1972), pp. 116–18.

11. DO (41) 26th meeting, 8 May 1941, CAB 69/2. It must be presumed that this information was obtained from a well-placed source in the Vichy government (see Halifax to FO #2101, 10 May 1941, FO 371/27349–E 2118/2118/89).

12. At the end of May, Rahn did in fact recommend the dispatch of a large German force to prevent an Anglo–Gaullist conquest of the Levant. He seems to have been unaware of the plans for an invasion of the Soviet Union (Rahn to Berlin #72, 31 May 1941, GFM T-120–70/50358-9).

13. Winant (London) conveying message from Eden to S. of S. #1906, 13 May 1941, *FRUS* 3 (1941):703–5.

14. Engert to S. of S. #144, 14 May 1941, *FRUS* 3 (1941):705–7.

15. Dentz to War Ministry #201, 12 May 1941, Guerre 1939–1945, Vichy–Europe 342. Conty reported this protest to Havard and suggested that Darlan might have concluded the agreement with Abetz behind Pétain's back (see Havard to FO #129, 13 May 1941, FO 371/27349–E 2192/2118/89).

16. DO (41) 26th meeting, 8 May 1941 and approved draft telegram to Wavell, CAB 69/2.

17. See chapter 3 of this book. As Eden argued at the 8 May Defence Committee meeting, it was not safe to assume that the Gaullists would be welcomed on their entry into Syria (DO [41], op. cit.)

18. DO (41), supra.

19. PREM 3, 422/6. Churchill appears to have been strongly influenced by Spears' advocacy of Free French intervention (see MEC, Spears Papers I [Cairo Diary], 11 May 1941).

20. DO (41), op. cit.

21. The bombing proved largely ineffective (see Havard to FO, 16 May 1941, FO 371/27349–E 2494/2118/89).

22. DO (41) 29th meeting, CAB 69/2; MacMichael to CO #645 (13 May 1941), #25 to FO (14 May 1941), CO to MacMichael #788 (15 May 1941) and minute by Crosthwaite, FO 371/27284–E 2263/11/89.

23. Churchill to de Gaulle, 14 May 1941 and de Gaulle to Churchill, 15 May 1941, Charles de Gaulle, *Mémoires de Guerre* (Paris, 1954) 1: 404 and 408.

24. Havard to FO #131, 14 May 1941, FO 371/27349–E 2227/2118/89.

25. Lord Wilson, *Eight Years Overseas* (London, 1948), p. 110; R. J. Collins, *Lord Wavell—A Military Biography* (London, 1947), pp. 420–21; Geoffrey Warner, *Iraq and Syria, 1941* (University of Delaware, 1974), p. 112.

26. One of the men chosen for the operation had recently sunk a British coast guard vessel aboard which he had himself been serving as a *Haganah* plant; the vessel had been used to intercept illegal Jewish immigrants to Palestine (see David Hacohen, *Et lesaper* [A Time to Tell] [Tel-Aviv, 1981], pp. 165–71; for an English-language excerpt from Hacohen's book, see the *Jerusalem Post International Edition*, 19–25 December 1982).

27. CZA S25/8883; various papers in Haganah Archive, Tel-Aviv, shown to author on condition of not citing specific files; David ha-Cohen, *Et lesaper*; Zerubavel Gil'ad, editor, *Sefer ha-Palmah* [Official History of the *Palmach*] (Tel-Aviv, 1953), 1: 45–47; Yig'al Allon, *Ma'arachot ha-Palmah* [Campaigns of the *Palmach*] (Tel-Aviv, 1965), pp. 15–18.

28. Despite their official thirty-year rule, the archival authorities at the Quai d'Orsay refuse to release the papers of the Beirut High Commission for this period, although they acknowledge that they possess them. The latest Israeli attempt to uncover the truth about the fate of the *Sea Lion* was undertaken during the occupation of Beirut in 1982 (see *Times* [London], 16 November 1982, p. 1 [cont'd. on p. 6]).

29. Ben-Tsiyon Dinur, general editor, *Sefer Toldot ha-Haganah* [Official History of the *Haganah*] (Tel-Aviv, 1956–1972), 3: 363–64.

30. A friend of Antony Palmer's who also served with the SOE in the Middle East

during the war, claims that many of the officers responsible for planning special opera-tions were ill-experienced amateurs who "did not know their asses from their elbows" and ended up sending capable men like Palmer to their deaths (interview with Richard Usborne, London, 12 January 1985; see also Viscount Chandos, *Memoirs of Lord Chandos* [London, 1962], p. 239).

31. Memoranda by COS and FO, 15 May 1941, FO 371/27291–E 2578/34/89.

32. Spears Mission Middle East to WO, 19 May 1941, FO 371/27294–E 2479/62/89; Lampson to FO #1424, 19 May 1941, FO 371/27323–E 2378/76/89; Wavell to WO #0/65504, 19 May 1941, FO 371/27323–E 2400/76/89; Collins, *Lord Wavell,* p. 420. Wavell confirmed these reports in his telegram to the WO.

33. Halifax to FO #2142, 14 May 1941, FO 371/27042A–E 2258/44/65; WM (41) 51st meeting, conclusions, minute 3 (confidential annex), CAB 65/22.

34. DO (41) 32nd meeting, 20 May 1941, CAB 69/2.

35. Ibid., COS #112 to Cairo, 20 May 1941.

36. Ibid.

37. MEC, Spears Papers I (Cairo Diary), 19 May 1941.

38. Wavell to WO #0/65982, 21 May 1941, PREM 3, 422/6.

39. Ibid., minute by Dill for P.M.

40. P.M. to Wavell via WO #028, 21 May 1941, PREM 3, 422/6. Churchill also rebuked Spears for his conduct, instructing him to send all future communications through GHQ Middle East. This prompted an impassioned letter of protest from Spears (Spears to Churchill, 6 June 1941, PREM 3, 407A). In his memoir of this period, Spears seems to make the improbable suggestion that Wavell's subsequent removal from the Middle Eastern command was the result of Churchill's unease over this incident: "So Wavell had won his point, though he did not know at what cost to himself. Nor did I at the time" (Major-General Sir Edward L. Spears, *Fulfilment of a Mission* [London, 1977], p. 94).

41. Lampson to FO #1458, 21 May 1941, FO 371/27323–E 2450/76/89; Catroux to de Gaulle, 21 May 1941, de Gaulle, *Mémoires de Guerre,* 1:411–12. It appears that Dentz had actually considered withdrawing troops from Syria so as to concentrate them for a defense of Lebanon against British attack, but had been dissuaded from this course of action by Rudolf Rahn (report by Rahn, 30 July 1941, *DGFP* D XIII, #165).

42. Collins, *Lord Wavell,* p. 421; Georges Catroux, *Dans la bataille de Méditer-ranée* (Paris, 1949), pp. 126–29.

43. This is Spears' version of how de Gaulle paraphrased his own words to Catroux, MEC, Spears Papers I (Cairo Diary), 30 May 1941.

44. Spears to Spears Mission London #1449, 20 May 1941, FO 371/27323–E 2444/76/89.

45. Engert to S. of S. #163, 23 May 1941, *FRUS* 3 (1941): 713–14.

46. R. T. Thomas (*Britain and Vichy* [London, 1979], chapter 6) argues that, through early 1941, Churchill backed the Free French against the FO's inclination to seek accommodation with Vichy, whereas later on, it was Eden who supported de Gaulle in the face of the prime minister's increasing hostility.

47. PREM 3, 422/2.

48. Memorandum by Eden, 27 May 1941, WP (41) 116, CAB 66/16.

49. DO (41) 35th meeting, 27 May 1941, CAB 69/2. The Turks proved unwilling to involve themselves in the operation. For a detailed look at the Turkish factor in the Levant problem at this juncture, see Yosef Olmert, "Britain, Turkey and the Levant Question during the Second World War," *Middle Eastern Studies,* 23, no. 4 (October 1987): 437–52.

50. Michael J. Cohen, "A Note on the Mansion House Speech, May 1941," *Asian and African Studies*, 2, no. 3 (1977): 375–86. From Cairo, Ambassador Lampson had been pressing for a similar scheme, minus the pro-Zionist element.

51. *Times* (London), 30 May 1941, p. 5.

52. WM (41) 56th meeting, minute 4, 2 June 1941, CAB 65/18. Yehoshua Porath (*Be-mivchan ha-ma'aseh ha-politi* [In the Trial of Political Action] [Jerusalem, 1985], pp. 259–63) unconvincingly argues that Eden's decision to deliver his speech prior to formal cabinet approval of the policy arose from his wish to block consideration of Churchill's pro-Zionist federation scheme. Given the extreme vagueness of Eden's words, it is not at all apparent how the Mansion House address could have served to preempt cabinet consideration of Churchill's more detailed plan. It seems more likely that Eden's sense of urgency reflected the imminence of a British military move into the Levant.

53. De Gaulle to Free French Delegation in London, 31 May 1941, de Gaulle, *Mémoires de Guerre*, 1:412.

54. Lampson to FO #1684, 4 June 1941 and Spears to London via Lampson's #1690 and #1702, 5 June 1941, FO 371/27325–E 2821/76/89.

55. Churchill to de Gaulle, 6 June 1941, de Gaulle, *Mémoires de Guerre*, 1:415.

56. De Gaulle to Catroux, 28 May 1941, Charles de Gaulle, *Lettres, notes et carnets, Juin 1940–Juillet 1941* (Paris, 1981), 1:339; text of Catroux's declaration contained in Lampson to Eden #1756, 8 June 1941, FO 406/79–E 2915/62/89; text of British guarantee, E 4169/62/89; A. B. Gaunson, "Churchill, de Gaulle, Spears and the Levant Affair, 1941," *The Historical Journal*, 27, no. 3 (1984): 697–713; Martin L. Mickelsen, "Another Fashoda: The Anglo–Free French Conflict over the Levant, May–September 1941," *Revue française d'histoire d'outre-mer*, 63, no. 230 (1976): 75–100. Mickelsen incorrectly writes that "General de Gaulle was finally compelled to accept the reference to the British guarantee in the Free French proclamation" (p. 81). This line in the Free French proclamation actually referred to the British promise to afford Syria and Lebanon all the benefits enjoyed by other countries fighting on the Allied side, such as inclusion in the sterling bloc.

57. DO (41) 39th meeting, 5 June 1941, CAB 69/2.

58. MEC, Spears Papers I (Cairo Diary), 6 June 1941.

59. Rahn's report, op. cit.

60. Memorandum by Dentz circulated to all *Services Spéciaux* officers, 21 May 1941, found among papers captured by the British in Jezireh and forwarded to Beirut in 1944, #344, FO 226/265; also found in Guerre 1939–1945, Vichy–Levant 43.

61. Copy of report by Repiton-Preneuf to Catroux, 23 May 1941, FO 371/27291–E 3218/34/89. According to Christopher Buckley (*Five Ventures. Iraq—Syria—Persia—Madagascar—Dodecanese* [London, 1954], pp. 47–48) Collet's original plan included the kidnapping of Dentz, who had been scheduled to pay an inspection visit to southern Syria; see also Anthony Mockler, *Our Enemies the French* (London, 1976), pp. 65–72.

62. Memorandum on an interview with Colonel Collet by Major-General Spears, 26 May 1941, FO 371/27291–E 3217/34/89.

63. For conflicting assessments of the likelihood of an outright British invasion, see Jules Henry (Ankara) to Vichy #797, 21 May 1941 and Dentz to Vichy #841–842, 28 May 1941, Vichy–Levant 43.

64. Rahn's report, op. cit.

65. Report by Bonichon, 7 June 1941 and report by Chief-Adjutant René Fauqueux of the Rayack air base, 11 June 1941, SHAT, Vichy Levant Army–2ème Bureau, 4 H

276/7; anonymous, handwritten denunciation (apparently written in left hand) by officer in the *Service des Renseignements*, 7 June 1941, 4 H 276/3bis.

66. "Note sur l'activité 'Gaulliste' en T.S.M.F.", undated, but apparently written in May 1941, SHAT, 4 H 276/7.

67. Lampson to FO #465, transmitting copy of 14 May 1941 report by Repiton-Preneuf, FO 371/27349–E 3202/2118/89.

68. Memorandum on an interview with Collet by Spears op. cit.

69. Achenbach (Paris) to Berlin #1690, 1 June 1941, *DGFP* D XII, #581.

70. Ribbentrop to Rahn #500, 3 June 1941, *DGFP* D XII, #587.

71. FO to Ankara #1207, 28 May 1941, FO 371/27323–E 2598/76/89; Ankara to FO #1373, 4 June 1941, FO 371/27294–E 2830/62/89; I. S. O. Playfair, et al. *The Mediterranean and the Middle East* (London, 1956), 2: 203–5; Buckley, *Five Ventures*, pp. 49–53; Warner, *Iraq and Syria, 1941* pp, 137–39.

72. Yig'al Allon, *Ma'arachot ha-Palmah*, pp. 15–18; segment written by Moshe Dayan in Zerubavel Gil'ad, ed., *Magen be-Seter* [Secret Defense] (Jerusalem, 1952), pp. 127–45; various files in the Haganah Archive, Tel-Aviv. *Haganah* commandos also played a leading role in going ahead of the main coastal attack force to try to prevent Vichy bridge demolition and to seize guardposts on the night of 7/8 June. It was in one such incident that Moshe Dayan lost his eye. In addition, at least one major sabotage operation was carried out by a *Haganah* cell in Aleppo. In the official history of British wartime intelligence, F. H. Hinsley mentions the importance of the topographical reconnaissance undertaken before the invasion without identifying the *Haganah* as a participant in this work (*British Intelligence in the Second World War* [London, 1979], 1:425). See also Buckley (*Five Ventures*, p. 56), who makes no mention of *Haganah* participation in the rearguard attack at Iskanderun.

73. Troupes Levant to Vichy #231, 4 June 1941, Vichy–Levant 38.

74. Wilson, *Eight Years Overseas*, p. 114–15; Buckley, *Five Ventures*, pp. 53–58; Playfair, *The Mediterranean*, p. 205; Mockler, *Our Enemies*, p. 96–97. The Vichy forces were ordered to treat Free French prisoners taken in battle as traitors who were to be tried by military courts and, in some cases, executed (Huntziger to Dentz 10/CAB, undated, Vichy–Levant 38). No record has been found of any such executions actually taking place.

75. Eastern Department minutes, June 1941, FO 371/27295–E 3018/62/89.

76. Undated report on British military performance by Yitshaq Sadeh (chief of *Haganah*), Haganah Archive, Tel-Aviv.

77. Mockler, *Our Enemies*, pp. 91 and 160. Indeed, de Gaulle suspected Wavell of deliberately sabotaging the whole operation in advance out of anger at having had his hand forced over the matter! (MEC, Spears Papers I [Cairo Diary], 5 June 1941.)

78. Playfair, *The Mediterranean*, p. 210–14; Buckley, *Five Ventures*, chapters 3 and 4.

79. "Note sur la possibilité d'un repli vers le nord" signed by Dentz, 19 June 1941, SHAT 4 H 281/6.

80. *Délégation française auprès de la commission allemande d'armistice*, (Paris, 1957), 4:540–47; Geo London, *L'amiral Esteva et le général Dentz devant la Haute Cour de Justice* (Lyon, 1945), pp. 217–21; André Laffargue, *Général Dentz, Paris–Syrie 1941* (Paris, 1954), pp. 116–35; George Kirk, *The Middle East in the War* (London, 1953), pp. 99–101; Buckley, *Five Ventures*, p. 118. Dentz's fluctuating attitude to the question of German air support is dealt with in detail in the above literature.

81. Buckley, *Five Ventures*, p. 112.

82. Note by von Grote and Schleier (Paris) to Berlin #1899, 26 June 1941, GFM T-

120–2207/474560-3; Melka, "Darlan," pp. 73–80. General Weygand's staunch opposition to the implementation of the Paris Protocols and Darlan's inability to secure tangible political concessions from the Germans were undermining the entire framework of Franco–German military collaboration during June 1941 (see Abetz to Berlin #1761, 11 June 1941, GFM T-120–70/50423-8; Paxton, *Vichy France*, p. 118–24; Hirszovicz, *The Third Reich*, pp. 173–76). Benoist-Méchin (*De la défaite*, p. 228) reports that in the second week of July, Darlan advocated sending virtually the entire Toulon fleet pell-mell into the eastern Mediterranean in an effort to reverse the situation, but that Admiral Auphan talked him out of the idea.

83. Knatchbull-Hugessen (Ankara) to FO #1606, 30 June 1941, FO 371/27352–E 3481/3408/89; Kelly (Berne) to FO, undated, E 3412/3408/89; Ankara to FO #1578, 27 June 1941, E 3413/3408/89; Ankara to FO #1589, 30 June 1941, FO 371/27296–E 3418/62/89; Rahn's report, op. cit.; Outrey (Ankara) to Vichy #1103–1105 (19 June 1941), Dentz to Vichy #789 (21 June 1941) and #980 (25 June 1941), Vichy–Levant 38; Outrey to Vichy #1142–1145, 9 July 1941 and Benoist-Méchin to Vichy via Outrey's #1093–1095, 1 July 1941, Vichy–Levant 39; Benoist-Méchin, *De la défaite*, chapter 14; Rahn, *Ruheloses Leben*, pp. 169–70.

84. Engert to S. of S. #223, 18 June 1941, *FRUS* 3 (1941):743–44; Halifax to FO #2826, 18 June 1941, FO 371/27326–E 3169/76/89; London, *L'amiral Esteva*, pp. 231–35.

85. Rahn's report, op. cit.; Rahn, *Ruheloses Leben*, p. 171–72; Benoist-Méchin, *De la défaite*, pp. 194–95; Playfair, *The Mediterranean*, pp. 216–18.

86. Ankara to FO #1597, 29 June 1941, FO 371/27296–E 3420/62/89; Lampson to FO #2077, 1 July 1941, FO minutes and FO to Ankara #1485, 2 July 1941, FO 371/27297–E 3485/62/89.

87. Warner, *Iraq and Syria, 1941*, p. 153.

88. Playfair, *The Mediterranean*, p. 222; Buckley, *Five Ventures*, p. 137. The figures cited include prisoners of war and deserters.

89. Hinsley, *British Intelligence*, pp. 424–25.

90. Benoist-Méchin, *De la défaite*, p. 184.

91. Only Georges Catroux (*Dans la bataille de Mediterranée* [Paris 1949], pp. 142–43) inexplicably argues that Dentz's resistance to the invasion was essentially pro forma.

92. Adrienne Hytier, *Two Years of French Foreign Policy* (Paris, 1958), pp. 275–85.

93. Report by Berthoud, just back from Beirut, transmitted in Lampson's #495, 30 May 1941, FO 371/27296–E 3201/62/89.

94. Commander-in-Chief Middle East to WO #0/75935, 24 June 1941, WO 106/3073–M.O.5.

95. Christopher M. Andrew and A. S. Kanya-Forstner, *France Overseas: The Great War and the Climax of French Imperial Expansion* (London, 1981), pp. 250–51; see also D. Bruce Marshall, *The French Colonial Myth and Constitution-Making in the Fourth Republic* (New Haven: Yale, 1973), chapter 3.

96. Article in *Orient*, 19 June 1941, included in intelligence report of 28 June 1941, Vichy–Levant 37.

97. Interview with Richard Usborne (London, 12 January 1985); MEC, Spears Papers I (Cairo Diary), report to Lyttelton, 18 July 1941. Spears seems to have had a rather cavalier attitude toward some of these incidents.

98. Spears, *Fulfilment*, pp.11–12.

99. COS (41) 213th meeting, 16 June 1941, CAB 79/2. Frustrated and enraged, Spears lashed out savagely at the Middle East command through the safe medium of

his diary: "They are swine. . . . These people make me sick at heart—I want to have the opportunity of telling Winston I am fed up" (MEC, Spears Papers I [Cairo Diary], 15 June 1941).

100. Halifax to FO #2826 (18 June 1941), Lampson to FO #1916 (20 June 1941) and COS (41) 219th meeting, 20 June 1941, FO 371/27326–E 3169/76/89; DO (41) 43rd meeting, 19 June 1941, CAB 69/2; MEC, Killearn Diaries, 19 June 1941; de Gaulle, *Mémoires de Guerre* 1:425–26; see also Spears to Spears Mission ELS/183, 28 June 1941, FO 371/27352–E 3482/3408/89.

101. MEC, Spears Papers I (Cairo Diary), 20 June 1941; see also de Gaulle to FO via Cairo's #1932, 21 June 1941, FO 371/27326–E 3230/76/89 (also in de Gaulle, *Mémoires de Guerre* 1:428–29).

102. De Gaulle to Catroux, 24 June 1941, de Gaulle, *Mémoires de Guerre* 1:430–31.

103. Minute by P.M., substance of which is transmitted to Lyttelton by Eden, 3 July 1941, FO 371/27298–E 3570/62/89.

104. Morton to Crosthwaite, 4 July 1941, FO 371/27298–E 3638/62/89; Lyttelton to Eden #1 TWIST, 6 July 1941, E 3684/62/89; Free French memo, 6 July 1941, FO 371/27299–E 3776/62/89; also in Guerre 1939–1945, Londres C.N.F. 39; Dejean and Cassin to de Gaulle #4828/AP, 7 July 1941, Londres C.N.F. 37; this correspondence between Free French in London and de Gaulle is also to be found in de Gaulle, *Mémoires de Guerre,* 1:436–40.

105. De Gaulle to Free French Delegation in London, 13 July 1941, de Gaulle, *Mémoires de Guerre,* 1:441.

106. DO (41) 49th meeting, 9 July 1941, CAB 69/2. Churchill raised particularly vociferous objections to de Gaulle's proposed amendment, arguing that "in fact, we might later derive advantage from the fact that this amendment had been proposed and rejected. It was not our intention to perpetuate the French position in the Levant."

107. Note by Rochat, 8 July 1941, Vichy–Levant 39; Leahy to Washington, 9 July 1941 (as communicated to FO), FO 371/27299–E 3747/62/89.

108. P.M. to Lyttelton, 11 July 1941, PREM 3, 422/6. Churchill's hopes for a more general accommodation with Vichy had just been raised by the secret visit to London of Georges Groussard, a confidant of General Huntziger. On his return to France, Groussard contacted London to ask for a cooperative attitude in the settlement of the Levant dispute as a sign of good will, and the British responded with an assurance that French rights in the region would be respected (P.M. to Lyttelton #2387 TWIST, 9 July 1941, FO 371/27300–E 3853/62/89). Churchill's cable to Lyttelton states that "our talks with him [Groussard] were on the dead level," thus appearing to confirm Groussard's claim to have met with Churchill, for which R. T. Thomas (*Britain and Vichy,* note 8 to chapter 5) finds no evidence in the British records. John Colville's diary entry for 20 June 1941 (*The Fringes of Power, 10 Downing Street Diaries, 1939–1955,* [New York, 1986], p. 403) mentions that "an emissary from Pétain came to see the P.M., sponsored by 'C' [chief of the Secret Intelligence Service]." See also Georges Groussard, *Service Secret 1940–1945* (Paris, 1964), chapter 2 and pp. 222–23.

109. Chandos, *Memoirs,* pp. 245–46.

110. Auchinleck to WO #0/81875, 15 July 1941, FO 371/27301; Lyttelton to P.M. #2 MAXIM, 18 July 1941, FO 371/27302–E 4062/62/89.

111. Ibid.; MEC, Spears Papers I (Cairo Diary), 17 July 1941. See also A. B. Gaunson's account, "Churchill, de Gaulle, Spears" and his *The Anglo–French Clash in Lebanon and Syria, 1940–1945* (London, 1987), pp. 53–59. Gaunson correctly stresses the destructive effect of the personal antagonism between Churchill and de Gaulle on efforts to reconcile Anglo–Free French differences. His choice of the secret protocol

as an illustration of this point appears flawed, however. Gaunson argues that General Wilson's acceptance of the protocol enjoyed Churchill's "blessing in advance, through his wire to Lyttelton." As Gaunson himself points out, though, Churchill's instructions to Lyttelton were only that he should accede to Vichy's demand for the exclusion of the Free French from the negotiations. It is highly unlikely that Churchill would have approved of the secret clause facilitating the repatriation of Vichy forces from the Levant. In any case, Wilson himself was unaware of the prime minister's cable to Lyttelton.

112. In his memoirs (*Dans la bataille,* p. 100), Catroux rather lamely claims that he believed Wilson's assertion that he had previously cleared his armistice proposals with de Gaulle. This was an apparent reference to the Cairo terms, with the substance of which Catroux must have been familiar. Contradicting himself, Catroux later defends his handling of the situation by arguing that "placed closer to the realities than General de Gaulle, I had a better sense than he of what was possible and what was not" (p. 164).

113. FO to Lyttelton #9, 17 July 1941, FO 371/27301–E 4003/62/89.

114. P.M. to de Gaulle, 20 July 1941, PREM 3, 422/6.

115. Free French Delegation to de Gaulle #160a/AO, 23 July 1941, Londres C.N.F. 37.

116. MEC, Spears Papers I (Cairo Diary), 20 July 1941.

117. Ibid., 21 July 1941.

118. Ibid.; Lyttelton to P.M. via Lampson's #8 LIMIT, 21 July 1941, FO 371/27302–E 4044/62/89; Chandos, *Memoirs,* pp. 247–50. Lyttelton (who later became Lord Chandos) conjectures that de Gaulle's fit of rage was partly an act designed to exploit the fact that "the English-speaking races hate scenes" (p. 249).

119. MEC, Killearn Diaries, 21 July 1941.

120. MEC, Spears Papers I (Cairo Diary), 21 July 1941.

121. Lyttelton to P.M., op. cit.; text of de Gaulle–Lyttleton agreements in FO 371/27302–E 4146/62/89; for accounts of this period see also de Gaulle, *Mémoires de Guerre,* 1:165–70 and 445–59; M.-C. Davet, *La double affaire de Syrie* (Paris, 1967), chapter 15; Howard Sachar, *Europe Leaves the Middle East, 1936–1954* (New York, 1972), pp. 179–217; Llewellyn Woodward, *British Foreign Policy in the Second World War* (London, 1970), chapter 17; Arnold Toynbee, ed., *Hitler's Europe* (Oxford, 1954), pp. 451–56.

Chapter 5

1. Dentz was subsequently released, and allowed to return to France. After the Liberation, he was arrested and tried for his role in facilitating the German use of Levant airfields in 1941. The court's death sentence was commuted to one of life imprisonment by de Gaulle in June 1945 (see Geo London, *L'amiral Esteva et le général Dentz devant la Haute Cour de Justice* [Lyon, 1945]).

2. De Gaulle to P.M. via Cairo #2326, 25 July 1941, FO 371/27302–E 4140/62/89; Admiralty correspondence regarding repatriation procedure, July 1941, FO 371/27352–E 4168/3408/89; Lyttelton to de Gaulle, 1 August 1941, FO 371/27303–E 4330/62/89; Lyttelton to FO via Cairo's #25 LIMIT, 1 August 1941 and FO to Cairo #2713, 2 August 1941, E 4300/62/89; Spears to Spears Mission via Cairo's #2490, 10 August 1941, FO 371/27305–E 4557/62/89; memorandum by Huntziger, 17 August 1941, Guerre 1939–1945, Vichy–Levant 37; Charles de Gaulle, *Mémoires de Guerre* (Paris, 1954) 1:171; M.-C. Davet, *La double affaire de Syrie* (Paris, 1967), pp. 195–201. In

violation of the terms of the armistice convention, Dentz's officers forced their troops to sign formal pledges not to join the Allied forces.

3. De Gaulle, *Mémoires de Guerre,* 1:171.

4. Viscount Chandos, *The Memoirs of Lord Chandos* (London, 1962), pp. 252–53.

5. Report by Collet, 27 July 1941, Guerre 1939–1945, Londres C.N.F. 39; also found in Lampson to FO #714, 4 August 1941, FO 371/27308–E 5254/62/89. Glubb Pasha was later to claim that it was not until after the armistice that he was informed that the Free French were to assume control of the Levant. Accordingly, his propaganda line in eastern Syria had concentrated on the theme of liberation from French rule as such, rather than Vichy rule specifically (Brigadier John B. Glubb, *The Story of the Arab Legion* [London, 1948], pp. 344–45); however, in an interview granted toward the end of his life, Glubb admitted that he had been fully aware of the Gaullists' prospective role in the Levant (A. B. Gaunson, *The Anglo–French Clash in Lebanon and Syria, 1940–1945* [London, 1987], pp. 23–24).

6. MacMichael to CO #788, 2 June 1941, FO 371/27325–E 2809/76/89; Spears to Lyttelton #1, 30 July 1941, FO 371/27304–E 4333/62/89; Auchinleck to WO #0/87851, 2 August 1941, E 4396/62/89; Lampson to FO #723, 6 August 1941, FO 371/27308–E 5256/62/89; MEC, Spears Papers I (Cairo Diary), 29 and 30 July 1941; de Gaulle, *Mémoires de Guerre,* 1:172–73; Georges Catroux, *Dans la bataille de Méditerranée* (Paris, 1949), p. 175; Anthony Mockler, *Our Enemies the French* (London, 1976), chapter 24. Mockler argues that Colonel Bouvier had helped incite this confrontation by carrying on separate discussions with both Free French and British regarding the transfer of power in the Jebel; however, in view of the pro-Allied sympathies he had manifested in the past, it seems likelier that Bouvier was himself confused by the duality of authority than that he deliberately sought to sow dissension between the victors.

7. MEC, Spears Papers I (Cairo Diary), 2 August 1941.

8. Lyttelton to P.M. #29 LIMIT, 2 August 1941, FO 371/27304–E 4353/62/89.

9. Lyttelton to FO via Spears' #2, 10 August 1941, FO 371/27305–E 4577/62/89; Spears to WO #36 for Spears Mission London, 12 August 1941, E 4648/62/89; Catroux, *Dans la bataille,* p. 184. A Vichy espionage cell was actually uncovered by the British in September 1941 (see note by du Paty de Clam and Admiral Platon, October 1942, Vichy–Levant 27).

10. Engert to S. of S. #332 and #333, 5 August 1941, *FRUS* 3 (1941):782–83.

11. Chandos, *Memoirs,* pp. 255–57. See also CO correspondence of early July 1941 in FO 371/27304–E 4453/62/89. This appeasement of de Gaulle did not sit well with much of the British military establishment. A report by military intelligence in mid-August argued that French and Syrian objectives were completely incompatible and that it was in Britain's best interest to side with the latter:

> At present, we appear to be subordinating vital British interests to Free French amour propre. It must, in fact, be put quite clearly to De Gaulle that the British Empire and the U.S.A. are quite capable of winning this war without him amd that if he continues in his present intransigent mood, H.M.G. can well afford to let him slide into oblivion (M.I.2 note on relations with Free French in Syria, 17 August 1941, WO 208/1596).

12. Spears was knighted in 1942.

13. Martin Gilbert, *Winston S. Churchill* (London, 1976), 5: 3–4.

14. Randolph Churchill, *Lord Derby* (London, 1959), chapter 16; Gilbert, *Winston S. Churchill* 3: chapter 19; Major-General Sir Edward L. Spears, *Assignment to*

Catastrophe (London, 1959), p. 175; William L. Shirer, *The Collapse of the Third Republic* (New York, 1969), pp. 844–46. For an account of Spears' post-World War I dealings with the British "master spy", Sidney Reilly, see Christopher Andrew, *Her Majesty's Secret Service* (New York, 1986), pp. 287–88.

15. Spears, *Assignment,* p. 538. On parting from a friend at Noirt, Spears "knew that the last tie that bound me to the France of my youth was severed" (p. 539).

16. Ibid., p. 620.

17. Anne Collet, *The Road to Deliverance. Damascus–Jerusalem–Damascus. 1940–June 1941.* (Beirut, 1942), pp. 137–38.

18. Spears War Mission Diary, Duala, 11 October 1940, WO 178/10; see also entry for 30 September 1940. In December 1940, Churchill's private secretary described Spears' relationship with de Gaulle as "correct though not cordial" (John Colville, *The Fringes of Power, 10 Downing Street Diaries 1939–1955* [New York, 1986], 13 December 1940, p. 312; see also entry for 10 November 1940, p. 290).

19. WO correspondence, 9–18 June 1941, FO 371/27295–E 3129/62/89.

20. Spears to WO via Wavell's #0/76248, 25 June 1941, FO 371/27291–E 3356/34/89.

21. COS to Wavell #139, 30 June 1941 and Morton (CFR) to Strang (FO), 27 June 1941, FO 371/27291–E 3356/34/89.

22. Shuckburgh (WO) to Morton, 28 June 1941, FO 371/27291–E 3356/34/89.

23. MEC, Spears Papers I (Cairo Diary), 23 June 1941.

24. MacMichael to CO #928, 26 June 1941, FO 371/27296–E 3406/62/89; Morton to Strang, 27 June 1941, FO 371/27291–E 3356/34/89.

25. MEC, Killearn Diaries, 8 and 9 July 1941. Regarding the *Providence* affair, see chapter 5 of this book.

26. Lyttelton to FO, 11 July 1941, FO 371/27346–E 3746/1964/89; MEC, Killearn Diaries, 14 July 1941.

27. Standing Interdepartmental Committee on Administration of Occupied Territories (Syria), 1st and 2nd meetings, 10 and 14 July 1941, WO 106/3075–M.O.5; WO to Commander-in-chief Middle East #77417, 11 July 1941, FO 371/27299–E 3794/62/89; minute by S. of S. for War and minute by Morton, 14 July 1941 and FO to Lyttelton, 15 July 1951, PREM 3, 422/6.

28. Spears to Spears Mission ELS/245, 19 July 1941, FO 371/27302–E 4110/62/89; see also de Gaulle to Churchill, 29 June 1941, Londres C.N.F. 39 (also in FO 371/27296–E 3436/62/89).

29. Spears to Spears Mission ELS/211, 8 July 1941, WO 106/3074–M.O.5.

30. Catroux (*Dans la bataille,* p. 193) identifies the armistice crisis as the turning point in Spears' relationship with de Gaulle. The Free French consul in Jerusalem also thought Spears' animosity toward de Gaulle arose from the latter's refusal to serve as Spears' tool (report by Wilensky on conversation with du Chaylard, 15 November 1943, CZA S25/5577).

31. Lyttelton to P.M., 15 August 1941, PREM 3, 422/14.

32. MEC, Spears Papers I (Cairo Diary), entry summarizing second half of August 1941.

33. Ibid.

34. François Kersaudy, *Churchill and de Gaulle* (New York, 1983), p. 151; Martin L. Mickelsen, "Another Fashoda: The Anglo–Free French Conflict over the Levant, May–September 1941," *Revue française de l'histoire d'outre-mer,* 63, no. 230 (1976), pp. 75–100.

35. Great Britain, *Parliamentary Debates,* (Commons) vol. 8 (London, 1941), p. 75.

36. Record of Churchill–de Gaulle meeting, 12 September 1941, PREM 3, 422/3.

37. Spears to Spears Mission London via Auchinleck's #92464, 14 August 1941, PREM 3, 422/14.

38. Free French Delegation in London to de Gaulle #112a/AP, 21 July 1941, Londres C.N.F. 37; note by General Catroux, 24 July 1941, Vichy–Levant 39; note de service #125, 10 July 1941, Vichy–Levant 39. The Vichy authorities formulated various vague plans for sabotaging the Gaullist administration in the Levant (see memo from Huntziger to Darlan [15 September 1941], note by Lagarde [4 October 1941], note from Huntziger to Darlan [21 October 1941] and Darlan to Huntziger [4 November 1941], Vichy–Levant 19). As late as October 1942, talk persisted within the Vichy War Ministry of laying the groundwork for a pro-Vichy Arab rebellion in Syria, to be synchronized with a German offensive in the Middle East. Rudolf Rahn encouraged these pipe dreams, which were taken less seriously by the Vichy Foreign Ministry (see note by Dentz, 3 October 1942 and note by du Paty de Clam and Admiral Platon, October 1942, Vichy–Levant 27). As one Foreign Ministry official pointed out, Catroux was clearly doing his best to limit the extension of British influence in the Levant, and it made no sense to interfere with his effort (note for Darlan from Foreign Ministry's Africa–Levant Dept., 22 November 1941, Guerre 1939–1945, Alger CFLN-GPRF 27).

39. Lyttelton to FO via Cairo's #3769, 1 December 1941, FO 371/27318–E 7988/62/89.

40. Spears to London #240, 23 September 1941, FO 371/27310–E 6012/62/89; see also Auchinleck to WO #144, 2 September 1941, FO 371/27308–E 5482/62/89. An Eastern Department minute attached to the latter telegram noted that "it begins to look as if Free French Syria is a greater danger to our position in the Middle East than Vichy Syria."

41. P.M.'s minute, 25 September 1941 and minute from Eden to P.M., 19 September 1941, FO 371/27311–E 6171/62/89.

42. Dispatch from Somerville Smith to Mack, 2 August 1941, FO 371/27304–E 4355/62/89.

43. He had benefited from his rivals' period of exile after the Shahbandar murder (Patrick Seale, *The Struggle for Syria* [Oxford, 1965], pp. 26–27).

44. Spears Mission first weekly situation report, 19 August 1941, FO 371/27307–E 5054/62/89. In view of their earlier dealings with representatives of the Axis powers, the nationalist leaders in the Levant were uncertain how they would be treated under Allied occupation. Shukri al-Quwatli had thought it best to leave for Saudi Arabia at the time of the Allied invasion. The British, ever pragmatic, authorized Ibn Saud to assure al-Quwatli and his colleagues that a cooperative attitude on their part would be reciprocated (Stonehewer-Bird [Jedda] to FO #198, 11 June 1941 and FO to Jedda #138, 20 June 1941, FO 371/27295–E 3088/62/89; Wikely [Jedda] to FO #265, 9 August 1941 and Eastern Department minutes, FO 371/27330–E 4533/69/89).

45. Lyttelton to FO via Cairo's #54 LIMIT, 26 August 1941, FO 371/27307–E 5055/62/89. A deferment of treaty talks until after the war appears to have been in line with American wishes as well. U.S. Consul-General Engert told a staff member of the British embassy in Cairo that a Franco–Levantine modus vivendi was preferable to a wartime treaty:

> He emphasized strongly that in any case, at the end of the war, no power on earth would be able to force Syria or the Lebanon to continue under the French, and he hinted ultimate solution might be some form of federation with Palestine

and Trans-Jordan under British auspices. It seemed quite clear that he had received these views from Washington, particularly as he asked that no mention of the matter should be made to the French (Lyttelton to P.M. via Cairo's #27 LIMIT, 31 July 1941, FO 371/27303–E 4320/62/89).

46. Catroux to de Gaulle #100, 4 September 1941, Londres C.N.F. 39; Spears to London via Auchinleck's #02265, #03480, #03490, #03491, etc., 12–15 September 1941, FO 371/27309–E 5639/62/89; political report by Gardener (Damascus) forwarded to Cairo by Spears on 11 October 1941, FO 371/27316–E 7439/62/89. For a detailed analysis of the political calculations and maneuvers surrounding the appointment of Sheikh Taj al-Din, see Asher Susser, "Western Power Rivalry and its Interaction with Local Politics in the Levant, 1941–1946" (Ph.D. diss., Tel-Aviv University, 1986), pp. 110–21. Susser notes that Jamil Mardam, ever flexible in his approach to politics, sought the post of prime minister in the new cabinet, but was spurned by Taj al-Din.

47. Spears to Lampson #244, 23 September 1941, FO 371/27312–E 6303/62/89; text of Catroux's proclamation in E 6250/62/89; record of de Gaulle's meeting with Churchill, Lyttelton et al., 1 October 1941, FO 371/27313–E 6507/62/89; Spears to Lampson #290, 8 October 1941, FO 371/27315–E 7221/62/89. Catroux's decision to issue his unilateral declaration of Syrian independence had not, in fact, enjoyed de Gaulle's full support (see record of de Gaulle–Eden meeting, 19 September 1941, MEC, Spears Papers II/4).

48. Lyttelton to FO via Cairo's #3807, 3 December 1941, FO 371/27369–E 8002/6937/89; Spears' monthly report for December 1941, FO 406/80–E 573/207/89.

49. The November 1941 correspondence relating to the issue of the proclamation of Lebanese independence is far too extensive to cite in detail. It is contained in FO 371/27367, /27368 and /27369.

50. Minute by Caccia, 3 November 1941, FO 371/27367–E 7201/6937/89.

51. Catroux to Lyttelton, 12 November 1941, FO 371/27368–E 7554/6937/89.

52. Lyttelton to FO via Cairo's #3653, 21 November 1941, FO 371/27368–E 7698/6937/89.

53. Ibid., FO to Cairo #4091, 22 November 1941.

54. Cairo–London correspondence, 15–20 November 1941, FO 371/27368–E 7534–7674/6937/89.

55. Eden to De Gaulle, undated and Eastern Department minutes, FO 371/27369–E 7751/6937/89. Eden threatened that if Catroux issued the declaration without including the amendments, Britain would withhold recognition of Lebanese independence. Dejean, in charge of foreign affairs for the Free French, reported to the Foreign Office that de Gaulle "had been rather upset" by Eden's letter. "It was quite clear however that M. Dejean had been delighted. He seemed quite hopeful that if the General received one or two letters like that he would grow out of his present habit of going back on his subordinates" (minute by Caccia, 26 November 1941, FO 371/27369–E 7811/6937/89).

56. Minute by Caccia, 24 November 1941, FO 371/27369–E 7737/6937/89.

57. WO correspondence, 23–27 September 1941, FO 371/27310–E 5943/62/89 and FO 371/27311–E 6174/62/89; series of reports from Spears, 3–4 October 1941, FO 371/27312–E 6279/, E 6297/ and E 6298/62/89; Catroux to de Gaulle #1440, 9 October 1941, Londres C.N.F. 39. In the course of this enterprise, one Lieutenant Somberbieille had seized the relative of a sheikh as a hostage and murdered him.

58. Spears to Wilson (Cairo) #284, 4 October 1941, FO 371/27312–E 6374/62/89;

Wilson to Spears via Cairo's #250, E 6324; Spears to Wilson #287 and #288, 5 October 1941 and Wilson's #11208, 6 October 1941, E 6385; Spears to Wilson #292, 8 October 1941, FO 371/27313–E 6496/62/89; Auchinleck to WO #12474, 9 October 1941, E 6514; Lyttelton–FO correspondence, 19–20 October 1941, E 6797; Spears to Lampson #265, 30 September 1941, FO 371/27314–E 6874/62/89; Lyttelton to FO via Cairo's #3429, 1 November 1941, FO 371/27315–E 7124/62/89; MacMichael to CO #C.S. 536/III, 23 October 1941, FO 371/27318–E 7938/62/89.

59. Auchinleck to WO #28514, 20 November 1941 and minutes by Crosthwaite, FO 371/27364–E 7675/5729/89; Auchinleck to WO #144, 2 September 1941, FO 371/27308–E 5482/62/89; Spears' #185, 29 September 1941, FO 371/27311–E 6107/62/89; Commandant Kolb-Bernard to Admiral Muselier, 6 October 1941, FO 371/27319–E 8111/62/89.

60. Report by British liaison officer in Beirut, 28 October 1941, transmitted in Lyttelton's #5, 20 November 1941, FO 371/27318–E 8034/62/89.

61. Lyttelton to FO via Cairo's #3769, 1 December 1941, FO 371/27318–E 7988/62/89.

62. Spears to Lyttelton, 25 November 1941, MEC, Spears Papers II/5.

63. Lyttelton to FO via Cairo's #3701, 24 November 1941, FO 371/27369–E 7768/6937/89.

64. Spears to London via Auchinleck's #29958, 23 November 1941, FO 371/27369–E 7737/6937/89.

65. Lyttelton to FO via Cairo's #3701, op. cit. and marginalia by Eden.

66. Ibid., minutes by Mack and Caccia.

67. The text of the declaration can be found in Albert Hourani, *Syria and Lebanon, A Political Essay* (Oxford, 1946), pp. 378–81.

68. FO minutes, op. cit.

69. Lyttelton to FO via Cairo's #3925, 13 December 1941, FO 371/27369–E 8255/6937/89; Lyttelton to FO via Cairo's #342, 22 January 1942, FO 371/31337–E 606/49/65.

70. Copy of record of War Cabinet meeting chaired by Eden, 30 September 1941, FO 371/28214–Z 8508/11/17.

71. Ibid., minute by Churchill, 4 October 1941.

72. Spears to Lyttelton, 18 October and 13 November 1941 and other correspondence over the future of the Spears Mission, MEC, Spears Papers II/1.

73. Spears to Lyttelton (in London) via Cairo's #3172, 9 October 1942, FO 371/27313–E 6480/62/89.

74. Letter from Gilbert Mackereth to Anthony Eden, 25 May 1945, FO 371/45596–E 3640/52/89.

75. War Office outline of Spears Mission's organization, 5 December 1943, FO 371/35213–E 7653/2154/89; 1944 table of comparison showing sections strength of the Spears Mission and the General Delegation, MEC, Spears Papers II/6.

76. Spears to Lyttelton (London) via Cairo's #3170, 9 October 1941, FO 371/27313–E 6479/62/89.

77. Eden to Spears enclosing official instructions, 6 February 1942, FO 406/80–E 280/279/89; Major-General Sir Edward L. Spears, *Fulfilment of a Mission* (London, 1977), p. 165. In his new capacity as minister in Beirut, Spears would report directly to the FO, while in his role as chief of the mission to the Free French, he would continue to report to the minister of state in Cairo (FO to Lyttelton #111, 7 January 1942, FO 371/31480–E 438/279/89).

78. Spears to Hamilton (Beirut), 29 January 1942, MEC, Spears Papers II/6.

Chapter 6

1. Report by Rosa (Banking and Exchange advisor in Beirut) to Fraser (Treasury), 5 October 1941, FO 371/27288–E 6966/11/89.

2. Stephen H. Longrigg, *Syria and Lebanon under French Mandate* (Oxford, 1958), p. 272.

3. Spears to Cairo #137, 2 September 1941 and #165, 9 September 1941, FO 371/27311–E 6176/62/89, also in FO 406/79.

4. Spears to Auchinleck #178, 12 September 1941, FO 371/27287–E 5730/11/89.

5. Auchinleck to WO #04697, 20 September 1941, FO 371/27287–E 6010/11/89; Lampson to FO #3315, 22 October 1941, FO 371/27288–E 6913/11/89.

6. Georges Catroux, *Dans la bataille de Méditerranée* (Paris, 1949), pp. 195–96).

7. Auchinleck to WO #04697, 20 September 1941, FO minutes and FO to Cairo #3409, 2 October 1941, FO 371/27287–E 6010/11/89; Spears to Lyttelton #406 transmitted to London in Auchinleck's #25336, 12 November 1941, FO 371/27288–E 7463/11/89.

8. Dejean to Eden, 6 October 1941, FO 371/27287–E 6419/11/89; Lampson to FO #3315, 22 October 1941, FO 371/27288–E 6913/11/89; report by Spears on first year of Wheat Office, 19 June 1943, FO 371/35200–E 3698/159/89; Spears, *Fulfilment of a Mission* (London, 1977), pp. 175–76. After the failure of the first wheat plan, Spears claimed it had actually been Lyttelton's brainchild rather than his own.

9. Howard M. Sachar, *Europe Leaves the Middle East, 1936–1954* (New York, 1972), p. 250.

10. De Gaulle to Catroux #1628b/ECO/22, 26 February 1942, Guerre 1939–1945, Londres C.N.F. 59.

11. French National Committee (FNC) to Catroux #4082b/Col., 9 May 1942, Londres C.N.F. 59; report by Spears on first year of Wheat Office, op. cit.

12. Catroux, *Dans la bataille,* p. 270; see also Spears, *Fulfilment,* chapter 13.

13. Unsigned 1943 Free French report on British interference in Levant affairs since 1941, Londres C.N.F. 41; Catroux, *Dans la bataille,* chapter 29.

14. Catroux to FNC #589/CH, 20 May 1942, Londres C.N.F. 59; minutes of Cairo meetings, 11–13 May 1942, FO 371/31472–E 3310/207/89; see also report by Spears on first year of Wheat Office, op. cit.

15. Note for FNC, 15 August 1942 and FNC to Catroux #4715b/Diplo/400, 27 May 1942, Londres C.N.F. 59.

16. Note for FNC, supra.

17. Catroux, *Dans la bataille,* p. 272.

18. A Jewish Agency observer speculated that, apart from his own financial stake in the matter, Barazi was also interested in impeding Syrian grain sales to Lebanon, in the hope of using the issue as a means of pressuring the Lebanese into a political union with Syria (Epstein's report to Kaplan on the OCP, Jerusalem, 22 October 1942, BGA, Section 3 Papers).

19. Spears claimed that the regional quotas were actually filled. According to the estimate of a Jewish Agency representative, however, only 40 percent of existing Syrian stocks were released as of three months after the harvest report by Spears on first year of Wheat Office, op. cit.; Spears, *Fulfilment,* chapter 14; Epstein's report to Kaplan on the OCP, *supra*).

20. Sachar, *Europe Leaves the Middle East,* pp. 226–28.

21. Beirut's #214/CH, 28 February 1942, Londres C.N.F. 40; Engert to S. of S. #64, 3 March 1942, *FRUS* 4 (1942): 644–46; Spears Mission to Cairo #670, 19 Febru-

ary 1942, FO 406/80–E 1312/207/89; Spears Mission to Cairo #680, 26 February 1942, E 1369/207/89; Spears Mission to Cairo #692, 5 March 1942, E 1564.

22. Beirut to Lyttelton #696, 4 March 1942, FO 371/31471–E 1552/207/89; see also Beirut to FO #707, 7 March 1942, E 1538; various reports on Shukri al-Quwatli, FO 226/310, *passim.*

23. Beirut to FO #707, 7 March 1942, FO 371/31471–E 1538/207/89. From Damascus, Gardener wrote in a similar vein (dispatch from Gardener, 22 February 1942, E 1859).

24. Cornwallis to FO #239, 2 March 1942, FO 371/31481–E 1164/292/89.

25. FO to Cairo (repeated to Beirut) #257, 2 March 1942, FO 371/31471–E 1369/207/89; Cornwallis to FO #239, 2 March 1942 and FO to Beirut #51, 3 March 1942, FO 371/31481–E 1408/292/89; Beirut to FO #699, 4 March 1942 and FO to Beirut #693, 5 March 1942, E 1462; Beirut to FO #701, 6 March 1942, E 14944; Beirut to FO #705, 7 March 1942, E 1528. As one Eastern Department official put it: "Our support of the present [Syrian] Government should not entail measures which will gratuitously antagonise the leaders of the largest party in Syria" (minute by Caccia, FO 371/31481–E 1408/292/89).

26. Dispatch from Hamilton, 21 February 1942, FO 371/31471–E 1860/207/89; Bishara al-Khoury, *Haqa'iq lubnaniyyah* [Lebanese Realities] (Beirut, 1960), 1:242–43.

27. Spears to FO, 7 April 1942 and FO to Spears #43, 12 April 1942, FO 371/31471–E 2224/207/89; Spears to FO #49, 14 April 1942, E 2360/207/89; Matthews (London) to S. of S. #1986, 20 April 1942, NA, SD 890E.00/103.

28. Spears to FO #83, 24 April 1942, FO 371/31472–E 2576/207/89.

29. Spears to FO #82, 24 April 1942, FO 371/31472–E 2569/207/89.

30. Casey to FO #467 and #468, 22 April 1942 and FO to Casey #805, 25 April 1942, FO 371/31472–E 2503/207/89. Casey, a former Australian cabinet minister and ambassador to the United States during 1940–1942, had no prior experience of the Middle East and seemed inclined to follow Spears' lead on Levant policy throughout his tenure as minister of state. He was later to convey his impression of Spears in the following succinct terms:

When we first met in Cairo in 1942, each of us believed that he had never met the same sort of person before. Although wholly different persons, we became good friends. Louis Spears is strong meat, but very good and unusual meat (Lord Casey, *Personal Experience* [London, 1962], p. 148).

31. Epstein to Shertok, record of conversation with Naccache, 21 January 1942, CZA S25/5630.

32. On al-Khoury's relationship with the British, see Asher Susser, "Western Power Rivalry and its Interaction with Local Politics in the Levant, 1941–1946" (Ph.D. diss., Tel-Aviv University, 1986), p. 189.

33. Catroux to de Gaulle #508/CH, 29 April 1942, Londres C.N.F. 40.

34. Ibid.

35. De Gaulle to Catroux, 4 May 1942, Londres C.N.F. 40; also in Charles de Gaulle, *Mémoires de Guerre* [Paris, 1954], 1:593–94.

36. Murray to Hull and Welles, 3 November 1941, NA, SD 890D.01/564; State Department press release, 29 November 1941, *FRUS* 3 (1941):806–7; memorandum by Welles on conversation with Halifax, 2 March 1942, *FRUS* 4 (1942):644. In the words of Paul Alling of the Near Eastern and African Affairs Department (NEA) of the State Department:

If the American Government should extend full recognition to Syria and the Lebanon at this time, when independence is not a fact and with what amounts to puppet governments in office there, we would not only do violence to the high standard we have set in international relations but our prestige would suffer in the very area we are endeavoring to influence (memorandum, 11 May 1942, NA, SD 890D.01/604).

37. S. of S. to Engert #51 (24 April 1942), #57 (28 April 1942) and Engert to S. of S. #155 (1 May 1942), *FRUS* 4 (1942):591–92 and 595; Spears to FO #87, 28 April 1942, FO 371/31472–E 2698/207/89; Spears to FO #90, 28 April 1942, E 2700.

38. Letters from Dejean to Eden and Peake to Caccia, April 1942, FO 371/31472–E 2742/207/89.

39. Minutes of Cairo meetings, 11–13 May 1942, FO 371/31472–E 3310/207/89; Engert To S. of S. #195, *FRUS* 4 (1942):596–98.

40. De Gaulle to Catroux #4714b/CAB, 28 May 1942, Londres C.N.F. 40. It can safely be assumed that the British were responsible for this leak.

41. Dejean to Peake, 30 May 1942, FO 371/31473–E 3443/207/89; aide-mémoire for FNC, E 3764; Spears' weekly political summary #13, 2 July 1942, E 3977; B. H. Liddell Hart, *History of the Second World War* (New York, 1982), chapter 19.

42. Catroux, *Dans la bataille,* pp. 266–67.

43. Spears to FO #222, 14 June 1942, FO 371/31473–E 3654/207/89.

44. Ibid., FO to Spears #243, 19 June 1942.

45. Spears to FO #260, 25 June 1942, FO 371/31473–E 3833/207/89.

46. Ibid., minute by Sir Maurice Peterson.

47. Lampson to FO #122, 21 June 1942, FO 371/31473–E 3998/207/89; Casey to FO #949, 28 June 1942, E 3885; Spears to Casey #176, 29 June 1942, E 3891; Spears to FO #69, 3 July 1942, E 4025; Shone (Cairo) to FO #2143, 12 November 1943, FO 371/35184–E 6873/27/89; see also report on Lebanese political personalities, 1942–1943, "Bishara al-Khoury," Londres C.N.F. 61.

48. Spears to FO #329, 16 July 1942, FO 371/31474–E 4277/207/89; Spears to FO #333, 18 July 1942, E 4285; Spears to FO #354, 24 July 1942, E 4431.

49. Spears to FO #358, 25 July 1942 and #359, 26 July 1942, FO 371/31474–E 4447/207/89; Hamilton to Casey #241, 28 July 1942, E 4486. Ankara served as Vichy's base for Levant-watching.

50. Spears to FO #357, 25 July 1942, FO 31474–E 4441/207/89; Spears to FO #360, 25 July 1942, E 4448.

52. Minute by P.M., on Spears' to FO #357, supra.

52. Ibid., minute by Caccia.

53. FO to Casey (for Spears) #1709, 31 July 1942, FO 31474–E 4441/207/89.

54. Spears' weekly political summary for Lebanon, 29 July 1942, FO 371/31474–E 4507/207/89.

55. Spears to FO #383, 4 August 1942, FO 371/31474–E 4640/207/89.

56. Casey to FO #1207, 3 August 1942, FO 371/31474–E 4596/207/89.

57. Draft agreements and memoranda on Haifa–Tripoli railway, July–December 1942, FO 371/31486 and /31487, *passim.*

58. Minute by Beckett, 8 July 1942, FO 371/31468–E 4009/183/89.

59. Memorandum by Spears, 20 June 1942 and dispatch to Casey, 21 June 1942, FO 371/31468–E 3941/183/89; Eastern Department minutes and 20 July 1942 dispatch to Spears, E 4009.

60. Gwynn to S. of S. #246, 13 July 1942 and #258, 22 July 1942, *FRUS* 4

(1942):598–604. This tendency to distinguish between the attitudes of the Ninth Army and the Spears Mission toward the Free French was shared by both the Gaullists and the Foreign Office. It was, of course, disputed by the Spears Mission itself. In 1943, Daniel Lascelles, Spears' devoted deputy, was to express his resentment:

> The fact is that there is hardly a British official or officer in these States who would not in his heart of hearts be delighted to see the last of the French, whether this meant the emergence of real independence or of a state of more or less overt dependence on ourselves. But . . . all those who hold these private views have been extremely careful to keep them to themselves or at any rate "in the family."

Lascelles claimed that during the period of General Wilson's command there was a particularly strong tendency among officers to pose before the French as "bluff and honest soldiers" while letting the Spears Mission take care of the dirty work (dispatch from Lascelles to Peterson, 9 August 1943, FO 226/243, #30/G [II]).

61. Welles to Winant #3272, 15 July 1942 and Winant to S. of S. #3975, 18 July 1942, *FRUS* 4 (1942): 600–1; see also memorandum by Welles based on talk with the British ambassador, 14 August 1942, NA, SD 890D.00/906.

62. Casey to FO #1048, 17 July 1942, FO 371/31480–E 4263/279/89.

63. Ibid., minute by Peterson.

64. John Harvey, ed., *War Diaries of Oliver Harvey* (London, 1978), 26 July 1942.

65. Minute by Peterson, 12 August 1942, FO 371/31474–E 4725/207/89.

66. Peake (British Mission to FNC) to FO #88 SAVING, 9 June, 1942, FO 371/32010–Z 4877/298/17; Parr (Brazzaville) to FO #364, 9 June 1942, Z 4942; Parr to Eden, 30 June 1942, Z 5391; synopses of de Gaulle–Churchill meetings by Morton and by Dejean, 10 June 1942, FO 371/32097–Z 4949/4949/17 and Z 5123 (see also the summary in de Gaulle, *Mémoires de Guerre,* 1:604–7); telegram from de Gaulle to Free French representatives in Africa and the Middle East, 14 June 1942 and to Catroux, 18 June 1942, de Gaulle, *Mémoires de Guerre,* 1:607–9; François Kersaudy, *Churchill and de Gaulle* (London, 1981), chapter 8; J.-B. Duroselle, *L'Abîme–1939–1945* (Paris, 1982), pp. 351–57. In his memoirs, de Gaulle indicates that once the United States had assumed the leadership of the Allied war effort, the British chose to concentrate their own resources on the defense and expansion of their empire in the Middle East. Although this statement ostensibly refers to military operations against the Axis powers, de Gaulle includes Syria in the list of countries on which the British are supposed to have set their sights (de Gaulle, *Mémoires de Guerre,* 2:5).

67. I. S. O. Playfair et al. *The Mediterranean and Middle East* (London, 1959), 3: chapter 14.

68. Records of Cairo meetings, 8–10 August 1942, FO 371/31475–E 5070/207/89.

69. De Gaulle to Pleven and Dejean, 24 August 1942, Londres C. N. F. 38; "Revue de la situation en Syrie et Liban," August 1942, Londres C.N.F. 42.

70. De Gaulle to Dejean and Pleven #1133/CH, 1 September 1942, Londres C.N.F. 38. In a telegram sent on 17 August to René Pleven, de Gaulle made a point of emphasizing that the British military was collaborating fully with Free France in the administration of the Levant. It was the Spears Mission that was creating all the trouble (Charles de Gaulle, *Lettres, notes et carnets, 1941–1943* [Paris, 1982], pp. 345–46).

71. Letter from de Gaulle to Casey and enclosed memorandum, 7 September 1942, FO 371/31477–E 5559/207/89; see also de Gaulle, *Mémoires de Guerre,* 2:20. Although the FO resented what it perceived as the arrogant tone of de Gaulle's communication, Maurice Peterson found merit in many of the points he made. This may well have been

more out of hostility toward Spears than sympathy for the Free French. (Eastern Department minutes, E 5559).

72. Telegrams from de Gaulle to Churchill, 15 August 1942, FO 371/31475–E 5072/ 207/89; Churchill to de Gaulle, 22 August 1942, E 5073; letter from de Gaulle to Churchill, 24 August 1942, E 5167; also in PREM 3, 422/10 and Charles de Gaulle, *Mémoires de Guerre,* 2:353–54 and 357–59.

73. Spears' Levant Diary, 23–24 August 1942, MEC, Spears Papers I/1.

74. Casey to FO #1396, 25 August 1942, FO 371/31475–E 5075/207/89; see also minute from Churchill to Eden, 19 September 1942, PREM 3, 422/14.

75. FO to Casey #1977, 28 August 1942, FO 371/31475–E 5057/207/89; Casey to Beirut #303, 31 August 1942, E 5177.

76. De Gaulle to P.M. via Spears' #301 to Casey, 1 September 1942, FO 371/ 31476–E 5184/207/89.

77. De Gaulle to Pleven #1024, 16 August 1942, Londres C.N.F. 45; Spears to FO #441, 25 August 1942, FO 371/31475–E 5084/207/89.

78. Minute by Strang on talk with Dejean, 24 August 1942, FO 371/31475–E 5133/207/89.

79. Halifax (Washington) to FO #4284, 24 August 1942, FO 371/31475–E 5074/ 207/89; Campbell (Washington) to FO #4195, 18 August 1942, FO 371/31474–E 4900/ 207/89 and #4216, 19 August 1942, E 4907.

80. Gwynn to S. of S. #300, 23 August 1942, *FRUS* 4 (1942):620.

81. Casey to FO #1469, 5 September 1942, FO 371/31476–E 5259/207/89; Eastern Department minutes, FO 371/31475–E 5015/207/89; Casey to Beirut (for de Gaulle) #323, 5 September 1942, FO 371/31476–E 5260/207/89; Gwynn to S. of S. #319, 1 September 1942, *FRUS* 4 (1942):626–27.

82. De Gaulle to Pleven #1024, op. cit.; Spears to FO #423, 21 August 1942, FO 371/31474–E 4938/207/89. The notion of the Soviets establishing a diplomatic presence in the Middle East alarmed the Foreign Office (see Eastern Department minutes, E 4938). De Gaulle also met with Wendell Wilkie during the latter's brief stopover in Beirut in September, but failed to swing his opinion decisively in favor of the Free French (see de Gaulle to FNC, 10 September 1942, Londres C.N.F. 43; Spears to FO #517, 14 September 1942, FO 371/31477–E 5488/207/89 and #512, 14 September, E 5511; de Gaulle, *Mémoires de Guerre,* 2:27–28).

83. Dejean to de Gaulle #Diplo/556, 18 August 1942, Londres C.N.F. 45.

84. Minute by Strang on meeting with Dejean, 29 August 1942, FO 371/31475–E 4133/207/89.

85. Dejean to de Gaulle #9094 Diplo/615, 3 September 1942, Londres C.N.F. 38.

86. De Gaulle to Dejean #1163/CH, 4 September 1942, Londres C.N.F. 38; also in de Gaulle, *Lettres, 1941–1943,* p. 369.

87. Letter from Clayton to Hopkinson, 7 September 1942 and Eastern Department minutes, FO 371/31477–E 5600/207/89; minute by P.M., 10 September 1942, PREM 3, 422/10.

88. Minute by P.M., supra.

89. Spears to FO #419, 19 August 1942, FO 371/31474–E 4901/207/89; Casey to FO #3196, 25 August 1942, FO 371/31475–E 5075/207/89. Spears himself reports in his memoirs that he induced the Ninth Army commander to demand the arrest of Murshid and the declaration of a state of siege in the Alawite territory as a means of "testing" de Gaulle (Spears, *Dans la bataille,* p. 219).

90. Report from staff officer (Intelligence) Levant area to staff officer (Intelligence) Mediterranean, 18 August 1942, MEC, Spears Papers II/6.

91. Minute by Peterson, 16 October 1942, FO 371/31480–E 7045/279/89.

92. Harvey, *War Diaries,* 14 September 1942.

93. Casey to FO #1396, 25 August 1942, FO 371/31475–E 5075/207/89. A. B. Gaunson seems to misinterpret the impact of de Gaulle's visit when he writes: "De Gaulle's tactics in the Levant seemed about to achieve the dismissal of Spears" (A. B. Gaunson, *The Anglo–French Clash in Lebanon and Syria, 1940–1945* [London, 1987], p. 102). De Gaulle's tactics actually helped *prevent* Spears' dismissal.

94. Eastern Department minutes (based on information provided by Dejean), 7 September 1942, FO 371/31476–E 5260/207/89.

95. Dejean to de Gaulle Diplo/643, 10 September 1942, Londres C.N.F. 43; Dejean to de Gaulle #9492 and #9496 Diplo/656, 12 September 1942, Londres C.N.F. 38.

96. Rooker (FO liaison with FNC) to FO #128 and #129, 9 September 1942, FO 371/31477–E 5341/207/89; Dejean to de Gaulle Diplo/643, 10 September 1942, Londres C.N.F. 43.

97. Helleu (Cairo) to de Gaulle (reporting on talk with Casey), 11 September 1942, Londres C.N.F. 38; canceled telegram from Philip to de Gaulle, 12 September 1942, Londres C.N.F. 43 (the gist of this rather harshly worded telegram was conveyed to de Gaulle in other cables).

98. De Gaulle to Pleven #1230/CH, 12 September 1942, Londres C.N.F. 38; also in de Gaulle, *Lettres, 1941–1943,* pp. 389–90.

99. Spears to FO #515, 14 September 1942, FO 371/31477–E 5517/207/89; see also Gwynn to S. of S. #342, 12 September 1942 and #344, 14 September 1942, *FRUS* 4 (1942):632–34.

100. Spears to FO #480, 5 September 1942, FO 371/31476–E 5258/207/89.

101. Dispatch from Spears to Casey, 16 September 1942, FO 371/31477–E 5602/207/89.

102. Ibid., minute by Eyres.

103. Spears to FR #523, 17 September 1942 and minute by P.M., 19 September 1942, FO 371/31477–E 5534/207/89; dispatch from Spears to Casey, 21 September 1942 and Eastern Department minutes, FO 371/31478–E 5856/207/89. Spears protested to Casey that General Alexander should not have been consulted about this matter because it lay exclusively within Spears' sphere of responsibility.

104. Eastern Department minutes, 23–25 September 1942, FO 371/31477–E 5626/207/89.

105. Harvey, *War Diaries,* 22 September 1942.

106. Ibid., 1 October 1942. See also record of 30 September Churchill–de Gaulle meeting, FO 371/31950 as quoted in Kersaudy, *Churchill and de Gaulle,* pp. 202–9.

107. Churchill's secret session speech of 10 December 1942 as quoted in Martin Gilbert, *Winston S. Churchill,* vol. 7 (Boston, 1986) :277–78. In his memoirs, Churchill played down the significance of this friction with de Gaulle:

> He . . . felt it to be essential to his position before the French people that he should maintain a proud and haughty demeanour toward "perfidious Albion," although an exile dependent upon our protection and living in our midst. He had to be rude to the British to prove to French eyes that he was not a British puppet. He certainly carried out this policy with perseverance (Winston Churchill, *The Second World War* [Boston, 1949] 3 [Their Finest Hour]:509).

108. Record of conversation between Dejean and Sargent, 2 October 1942, Londres C.N.F. 43; Winant to S. of S. #5615, 8 October 1942, *FRUS* 4 (1942):636.

109. Harvey, *War Diaries,* 2 October 1942.

110. Draft text of interpretive agreement, October 1942, FO 371/31478–E 5955/207/89; Eastern Department minutes and FO to Casey #2489, 16 October 1942, FO 371/31479–E 5989/207/89.

111. Casey to FO #1729, 11 October 1942 FO 371/31479–E 5989/207/89. The British military authorities concurred with Casey's views (letter from Major-General John Kennedy to Peterson, 16 October 1942, FO 371/31479–6050/207/89).

112. Catroux, *Dans la bataille,* p. 287–91.

113. FO to Casey #2504, 18 October 1942, FO 371/31479–E 5989/207/89; Harvey, *War Diaries,* 18 October 1942.

114. Eastern Department minutes and letter from Peterson to Helleu, 12 November 1942, FO 371/31479–E 6471/207/89; FO to Casey #2929, 27 November 1942, E 6929; minute by Peterson, 17 November 1942, E 7003.

115. Hopkinson to Peterson via Casey's #1944, 16 November 1942, FO 371/31479–E 8779/89; S. of S. to Wadsworth (Beirut) #262, 2 December 1942, *FRUS,* 4 (1942):637; FO minute, 14 December 1942, FO 371/32153–Z 10307/8463/17; also in de Gaulle, *Mémories de Guerre,* 2:426–27; de Gaulle to Catroux, 11 November 1942, de Gaulle, *Mémoires de Guerre,* 2:395–96. This agreement had been further delayed in part by British concern about the possibility of a nasty public reaction by de Gaulle to his exclusion from the North African administration (memorandum reviewing relations with de Gaulle, 7 August 1943, WP [43] 341, FO 371/3604–Z 7763/665/17).

Chapter 7

1. British support for de Gaulle was crucial in gaining American acceptance of a role for him in the Algerian administration. It was largely Eden's pressure that induced Churchill to lend this support, although it was a matter of months before even the British extended formal recognition to the FCNL. See Jean-Baptiste Duroselle, *L'Abîme—1939–1945* (Paris, 1982), chapter 14; François Kersaudy, *Churchill and de Gaulle* (London 1981), pp. 264–95; John Harvey, *War Diaries of Oliver Harvey* (London, 1978), 13 July 1943.

2. Gwynn to S. of S. #455, 16 November 1942, *FRUS* 4 (1942):666; see also 660 ff.

3. Spears to FO #579, 15 October 1942, FO 371/31468–E 6032/183/89; Spears to FO #4, 9 January 1943, FO 371/35174–E 559/27/89; personal note from Spears to P.M., 2 February 1943, FO 226/243–#30/G (I); letter from Spears to Macmillan, 30 March 1943, FO 226/243–#30/G (II); Spears' Levant Diary, 12 February 1943, MEC, Spears Papers I/1.

4. George Kirk, *The Middle East in the War* (Oxford, 1953), p. 117.

5. Interview with Prof. Maxime Rodinson (who was himself a member of the Communist Party who resided in Lebanon throughout the war years), Paris, 2 May 1985; report by Free French officer just arrived in Algiers from Levant, November 1943, Guerre 1939–1945, Alger CFLN-GPRF 999. Rodinson reports that the leftist republican movement in Beirut came to a head in the fall of 1943, when vague plans for an armed coup were hatched by Capitaine de Gendarmerie Montezer, an adventurer who claimed to represent a left-wing masonic lodge in Toulouse and who proposed to reestablish the "true Gaullism" in the Levant. Following a series of chaotic meetings attended by hundreds of disaffected Free French soldiers and sailors, the military command took steps to liquidate the movement through the use of reassignments to disperse its key

members. As seen in chapter 9 of this book, however, political factionalism of this sort continued to afflict the Free French administration of the Levant well into 1944.

6. Letter from Lépissier to Cassin transmitted by Lascelles (Beirut), 5 April 1943, FO 371/35176–E 2184/27/89.

7. Minute by Rooker on 26 April 1943 talk with Cassin, FO 371/35176–E 2184/27/89.

8. Minutes by Peterson, 8 and 12 January 1943, FO 371/35174–E 273/27/89.

9. "Note relative à l'affaire des elections" (unsigned), 30 November 1942, Guerre 1939–1945, Londres C.N.F. 40. The corrupt Husni Barazi was replaced as Syrian premier by Jamil Ulshi in January 1943, while Taj al-Din's death led to the assumption of presidential powers by the Syrian Council of Ministers. These were regarded as purely superficial changes by all concerned (see Spears' weekly political summary #27, 7 October 1942, FO 371/31478–E 5922/207/89; Spears to FO #33, 14 January 1943, FO 371/35174–E 313/27/89; Spears to FO #48, 17 January 1943, E 342).

10. Catroux to FNC #307/CH, 6 March 1943 and #318/CH, 8 March 1943, Londres C.N.F. 41.

11. Yehoshua Porath, *Be-mivchan ha-ma'aseh ha-politi* [In the Trial of Political Action] (Jerusalem, 1985), pp. 55–64; Great Britain, *Parliamentary Debates* 5th ser., 387 (24 Feb. 1943), p. 139.

12. Catroux to FNC #318/CH, 8 March 1943, Londres C.N.F. 41. See also letter from Massigli to Helleu, 26 March 1943, Londres C.N.F. 44.

13. Spears to FO #121, 21 February 1943, FO 371/35175–E 1082/27/89. Was Catroux deliberately trying to lull Spears' suspicions so as to facilitate the gaining of treaty rights for France?

14. Report by Bernard Joseph (head of Jewish Agency's Political Department) on secret talk with Naccache in late December 1942, CZA, S25/4549; Beirut to FNC #1689/CH, 14 December 1942, Londres C.N.F. 45; Catroux to FNC #425/CH, 25 March 1943, Londres C.N.F. 41; Wadsworth to S. of S. #51 (29 January 1943), #100 (5 March 1943), #109 (19 March 1943) and #115 (23 March 1943), *FRUS* 4 (1943)956–65; Spears to FO #198, 19 March 1943, FO 371/35176–E 1602/27/89.

15. Spears to Fo #198, supra.

16. Catroux to FNC #367/CH, 16 March 1943 and #421/CH, 24 March 1943, Londres C.N.F. 41.

17. Interview with Sir Richard Beaumont (London, 27 August 1987).

18. Report by Lascelles, 13 March 1943, FO 226/240–9/80/43. In a bizarre misunderstanding, al-Quwatli was reported to have mistaken Lascelles, fluent French speaker that he was, for a Frenchman—possibly an *agent provocateur.* The matter was eventually clarified, but a flabbergasted Lascelles remarked: "I have been taken before now for a Portugese [sic]—and minded less" (exchange of notes between Furlonge and Lascelles, 18 March 1943).

19. Lascelles to Gardener, 23 April 1943, FO 226/240–9(IV)/163/43.

20. Lascelles to Gardener, 27 April 1943, FO 226/240–9(IV)/171/43.

21. Report by Lascelles, 28 April 1943, FO 226/240–9(IV)/178/43.

22. For a detailed analysis of this complicated bargaining process, see Asher Susser, "Western Power Rivalry and its Interaction with Local Politics in the Levant, 1941–1946" (Ph.D. diss., Tel-Aviv University, 1986), pp. 270–85.

23. Spears to FO #212, 23 March 1943, FO 371/35176–E 1717/27/89; Spears to FO #215, 25 March 1943, E 1730; Spears to FO #224, 25 March 1943, E 1792.

24. Spears to FO #29, 27 March 1943, FO 371/35176–E 1965/27/89.

25. Minute by Crosthwaite, FO 371/31479–E 7507/207/89. The idea seems to have

been to exclude pro-Axis figures from political office, but, given the fickleness of political loyalties in the region, this label could have been extended to include most of the local leadership.

26. Memorandum by Furlonge (political officer in Beirut), 10 February 1943, FO 371/35175–E 1273/27/89.

27. Helleu to FNC #488/CH, 8 April 1943, Londres C.N.F. 44; see also Helleu to FNC #472, 4 April 1943.

28. MEC, Coghill Diary, note #41; Helleu to FNC #590/CH, 25 April 1943, Londres C.N.F. 44; *Cabinet politique*'s monthly review for Syria and Lebanon, April 1943, Londres C.N.F. 42; note by Benoist's office (Cairo), 28 April 1943, Londres C.N.F. 41.

29. Dispatch from Spears to Casey, 24 March 1943, FO 684/14–20/E; Helleu to FNC #728/CH, 16 May 1943, and FNC to Helleu Diplo/358, 27 May 1943, Londres C.N.F. 44.

30. Spears' undated memorandum, March 1943, FO 371/35177–E 2488/27/89; notes on Spears' meeting with Massigli in London, 15 July 1943, FO 371/35179–E 4286/27/89.

31. Helleu to FNC #621/CH, 30 April 1943 and FNC to Helleu Diplo/336, 15 Mary 1943, Londres C.N.F. 59.

32. Correspondence over wheat scheme, May 1943, FO 371/35199–E 2772/, E 2937/, E 2983/, E 3013/, E 3017/, E 3035/159/89, *passim*; Spears to FO #313, 20 May 1943, FO 371/35200–E 3128/159/89; Spears to FO #315, 31 May 1943, E 3205; Helleu to FNC #712 (18 May 1943), #759/CH (20 May 1943) and Diethelm (*Commissariat des Finances*) to Rauzan (Beirut) #9728c/Diplos (31 May 1943), Londres C.N.F. 59; Admiral Auboyneau (Cairo) to de Gaulle, 1 June 1943, Londres C.N.F. 44.

33. FNC to Helleu #9209c Diplo/345, 22 May 1943 and Helleu to FNC #751/CH and #803/CH, 25 May 1943, Londres C.N.F. 41.

34. Auboyneau to de Gaulle #40, 29 May 1943, Alger CFLN-GPRF 1468.

35. Major-General Sir Edward L. Spears, *Fulfilment of a Mission* (London, 1977), p. 208.

36. Spears' weekly political summary #62, 9 June 1943, FO 371/35177–E 3386/27/89.

37. Spears' "Comments on MSC (42) 3 and 9," 14 February 1943, FO 371/35177–E 2488/27/89.

38. Letter marked "private and personal" from Spears to Eden, 2 April 1943, FO 371/35177–2346/27/89. The enlistment question had actually been resolved on British terms (with 10,000 Syrians and Lebanese to be called up) by the time Spears wrote this letter.

39. Letter marked "private and personal" from Eden to Spears, 21 April 1943, FO 371/35177–E 2346/27/89.

40. Arab Federation Report, ME (0) (42) 4, 9 January 1942, FO 371/31337–E 436/49/65; Porath, *Be-mivchan,* pp. 120–62.

41. Glubb Pasha, "A Further Note on Peace Terms in the Middle East," 25 May 1943, MEC, Spears Papers III/5; see also his "Note on Post-War Settlements in the Middle East" (written in 1942), Spears Papers III/5.

42. In 1942, MacMichael had referred to French interests in the Levant as being "largely ecclesiastical" (dispatch from MacMichael to Lord Cranborne [colonial secretary], 5 September 1942, FO 371/31338–E 5802/49/65).

43. "Resolutions on the Political Situation in the Middle East," May 1943, MEWC (43) 25, FO 371/34975–E 3234/2551/65; see also Porath, *Be-mivchan,* pp. 302–3.

44. Ibid., minute by Peterson, 7 June 1943.

45. Ibid., note from Eden to P.M. (drafted by Cadogan), 10 June 1943. Also see Porath, *Be-mivchan,* pp. 302–3.

46. Minute by R. M. A. Hankey, 8 July 1943, FO 371/35178–E 3893/27/89.

47. Free French copy of parliamentary address by Lord Moyne, with marginalia (9 June 1942), Beirut to FNC #1405, 12 October 1942, Beirut to FNC #1654, transmitting report from du Chaylard in Jerusalem, 9 December 1942, Londres C.N.F. 207.

48. Dossier labeled "Questions Arabes," Londres C.N.F. 148. This file contains a confidential report on Arab federation and the hindrance posed to it by the French mandate in Syria, which was prepared for the Foreign Office by the Foreign Research and Press Service at Balliol College, Oxford, 20 June 1941; see also dispatch from Massigli (London) to Catroux (Algiers), 6 April 1943, Londres C.N.F. 41.

49. See Massigli to Catroux, supra; Cairo to FNC, 3 March 1943, Londres C.N.F. 41; Beirut to FNC #188/CH (transmitting report from Maigret in Jeddah), 11 February 1943, Londres C.N.F. 44.

50. Beirut to FO #358, 22 June 1943, FO 371/35213–E 3617/2154/89. Eyres of the Eastern Department noted on 18 June: "We had not heard of Sir E. Spears' impending arrival, but I understand that the arrangements were made on the highest level" (E 3555).

51. Memorandum by Spears, 5 July 1943 (date marked with question mark), FO 371/35178–E 3893/27/89. Very similar views were expressed by Freya Stark of the Ministry of Information (and a friend of Spears). She argued that France's anachronistic insistence on direct administration in Syria and Lebanon was inconsistent with the subtler methods by which the British exerted political influence in the region. It would therefore be best to remove this potential source of tension altogether. She also advocated the establishment of a left-wing, anti-imperialist postwar government in Paris (memorandum by Freya Stark, 29 September 1943, FO 371/35182–5789/27/89; see also Freya Stark, *Dust in the Lion's Paw* [London, 1961], pp. 130 and 135).

52. Minute from P.M. to Eden, 12 July 1943, FO 371/35178–E 3893/27/89.

53. Harvey, *War Diaries,* 21 May 1943. Official U.S. and British recognition of the FCNL was not to be granted until August, two months after its creation.

54. Ibid., 6 July 1943.

55. Ibid., 13 July 1943.

56. Memorandum signed by Eden, FO 371/35178–E 3893/27/89.

57. Minute from P.M. to Eden, 15 July 1943, FO 371/35178–E 3893/27/89.

58. Helleu to FNC #986/CH, 22 June 1943 and #1014/CH, 26 June 1943, Londres C.N.F. 44; Lascelles to FO #379, 29 June 1943, FO 371/35178–E 3785/27/89; Minute from P.M. to Eden, 28 June 1943, PREM 3, 422/12.

59. Helleu to FNC #1014/CH, supra.

60. Ibid.

61. Lascelles to FO #379, 29 June 1943, Eastern Department minutes and FO to Lascelles, FO 371/35178–E 3785/27/89.

62. Minute from P.M. to Eden, 28 June 1943, PREM 3, 422/12.

63. WM (43) 89th meeting, item 3, 28 June 1943, CAB 65/34.

64. London to Helleu Diplo/422 (26 June 1943), "Elements de réponse aux questions de Foreign Office" (12 July 1943), FCNL (Algiers) to London #347 (14 July 1943) and Massigli (London) to Algiers Diplo/42 (15 July 1943), Londres C.N.F. 44; P.M. to Commander-in-chief Middle East via Air Ministry's #0Z.1881, 3 July 1943, PREM 3, 422/12; Spears' Levant Diary, 7 July 1943, MEC, Spears Papers I/1; FO minutes prepared for meeting with Massigli, 13 July 1943, FO 371/35179–E 4403/27/89.

Benoist, the Free French representative in Cairo, also expressed dismay over Helleu's support for Mukaddam (Benoist to FCNL #264, 6 July 1943, Londres C.N.F. 44).

65. Memorandum for Massigli in preparation for his meeting with Cadogan, 12 July 1943, Londres C.N.F. 44.

66. Helleu to London #1026, 28 June 1943 and #1106/CH, 19 July 1943, Londres C.N.F. 44; Helleu to FCNL #125/CH, 28 June 1943, Londres C.N.F. 41; Spears to FO #449, 9 August 1943, FO 371/35180–E 4697/27/89; McClenahan (military intelligence representative in Cairo) to Washington, D.C., 29 August 1943, NA, OSS 226/44428; Spears, *Fulfilment*, p. 222.

67. Casey to Cadogan (12 July 1943), Spears to Cadogan (13 July 1943) and Cadogan to Spears and Casey (14 July 1943), FO 371/35178–E 4112/27/89.

68. FO minutes, 11–15 May 1943, FO 371/35177–E 2759/27/89; Spears' Levant Diary, 7 July 1943 and record of that day's meeting with Massigli, Casey, and Churchill, MEC, Spears Papers I/1; note from Spears to R. M. A. Hankey, 13 July 1943 and Eastern Department minutes, FO 371/35178–E 4070/27/89.

69. FO notes on meeting of Spears, Casey, and Massigli, 15 July 1943, FO 371/35179–E 4286/27/89; Spears' Levant Diary, 15 July 1943, MEC, Spears Papers I/1.

70. De Gaulle (Algiers) to Massigli, 17 July 1943, Charles de Gaulle, *Mémoires de Guerre* (Paris, 1956), 2:516–17. J.-B. Duroselle has noted that de Gaulle's penchant for monopolizing the conduct of Free French diplomacy created tension between Massigli and him. In the final reckoning, despite Massigli's long-standing diplomatic experience, his views carried little weight with the general (Duroselle, *L'Abîme*, pp. 475–76).

71. MSC (43) 4 (22 July 1943), FO to Beirut #21 (27 July 1943) and minute by Morton (28 July 1943), PREM 3, 422/14; Spears' Levant Diary, 7 July 1943, MEC, Spears Papers I/1.

72. Minute by Caccia, 8 April 1943 and FO to Casey #1214, 14 April 1943, FO 371/35213–E 2160/2154/89; Casey to FO #1356, 3 June 1943 and FO minutes, E 3242.

73. Spears' Levant Diary, 25 June 1943, MEC, Spears Papers I/1.

74. Eden to Spears, 27 July 1943, FO 371/35213–E 4229/2154/89.

75. Ibid., minute by Peterson, 21 July 1943.

76. Spears' Levant Diary, 15 July 1943, MEC, Spears Papers I/1.

77. Helleu to Catroux #784/CH, 22 May 1943 and Catroux to Helleu CAB/9372c, 25 May 1943, Londres C.N.F. 41.

78. Helleu to FCNL #1002/CH, 24 June 1943, Londres C.N.F. 41; Lascelles to FO #363, 23 June 1943, FO 371/35177–E 3651/27/89; Lascelles to FO #370, 26 June 1943, FO 371/35178–E 3702/27/89; Wadsworth to S. of S. #214, 24 June 1943, *FRUS* 4 (1943):976–78.

79. Letter from Nahas Pasha to Catroux, 10 July 1943, FO 371/35179–E 4302/27/89.

80. Secret letter from Helleu to Massigli, 26 July 1943, Alger CFLN-GPRF 1468. Helleu requested that Massigli show this letter to de Gaulle.

81. Dispatch from Lascelles to Eden, 20 July 1943, FO 226/243, #30/G (II). Lascelles reported that Helleu had just appointed Mme. Paris, his former mistress and "one of the worst of the 'bad gang'," as an assistant aide-de-camp.

82. Lascelles to FO #42, 21 July 1943, FO 371/35179–E 4263/27/89; Levant weekly political summary #68, 21 July 1943, E 4281; Spears' weekly political summary #69, 28 July 1943, FO 371/35179–E 4459/27/89.

83. Lascelles to FO #395, 7 July 1943, FO 371/35178–E 3966/27/89.

84. Report for Jewish Agency entitled "Michtav mi-Beirut" [a letter from Beirut], 25 September 1943, BGA, section 3 papers (also in CZA, S25/5577).

85. Helleu to FNC #868/CH, 2 June 1943, Londres C.N.F. 44; Spears' weekly political summary #63, 16 June 1943, FO 371/35177–E 3501/27/89; summary of #64 (by Lascelles), 23 June 1943, E 3691.

86. Lascelles to FO #404, 12 July 1943 and minute by Hankey, FO 371/35178–E 4036/27/89.

87. Spears' weekly political summary #69, op. cit.; Spears to FO #459, 18 August 1943, FO 371/35180–E 4900/27/89.

88. FO minutes, July 1943, FO 371/35178–E 3966/27/89; Spears to FO #470, 24 August 1943, FO 371/35180–E 5070/27/89; dispatch from Baxter (approved by Eden) to Campbell, 16 August 1943, FO 371/35179–E 4520/27/89. The aide-mémoire Campbell presented to American Secretary of State Cordell Hull noted significantly that "should an Arab federation ever come into being it is highly probable that teaching and use of English [in Syria] will in order to secure conformity, tend largely to supersede that of French" (British embassy to S. of S., 18 September 1943, *FRUS* 4 [1943]:989–91).

89. Spears to FO #477, 26 August 1943, FO minutes and FO to Spears #405, 29 August 1943, FO 371/35180–E 5088/27/89; see also E 7183.

90. Spears to FO #435, 1 August 1943, FO 371/35179–E 4517/27/89; Spears to FO #442, 5 August 1943, E 4611; Wadsworth to S. of S. #242, 2 August 1943 and #244, 4 August 1943, *FRUS* 4 (1943):980–85. The Christian-Muslim ratio was thus altered from the previous one of 5.5:5 to that of 6:5. This arrangement has remained intact to the present day (although, unfortunately, the same can hardly be said of Lebanon itself).

91. Undated 1943 report on Lebanon by E. Epstein, CZA, S25/9027; Albert Hourani, *Syria and Lebanon, A Political Essay* (Oxford, 1946), pp. 133–35 and 257; Kamal S. Salibi, *The Modern History of Lebanon* (New York, 1965), pp. 171–88; Howard Sachar, *Europe Leaves the Middle East, 1936–1954* (New York, 1972), pp. 299–301; author's interview with Dr. Eliahu Elath (Epstein), (Jerusalem, 22 May 1988).

92. Report by officer just back from Levant, November 1943, Alger CFLN-GPRF 999; Georges Catroux, *Dans la bataille de Méditerranée* (Paris, 1949), chapter 44.

93. Spears to FO #467, 22 August 1943, FO 371/35180–E 4974/27/89; Spears to FO #90, 6 September 1943, FO 371/35182–E 5539/27/89; dispatch from Massigli to Helleu, 21 September 1943, Alger CFLN-GPRF 999.

94. R. W. McClenahan (U.S. military intelligence, Cairo) to Washington, D.C., 14 April 1943, NA, OSS 226/34139.

95. Interview with Sir Richard Beaumont (London, 27 August 1987).

96. Memorandum by Furlonge for Spears, 17 February 1943, FO 226/240–9/48/43; BSM Zahle to BSM Beirut, 11 June 1943, 9(VI)/269/43 and FO 226/240–249, *passim;* Spears to FO #467, 22 August 1943, FO 371/35180–E 4974/27/89; Spears to FO #482, 26 August 1943, E 5120; FO minute by Peterson reporting on complaint by Viénot (French representative in London), 13 September 1943, FO 371/35181–E 5525/27/89; Spears to FO #97, 17 September 1943, FO 371/35182–E 5817/27/89; Eliahu Sasson, "Le-goraloh ha-medini shel ha-Levanon" [Of Lebanon's Political Fate], 4 October 1943, CZA, S25/5577; report for Jewish Agency, [a letter from Beirut], op. cit.; undated report on Lebanese elections by *Sûreté-Générale*, Alger CFLN-GPRF 1004; Wadsworth to S. of S. #280, 22 September 1943, *FRUS* 4 (1943):992–93; Camille Chamoun, *Mudhakkiratiy* [My Memoirs] (Beirut, 1969), 1:23.

97. Spears' weekly political summary #74, 1 September 1943, FO 371/35181–E 5281/27/89; Wadsworth to S. of S. #266, 3 September 1943, *FRUS* 4 (1943):987–89; report for Jewish Agency [a letter from Beirut]," supra; Salibi, *Modern History,* p. 186. The

level of participation in the elections was unusually high by the apathetic standards of the Levant; approximately 60 percent of eligible voters cast their ballots (excluding ballots that were cast twice), as compared with only some 15–25 percent in the Syrian elections.

98. Spears' weekly political summary #74, supra.

99. Dispatch from FCNL to Helleu, 21 September 1943, Alger CFLN-GPRF 999; Spears to FO #519, 16 September 1943, FO 371/35182–E 5560/27/89. The Jewish Agency received a report according to which Chataigneau returned to Beirut with instructions from Catroux that Bishara al-Khoury's bid for the presidency should be supported by the General Delegation (report for Jewish Agency, [a letter from Beirut], op. cit.).

100. In his memoirs, al-Khoury claims that Edde recognized that Al-Khoury's election to the presidency was ultimately inevitable, and argues that Edde agreed to the Anglophile Chamoun as a compromise candidate only in the hope of provoking the French into suspending the whole process (Bishara al-Khoury, *Haqai'iq lubnaniyyah* [Lebanese Realities] [Beirut, 1960], 1:259–62). See also Chamoun, *Mudhakkiratiy,* pp. 23–24.

101. Helleu to Massigli #1360/CH (25 September 1943), #1381/CH (4 October 1943) and unsigned report (4 October 1943), Alger CFLN-GPRF 999; Spears to FO #532, 20 September 1943, FO 371/35182–E 5674/27/89 and #547, 28 September 1943, E 5799; Wadsworth to S. of S. #280, 22 September 1943, *FRUS* 4 (1943):992–93; report for Jewish Agency [a letter from Beirut], op. cit.; "Of Lebanon's Political Fate," op. cit.; Hourani, *Syria and Lebanon,* pp. 257–58. Whereas, in his cables to London, Spears downplayed the importance of his role in this process, he clearly felt the need to gloat over his victory to someone. In a lengthy letter sent to Casey, he described his crucial meeting with al-Khoury as follows:

> I sent for Beshara and following my constant tactics of always insisting that we were taking no direct part in the matter and were only giving advice upon request, I got him with great difficulty to consent to stand down himself but he would only do so in favour of one man, Shamoun. Now I knew that Shamoun was anathema to the French but kept this to myself, merely urging Beshara to come to an understanding direct with Edde on the subject.

> Negotiations between the parties were initiated, when as I expected, the French, finding out about it, went up in smoke. They begged me to use all my influence to prevent Shamoun's election and put their maximum pressure on Edde to make him withdraw his offer to stand down in Shamoun's favour.

> From that moment on it was comparatively easy sailing (personal and secret letter from Spears to Casey, 21 September 1943, FO 226/240–9(13)/646/43).

Spears sent a copy of this letter to High Commissioner MacMichael in Palestine, requesting that he destroy it after having read it. MacMichael responded with a note of congratulations, reporting that: "The document is being consigned to the flames, but seems to burn with a bluish excellence" (FO 226/240–9/647/43). At several decades' remove, however, Spears' immodest self-evaluation seems rather risible. On being shown the text of this letter, both Professor Albert Hourani and Sir Richard Beaumont were struck by its overblown tone; certainly al-Khoury was no innocent instrument of Spears' anti-French wiles. Once again, the question of who used whom in these intrigues is a moot one.

102. Reports from Beirut to Algiers, September–October 1943, op. cit.

103. Wadsworth to S. of S. #280, op. cit.

104. Eliahu Sasson, "Yedi'ot arviyot" [Arab Information], 29 September 1943, BGA, section 3; Sasson, "Le-goraloh," 4 October 1943, op. cit. The latter report is also to be found in Eliahu Sasson, *Ba-derekh el ha-shalom: igrot ve-sichot* [On the Road to Peace: Letters and Conversations] (Tel-Aviv, 1978) pp. 261–76; also see pp. 219–26 for indications of al-Khoury's earlier, less favorable attitude toward the Muslims and Arab nationalism. Sasson argued that his political transformation did not represent a betrayal of Maronite interests, but rather a practical reappraisal of where those interests lay.

An American military intelligence report on the Lebanese elections, dated 1 November 1943 (NA, OSS 226/49772), consists almost entirely of a word-by-word translation of Sasson's 4 October 1943 report. The source cited is "a trained journalist-observer in the Middle East" with a reliability rating of A1. Even the few passages not found verbatim in the Hebrew original are hostile in tone to Arab nationalism and include a criticism of George Wadsworth as being "frankly pan-Arabist." No attempt was even made to correct Sasson's occasionally idiosyncratic English. The Israeli archives frequently contain English versions of reports, and this is clearly one of them. One might wonder how many other reports were prepared for American intelligence in the Middle East by analysts from other countries.

Chapter 8

1. Helleu to FCNL #1340/CH, 22 September 1943, Alger CFLN-GPRF 999.

2. Note from Catroux to Massigli, 30 September 1943 and unnumbered cable from Massigli to Helleu, 1 October 1943, Alger CFLN-GPRF 999.

3. Spears to FO #581, 16 October 1943, FO 371/35182–E 6294/27/89; Spears to FO #589, 20 October 1943, E 6384; see also Helleu to Massigli #1391/CH, 9 October 1943, Alger CFLN-GPRF 999.

4. Bishara al-Khoury, *Haqa'iq lubnaniyyah* [Lebanese Realities] (Beirut, 1960), 1:264.

5. Kamal S. Salibi, *The Modern History of Lebanon* (New York, 1965), pp. 171–88; Walid Khalidi, *Conflict and Violence in Lebanon* (Harvard, 1979), note 27 to chapter 1; Elie Kedourie, *Islam in the Modern World* (New York, 1981), pp. 90–91. Kedourie writes as follows of al-Khoury's decision to enter into the pact:

> This radical departure in Maronite politics, so fraught with dangers and so heavy with future disasters, was undoubtedly effected under British influence. . . . We do not know whether those Maronite leaders who set their community on this perilous path weighed the risks of this adventure, or whether in their eagerness for power they persuaded themselves that General Spears . . . was an immortal god who would forever watch over their welfare.

6. Spears' weekly summary #80, 13 October 1943, FO 371/35182–E 6203/27/89; Helleu to Massigli #1394/CH, 9 October 1943, Alger CFLN-GPRF 999.

7. Spears' weekly political summary #80, supra.

8. Spears' weekly summary #82, FO 371/35182–E 6293/27/89.

9. Spears to FO #573, 14 October 1943, FO 371/35182–E 6214/27/89; Spears to FO #575, 14 October 1943, E 6219.

10. FO minutes and #176 to Spears, FO 371/35183–E 6451/27/89.

11. Spears to FO #588, 26 October 1943, FO 371/35183–E 6451/276/89; see also #599, 26 October, E 6459.

12. Spears to FO #609, 2 November 1943, FO 371/35183–E 6631/27/89.

13. Richard Law's response to a question in Parliament, 27 October 1943, FO 371/35183–E 6555/27/89.

14. Spears' weekly political summary #83, 3 November 1943, FO 371/35183–E 6713/27/89.

15. Beirut to FCNL #1489/CH, 1 November 1943, Alger CFLN-GPRF 999.

16. These two figures were particularly suspected by the French due to their history of involvement in Arab affairs since the Arab Revolt in World War I. Clayton had served as liaison officer in Damascus in 1920, and Newcombe had been an associate of T. E. Lawrence, that archetypal embodiment, in French eyes, of Arabophilism and British expansionism in the Middle East.

17. Helleu to Massigli #1412/CH, 13 October 1943, Alger CFLN-GPRF 999; note from Viénot, 25 October 1943, FO 371/35183–E 6544/27/89; Casey to FO #2461, 1 November 1943, E 6610.

18. See Jean-Baptiste Duroselle, *L'Abîme—1939–1945* (Paris, 1982), pp. 484–85.

19. See Wm. Roger Louis, *Imperialism at Bay* (Oxford, 1978), chapters 11, 14 and *passim* for a discussion of the British response to the American critique of imperialism.

20. For an analysis of Pleven's views see FO minutes, November 1943, FO 371/35183–E 6736/27/89. For de Gaulle's outlook, see D. Bruce Marshall, *The French Colonial Myth and Constitution-Making in the Fourth Republic* (New Haven: Yale, 1973), p. 100:

> At no time did he imagine France at the center of a network of autonomous states bound together in the fashion of the British Commonwealth, only by ties of economic interest, culture and tradition. Instead, his attitude took for granted the universalistic ideas of equality and liberty that bind citizens within the historic community of the nation. Where cultural differences and economic conditions made such links inadequate, it was necessary to supplement them with administrative controls and, in some cases, with the use of force.

21. Pierre Rondot, *The Changing Patterns of the Middle East, 1919–1958* (New York, 1961), pp. 97–99. See Robert Montagne, "French Policy in North Africa and in Syria," *International Affairs*, 16, no. 2 (March/April 1937): 263–79; Robert Montagne, "La politique de la Grande-Bretagne dans les 'pays arabes'," *Politique étrangère*, (November 1946), 2:498–514. On page 265 of the first article, Montagne writes:

> Because of his Latin origins the Frenchman always feels himself something of a missionary. He must teach the world, or show it what he believes to be the truth, his truth.

22. Note from Boegner to Helleu, 20 October 1943 and Helleu to FCNL #1453/CH, 23 October 1943, Alger CFLN-GPRF 999.

23. Casey to FO #298, 16 October 1943, FO 371/35182–E 6220/27/89.

24. Spears to FO #582, 16 October 1943, FO 371/35182–E 6250/27/89.

25. See political report by Chataigneau for Massigli, 1 November 1943, Alger CFLN-GPRF 1005.

26. Note from Catroux to Massigli, 8 November 1943, Alger CFLN-GPRF 1005.

27. Benoist to de Gaulle and Massigli, #222, 23 October 1943, Alger CFLN-GPRF 999.

28. Ibid.

29. Note by Catroux for Massigli, 8 November 1943, Alger CFLN-GPRF 1005.

30. The series of documents entitled "Séances du CFLN" consists of nothing but lists of official decisions by the committee without any record of the deliberations that led up to those decisions.

31. Spears to FO #578, 16 October 1943, FO 371/35182–E 6222/27/89; Spears to FO #619, 5 November 1943, FO 371/35183–E 6710/27/89; Wadsworth to S. of S. #302, 5 November 1943, *FRUS* 4 (1943):1001; Chataigneau's report on the November crisis, 9 December 1943 and FCNL to Beirut #521, 16 December 1943, Alger CFLN-GPRF 1000. By mistake, the November 5 communiqué was issued in the name of the FCNL itself rather than that of the General Delegation as had been intended.

32. Spears to FO #620, 6 November 1943, FO 371/35183–E 6733/27/89; Spears' #627, 8 November 1943, E 6776; Spears' #628, 8 November, E 6811; Wadsworth to S. of S. #305, 8 November 1943 and #306, 9 November 1943, *FRUS* 4 (1943):1003–6.

33. Wadsworth's #306, supra.

34. Spears to FO #628, 8 November 1943, FO 371/35183–E 6811/27/89.

35. Wadsworth to S. of S. #309, 10 November 1943 and Kirk (Cairo) to S. of S. #2032, 11 November 1943, *FRUS* 4 (1943):1009–11; Spears to FO #636, 10 November 1943, FO 371/35183–E 6830/27/89; Spears to FO #637 and #638, 11 November 1943, FO 371/35184–E 6848/27/89; Helleu to Algiers #1525/CH, 11 November 1943, Alger CFLN-GPRF 1575; Sir Edward L. Spears, *Fulfilment of a Mission* (London, 1977), pp. 224–27; Howard Sachar, *Europe Leaves the Middle East, 1936–1954* (New York, 1972), pp. 304–5. The pro-British Lépissier and Colonel Gennardi were placed under house arrest at this time (Spears to FO #708, 18 November 1943, FO 371/35188–E 7132/27/89).

36. The head of the British Security Mission in the Levant was convinced that Spears could easily have restrained the Lebanese had he wanted to: "I consider Spears at least 75% responsible for all the trouble here" (MEC, Coghill Diary, 28 November 1943).

37. See Helleu, letter to *Le Figaro*, 20/21 October 1951. In the 17 October issue, Catroux had written:

> I must say explicitly that the Delegate General carries the entire responsibility for these decisions, of which the Algiers Committee was informed only by the Reuters dispatches which arrived before the official reports from Beirut.

(I wish to thank Dr. Henri Lerner for drawing my attention to these letters.)

38. George Kirk, *The Middle East in the War* (Oxford, 1953), p. 279, note 2.

39. Catroux to Algiers #392–399, 17 November 1943, Alger CFLN-GPRF 1575. See also Macmillan's report on a conversation with Catroux in which the latter assessed Helleu's behavior in the following terms: "Being a man without character, weak and given to strong drink he probably misinterpreted a general statement of support which he had received from De Gaulle" (Macmillan to FO #2540, 1 December 1943, FO 371/35194–E 7582/27/89).

40. Catroux to Algiers #392–399, supra.

41. "Note circulaire pour diffusion générale" by General de Lavalade, 2 December 1943, Alger CFLN-GPRF 1000.

42. Ibid. See also Spears to FO #642, 11 November 1943, FO 371/35184–E 6857/27/89.

43. The head of the Phalangists, Pierre Gemayel, was later to tell a Jewish Agency

representative that, while he regretted the outcome of the Novembver 1943 crisis, he had felt obliged to throw his party's support behind the anti-French movement for fear of losing political ground to other groupings (letter from Hadad [Beirut], 25 December 1943, CZA, S25/5577). Maxime Rodinson recalls that the anti-British broadcasts by French radio in Beirut during the first days of the crisis reminded him of the German propaganda directed at French troops from behind the Siegfried Line during the Phony War (interview with Prof. Maxime Rodinson, Paris, 2 May 1985).

44. Spears to FO #651, 12 November 1943, FO 371/35184–E 6905/27/89; Spears to FO #654 and #655, 12 November 1943, E 6907; Hadad's "Letter from Beirut no. 2" (English version), 26 November 1943, CZA, S25/5577; Spears, *Fulfilment,* chapter 17.

45. Commander-in-chief Middle East to WO #5342, 13 November 1943, FO 371/35186–E 7004/27/89; Hadad's "Letter from Beirut no. 2," supra. William McGaffin of the Associated Press informed U.S. military intelligence that "the Spears Mission, on more than one occasion, assisted American correspondents in circumventing French censorship, thereby enabling them to send out much fuller accounts" (Cairo military intelligence report #12385, 5 January 1944, NA, OSS 226/53729). One hundred and seventeen casualties resulted from Franco–Lebanese confrontations according to the official Lebanese report published in April 1944, not more than 140 as Spears had reported (minutes by Stewart and Hankey, 24 April 1944, FO 371/40111–E 2299/20/88).

46. U.S. military intelligence report #12313, 31 December 1943, based on observations of Donald MacKenzie of the *New York Daily News,* NA, OSS 226/53572. Spears also had motorcyclists cross the Palestine frontier to deliver news accounts to a radio station that he had established some time earlier as a provision for just such a situation. The station's broadcasts were directed at Cairo, as a means of maintaining communications in case the French blocked all other means of contact; however, the broadcasts were also picked up by the Lebanese public, which was informed of the correct radio frequency by advertisements placed in newspapers by the Spears Mission (Spears, *Fulfilment,* p. 229). This was in addition to the inflammatory critiques of French policy which were regularly broadcast by the Arabic-language Jaffa radio during the crisis (Richard Pearse, *Three Years in the Levant* [London, 1949], pp. 73–74).

47. Memorandum of 15 November 1943, FO 898/197.

48. Casey to FO #2558, 11 November 1943, FO 371/35184–E 6881/27/89; Casey Diary extracts, 11 November 1943, MEC, Spears Papers III/4.

49. Wadsworth to S. of S. #327, 22 November 1943, NA, SD 890E.00/255.

50. Casey to FO via Mideast Command to Air Ministry #KK/138, 11 November 1943, FO 371/35184–E 6881/27/89.

51. Ibid., FO to Casey #3548, 12 November 1943.

52. Ibid., minute by Peterson.

53. Spears to FO #654 and #655, 12 November 1943, FO 371/35184–E 6907/27/89; FO to Spears #528, 13 November 1943, FO 371/35185–E 6913/27/89; Spears to FO #674, 14 November 1943, FO 371/35186–E 6972/27/89; Spears to FO #675, 14 November 1943, E 6973; MEC, Coghill Diary, note 50. When the French launched a brief attack against Arslan's stronghold, the Foreign Office did authorize Spears to give refuge to the two ministers at the British Legation in Beirut; however, they decided not to leave after Catroux, just arrived in Beirut, called off the attack (Spears to FO #688, #692 and #693, 16 November 1943, FO 371/35187–E 7052/27/89; Spears to FO #522, 17 November 1943, E 7096).

54. Spears to Fo #661, 13 November 1943, FO 371/35185–E 6948/27/89; FO correspondence with Cairo, Jedda, and Baghdad, 12–13 November 1943, E 6929, E 6932, E

6933 and E 6934; Shone (Cairo) to FO #2143, 12 November 1943, FO 371/35184–E 6873/27/89; Cornwallis (Baghdad) to FO #1085, 15 November 1943, FO 371/35186–E 7014/27/89; Spears, *Fulfilment,* pp. 241–43.

55. WM (43) 153rd meeting, minute 1, 12 November 1943, CAB 65/36. Macmillan was actually in southern Italy during the first few days of the crisis, leaving his deputy Makins to deal with the FCNL.

56. Ibid., WM (43) 154th meeting, minute 2, 15 November 1943.

57. Copy of Churchill's #504 to Roosevelt of 13 November 1943 as included in FO to Halifax (Washington) #7829, 13 November 1943, FO 371/35188–E 7116/27/89.

58. Halifax to FO #5175, 15 November 1943, FO 371/35186–E 7032/27/89.

59. Viénot to FCNL #1319–1320, 20 November 1943, Alger CFLN-GPRF 1000.

60. Memorandum by Paul Alling, 12 November 1943, NA, SD 890.E.00/228.

61. S. of S. to Wadsworth #269, 12 November 1943 and S. of S. to Wiley #2139, 12 November, *FRUS* 4 (1943):1022; see also Duroselle, *L'Abîme,* pp. 490–91.

62. Makins (Algiers) to FO #2373, 16 November 1943, FO 371/35187–E 7079/27/89; Makins to FO #2341, 14 November 1943, FO 371/35185–E 6953/27/89; Viénot (London) to FCNL #1240–1241, 16 November 1943, Alger CFLN-GPRF 999.

63. Charles de Gaulle, *Mémoires de Guerre* 2: (Paris, 1956) 148–49 and 547–48.

64. Report from Murphy via Wiley's #1990, 13 November 1943, *FRUS* 4 (1943): 1026–27.

65. Casey to FO #2540, 13 November 1943, FO 371/35185–E 6926/27/89; Casey (from Beirut) to FO via Spears' #667, 14 November 1943, E 6963 and #668, 14 November 1943, E 6967.

66. Casey to FO #2593, 15 November 1943, FO 371/35186–E 7010/27/89 and #2598, 15 November, # 7012.

67. Spears to FO #689, 16 November 1943, FO 371/35187–E 7050/27/89.

68. Harold Macmillan, *War Diaries—The Mediterranean, 1943–1945* (London, 1984), 17 November 1943.

69. Ibid., 16 November 1943.

70. Ibid., 19 November 1943.

71. FO to Casey #3621 and #3623, 17 November 1943 and minutes by Peterson and R. M. A. Hankey, FO 371/35187–E 7102/27/89; WM (43) 156th meeting, minute 3, 17 November 1943, CAB 65/36.

72. Records of discussions among Peterson, Hankey; and Calthrope, 19 November– 5 December 1943, FO 371/35213–E 7441/ and 7653/2154/89.

73. Ibid., minute by Hankey.

74. Spears to FO #704, 18 November 1943, FO 371/35188–E 7111/27/89.

75. Casey to FO #2624, 18 November 1943, FO 371/35188–E 7119/27/89.

76. WM (43) 157th meeting, 18 November 1943, CAB 65/36; Casey Diary, 19 and 27 November 1943, MEC, Spears Papers III/4. See also the minute by Peterson entitled "The French Case in Lebanon," which argues that the French would not have been criticized if they had restricted their action to the dissolution of the Lebanese Parliament. Alexander Cadogan indicated his full agreement with this analysis in FO 371/35189–E 7183/27/89.

77. Casey to FO via Spears' #717 and #718, 19 November 1943 and Casey to FO #2644, 21 November 1943, FO 371/35188–E 7160/27/89.

78. Dispatch from de Gaulle to Catroux, 13 November 1943, de Gaulle, *Mémoires de Guerre,* 2:597; Macmillan to FO #2409 and #2410, 19 November 1943, FO 371/ 35188–E 7155/27/89.

79. Telegram from de Gaulle to Helleu, 13 November 1943, de Gaulle, *Mémoires de Guerre*, 2:598.

80. Helleu to de Gaulle #1601/CH, #1602/CH and #1606/CH (18 November 1943), Helleu to FCNL #428–429 (18 November 1943) and Helleu to de Gaulle #1672/CH (19 November 1943), Alger CFLN-GPRF 1575; memorandum sent by Helleu to Massigli, 19 November 1943, Alger CFLN-GPRF 1000.

81. Spears to FO #702, 17 November 1943, FO 371/35187–E 7109/27/89; Catroux to de Gaulle, 19 November 1943, de Gaulle, *Mémoires de Guerre*, 2:599.

82. Macmillan to FO #2417, 19 November 1943, FO 371/35189–E 7165/27/89; Macmillan to FO #2432, 20 November 1943, FO 371/35190–E 7190/27/89.

83. Minute by Eden and FO to Algiers #2721, 20 November 1943, FO 371/35190–E 7190/27/89.

84. Macmillan to FO #2433, 20 November 1943, FO 371/35190–E 7204/27/89.

85. FO to Macmillan #2744, 21 November 1943, FO 371/35190–E 7194/27/89; WM (43) 159th meeting, 21 November 1943, CAB 65/36.

86. Wadsworth to S. of S. #327, 22 November 1943, *FRUS* 4 (1943:1040–43).

87. FO to Macmillan #2761, 23 November 1943, FO 371/35190–E 7248/27/89; WM (43) 160th meeting, minute 4, 22 November 1943, CAB 65/36.

88. Spears to FO #723, 21 November 1943, FO 371/35189–E 7191/27/89; Catroux to FCNL #456–461, 20 November 1943 and Catroux to de Gaulle #1635/CH, 21 November 1943, Alger CFLN-GPRF 1005; Catroux to FCNL #481–482, 22 November 1943, Alger CFLN-GPRF 1575.

89. See Catroux to de Gaulle #1614, 23 November 1943 and dispatch from Massigli to Chataigneau, 25 November 1943, Alger CFLN-GPRF 1468.

90. Catroux to CFLN #1639/CH, 21 November 1943 and de Gaulle to Helleu #DGH/783, 21 November 1943, Alger CFLN-GPRF 1005.

91. De Gaulle to Catroux #446, 21 November 1943, Alger CFLN-GPRF 1468; also in Charles de Gaulle, *Lettres, notes et carnets, Juin 1943–Mai 1945*, (Paris, 1983), 3:113–14.

92. Unnumbered telegram from de Gaulle to Catroux, 22 November 1943, Alger CFLN-GPRF 1468; also in de Gaulle, *Lettres, 1943–1945*, 3:114–15).

93. Catroux to FCNL #488–491, 22 November 1943, Alger CFLN-GPRF 1575; see also Spears to FO #735, 22 November 1943, FO 371/35191–E 7252/27/89.

94. Catroux to de Gaulle #1614/CH, 23 November 1943, Alger CFLN-GPRF 1468.

95. Catroux to FCNL #497–498 and #500–501, 23 November 1943, Alger CFLN-GPRF 1575.

96. Personal letter from Massigli conveyed to Catroux by Ostorog, 25 November 1943, Alger CFLN-GPRF 1468; see also Massigli to Catroux #454, 24 November 1943, Alger CFLN-GPRF 1578.

97. Massigli to Catroux #451, 23 November 1943, Alger CFLN-GPRF 1578.

98. Catroux to FCNL #502, 24 November 1943, Alger CFLN-GPRF 1575; Spears to FO #761, 24 November 1943, FO 371/35192–E 7347/27/89; Macmillan to FO #2463 (copy to Spears), 23 November 1943, FO 371/35191–E 7299/27/89. In his #2470 (24 November 1943, FO 371/35192–E 7319), Macmillan reported:

Most interesting immediate feature in the picture is a further defeat of de Gaulle. Massigli says that he feels the difference between his almost dictatorial authority a few months ago and the present situation. The new members of the

Cabinet [that is, FCNL] are much more independent-minded than the old and the new assembly is confronting de Gaulle who has no Parliamentary experience with a new problem.

99. Massigli to Catroux #442, 23 November 1943, Alger CFLN-GPRF 1468.

100. Spears to FO #745, 24 November 1943, FO 371/35192–E 7324/27/89.

Chapter 9

1. U.S. military intelligence report #11879, 4 December 1943, NA, OSS 226/52142.

2. Although the British ultimatum had not been issued publicly, and the FCNL had ostensibly acted on its own in restoring the Lebanese government, the substance of the British role in the affair was soon a matter of common knowledge.

3. Spears to FO #789, 30 November 1943, FO 371/35194–E 7555/27/89; Spears to FO #778, 28 November 1943, FO 371/35193–E 7486/27/89.

4. Note by Meyrier, 6 December 1943, Guerre 1939–1945, Alger CFLN-GPRF 1006; CFLN instructions on Levant policy, 8 December 1943, Alger CFLN-GPRF 1000. Chataigneau, writing in support of Catroux's views, argued that before long, the Maronites in Lebanon, as well as other regional minorities, would turn back to France out of fear of Muslim intolerance and pan-Arab nationalism. Given a liberal policy, France could exploit these sectarian tensions to restore her position (Chataigneau to Massigli, 29 November 1943, Alger CFLN-GPRF 1000).

5. Spears to FO #774, 27 November 1943, FO 371/35193–E 7445/17/89.

6. FO to Spears #596, 28 November 1943, FO 371/35192–E 7319/27/89.

7. Harold Macmillan, *War Diaries—The Mediterranean 1943–1945* (London, 1984), 26 November 1943.

8. Ibid.

9. Ibid.

10. Ibid., 27 November 1943. In fact, Macmillan remained at his post.

11. Spears to FO #784, 30 November 1943, FO 371/35194–E 7564/27/89.

12. Ibid. In the margin next to this passage, Hankey commented: "Like Zionist propaganda."

13. Spears to FO #787, 2 December 1943, FO 371/35194–E 7594/27/89.

14. Catroux to FCNL #533, 27 November 1943, Alger CFLN-GPRF 1005.

15. Macmillan to FO #2540, 1 December 1943, FO 371/35194–E 7582/27/89; note by Meyrier, 6 December 1943, Alger CFLN-GPRF 1006.

16. FCNL instructions on Levant policy, 8 December 1943, Alger CFLN-GPRF 1000.

17. Ibid.

18. Casey to FO #2756, 6 December 1943, FO 371/35194–E 7647/27/89; Spears' dispatch #82, 10 December 1943, FO 371/35196–E 8103/27/89; Spears to FO #844, 19 December 1943, FO 371/35196–E 7959/17/89; Spears to FO #855, 24 December 1943, E 8054; Spears' weekly political summary #90, 22 December 1943, FO 371/40299–E 98/23/89. For the texts of the power-transfer agreements, see Albert Hourani, *Syria and Lebanon, A Political Essay* (Oxford, 1946), pp. 381–84.

19. Record of Cairo meeting including Spears, Eden, Cadogan, Lampson, and Casey, 7 December 1943, MEC, Spears Papers III/4; Macmillan, *War Diaries*, 7 December 1943; memorandum by Moyne, 9 December 1943, P. (M) (43) 27, CAB 95/14; Macmillan to FO #2623, 10 December 1943, FO 371/35195–E 7772/27/89; Spears to

FO #839, 17 December 1943, E 7945. The Foreign Office decision to push for the negotiation of Franco–Levantine treaties during wartime was approved by the prime minister (see minutes by R. M. A. Hankey, 3 and 11 December 1943, FO 371/35194–E 7564/17/89).

20. The Spears Mission's resentment at what was seen as London's pro-French tilt was encapsulated in a minute by Lascelles, written about a dispatch Baxter had sent to Spears reiterating Britain's continued recognition of the French mandate:

> This dispatch can only be described as a Papal Bullock. Its forepart is marked "UNQUESTIONABLE DOGMA"; and—since it has been well said that there is no dogma without its stigma—its hinder part is marked "Charles Baxter." . . .

> The only logical inference . . . would seem to be that any group of Frenchmen whom we for our own purposes had chosen to recognise as allies would ipso facto have been entitled to exercise the mandate in the Levant on behalf of the French State. The Free French in the early days were only a few thousand strong, but numbers and importance apparently make no difference to the principles involved. Had the Count of Paris and his valet been the only Frenchmen to rally to our cause we should, I suppose, have been obliged to instal them in the Levant as the MANDATORY AUTHORITY. No formal recognition, it is to be noted, would have been required for this mere "change in the organs of government": the fact that *we* recognised the count as "exercising governmental functions" over Pondicherry, Chandergore, etc. would have been quite sufficient (Lascelles' 5 February 1944 minute on Baxter's despatch #7, 12 January 1944, FO 226/252–27/14/44).

21. Undated memorandum by Catroux (presumably written in December 1943), Alger CFLN-GPRF 1005.

22. Catroux to de Lavalade, 26 December 1943, Alger CFLN-GPRF 1001.

23. Dispatch from Spears to Eden #83 (enclosing copy of *En Route*), 14 December 1943, FO 371/36109–Z 12677/12677/17.

24. Ibid.

25. Report by Oliva-Roget, 18 December 1943, Alger CFLN-GPRF 1006.

26. See, for example, dispatch from Viénot (London) to Massigli (reporting on conversation with Monsieur Tallec, just arrived from Beirut), 21 December 1943, Guerre CFLN-GPRF 1000; see also unsigned, undated report to Catroux, Londres C.N.F. 42, complaining that *Services Spéciaux* officers are forced to spend too much of their time monitoring the activities of their English colleagues. Lebanese and Syrians observed in the company of British officers were regularly blacklisted. The British were, of course, perfectly aware that their movements were being reported, and delighted in confusing the informers (see Richard Pearse [a British Field Security Officer in Syria], *Three Years in the Levant* [London, 1949], pp. 200–1 and 261–62).

27. OSS report from Cairo #G-7633, 12 May 1945, NA, OSS 226/L56530. Sir Richard Beaumont, British vice-consul in Damascus during the war, characterizes French suspicions of Altounyan and Stirling as absurd, arguing that both these men were "over the hill" by the 1940s (interview with Sir Richard Beaumont, London, 27 August 1987). Lascelles appears to have had a similar view, as seen in his memorandum of 6 January 1943, which maliciously parodied a letter in which Altounyan had offered Spears his advice on how to arrange the Syrian elections (FO 226/240–9/3/43 and 9/4/43).

28. MEC, Coghill Diary, notes #23, #24, and #64; Lyttelton to CO via Lampson's

#2364, 29 July 1941, FO 371/27303–E 4248/62/89; SIME/009/104, 11 March 1944, FO 921/177–22 (6). The French security service reported in August 1944 that officers in the Syrian police and gendarmerie were in the pay of Coghill's BSM (report by *Sûreté aux Armées,* Damascus, 4 August 1944, Alger CFLN-GPRF 1003).

29. Interview with Richard Usborne (London, 12 January 1985).

30. Shlomo Kostika's Diary, undated entries describing "Ha-tochnit ha-surit" (the Syrian Plan), Haganah Archive, Tel-Aviv; Zerubavel Gil'ad, ed., *Magen be-Seter* [Secret Defense] (Jerusalem, 1952), pp. 154–65. The SOE kept the existence of this network secret from the French. Yerucham Cohen, a member of the *Haganah* network in Lebanon, describes being mistaken for an Axis agent by French security and jailed for weeks before his British contacts managed to get him out, claiming he was a deserter from the British army. His new cover was so convincing that the mandatory authorities in Palestine imprisoned him again before the matter was finally cleared up (interview with Yerucham Cohen, Tel-Aviv, June 1985). The French actually set up an anti-German sabotage network of their own that included Jews recruited from Palestine (MEC, Coghill Diary, note #31; SIME/009/104, 11 March 1944, FO 921/177–22 [6]).

31. See for instance, report by *Sûreté aux Armées* (7 August 1944, Alger CFLN-GPRF 1003) regarding the remarks of Captain Nairn, the British political officer in Sidon, in conversation with notables of Nabatiyeh, to the effect that the Levant would be included in a post-war Arab federation.

32. "Note d'information de la section politique," Damascus Delegation, 9 August 1944, Alger CFLN-GPRF 1003.

33. Political report from Beynet to Massigli, 22 August 1944, Alger CFLN-GPRF 1003. In his memoirs, Stirling gives vent to his resentment of the Free French presence in Syria, while claiming to have scrupulously avoided provoking the Arabs against them:

> Had I wanted to I could so very easily have stirred up the Arabs to revolt against the continued domination of France; but I steadily adhered to the policy laid down by my chief, General Spears. No action of mine ever harmed the relations between the Arabs and the French (Lt.-Col. W. F. Stirling, *Safety Last* [London, 1953], p. 221).

As far as the French were concerned, of course, the problem lay precisely in the loyal adherence of Stirling and his colleagues to Spears' policy.

34. Beaumont traces Oliva-Roget's hostility toward him to the following incident: After the reinstatement of the Lebanese government, a cheering crowd gathered in front of the British consulate in Damascus. The British consul, new at his post, asked Beaumont whether or not he should step out onto the balcony to greet the people. Beaumont encouraged him to do so "by all means." Within minutes, Oliva-Roget was on the phone to complain about the disloyalty of this action; Beaumont simply told him: "Je ne dois pas vous rendre compte. C'est votre préoccupation" (interview with Sir Richard Beaumont, London, 27 August 1987).

35. See Pearse, *Three Years,* pp. 11–12.

36. Report by Oliva-Roget, op. cit.; see also Chataigneau's summary of the report as sent to Massigli, 21 December 1943, Alger CFLN-GPRF 1000.

37. Report by the political service of the General Delegation, Tyre branch, 6 September 1944 (summarizing conversation between Major Altounyan and the French political officer in Tyre), Alger CFLN-GPRF 1003.

38. Report #543 to U.S. military intelligence by Duncan MacBryde, the assistant military attaché in Beirut, detailing his conversation with the chief of the British

military liaison unit to French GHQ in the Levant, 28 July 1944, NA, OSS 266/87731. For background on Lt.-Col. Alessandri, see FO record of London discussion among Spears, Casey, and Massigli, 15 July 1943, FO 371/35179–E 4286/27/89. The British files on "Colonel Alessandri and the Bureau Noir" (listed under FO 371/40349 ff.) remain classified. The French archives, of course, contain no mention of the subject. Alessandri was either removed from the scene or instructed to freeze his operations at the end of 1944 when the French became aware that British intelligence was investigating the matter (dispatch from Shone to Baxter, 20 January 1945 and minute by Baxter, FO 371/45612–E 778/778/89); see also Pearse, *Three Years*, p. 197.

39. Spears to FO #13 SAVING, 21 February 1944, FO 371/40300–E 1490/23/89; Spears to Eden dispatch #15, 25 February 1944, E 1553/23/89; minute by Peterson, E 1595; Spears' weekly political summary #100, 1 March 1944, E 1674; Spears to FO #114, 3 March 1944, FO 371/40310–E 1458/217/89; Spears to FO #129, 8 March 1944, FO 371/40311–E 1458/217/89; Spears to FO #134, 9 March 1944, E 1620; SIME/009/ 104, 11 March 1944, FO 921/177–22 (6).

40. Report by American naval liaison officer in Beirut, 30 December 1943, NA, OSS 226/55187; report #350 by Major Virgil Jackson (U.S. military attaché in Beirut), 3 March 1944, NA, OSS 226/63603. The *Cagoule* was a conspiratorial, right-wing, antirepublican organization that had gained some adherents in French government, military, and police circles during the turbulent 1930s.

41. Spears to FO #128, 8 March 1944, FO 371/40300–E 1568/23/89.

42. Chataigneau to Massigli #292, 5 March 1944 and dispatch from Ostorog to de Guiringaud (Algiers), 28 February 1944, Alger CFLN-GPRF 1001.

43. Report #14605 furnished to OSS on "Views of U.S.A. representative [in Lebanon]," 4 January 1945, NA, OSS 226/58212. Spears actually claimed to have sought to tone down the language of the Levant governments' *démarches* over the Beynet issue. Wadsworth was rebuked by the State Department after a French protest over his behavior (dispatch from Ostorog to de Guiringaud, 23 March 1944, Alger CFLN-GPRF 1001).

44. Egyptian consul to Cairo, 8 March 1944 and marginalia by Free French authorities, Alger CFLN-GPRF 1001.

45. Chataigneau to Massigli #275/CH, 2 March 1944 and Massigli to Chataigneau #220, 4 March 1944, Alger CFLN-GPRF 1001.

46. Chataigneau to Massigli #296 and #298/CH, 7 March 1944, FCNL cable to Beynet canceled by de Gaulle, Beirut to FCNL #319/CH, 10 March 1944, Alger CFLN-GPRF 1001; Spears to FO #13 SAVING, 21 February 1944, FO 371/40300–E 1490/23/89; Spears to FO #133, 9 March 1944, E 1610; Cooper (Algiers) to FO #346, 16 March 1944 and #381, 28 March 1944, E 1774; see also "Instruction secrete fixant les attributions militaires de général d'armée Beynet," Algiers, 11 May 1944, Alger CFLN-GPRF 1002. The trouble over Beynet's appointment had provoked the passage of a resolution by the French Consultative Assembly in Algiers calling for a suspension of the appointment until the assembly had had a chance to debate it in full. De Gaulle had responded characteristically by rejecting the notion that the assembly had any business meddling in executive affairs (resolution by the Provisional Consultative Assembly and note by de Gaulle, 3 March 1944, Alger CFLN-GPRF 1001).

47. See chapter 6 in this book.

48. Chataigneau to Massigli #34/CH (10 January 1944), dispatch from Chataigneau to Massigli (25 January 1944) and Viénot to Massigli Diplo/1232 (9 March 1944), Alger CFLN-GPRF 1001; Beynet to FCNL #460/CH, 16 April 1944, Alger CFLN-GPRF 1002; Albert Hourani, *Syria and Lebanon*, pp. 288–91. Repeated French demands for

inclusion in the MESC were dismissed out of hand by the Foreign Office on the grounds that the supplies and shipping facilities controlled by the council were exclusively British and American (note from FCNL to FO, 20 May 1944 and FO minutes, FO 371/40336–E 3479/3479/89). The head of the Spears Mission's Economic Section hoped to see to it that the Supervisory Council gave Britain the sort of grip on the Levant economy that the French had enjoyed through control of the Common Interests. The MESC favored greater participation by the Syrian and Lebanese governments, for fear that an anti-British backlash might otherwise result (report by John Bennet [of the MESC] after late February 1944 trip to the Levant, FO 922/202–GO/822).

49. Syrian Interior Minister Lutfi al-Haffar told Eliahu Sasson of the Jewish Agency that the British were actually pressing his government to take over functions from the French faster than it could handle. He added that the Syrian leadership had no illusions about British motives, and was convinced that the British were ingratiating themselves with the Levant governments only as a means of integrating the states into their regional sphere of influence (memorandum by E. Sasson, 7 March 1944, reporting on second conversation with Lutfi al-Haffar, BGA, Section 3 papers).

50. A majority of the *troupes spéciales* consisted either of members of minority groups or of Sunnis from rural regions. These were the people least responsive to the nationalist ideology of the urban-based, National Bloc, and the Bloc's leaders feared that the *troupes spéciales* might yet be used against them by the French (Asher Susser, "Western Power Rivalry and its Interaction with Local Politics in the Levant, 1941–1946" [Ph.D. diss. Tel-Aviv University, 1986], pp. 503–4).

51. Holmes to WO #5388, 4 January 1944, FO 371/40310–E 217/217/89; Cooper to FO #139, 26 January 1944, E 612; Spears to FO #46, 28 January 1944, E 656; M.I.2 (WO) to FO, 28 January 1944, summarizing Franco–British staff talks in Levant, E 668; Spears' weekly summary #94, 19 January 1944, FO 371/40299–E 764/23/89; Spears' weekly summary #98, 16 February 1944, FO 371/40300–E 1483/23/89; Spears' weekly summary #99, 23 February 1944, E 1487; dispatch from Catroux to de Gaulle, 28 January 1944, Alger CFLN-GPRF 1001.

52. Dispatch from Catroux to de Gaulle, 28 January 1944, Alger CFLN-GPRF 1001.

53. Spears to FO #108, 28 February 1944, FO 371/40310–E 1357/217/89.

54. Spears to FO #201, 11 April 1944, FO 371/40311–E 2259/217/89.

55. "Direction Générale des Services Spéciaux: Bulletin de Renseignement," 11 September 1944, Alger CFLN-GPRF 1002.

56. See Itamar Rabinovich, "The Compact Minorities and the Syrian State, 1918–1945," *Journal of Contemporary History,* 14, no. 4 (1979), pp. 693–712; also Albert Hourani, *Syria and Lebanon,* p. 289.

57. British Security Mission report, 26 May 1944, FO 684/15 (I); report by *Sûreté aux Armées,* Damascus, 31 May 1944, Alger CFLN-GPRF 1002.

58. Report from Furlonge to Spears, 4 March 1944, FO 226/252–27/36/44 and *passim;* dispatch from Spears to Eden, 12 April 1944, FO 371/40301–E 2451/23/89; Beynet to Massigli #388/CH, 25 March 1944, Alger CFLN-GPRF 1001.

59. Spears saw the signs of a renewed Franco–Maronite flirtation as resulting from fears that Lebanon would be handed back to unrestricted French control after the war:

> Most of . . . [the Maronites] know perfectly well that a completely independent Lebanon unprotected by any great power is ridiculous, but few of them would willingly return to being dominated by the French. On the other hand, if it were compatible with British policy and if we could state this, they would be only too

glad to have the same sort of relations with Great Britain as Transjordan will have when the Mandate is surrendered, and they might even wish for far more help, advice and even interference than would be acceptable, for instance, to the Iraqis (memorandum by Spears, 17 June 1944, FO 226/252–27/97/44.)

60. Kamal S. Salibi, *The Modern History of Lebanon* (New York, 1965), pp. 112–14.

61. Political report from Beynet to Massigli (27 April 1944), Beynet to Massigli #501/CH (28 April 1944), Massigli to Beynet #421 (2 May 1944), Alger CFLN-GPRF 1006; Spears to FO #230, 27 April 1944, FO 371/40111–E 2599/20/88.

62. Beynet to Massigli #501/CH (28 April 1944), #513/CH (30 April 1944), #518/CH (1 May 1944), unnumbered telegram from Beynet to Massigli (5 May 1944) and memorandum on political situation in Lebanon (25 May 1944), Alger CFLN-GPRF 1006; Spears to FO #239, 30 April 1944, FO 371/40111–E 2655/20/88; Cooper to FO #508, 1 May 1944 and FO to Cooper #429, 3 May 1944, E 2704; Cooper to FO #529, 5 May 1944, E 2770; Spears to FO #255, 5 May 1944, E 2762. In the end, fourteen of the antigovernment demonstrators were sentenced to terms of no more than two years each by a Lebanese court. The man responsible for shooting the French soldier turned out to be an Egyptian journalist associated with the Arab nationalist movement. At the time of his arrest in Beirut in August he was in the car of the U.S. consul to Damascus (although not necessarily with the latter's knowledge). A French military court later sentenced him to a mere sixteen months in prison (Vaux [Cairo] to FCNL #289, 3 May 1944 and Beynet to Algiers #869/CH, 14 August 1944, Alger CFLN-GPRF 1006; Spears' weekly political summary #119, 12 July 1944, FO 371/40301–E 4384/23/89; Beirut report #G-6850, 2 January 1945, NA, OSS 226/109877). In mid-May, the Lebanese government was alerted yet again to the possibility of a coup attempt by right-wing French officers, but nothing came of it (report #G-3459, 18 May 1944 and #G-3837, 9 June 1944, NA, OSS 226/74619 and /78687, respectively).

63. FO to Spears #130 (transmitting message from P.M.), 10 March 1944, MEC, Spears Papers II/7.

64. Minute from Eden to P.M., 19 March 1944, PREM 3–423/15.

65. Ibid., minute from P.M. to Eden, 2 April 1944.

66. Duff Cooper, *Old Men Forget* (London, 1954), pp. 322–23.

67. Dispatch from Cooper (Algiers) to Eden, 22 May 1944, PREM 3–423/15.

68. Ibid., minute from P.M. to Eden, 11 June 1944.

69. Spears' weekly political summary #114, 7 June 1944, FO 371/40301–E 3604/23/89; weekly summary #116, 21 June 1944, E 3987; Spears to FO #37, 24 June 1944, FO 371/40312–E 3738/217/89. The offer of 7,000 rifles came in response to a Syrian request for only 1,000 (minute by Peterson, FO 371/40313–E 4175/217/89).

70. Beynet to Massigli, political report on Syria (sent before confirmation of the British decision), 14 June 1944, Alger CFLN-GPRF 1002.

71. Cooper to FO #1192, 22 June 1944, FO 371/40313–E 3888/217/89.

72. Cooper to FO #24 SAVING, 3 July 1944, FO 371/40313–E 4057/217/89.

73. Spears' weekly political summary #117, 28 June 1944, FO 371/40301–E 4059/23/89. The Soviets established diplomatic relations in August 1944. Formal U.S. recognition of Syrian and Lebanese independence came one month later.

74. Eden to Cooper #259, 29 June 1944, FO 371/40312–E 3880/217/89; Spears to FO #394, 3 July 1944, FO 371/40313–E 3893/217/89; Cooper to FO #1242, 4 July 1944, E 3903; FO to Spears' #347, 6 July 1944 and minute by Peterson, E 4004; Spears to FO #412, 9 July 1944, E 4050; Spears to FO #420, 12 July 1944 and #423, 14 July 1944 and minutes by Hankey and Peterson, E 4175; Cooper to FO #1287, 14 July

1944, E 4174; FO minutes and FO to Cooper #77 SAVING, 1 August 1944, E 4122; FO minutes, July 1944, FO 371/40314–E 4277/217/89; Moyne to FO #1696, 19 July 1944, E 4308.

75. Note from Eden to P.M., 29 June 1944, FO 371/40313–E 4066/217/89.

76. Beynet to FCNL #763/CH (14 July 1944), note from Massigli to Duff Cooper (15 July 1944), Oliva-Roget (Damascus) to Beynet (18 July 1944) and various other reports from Beirut and Damascus (July 1944), Alger CFLN-GPRF 1002; copy of dispatch from Des Essars to Oliva-Roget (forwarded to Algiers on 1 August 1944) and three unnumbered reports from Beynet to Massigli (8 August 1944), Alger CFLN-GPRF 1003; Spears to FO #454, 24 July 1944, FO 371/40301–E 4412/23/89; Cooper to FO #1343, 28 July 1944, FO 371/40315–E 4476/217/89. The French had tapped many of the Syrian and Lebanese governments' telephone lines, giving them a clear picture of the degree to which the nationwide manifestations of anti-French sentiment were being centrally coordinated.

77. Spears to FO #434, 18 July 1944, FO 371/40314–E 4278/217/89.

78. Ibid., Spears to FO #435, 18 July 1944.

79. Ibid., minute by Hankey and FO to Spears #384, 22 July 1944.

80. FO to Spears #382, 19 July 1944, FO 371/40314–E 4368/217/89. General Holmes was to accompany Spears to London to present the military point of view.

81. Political report from Beynet to Massigli, 28 June 1944, Alger CFLN-GPRF 1002.

82. Chataigneau to Massigli, 12 July 1944 (transmitting report by Oliva-Roget), Alger CFLN-GPRF 1002.

83. Dispatch from Massigli (Algiers) to Viénot (London), 8 July 1944, Alger CFLN-GPRF 1002.

84. Memorandum from Massigli to Viénot, 12 July 1944, Alger CFLN-GPRF 1002.

85. Minute by Hankey, 15 August 1944, FO 371/40302–E 5409/23/89; record of conversation among top French and British officials, 23 August 1944, E 5185; aide-mémoire by Massigli, 24 August 1944, E 5144; letter from Massigli to Eden, 25 August 1944 and minute by Peterson, 28 August 1944, E 5342; FO to Moyne (Cairo) #3033, 30 August 1944, FO 371/40316–E 5207/23/89; minute by Peterson, 30 August 1944, E 5258. De Gaulle expressly ordered Massigli to avoid any direct contact with Spears in London (telegram from de Gaulle [Algiers] to Massigli [London], 25 July 1944, Charles de Gaulle, *Lettres, notes et carnets, Juin 1943–Mai 1945* [Paris, 1983], p. 271).

86. Oddly enough, Beynet reported that MacKereth was one of France's most committed foes in the British foreign service, a "spécialiste de l'action anti-française" (dispatch from Beynet to de Gaulle, 2 June 1944, Alger CFLN-GPRF 1002). For more background on MacKereth, and a compilation of his reports, see Michael G. Fry and Itamar Rabinovich, eds., *Despatches from Damascus: Gilbert MacKereth and British Policy in the Levant, 1933–1939* (Tel Aviv and Southern California, 1985).

87. Minute by Spears on Forester's #5, 21 August 1944, FO 371/40316–E 5105/217/89.

88. See chapter 6 of this book.

89. Dispatch from Beirut Chancery to FO Eastern Department, 10 August 1944, FO 371/40347–E 5186/5178/89; see also dispatch from MacKereth to Baxter, 2 September 1944, FO 371/40302–E 5588/23/89.

90. Minute by Hankey, FO 371/40302–E 5588/23/89.

91. MacKereth to FO #511, 16 August 1944, FO 371/40302–E 4980/23/89; Mac-Kereth to FO #515, 18 August 1944, E 5012; dispatch from MacKereth to Hankey, 29

August 1944, E 5498; Forester (Damascus) to FO #5 (transmitting report from MacKereth), 21 August 1944, FO 371/40316–E 5105/217/89.

92. Correspondence concerning Gilbert MacKereth, September–October 1944, MEC, Spears Papers II A/4; Major-General Sir Edward L. Spears, *Fulfilment of a Mission* (London, 1977), p. 295. MacKereth had sent many of his most incriminating cables by way of the Damascus consulate, so that they would escape the notice of Spears' devoted secretary (and future second wife), Nancy Maurice. When Spears returned to the region, he furiously searched all the Beirut cables for the texts of MacKereth's reports, but did not think of examining the correspondence of the Damascus consulate; hence his charge that some of the telegrams had been hidden (letter to author from Sir Richard Beaumont [who served as British vice-consul in Damascus during this period], April 1987).

93. Note from Eden to Spears, 25 August 1944, FO 371/40302–E 5237/23/89.

94. Extracts from conversation between Spears Eden, 1 September 1944, FO 371/40347–E 5415/5178/89.

95. Letter marked "private and personal" from Spears to Churchill, 2 September 1944, MEC, Spears Papers II/7.

96. Ibid., letter from Churchill to Spears, 3 September 1944.

97. Spears to FO #557, 11 September 1944, FO 371/40302–E 5575/23/89; Spears to FO #572, 14 September 1944, E 5681; Spears to FO #566, 13 September 1944, FO 371/40112–E 5663/20/88; Spears to FO #588, 21 September 1944, E 5811/20/88; Wadsworth to S. of S. #190, 15 September 1944, *FRUS* 5 (1944):777–79. The image that the new British line most readily evoked in Syrian minds was that of the Sykes–Picot agreement of World War I (see Moyne to FO #2264, 30 September 1944, FO 371/40304–E 5999/23/89).

98. Minute by Lawrence on Spears' #557, FO 371/40302–E 5575/23/89.

99. Spears' weekly political summary #130, 27 September 1944, FO 371/40304–E 6155/23/89; Spears to FO #589, 22 September 1944, FO 371/40303–E 5853/23/89; Spears to FO #590, E 5854; Wadsworth to S. of S. #193, 19 September 1944, *FRUS* 5 (1944):780–82. The British embassy in Washington, D.C., eventually managed to induce a reluctant State Department to respond to the Syrian protest by asserting that the United States had no objection to a Franco–Syrian treaty as such (record of conversation between Wright of British embassy and NEA staff, 28 September 1944 and Wadsworth to S. of S. #217, 11 October 1944, *FRUS* 5 (1944):791–92 and 800–1; Halifax to FO #5601, 15 October 1944, FO 371/40305–E 6309/23/89.

100. Eastern Department minutes on Spears' #572, 14 September 1944, FO 371/40302–E 5681/23/98.

101. 25 September 1944 minute by R. M. A. Hankey on Spears' #593 of 23 September, FO 371/40303–E 5827/23/89.

102. Retrospective summary written in January 1945, Spears Levant Diary, MEC, Spears Papers I/1.

103. Spears to FO #604, 25 September 1944 and minute by Eden, FO 371/40304–E 5887/23/89; FO to Spears #565, 2 October 1944, E 5900.

104. Minutes from Churchill to Eden, 27 September and 2 October 1944, FO 371/40303–E 5855/23/89.

105. Churchill to Spears via FO's #567, 3 October 1944, PREM 3–423/11.

106. Ibid., minute from P.M. to Eden, 3 October 1944.

107. Minute from Eden to P.M., 5 October 1944 and P.M. to Eden, 6 October, PREM 3–423/11.

108. Eden to FO via Clark-Kerr's #2792 from Moscow, 11 October 1944, FO to Eden #3727, 16 October 1944 and FO minutes, FO 371/40318–E 6370/217/89; minutes of Cairo conference (Churchill, Eden, Paget et al.), 20 October 1944, E 6652; also in PREM 3–423/11.

109. Letter from Moyne to Spears, 11 October 1944, MEC, Spears Papers II/6; see also letter from Moyne to Eden, 23 October 1944, FO 371/40318–E 6042/217/89. The British Middle Eastern authorities strongly suspected the French of distributing arms in Syria's tribal zones and argued that the continued arming of the gendarmerie was a necessary countermeasure (Spears to FO #42 and #43, 25 October 1944, FO 371/40318–E 6580/217/89; Paget to WO #CGS/2387, 6 November 1944, E 6935).

110. FO briefs for Eden and Cadogan, November 1944, FO 371/40306–E 7099/23/89; letter from Bidault (French foreign minister) to Duff Cooper (British minister in Paris), 11 November 1944, FO 371/40318–E 7374/217/89; record of Anglo-French talks in Paris, 11–12 November 1944, E 7627; record of 11 November 1944 meeting including de Gaulle, Bidault, Churchill, and Eden, in Charles de Gaulle, *Mémoires de Guerre*, 3:350–59.

111. Letter from Spears to Churchill, 24 October 1944, MEC, Spears Papers II/7.

112. Retrospective summary of events, Spears Levant Diary, January 1945, MEC, Spears Papers I/1.

113. FO to Spears #648, 4 December 1944, FO 371/40347–E 7473/5178/89.

114. FO 371/40347–E 7675/, E 7608/, E 7818/5178/89, *passim*. Stephen Longrigg's *Syria and Lebanon under French Mandate* (Oxford 1958) p. 346, note 1 maintains the myth of Spears' voluntary departure.

115. Spears Levant Diary, January 1945, op. cit.

116. Report on "Évolution des relations franco–syriennes" (written after May 1945), pp. 88–89, SHAT, Papiers Beynet (1 K 230) I; report #G-6766, 20 December 1944, NA, OSS 226/L50738.

117. Report by Spears, 8 December 1944, FO 371/40307–E 7799/23/89.

118. Eastern Department minutes, FO 371/40307–E 7799/23/89.

Chapter 10

1. MEC, Coghill Diary, note #55.

2. Eden to Shone #210, 20 December 1944, FO 371/40347–E 7753/5178/89. The U.S. Department of State had recently been emphasizing American opposition to the French quest for a privileged status in Syria and Lebanon (Phillip Baram, *The Department of State in the Middle East, 1919–1945* [Philadelphia, 1978], chapter 7).

3. Killearn to FO #2713, 23 December 1944, FO 371/40307–E 7871/23/89; see also Grigg to FO via Shone's #2, 16 January 1945, FO 371/45556–E 403/8/89. In a speech to British Ministry of Information officials in Cairo, Brigadier Clayton spoke of the "shattering effect" the reestablishment of the French in the Levant would have on Britain's position in the Arab world (report by U.S. naval liaison officer in Beirut, 27 December 1944, NA, OSS 226/115697).

4. Shone to FO #832, 30 December 1944, FO 371/45556–E 8/8/89; Shone to FO #3 SAVING, 4 January 1945, E 251; Shone to FO #5, 2 January 1945, E 80; dispatch from Shone to Baxter, 25 April 1945, FO 371/45596–E 2873/52/89; minute by Beith (Eastern Dept.), 29 November 1945, E 9230; see also report #30674, 23 December 1944, NA, OSS 226/L51561.

5. Memorandum by Butler, 8 November 1944, FO 371/40306–E 7056/23/89; Sir Maurice Peterson, *Both Sides of the Curtain* (London, 1950), p. 237.

6. Memorandum by Hankey, 12 January 1945 and minutes by Cadogan and Eden, FO 371/45557–E 758/8/89; FO to Shone #226, 2 May 1945, FO 371/45563–E 2728/8/89. Duff Cooper argued that arbitration of the dispute would be the worst possible role for Britain to play because it would only earn it the hatred of both sides. In his view, relations with France ought to take precedence over Middle Eastern concerns and the French should therefore be left to do as they pleased in the Levant (note from Cooper to Butler, 13 February 1945, FO 371/45561–E 1631/8/89).

7. Minute from P.M. to Eden, 11 January 1945, FO 371/45557–E 696/8/89.

8. Report on Alawite situation by *Sûreté aux Armées* (transmitted by Beynet to Massigli), 22 August 1944, Alger CFLN-GPRF 1003.

9. Spears to FO #77 SAVING, FO 371/40307–E 7630/23/89; Political Intelligence Centre Middle East (PICME) paper #71 (PIC/190/55), 9 December 1944, FO 371/45354–E 197/68/88; Wadsworth to S. of S. #257, 18 November 1944, *FRUS* 5 (1944):810–11. Most reports indicate that the Maronite Patriarch was not won over to the Mount Lebanon idea; however, a Jewish Agency representative reported that the Patriarch was attempting to bring about the fall of the al-Solh government as part of a general French attempt to capitalize on the departure of Spears by transforming Lebanon into an independent Christian homeland under French protection (report by A. H., Jerusalem, 1 January 1945, BGA, Section 3 papers).

10. Spears to FO #664, 14 October 1944, FO 371/40112–E 6296/20/88; Spears to FO #682, 22 October 1944, E 6522; Wadsworth to S. of S. #228, 20 October 1944, *FRUS* 5 (1944):803–5.

11. Spears to FO #44, 26 October 1944, FO 371/40318–E 6612/217/89.

12. Memorandum by Furlonge, 20 November 1944, FO 371/40318–E 7696/217/89; PICME paper #71, op. cit.

13. Young (Beirut) to FO #816, 24 December 1944, FO 371/40307–E 7874/23/89; Shone to FO #3, 17 January 1945, FO 371/45556–E 445/8/89; Shone to FO #16, 23 January 1945, FO 371/45557–E 565/8/89; dispatch from Shone to Eden, 22 January 1945, FO 371/45559–E 1086/8/89.

14. FO minutes on Shone to FO #3, supra; Grigg to FO #78, 25 January 1945, FO 371/45557–E 597/8/89.

15. Shone to FO #61, 6 February 1945, FO 371/45558–E 888/8/89; Shone to FO #66, 22 February 1945, FO 371/45560–E 489/8/89; Shone to FO #167, 12 March 1945, FO 371/45561–E 1722/8/89; dispatch from Shone to FO, 29 March 1945, FO 371/45562–E 2337/8/89.

16. Letter from Bidault to Cooper as transmitted to FO on 24 February 1945, FO 371/45560–E 1340/8/89; Cooper to FO #111 SAVING, 24 February 1945, E 1386.

17. Minute by Hankey, 31 March 1945, regarding discussion with War Office officials, FO 371/45561–E 1726/8/89.

18. Ibid., minute by Hankey, 16 March 1945; see also minutes by Butler and Baxter.

19. Shone to FO #53, 4 February 1945, FO 371/45558–E 821/8/89; FO to Shone #64, 7 February 1945, E 811; Shone to FO #54, 5 February 1945 and FO minutes, E 860.

20. Shone to FO #100, 14 February 1945, FO 371/45559–E 1112/8/89; report by Coghill, 10 February 1945, enclosed in Shone to Eden #34, 2 March 1945, FO 371/45561–E 1773/8/89; Shone to FO #78, 25 April 1945, FO 371/45563–E 2671/8/89.

Shone attributed these destabilizing tendencies to three familiar factors: "(a) the ineffectiveness of General Beynet; (b) the chaos in the local French administration; and (c) the power wielded by a small group of highly objectionable officials" (dispatch from Shone to Butler, 9 March 1945, FO 371/45561–E 1884/8/89). Topping Shone's list of objectionable officials in the Grand Serail was Count Ostorog, whom he described as a "smooth, able, unreliable Levantine."

21. Copy of report by N. E. Schooling to Brigadier Hogg (GHQ MEF), 22 March 1945, FO 226/287–#92 (I). (Brigadier Hogg was the future Lord Hailsham.)

22. Oral answers of 14 February 1945, Great Britain, *Parliamentary Debates* (Commons), 5th, 408 (London, 1945):197–98; Shone's weekly political summary #151, 21 February 1945, FO 371/45553–E 1647/5/89. Spears saw it as his role in Parliament to harass the government over its Levant policy as well as to function as a general spokesman for the Arab cause (FO 371/45559–E 1118/ and 1133/8/89, *passim*).

23. Record of Cairo conversation, 17 February 1945 and minute by Shone, FO 371/45580–E 1415/8/89; see also Churchill's statement in the House of Commons: Great Britain, *Parliamentary Debates* (Commons) 5th ser., 408 (London, 1945):1290.

24. Cooper to FO #407, 6 March 1945, FO 371/45560–E 1588/8/89; Shone to FO #150, 9 March 1945, FO 371/45561–E 1655/8/89.

25. Cooper to FO #160 SAVING, 28 March 1945 and FO to Cooper #611 SAVING, 9 April 1945, FO 371/45562–E 2102/8/89; Shone to FO #75, 20 April 1945, E 2560; Shone to FO #77, 25 April 1945, FO 371/45563–E 2670/8/89.

26. See *FRUS* 8 (1945):1035–46; Halifax to FO #1148 and #1149, 17 February 1945, FO 371/45560–E 1489/8/89.

27. For the decision to create the committee, see WM (43) 92nd meeting, minute 2, confidential annex, 2 July 1943, CAB 65/39. The Palestine Committee's final report of 20 December 1943 is in P.(M) (43) 29, CAB 95/14; see also memorandum by Moyne, 1 November 1943, P.(M) 15, CAB 95/14 and Yehoshua Porath, *Be-mivchan ha-ma'aseh ha-politi* [In the Trial of Political Action] (Jerusalem, 1985), pp. 142–62.

28. Memorandum by L. S. Amery, 31 July 1943, P.(M) (43) 3, CAB 95/14.

29. P.(M) (43) 3rd meeting, 16 November 1943, CAB 95/14.

30. Palestine Committee's final report, op. cit.; memorandum by Moyne, 16 November 1943, P.(M) (43) 24, CAB 95/14.

31. PHP (43) 41, 8 December 1943, FO 371/35195–E 7802/27/89.

32. Ibid. Annex A (Foreign Office note).

33. Memorandum by Oliver Stanley (head of the Colonial Office), 11 September 1945, P.(M) (44) 10, CAB 95/14; note by Eden, P.(M) (44) 11, CAB 95/14; Yehoshua Porath, *Be-mivchan,* pp. 142–62.

34. Copy of PHP memorandum and minute by Hankey, 4 April 1945, FO 371/45575–E 4613/8/89.

35. Cooper to FO #1395, 5 August 1944, FO 371/40301–E 4712/23/89.

36. Copy of JP (45) 35th meeting, 14 February 1945, FO 371/45592–E 1576/14/89.

37. Minute by Hankey, 3 May 1945, FO 371/45565–E 3387/8/89.

38. Ibid. J. G. Ward of the Foreign Office's PostWar Reconstruction Department noted in the margin: "Exactly—this is what the French suspect we are after. How right they are!"

39. Minute by Hankey, 3 March 1945, FO 371/45575–E 4613/8/89.

40. Ibid., minute by Ward, 23 April 1945.

41. Ibid., minute by F. R. Hoyer Millar (head of the Western Department, which was responsible for French affairs), 26 April 1945.

42. Ibid., canceled note from Baxter to Brigadier Hollis as redrafted by Hankey, 1 May 1945, FO 371/45575–E 4613/8/89.

43. Shone to FO #83, 27 April 1945, FO 371/45563–E 2706/8/89. Shone urged that Britain threaten to end its mediation efforts between the French and Levant governments unless the reinforcement order were canceled—hardly the sort of sanction the French were likely to respond to (Shone to FO #291, 1 May 1945, FO 371/45589–E 2772/12/89).

44. COS (45) 112th meeting, 29 April 1945, FO 371/45589–E 2851/12/89.

45. FO minute: "The Levant States," 18 May 1945, FO 371/45570–E 3828/8/89; Shone's weekly political summary #161, 1 May 1945, FO 371/45553–E 3177/5/89. The American government also voiced its opposition to the French move (Grew [Acting S. of S.] to Caffery [Paris] #1776, 30 April 1945, *FRUS* 8 (1945):1060–61).

46. Telegram from de Gaulle to Mast, 2 May 1945, Charles de Gaulle, *Lettres, notes et carnets, Juin 1943–Mai 1945* (Paris, 1983), 3:432–33.

47. WM (45) 53rd meeting, minute 2, 4 May 1945, CAB 65/50; FO to Cooper #895 (transmitting message from P.M. to de Gaulle), 4 May 1945, FO 371/45588–E 2733/12/89; Shone's weekly political summary #163, 15 May 1945, FO 371/45554–E 3725/5/89.

48. Copy of letter from de Gaulle to Churchill, 6 May 1945, FO 371/45589–E 2925/12/89; also in Charles de Gaulle, *Mémoires de Guerre* [Paris, 1959], 3:512–13).

49. FO minute: "The Levant States," 18 May 1945, op. cit., minute by Campbell on Cooper's #703, 5 May 1945, FO 371/45589–E 2889/12/89.

50. Shone to FO #329, 11 May 1945, FO 371/45563–E 3021/8/89; Shone to FO #335, 12 May 1945, E 3037; Shone's weekly political summary #163, 15 May 1945, FO 371/45554–E 3725/5/89.

51. Cooper to P.M. #705, 5 May 1945, FO 371/45589–E 2894/12/89; FO minutes to P.M., 8–14 May 1945, FO 371/45590–E 2979/12/89; FO to Cooper #956, 16 May 1945, E 3153; Cooper to FO #748, 18 May 1945, E 3188; Shone to FO #367, 18 May 1945, FO 371/45355–E 3197/68/88; Shone to FO #375, 19 May 1945, FO 371/45564–E 3212/8/89; Shone's #378, 20 May 1945, E 3210.

52. P.M.'s minute to Ismay for COS committee, 8 May 1945, FO 371/45589–E 2918/12/89; see also P.M.'s minute to Ismay of 10 May.

53. FO minute by Young, 8 May 1945, FO 371/45589–E 2978/12/89.

54. Cooper to FO #755, 21 May 1945, FO 371/45564–E 3217/8/89. W. H. Young of the Eastern Department noted in the margin: "To put it mildly!" Beynet told the Lebanese foreign minister that the question of reinforcements had become a personal issue between Churchill and de Gaulle (Shone to FO #342, 14 May 1945, FO 371/45563–E 3070/8/89).

55. Note from Holman (Paris) to Harvey, 31 May 1945, reporting on conversation with the chef de cabinet of Dantry, the French minister of reconstruction, FO 371/45571–E 3980/8/89.

56. Ibid., minute by Young; see also Cooper to FO #807, 1 June 1945, FO 371/45568–E 3630/8/89.

57. De Gaulle, *Mémories de Guerre*, 3:186. The exclusion of the Foreign Ministry from the decisionmaking process was itself doubtlessly a factor in sapping its enthusiasm for the general's policy.

58. Telegram from de Gaulle to Bonnet, 29 May 1945, de Gaulle, *Mémoires de Guerre*, 3:516.

59. Grigg via Shone's #322 to FO, 8 May 1945, FO 371/45589–E 2926/12/89. Shone shared Grigg's views (Shone to FO #364, 18 May 1945, FO 371/45564–E 3179/8/89),

although he was also prepared to restrain the Levant governments by leaving them in doubt over Britain's likely reaction to a French crackdown (Shone to FO #365, 18 May 1945, FO 371/45564–E 3185/8/89).

60. Minutes by Hankey and Baxter, 8 and 9 May 1945, FO 371/45590–E 3080/12/89.

61. Halifax to FO #3426, 16 May 1945, FO 371/45564–E 3198/8/89; FO to Halifax #5223, 21 May 1945, E 3225; aide-mémoire from British embassy to Department of State, 21 May 1945, *FRUS* 8 (1945):1084–85.

62. Halifax to FO #3529, 21 May 1945 and FO to Halifax #5335, 23 May 1945, FO 371/45564–E 3220/8/89; FO to Halifax #5478, 26 May 1945, FO 371/45565–E 3335/8/89; memorandum by Loy Henderson (chief of NEA), 21 May 1945, *FRUS* 8 (1945): 1085–87.

63. Memorandum from Henderson to Acting S. of S. Grew, 23 May 1945, *FRUS* 8 (1945):1093–95. The United States urged restraint on the French government at the end of May.

64. Cooper to FO #777 and #778, 26 May 1945, FO 371/45565–E 3411/8/89; Holman (Paris) to FO #786, 29 May 1945, FO 371/45566–E 3495/8/89; Holman to FO #794, 30 May 1945, E 3537.

65. Minute by Hankey, 18 February 1945, FO 371/45559–E 1098/8/89.

66. Grigg to FO #436, 13 May 1945, FO minutes and FO to Grigg #778, 15 May 1945, FO 371/45590–E 3026/12/89.

67. Minute by Eden, 21 May 1945, FO 371/45570– E 3829/8/89.

68. Wadsworth to Grew #161, 29 May 1945 and Grew to Wadsworth #156, 29 May 1945, *FRUS* 8 (1945): 1113–14; Halifax to FO #3238, 10 May 1945, FO 371/45590–E 2980/12/89; Halifax to FO #3259, 10 May 1945, E 2995.

69. Shone to FO #387, 23 May 1945, FO 371/45565–E 3324/8/89.

70. Shone to FO #319 and #320, 28 May 1945, FO 371/45565–E 3436/8/89; see also Shone's #405 of 25 May (E 3376) in which he had written: "If the [Syrian] Government were to give the word I think there is little doubt that a general attack on the French throughout the country would take place."

71. Reports had reached the General Delegation of a high-level Syrian–Lebanese conference at Shtaura on 19 May, at which it had been decided to undertake a joint coup de main against all French establishments in the two countries. In fact, British intelligence reported that, while such proposals had been made at the conference, more prudent counsels had ultimately prevailed. Nonetheless, as Shone pointed out, "if French believed that above measures were likely to be put into effect, this may have been immediate cause of their violent action in Syria" (Shone to FO #97, 3 June 1945, FO 371/45569–E 3719/8/89).

72. He was convinced that this was a cover for an observation post that would pass on information to the Syrians. At the time, the British thought the fire had been unintentionally directed against them (report from Hama by Colonel Jean, 27 May 1945, found by British in office of French political officer in Homs [Capt. Briot], FO 371/45582–E 6713/8/89).

73. Paget to WO #CIC/728, 26 May 1945, FO 371/45565–E 3415/8/89.

74. Shone to FO #421 and #422 (reporting on account by Young), 28 May 1945, FO 371/45566–E 3497/8/89. An unconfirmed report by the OSS was later to indicate that the French may have been planning an attack on Damascus as early as May 23, to include an assault on the Parliament while it was in session with a view to eliminating a large segment of the country's leadership. This seems an exaggerated account, although the French did end up seizing the Parliament building (with no deputies inside)

in the course of the fighting at the end of the month (report #G-7873, 14 June 1945, NA, OSS 226/135050).

75. Minute from S. of S. for War to P.M., 20 May 1945, FO 371/45564–E 3218/8/89; record of Churchill's meeting with Eden, chief of Imperial General Staff, and FO officials (Sir Orme Sargent and Ronald Campbell), 28 May 1945, E 3557; Paget to WO #GO/15917, 26 May 1945 and FO to Damascus #44 (transmitting P.M. to Paget), 28 May 1945, FO 371/45565–E 3407/8/89; FO minutes, 28 May 1945, E 3436 and E 3556.

76. Precisely how the fighting was precipitated was never determined. Hankey concluded: "Really the facts might show either that the French lost their heads at a certain moment or that they had a plan for a coup" (Minute by Hankey on Shone's #98, 3 June 1945, FO 371/45569–E 3753/8/89).

77. Young (Beirut) to FO #432, #433, #434 and #435 (reporting on telephone conversations with Shone, who was in Damascus at the time and unable to communicate directly with London), 29 May 1945, FO 371/45566–E 3498/8/89; Young to FO #436, 30 May 1945, E 3511; Shone's weekly political summaries #165, 29 May 1945, and #166, 5 June 1945, FO 371/45554–E 4606/ and E 4669/5/89; Paget to WO #GO/18445, 4 June 1945, FO 371/45569–E 3722/8/89. The total number of deaths by the end of the fighting in Syria was as follows: 55 French, 55 native troops under French command, 111 Syrian gendarmes, 2 British (killed by an explosion in the Parliament building during the French attack on it), and 833 civilians (WO casualty figures, FO 371/45578–E 5446/8/89).

78. Paget to WO #T/7, 3 June 1945, FO 371/45569–E 3722/8/89. A British military commission that later investigated the incident was unable to establish the circumstances of the victims' death beyond the fact that they had suffered fatal blows from sharp instruments (British Army Commission report, 9 June 1945, FO 371/45567–E 5193/8/89).

79. Shone to FO #18 SAVING, 19 June 1945, FO 371/45575–E 4581/8/89. For a vivid, eyewitness account of the fighting in Damascus, see Lt.-Col. W. F. Stirling, *Safety Last* (London, 1953), pp. 230–37.

80. Khalid al-Azm, *Mudhakkirat Khalid al-Azm* [Memoirs] (Beirut, 1973), 1:294–301.

81. Killearn to FO #1177, 29 May 1945, FO 371/45566–E 3530/8/89.

82. Grigg to FO #526, 30 May 1945, FO 371/45566–E 3547/8/89.

83. Young to FO #448 (transmitting personal message for Eden from Shone), 30 May 1945, FO 371/45568–E 3626/8/89.

84. Young to FO #439 (transmitting message from Shone), 30 May 1945, FO 371/45566–E 3543/8/89.

85. FO to Halifax #5688, 30 May 1945 and FO minutes, FO 371/45566–E 3552/8/89; WM (45) 58th meeting, conclusions, minute 2, 30 May 1945, FO 371/45568–E 3675/8/89; Halifax to FO #3803, 31 May 1945 and FO minutes, FO 371/45567–E 3576/8/89; CM (45) 3rd meeting, minute 2, 31 May 1945, CAB 65/53.

86. Minute by Speaight, 31 May 1946 (endorsed by Hoyer Millar, Harvey, and Sargent, with the latter expressing some scepticism), FO 371/49127–Z 6778/208/17.

87. FO to Cooper #1036, 31 May 1945, FO 371/45568–E 3677/8/89; Eden to Cooper #1037, 31 May 1945, FO 371/45566–E 3450/8/89.

88. Record of conversation between Massigli and Eden, 31 May 1945, FO 371/45570–E 3862/8/89. This diplomatic gaffe appears to have been the result of an honest, if stupid, mistake (see Winston S. Churchill, *The Second World War* [Boston, 1953], 6:561–66).

89. Two telegrams from de Gaulle to Beynet, 1 June 1945, de Gaulle, *Mémoires de Guerre*, 3:519–20.

90. Message from Paget to Beynet, 1 June 1945, FO 371/45580–E 5800/8/89.

91. Telegram from de Gaulle to Beynet, 3 June 1945, de Gaulle, *Mémoires de Guerre*, 3:531.

92. Beynet to de Gaulle #553–556, 3 June 1945, SHAT, Papiers Beynet (1 K 230) XII.

93. FO to Paris #1068, 3 June 1945, FO 371/45569–E 3746/8/89; Cooper to FO #828, 4 June 1945, E 3713; Cooper to FO #834, 4 June 1945, E 3760. The British military contingency plan in the event the *Jeanne d'Arc* did proceed with reinforcements to Beirut was to prevent it from berthing at the harbor, and to apprehend landing parties by the boatload if they attempted to row ashore (Chiefs of Staff to Commanders-in-Chief Middle East and Mediterranean #3605, 7 June 1945, FO 371/45571–E 3892/8/89.)

94. Record of 2 June 1945 press conference, de Gaulle, *Mémoires de Guerre*, 3:521–30.

95. Ibid., p. 198.

96. De Gaulle's press conference, *Mémoires de Guerre*, 3:521–30.

97. Minute by R. I. Campbell, 6 June 1945, FO 371/45571–E 3982/8/89.

98. Dispatch from Beynet to de Gaulle, 28 May 1945, SHAT, Papiers Beynet (1 K 230) XI.

99. Beynet to Bidault #1362, 1 June 1945 and #1466, 7 June 1945, SHAT, Papiers Beynet (1 K 230) XII.

100. Report by Oliva-Roget, June 1945, SHAT, Papiers Beynet (1 K 230) II. Oliva-Roget claimed that the British had expected the French to be overwhelmed by a Syrian onslaught, allowing them to step in and save the French from massacre; instead they blatantly prevented a French victory.

101. Report on "Évolution des relations franco-syriennes," pp. 107–08, SHAT, Papiers Beynet (1 K 230) I.

102. Report by Robert Sethian to Dr. William L. Langer (Washington, D.C.) on "French Dissensions in the Levant," 6 September 1945, NA, OSS 226/XL15239; Shone to FO #588, 26 June 1945, FO 371/45575–E 4573/8/89; Young to FO #49 SAVING, 1 October 1945, FO 371/45583–E 7549/8/89; author's interview with Dr. Maxime Rodinson (Paris, 2 May 1985).

103. Caffery (Paris) to Grew (acting S. of S.) #3269 (3 June 1945), Grew to French Ambassador Bonnet (8 June 1945), record of conversation between Lacoste (counselor in the French embassy) and NEA officials (20 June), *FRUS* 8 (1945):1134–54; diplomatic exchanges regarding possible format of Levant conference, 6–15 June 1945 and FO to Cooper #1131 and #1132, 15 June 1945, FO 371/45571–E 3971/8/89. An essentially substanceless Franco–Soviet pact had been signed in December 1944 (see A. W. DePorte, *De Gaulle's Foreign Policy 1944–1946* [Harvard, 1968], pp. 74–83).

104. Young to FO (transmitting message from Shone, in Damascus), 2 June 1945, FO 371/45568–E 3693/8/89; Shone to FO #111, 6 June 1945, FO 371/45571–ER 3905/8/89.

105. Personal minute from P.M. to Cadogan, 23 June 1945, FO 371/45575–E 4687/8/89.

106. John Harvey, ed., *War Diaries of Oliver Harvey* (London, 1978), 10 June 1945.

107. Shone's weekly political summary #166, 5 June 1945, FO 371/45554–E 4669/5/89; Paget to WO #GO/18445, 4 June 1945, FO 371/45569–E 3722/8/89; Young to FO #15 Remac, 4 June 1945, FO 371/45600–E 3692/170/89 and *passim*. Paget sought to

justify his seizure of the OCP's assets by claiming that the French had used OCP trucks for military purposes during the fighting. This charge appears to have been untrue (report #G-7827 "Account of Crisis: 28 May–1 June," 9 June 1945, NA, OSS 226/L57344). The commander-in-chief's conduct hardly followed the spirit of his instructions from Churchill:

> As soon as you are master of the situation, you should show every consideration to the French. We are very intimately linked with France in Europe and your greatest triumph will be to produce a peace without rancour (personal telegram from P.M. to Paget, 3 June 1945, FO 371/45569–E 3825/8/89).

108. Grigg to FO #559, 5 June 1945, FO 371/45570–E 3854/8/89; Grigg to FO #578, 8 June 1945, FO 371/45571–E 3973/8/89; FO to Halifax #6265, 13 June 1945, FO 371/45604–E 3880/420/89; Shone to FO #539, 15 June 1945, E 4188; Halifax to FO #4171, 15 June 1945, E 4206; Grigg to FO #613, 16 June 1945, E 4219. Shone was opposed to Grigg's proposal. Phillip Baram has noted that NEA did favor a positive response to a Syrian request later that year for arms shipments and loans, but the upper echelons in the State Department remained unwilling to involve the United States so deeply in the Levant (Phillip Baram, *The Department of State in the Middle East, 1919–1945* [Philadelphia, 1978], p. 251).

109. Halifax to FO #4018, 8 June 1945, FO 371/45655–UE 2435/2/53.

110. Alan Campbell-Johnson, *Eden, the Making of a Statesman* (New York, 1955), p. 221.

111. FO to Halifax #6288, 13 June 1945, FO 371/45655–UE 2435/2/53.

112. Minute from Churchill to Cadogan, 15 June 1945, FO 371/45655–UE 2710/2/53.

113. Shone to FO, June 1945, FO 371/45572–E 4062/8/89.

114. Minutes by Campbell and Cadogan on meetings with Massigli on 5 and 11 June 1945, FO 371/45572–E 4097/ and E 4100/8/89; FO to Cooper #1284 SAVING, 9 June 1945, E 4100.

115. Minute by Hoyer Millar, 10 June 1945, FO 371/45571–E 3963/8/89.

116. Minute by Oliver Harvey, 26 June 1945, FO 371/49068–Z 7882/13/17. Cadogan agreed with Harvey's sentiments, but expressed doubt whether there was much left to salvage for the French in the Levant (minute by Cadogan, 26 June 1945, FO 371/49068–Z 7882/13/17).

117. Minute by Hoyer Millar, 22 June 1945, FO 371/45572–E 4062/8/89.

118. Ibid., minute by Harvey, 22 June 1945. For a good account of the 1945 Levant crisis within the context of Britain's struggle to prevent the disintegration of its Middle Eastern empire, see Wm. Roger Louis, *The British Empire in the Middle East: 1945–1951* (Oxford, 1984), pp. 147–72.

119. Ibid., minute by Hankey, 24 June 1945.

120. Ibid.

121. Western Department memorandum, 6 August 1945, FO 371/45581–E 6051/8/89.

122. FO memorandum, 15 July 1945, FO 371/45579–E 5171/8/89.

123. Shone to FO #536, 14 June 1945, FO 371/45573–E 4227/8/89; Shone to FO #550, 18 June 1945, FO 371/45574–E 4288/8/89; Shone to FO #575, 22 June 1945, E 4422/8/89; Shone to FO #576, 22 June 1945, E 4431; Shone to FO #635 and Paget to WO #GO/27692, 6 July 1945, FO 371/45576–E 4907/8/89; Shone to FO #664 and #665, 13 July 1945, FO 371/45577–E 5160/8/89.

124. Shone to FO #505, 11 June 1945, FO 371/45572–E 4092/8/89; Shone to FO #562, 22 June 1945, FO 371/45574–E 4416/8/89.

125. Shone to FO #568, 21 June 1945, FO 371/45574–E 4421/8/89; Shone to FO #589, 26 June 1945, FO 371/45575–E 4566/8/89; Shone to FO #119, 30 June 1945, E 4699; Shone to FO #606, 1 July 1945, E 4700; Shone's weekly political summary #173, 31 July 1945, FO 371/45554–E 5992/5/89.

126. Grigg to FO #587, 12 June 1945, FO 371/45572–E 4094/8/89; Shone to FO #580, 23 June 1945, FO 371/45574–E 4429/8/89; Shone to FO #582, 23 June 1945, E 4450; Shone to FO #627, 6 July 1945, FO 371/45576–E 4913; Shone to FO #26 SAVING, 25 July 1945, FO 371/45579–E 5632/8/89. Azzam Pasha, the secretary-general of the Arab League, informed Grigg that, in addition to its public resolutions, the organization had also secretly voted to recommend that member states study the possibility of breaking all diplomatic, economic, and cultural links with France and perhaps even adopting active military measures in support of Syria and Lebanon (Grigg to FO #586, 13 June 1945, FO 371/45573–E 4160/8/89).

127. "Aperçu sur la situation politique en Syrie et au Liban, #2," August 1945, SHAT, Papiers Beynet (1 K 230) IV.

128. Shone to FO #746, 3 August 1945, FO 371/45579–E 5699/8/89.

129. Shone to FO #583, 23 June 1945, FO 371/45574–E 4451/8/89.

130. Grigg to FO #652, 30 June 1945, FO 371/45575–E 4697/8/89; Paget to WO #GO/25772, 29 June 1945, FO 371/45576–E 4799/8/89.

131. Shone to FO #602, 29 June 1945, FO 371/45577–E 4691/8/89.

132. Cooper to FO #882, 16 June 1945, FO 371/45574–E 4325/8/89; minutes by Hankey and Cadogan, 23 June 1945, FO 371/45575–E 4708/8/89; see also July 1945 summary of the diplomatic effort in FO 371/45577–E 5181/8/89.

133. Minutes by Hankey and Cadogan, supra; FO minutes and notes, 24 June–1 July 1945, FO 371/45575–E 4709/8/89; Mary Borden (Lady Spears), *Journey down a Blind Alley* (New York, 1946), pp. 360–64.

134. In response to a suggestion by Duff Cooper that de Gaulle's Anglophobia was partly understandable in view of Spears' past conduct, Churchill responded bitterly as follows:

I am very sorry to read your No. 836, the first paragraph of which shows that you are pursuing your old policy of ill-will against General Spears. What has happened now shows only too clearly the wisdom of the course he took. Mr. Shone, who took his place, has been forced into almost exactly the same position.

The reason I choose General Spears was that at the time he was on very good terms with De Gaulle and very friendly to the French.

The final line of the draft cable, which was later deleted, ran as follows: "He had one great advantage which I value very much in British Representatives, namely, that he was always capable of standing up to the arrogant bravado of General de Gaulle and others of his kidney" (P.M. to Duff Cooper marked "personal and top secret" #T.1088/5, 7 June 1945, PREM 3, 423/15 [in response to Coopers' #836 of 5 June, PREM 3, 423/15]).

135. Western Department memorandum, 6 August 1945, FO 371/45581–E 6051/8/89. Very similar ideas were being discussed in French government circles at the time, whereas de Gaulle himself was beginning to elaborate the notion of a European block independent of the Soviet Union, the United States, and of Britain as well (see De-Porte, *DeGaulle's Foreign Policy,* pp. 192–201 and 285–87.)

136. Halifax to FO #5110, 21 July 1945, FO 371/45578–E 5351/8/89; extract from record of 7th meeting at Potsdam, 23 July 1945, E 5483.

137. Western Department memorandum, op. cit.

138. Minutes, 5 and 6 August 1945, FO 371/45581–E 6051/8/89.

139. Note, 8 August 1945, FO 371/45581–E 6051/8/89.

140. Minute by Bevin, 16 August 1945, FO 371/45581–E 6094/8/89.

141. CP (45) 123, 20 August 1945 and CP (45) 125, 23 August 1945 as found in FO 371/45581–E 6248/8/89. From Beirut, Shone warned that the news alone of a temporary French security role would cause an explosion in the Levant (Shone to FO #820, 25 August 1945, FO 371/45581–E 6253/8/89). Similar sentiments were expressed by Loy Henderson of NEA in the American State Department (Balfour [Washington, D.C.] to FO #6074, 6 September 1945, FO 371/45582–E 6630/8/89).

142. Shone to FO #778, 14 August 1945, FO 371/45581–E 5963/8/89; dispatch from Shone to Campbell (FO), 15 August 1945, FO 371/45582–E 6300/8/89; Shone to FO #829, 28 August 1945, E 6347.

143. Note from Massigli to Bevin, 23 August 1945 and Bevin to Massigli, 3 September 1945, FO 371/45582–E 6321/8/89.

144. Note from Duff Cooper, 7 September 1945, FO 371/49069–Z 10478/13/17.

145. Ibid.

146. "Translation of Document Agreed with M. Chauvel for Submission to the British and French Governments," 25 September 1945, FO 371/45583–E 7608/8/89; CM (45) 39th meeting, 9 October 1945, E 7608.

147. "Translation of Memorandum Communicated by M. Chauvel," 25 September 1945, FO 371/45583–E 7608/8/89.

148. See minute by R. G. Howe, 10 October 1945, FO 371/45584–E 7794/8/89.

149. Cabinet memorandum by Bevin, 5 October 1945, CP (45) 206, FO 371/45583–E 7608/8/89; minute by R. G. Howe, 10 October 1945, FO 371/45584–E 7794/8/89; minutes by Harvey, 27 and 28 October 1945, E 8308. Bevin remained concerned that the Soviets might try to exploit Anglo–French differences over the Levant to undermine the effort to create a Western Block (minutes of meeting at Chequers including Bidault, Massigli, Attlee, and Bevin, 16 September 1945, FO 371/45582–E 6960/8/89).

150. Minutes by Harvey and Howe, 3 October 1945, FO 371/45583–E 7203/8/89; minutes by Howe and Baxter (Eastern Dept.) and Harvey and Rumbold (Western Dept.), 18 October 1945, FO 371/45584–E 8206/8/89; minute by Shone, 14 September 1945, FO 371/45582–E 6963/8/89; minute by Shone, 8 October 1945, FO 371/45584–E 7740/8/89; minute by J. Thyne Henderson (Eastern Dept.), 29 September 1945, FO 371/45583–E 7171/8/89.

151. Minute by Rumbold, 26 October 1945, FO 371/45584–E 8206/8/89.

152. Minutes by Rumbold and Harvey, 26 and 27 October 1945, FO 371/45584–E 8206/8/89.

153. Minute by Howe, 27 October 1945, FO 371/45584–E 8207/8/89; FO to Cooper #1706, 31 October 1945, E 8124; minute by Cadogan, 2 November 1945, FO 371/45585–E 8451/8/89.

154. Cooper to FO #1284, 16 November 1945, FO 371/45585–E 8833/8/89; see also DePorte, *DeGaulle's Foreign Policy,* chapter 9.

155. Memorandum by Loy Henderson on talk with Wright (counselor of the British embassy) (3 December 1945), communication from Department of State to British embassy (13 December 1945), Tandy (first secretary of British embassy) to Henderson, (13 December 1945), *FRUS* 8 (1945): 1174–82; Halifax to FO #8080, 4 December 1945, FO 371/45604–E 9434/420/89; Cooper to FO #1340, 5 December 1945, E 9478.

156. FO to Shone #911, 12 December 1945, FO 371/45586–E 9699/8/89. French text is in de Gaulle, *Mémoires de Guerre*, 3:639–40.

157. The salient passage in the Anglo–French evacuation agreement ran as follows:

The programme of evacuation will be drawn up in such a way that it will ensure the maintenance in the Levant of sufficient forces to guarantee security, until such time as the United Nations Organisation has decided on the organisation of collective security in this zone.

Until these arrangements have been carried out, the French government will retain forces regrouped in the Lebanon (R. G. Howe to Bevin, 18 January 1946, FO 371/52843–E 702/2/89).

158. Aide-mémoire from Massigli, 24 December 1945, FO 371/45591–E 10090/12/89; minute by Shone on 1 February 1946 meeting between Massigli and Sargent, FO 371/52843–E 1124/2/89. The British in Lebanon remained highly suspicious of French intentions in the country. In December, Ninth Army officers reported a sudden, and apparently orchestrated, effort by their French counterparts to establish friendly relations with them, "the idea being, of course that the locals sh[oul]d see all this back-slapping and conclude we're 'ganging up' with the French" (British legation minutes, 11 December 1945, FO 226/286, #91).

159. Letter from de Gaulle to Francisque Gay (temporarily in charge of the Ministry of Foreign Affairs), 4 January 1946, de Gaulle, *Mémoires de Guerre*, 3:645.

160. Note from Orme Sargent to Bevin, enclosing draft of joint directive, 12 February 1946, FO 371/52844–E 1611/2/89.

161. Note from R. G. Howe to Ernest Bevin, 18 January 1946. This memorandum reflected a consensus within the Foreign Office and was approved by Bevin.

162. Meeting Camille Chamoun at the opening of the United Nations General Assembly in January 1946, George Wadsworth had informed him of the State Department's objections to the 13 December statement and had given him to understand that the Americans would be sympathetic to a Syrian and Lebanese challenge in the United Nations (Camille Chamoun, *Marahil al-istiqlal* [On the Road to Independence] [Beirut, 1949], pp. 321–22).

163. Syrian–Lebanese letter to the Security Council, 4 February 1946, United Nations, *Journal of the Security Council,* 1st year, 1st sess., p. 139; FO to Shone #157, 22 February 1946, FO 371/52845–E 1822/2/89.

164. United Nations, *Journal of the Security Council,* p. 340.

165. Note from Sargent (FO) to Major-General Simpson (WO), 22 February 1946, FO 371/52845–E 1822/2/89. The entire Security Council debate is in United Nations, *Journal of the Security Council,* pp. 265–347.

166. Louis, *The British Empire,* p. 171, note 79.

167. Correspondence and minutes, February 1946, FO 371/52845–E 1675/, E 1728/, E 1822/2/89, *passim.*

168. Minute by Beith, 26 February 1946, FO 371/52845–E 1675/2/89.

169. Dispatch from Howe to Shone, 28 February 1946, FO 371/52844–E 1589/2/89.

170. See Shone's weekly political summaries for March 1946, FO 371/52857–E 2654/, E 2842/, E 3037/, E 3229/213/89; *New York Times,* 18 April 1946, p. 6 and 31; August 1946, p. 2. The French and British continued to the very end to suspect each other of planning to maintain local influence through surreptitious means (see, for example, *New York Times,* 27 May 1946, p. 11).

171. *New York Times,* 6 August 1946, p. 2.

Conclusion

1. In June 1945, when General Dentz's death sentence for his role in the events of May 1941 was commuted, Catroux remarked to the British military attaché in Paris that Dentz's life had been saved by Britain's recent intervention in the Syrian crisis. De Gaulle could not bring himself to see a man executed who had done so much to resist the British in the Levant (Holman [Paris] to Hoyer Millar, 23 June 1945, FO 371/45577–E 4661/8/89).

2. Sir Osbert Sitwell, *Great Morning!* (Boston, 1947), pp. 143–44. I am grateful to Richard Usborne for this reference.

3. MEC, Coghill Diary, explanatory note #25.

4. Report by Shone, 30 April 1945, FO 371/45564–E 3122/8/89.

5. Author's conversation with Prof. Albert Hourani (St. Antony's College, Oxford, 7 December 1984).

6. Memorandum by Rosa for Treasury, 20 October 1942, FO 371/31479–E 6165/207/89.

7. Dispatch marked "personal" from Caccia (Eastern Dept.) to Lascelles (Beirut), 21 April 1943, FO 371/35176–E 2284/27/89.

8. See Elie Kedourie, "Pan-Arabism and British Policy," *The Chatham House Version and Other Middle Eastern Studies—New Edition* (University Press of New England, 1984), chapter 8.

9. One prominent officer in the Free French movement was later to recognize bureaucratic infighting as a factor in Britain's wartime Levant policy, although he got the details all wrong. He portrayed Spears' policy as being, in part, the manifestation of a struggle between the pro-French policy of the Foreign Office and the Lawrencian dreams of the Colonial Office (Jacques Soustelle, *Envers et contre tout* [Paris, 1947], 1:340–41)!

10. Indeed, the Prime Minister tended to see criticism of Spears as a veiled form of attack against his own person:

> I object extremely to the theme on which the Foreign Office has now apparently set to work, that all the troubles have arisen through Spears' excessive championship of Lebanese and Syrian interests. This among other points is a reflexion on me (minute from P.M. to Eden, 28 January 1945, PREM 3–423/15).

11. This contradistinction between the outlooks of Churchill and de Gaulle was made by Lord Stockton (Harold Macmillan) during an interview broadcast on BBC Television on 20 December 1984. For an animated account of the relations between the two men, which, perhaps, understates the depth of the animosity that developed between them, see François Kersaudy, *Churchill and de Gaulle* (London, 1981).

12. Andrée Pierre-Vienot, "The Levant Dispute: The French Case," *London Quarterly of World Affairs* 11 (October 1945):219–28.

13. D. W. Brogan, "Franco-British Crisis," *The Spectator,* 13 July 1945.

14. See I. N. Clayton's record of his 30 September 1944 talk with Saadullah Jabri and Jamil Mardam, FO 226/266–352/31/44.

15. Interview with Sir Richard Beaumont (London, 27 August 1987).

16. See Louis, *The British Empire,* p. 124.

17. Joseph Schumpeter, *Imperialism and Social Classes* (New York, 1951).

BIBLIOGRAPHY

Archival Sources

Public Record Office, London

AIR 23   (Air Ministry—Overseas Air Commands)
CAB 65   (WM—War Cabinet meetings)
CAB 66   (WP—War Cabinet print [memoranda])
CAB 69   (Defence Committee)
CAB 79   (COS—Chiefs of Staff meetings)
CAB 80   (COS memoranda)
CAB 81   (Post-Hostilities Planning
          Subcommittee of the COS)
CAB 85   (Committee on Foreign [Allied] Resistance [CFR])
CAB 95   (Middle East and Palestine Committee)
CAB 128   (CM—postwar cabinet meetings)
FO 226   (Foreign Office papers—
          Beirut Legation and Spears Mission 1942–1945)
FO 371   (general correspondence)
FO 406   (confidential print)
FO 684   (Damascus Consulate)
FO 898   (Political Warfare Executive)
FO 921   (Minister of State Cairo's office)
FO 922   (Middle East Supply Centre)
PREM 3   (Premier's wartime papers on Syria)
WO 106   (War Office papers—
          Middle East correspondence)
WO 178   (War diaries: military missions)
WO 190   (MI 14 appreciation)
WO 193   (Special Operations Executive)
WO 208   (General Staff)

Middle East Centre, St. Antony's College, Oxford

Coghill Papers
Killearn Diaries
Spears Papers

Archive du Ministère
des Affaires Étrangères, Paris

E–Levant 1918–1929
  Syrie–Liban: 2ème partie, 1922–1929
E–Levant
  Syrie–Liban 1930–1940
Guerre 1939–1945
  Alger CFLN-GPRF
  Londres C.N.F.
  Vichy–Europe: Grande Bretagne
  Vichy–Levant
Papiers d'Agents
  Papiers Puaux

Service Historique de l'Armée de Terre, Paris

Papiers Beynet (1 K 230)
Sous-série 4 H (Levant)
  Cabinet militaire à Beirut 1941–1946
  Campagne de Syrie et Liban 1941
  2ème Bureau 1940–1941, 1941–1946

Archives Nationales, Paris

Papiers Catroux (72 AJ 428)
Papiers de Larminat (72 AJ 1915–1929)

Central Zionist Archive, Jerusalem

S25 papers   (Jewish Agency—Political Department)

Ben-Gurion Archive, Sde Boqer

Section 3 papers: 1940–1945

Haganah Archive, Tel-Aviv

Various files shown to author on condition of not being specifically cited.

National Archives and Records Service, Washington, D.C.

GFM T-120   (German Foreign Ministry papers on microfilm)
OSS 226   (Office of Strategic Services papers on Syria and Lebanon)
SD 890D and 890E   (State Department decimal files on Syria and Lebanon)

Interviews and conversations

Professor Albert Hourani (Oxford, 7 December 1984 and London, 5 August 1987)
Sir P. M. Crosthwaite (London, 5 January 1985)
Richard Usborne (London, 12 January 1985)

Prof. Maxime Rodinson (Paris, 2 May 1985)
Yerucham Cohen (Tel-Aviv, June 1985)
Sir Richard Beaumont (London, 27 August 1987)
Lord Hankey (Edenbridge, Kent, September, 1987)
Dr. Asher Susser (Tel-Aviv, 27 December 1987)
Dr. Eliahu Elath (Jerusalem, 22 May 1988)

Published Primary Sources

Délégation française auprès de la commission allemande d'armistice (*DFCAA*), Vol. 4 Paris, 1957.
Great Britain, *Parliamentary Debates* (*Commons*), various volumes from the war years: London, 5th ser.,(1941–45).
United Nations. *Journal of the Security Council.* 1st year, 1st sess., 1946.
U.S., Department of State. *Documents on German Foreign Policy, 1918–1945* (*DGFP*), series D, Vols. 11–13. Washington, D.C., 1960–64.
U.S., Department of State. *Foreign Relations of the United States* (*FRUS*), various volumes from the war years. Washington, D.C., 1958.

Memoirs and Secondary Literature

Abetz, Otto. *Das Offene Problem.* Cologne, 1951.
Allon, Yig'al. *Ma'arachot ha-Palmah* [Campaigns of the *Palmach*], Tel-Aviv, 1965.
Andrew, Christopher. *Her Majesty's Secret Service.* New York, 1986.
———and Kanya-Forstner, A. S. *France Overseas: The Great War and the Climax of French Imperial Expansion.* London, 1981.
Aron, Robert. *Histoire de Vichy.* Paris, 1954.
Azm, Khalid al-. *Mudhakkirat Khalid al-Azm* [Memoirs]. Vol. 1: Beirut, 1973.
Baram, Phillip. *The Department of State in the Middle East, 1919–1945.* Philadelphia, 1978.
Benoist-Méchin, Jacques. *De la défaite au désastre.* 2 vols. Paris, 1984–85.
Benoit, Pierre. *La Châtelaine du Liban.* Paris, 1924.
Borden, Mary. *Journey down a Blind Alley.* New York, 1946.
Buckley, Christopher. *Five Ventures. Iraq—Syria—Persia—Madagascar—Dodecanese.* London, 1954.
Burrows, Matthew. " 'Mission Civilisatrice': French Cultural Policy in the Middle East, 1860–1914." *The Historical Journal* 29 (1986): 109–35.
Campbell-Johnson, Alan. *Eden, the Making of a Statesman.* New York, 1955.
Casey, Lord. *Personal Experience.* London, 1962.
Catroux, General Georges. *Dans la bataille de Méditerranée.* Paris, 1949.
———*Deux missions en Moyen-Orient* (*1919–1922*). Paris, 1958.
———letter to *Le Figaro,* 17 October 1951.
Chamoun, Camille. *Marahil al-istiqlal* [On the Road to Independence]. Beirut, 1949.
———*Mudhakkiratiy* [My Memoirs]. Vol. 1. Beirut, 1969.
Chandos, Viscount. *Memoirs of Lord Chandos.* London, 1962.
Charles-Roux, F. *Cinq mois tragiques aux affaires étrangères.* Paris, 1949.
Churchill, Randolph. *Lord Derby.* London, 1959.

Churchill, Winston S. *The Second World War.* 6 vols. London, 1948–54.

"Cleante," "Siria e Libano nella politica franco-inglese." *Nuova Antologia,* August 1945, p. 314 ff.

Cohen, Michael J. "A Note on the Mansion House Speech, May 1941." *Asian and African Studies* 11 (1977): 375–86.

———*Palestine: Retreat from the Mandate.* New York, 1978.

Collet, Anne. *The Road to Deliverance. Damascus–Jerusalem–Damascus. 1940–June 1941.* Beirut, 1942.

Collins, R. J. *Lord Wavell—A Military Biography.* London, 1947.

Colville, John. *The Fringes of Power, 10 Downing Street Diaries 1939–1955.* New York, 1986.

Cooper, Duff. *Old Men Forget.* London, 1954.

Coulet, François. *Vertu des temps difficiles.* Paris, 1967.

Cumming, Henry H. *Franco–British Rivalry in the Post-War Near East.* Oxford, 1938.

Davet, M.-C. *La double affaire de Syrie.* Paris, 1967.

De Gaulle, Charles. *Lettres, notes et carnets.* 3 vols.:*1940–41, 1941–43, 1943–45.* Paris, 1981–83.

———*Mémoires de Guerre.* 3 vols. Paris, 1954–59.

De Larminat, Edgard. *Chroniques irrévérencieuses.* Paris, 1962.

DePorte, A. W. *De Gaulle's Foreign Policy 1944–1946.* Harvard, 1968.

Dinur, Ben-Tsiyon, general editor. *Sefer Toldot ha-Haganah* [Official History of the Haganah]. 3 vols. Tel-Aviv, 1954–1972.

Duroselle, Jean-Baptiste. *L'Abîme—1939–1945.* Paris, 1982.

Eliav, Ya'acov. *Mevukash* [Wanted]. Jerusalem, 1983.

Fraser-Tytler, W. K. *Afghanistan.* 3rd ed. London, 1967.

Fry, Michael G., and Rabinovich, Itamar, eds. *Despatches from Damscus: Gilbert MacKereth and British Policy in the Levant, 1933–1939.* Tel-Aviv University and University of Southern California, 1985.

Gaunson, A. B. *The Anglo-French Clash in Lebanon and Syria, 1940–1945.* London, 1987.

———"Churchill, de Gaulle, Spears and the Levant Affair, 1941." *The Historical Journal* 27 (1984):697–713.

Gil'ad, Zerubavel, ed. *Magen be-Seter* [Secret Defense]. Jerusalem, 1952.

———, ed. *Sefer ha-Palmah* [Official History of the *Palmach*]. 2 vols. Tel-Aviv, 1953.

Gilbert, Martin. *Winston S. Churchill.* Vols. 3–7. London and Boston, 1971–86.

Glubb, Brigadier John B. *The Story of the Arab Legion.* London, 1948.

Groussard, Georges. *Service Secret 1940–1945.* Paris, 1964.

Hacohen, David. *Et lesaper* [A Time to Tell]. Tel-Aviv, 1981.

Harvey, John, ed. *War Diaries of Oliver Harvey.* London, 1978.

Helleu, Jean. letter to *Le Figaro,* 20/21 October 1951.

Hinsley, F. H. et al. *British Intelligence in the Second World War.* Vol. 1. London, 1979.

Hirszovicz, Lukasz. *The Third Reich and the Arab East.* London 1966.

Hourani, Albert. *Arabic Thought in the Liberal Age.* Oxford, 1962.

———*Syria and Lebanon, A Political Essay.* Oxford, 1946.

Hytier, Adrienne. *Two Years of French Foreign Policy.* Paris, 1958.

Jäckel, Eberhard. *Frankreich in Hitlers Europa.* Stuttgart, 1966.

Julien, Charles-André. "French Difficulties in the Middle East." *Foreign Affairs* 24 (January 1946):325–36.

Kedourie, Elie. *The Chatham House Version and Other Middle Eastern Studies—New Edition.* University Press of New England, 1984.

———*England and the Middle East.* London, 1956.

———*Islam in the Modern World.* New York, 1981.

———review of Spears' *Fulfilment of a Mission* in *Times Literary Supplement,* 27 October 1978, p. 1257.

Kedward, H. R. *Resistance in Vichy France.* Oxford, 1978.

Kersaudy, François. *Churchill and de Gaulle.* (New York, 1983).

Khoury, Bishara al-. *Haqa'iq lubnaniyyah* [Lebanese Realities]. 3 vols. Beirut, 1960–61.

Khoury, Philip S. *Syria and the French Mandate.* Princeton, 1987.

Kirk, George. *The Middle East in the War.* London, 1953.

Kirkbride, Sir A. S. *A Crackle of Thorns.* London, 1956.

Laffargue, André. *Général Dentz, Paris–Syrie 1941.* Paris, 1954.

Langer, William L. *Our Vichy Gamble.* New York, 1947.

Leahy, William D. *I Was There.* New York, 1950.

Liddell Hart, B. H. *History of the Second World War.* New York: Perigree edition, 1982.

Lipschits, Isaac. *La politique de la France au Levant, 1939–1941.* Paris, 1963.

London, Geo. *L'amiral Esteva et le général Dentz devant la Haute Cour de Justice.* Lyon, 1945.

Longrigg, Stephen. *Syria and Lebanon under French Mandate.* Oxford, 1958.

Louis, Wm. Roger. *The British Empire in the Middle East: 1945–1951.* Oxford, 1984.

———*Imperialism at Bay.* Oxford, 1978.

Macmillan, Harold. *War Diaries—The Mediterranean 1943–1945.* London, 1984.

Marrus, Michael, and Paxton, Robert. *Vichy France and the Jews.* New York, 1983.

Marshall, D. Bruce. *The French Colonial Myth and Constitution-Making in the Fourth Republic.* New Haven: Yale, 1973.

May, Ernest R. "Cabinet, Tsar, Kaiser." pp. 11–36 in Ernest R. May, ed. *Knowing One's Enemies.* Princeton, 1984.

Melka, Robert, L. "Darlan between Britain and Germany 1940–41." *Journal of Contemporary History* 8 (1973): 57–80.

Mickelsen, Martin L. "Another Fashoda: The Anglo–Free French Conflict over the Levant, May–September 1941." *Revue française d'histoire d'outre-mer* 63 (1976): 75–100.

Mockler, Anthony. *Our Enemies the French.* London, 1976.

Monroe, Elizabeth. *Britain's Moment in the Middle East.* 2d ed. London, 1981.

———*The Mediterranean in Politics.* Oxford, 1938.

Montagne, Robert. "French Policy in North Africa and in Syria." International Affairs 16 (March–April 1937):263–79.

———"Le Panarabisme et la politique britannique en Orient." *Politique étrangère.* October 1946.

Nicosia, Francis. *The Third Reich and the Palestine Question.* Austin, 1985.

Olmert, Yosef. "Britain, Turkey and the Levant Question during the Second World War." *Middle Eastern Studies.* 23(October 1987):437–52.

———"British Policy Toward the Levant States, 1940–1945." Ph.D. dissertation, Department of Government, London School of Economics, 1983.

Paxton, Robert. *Vichy France.* New York, 1972.

Pearse, Richard. *Three Years in the Levant.* London, 1949.

Peters, Joan. *From Time Immemorial.*New York, 1984.

Peterson, Sir Maurice. *Both Sides of the Curtain*. London, 1950.

Pierre-Vienot, Andrée. "The Levant Dispute: The French Case." *London Quarterly of World Affairs* 11 (October 1945):219–28.

Playfair, I. S. O., C. J. C. Molory & Sir William Jackson, *The Mediterranean and the Middle East*. 6 vols. London, 1954–1988.

Porath, Yehoshua. *Be-mivchan ha-ma'aseh ha-politi* [In the Trial of Political Action]. Jerusalem, 1985.

Puaux, Gabriel. *Deux années au Levant*. Paris, 1952.

——letter to *Le Figaro*, 1/2 October 1949.

Queuille, Pierre. "La politique d'Hitler à l'egard de Vichy." *Revue d'histoire diplomatique* 3–4 (1983).

Rabinovich, Itamar. "The Compact Minorities and the Syrian State, 1918–1945." *Journal of Contemporary History* 14 (October 1979):693–712.

Rahn, Rudolf. *Ruheloses Leben*. Düsseldorf, 1949.

Rondot, Pierre. *The Changing Patterns of the Middle East, 1919–1958*. New York, 1961.

——"L'expérience du mandat français en Syrie et au Liban (1918–45)." *Revue des droits internationals publiques* 52 (1948):387–409.

——"Les mouvements nationalistes au Levant durant la deuxième guerre mondiale." *La guerre en méditerranée 1939–1945*. Paris, 1971, pp. 643–65.

Roshwald, Aviel. "The Spears Mission in the Levant: 1941–1944." *The Historical Journal* 29 (December 1986):897–919.

Sachar, Howard. *Europe Leaves the Middle East, 1936–1954*. New York, 1972.

Salibi, Kamal S. *The Modern History of Lebanon*. New York, 1965.

Sasson, Eliahu. *Ba-derekh el ha-shalom: igrot ve-sichot* [On the Road to Peace: Letters and Conversations]. Tel-Aviv, 1978.

Schumpeter, Joseph. *Imperialism and Social Classes*. New York, 1951.

Seale, Patrick. *The Struggle for Syria*. Oxford, 1965.

Shirer, William L. *The Collapse of the Third Republic*. New York, 1969.

Shorrock, William I. *French Imperialism in the Middle East*. Madison, 1976.

Silverfarb, Daniel. *Britain's Informal Empire in the Middle East. A Case Study of Iraq, 1929–1941*. Oxford, 1986.

Sitwell, Sir Osbert. *Great Morning!* Boston, 1947.

Soustelle, Jacques. *Envers et contre tout*. 2 vols. Paris, 1947–50.

Spears, Major-General Sir Edward L. *Assignment to Catastrophe*. reprint society ed. London, 1956.

——*Fulfilment of a Mission*, London, 1977.

——*Two Men Who Saved France—Petain and de Gaulle*. London, 1966.

Stark, Freya. *Dust in the Lion's Paw*. London, 1961.

Stirling, Lt.-Col. W. F. *Safety Last*. London, 1953.

Susser, Asher. "Western Power Rivalry and its Interaction with Local Politics in the Levant, 1941–1946." Ph.D. dissertation, Tel-Aviv University, 1986.

Thomas, R. T. *Britain and Vichy*. London, 1979.

Toynbee, Arnold, ed. *Hitler's Europe*. London, 1954.

von Hentig, Werner Otto. *Mein Leben. Ein Dienstreise*. Goettingen, 1962.

Warner, Geoffrey, *Iraq and Syria, 1941*. University of Delaware, 1974.

Wilson, Field-Marshall Lord. *Eight Years Overseas*. London, 1948.

Wolfers, Arnold. *Britain and France between Two World Wars*. New York, 1940.

Woodward, Llewellyn. *British Foreign Policy in the Second World War*. London, 1970.

Index